Committee House Judiciary

Investigation of the Employment of Pinkerton Detectives at

Homestead

Committee House Judiciary

Investigation of the Employment of Pinkerton Detectives at Homestead

ISBN/EAN: 9783337149833

Printed in Europe, USA, Canada, Australia, Japan

Cover: Foto ©Suzi / pixelio.de

More available books at **www.hansebooks.com**

52D CONGRESS, } HOUSE OF REPRESENTATIVES. { MIS. DOC.
1st Session. } { No. 335.

INVESTIGATION

OF THE

EMPLOYMENT OF PINKERTON DETECTIVES

IN CONNECTION WITH

THE LABOR TROUBLES

AT

HOMESTEAD, PA.

WASHINGTON:
GOVERNMENT PRINTING OFFICE.
1892.

INVESTIGATION OF THE EMPLOYMENT OF PINKERTON DETECTIVES IN CONNECTION WITH THE LABOR TROUBLES AT HOMESTEAD, PA.

PITTSBURG, Pa., *July 12, 1892.*

In the House of Representatives on May 12, 1892, Mr. Oates, from the Committee on the Judiciary, submitted the following report, which was adopted:

The House of Representatives having ordered this committee to report back the resolution proposing an investigation of the Pinkerton Detective Agency, the Committee on the Judiciary, having had the same under consideration, report therefor the following substitute and recommend its adoption:

"Whereas it has been alleged that a certain organization known as the Pinkerton detectives has been employed unlawfully and to the detriment of the public by railroad corporations engaged in the transportation of the United States mails and interstate commerce: Therefore, be it

"*Resolved,* That the Committee on the Judiciary be, and it is hereby, directed to investigate the said Pinkerton detectives, to wit: The character of their employment by corporations engaged in the transportation of interstate commerce or the United States mails, the numbers so employed, and whether such employment has provoked breaches of the peace or caused the destruction of property, and all the material facts connected with their alleged employment, and to report the same to this House by bill or otherwise at any time. And to this end, the said Committee on the Judiciary is hereby authorized and empowered to issue and cause to be served processes for the production of papers and to procure the attendance of witnesses, to administer oaths, and to employ a clerk and stenographer if necessary, and any subcommittee of said Judiciary Committee is hereby invested with like powers, for the purpose aforesaid, and may sit wherever deemed necessary, and during the sessions of the House. All of the expenses of such investigation shall be paid out of the contingent fund of the House upon proper vouchers, certified as correct by the chairman of the said committee or subcommittee, not to exceed the aggregate sum of two thousand dollars, which the Clerk of the House of Representatives is hereby directed to turn over to the chairman of such subcommittee, not exceeding one thousand dollars at a time, taking his receipt therefor, and which shall be accounted for by him to said clerk in the manner aforesaid, the same to be immediately available."

Also on July 6, 1892, in the House of Representatives, Mr. Williams, of Massachusetts, submitted the following—

Whereas the Pinkerton detective or private police force, to the number of several hundred, is now engaged in an armed conflict at Homestead, Pa., with the late employés of the Carnegie Iron Works at said place, and great loss of human life and destruction of property are likely to result from same; and

Whereas the Judiciary Committee has been directed by a resolution of the House to investigate the nature and character of the employment of Pinkerton detectives by corporations engaged in interstate commerce; therefore, be it

Resolved, That said committee shall investigate and report on the character of the employment of said forces in the present instance, and the causes and conditions of the sanguinary conflict now going on at Homestead, Pa.

Which was referred to the Committee on the Judiciary and was reported back favorably on July 7, 1892, and adopted with the following amendment:

That the committee be instructed to inquire whether or not the employment of Pinkerton detectives has any connection with the present system of Federal taxation.

In pursuance of the foregoing resolutions a subcommittee of the Committee on the Judiciary, consisting of Hon. William C. Oates, of

Alabama, chairman; Hon. C. J. Boatner, of Louisiana; Hon. William
D. Bynum, of Indiana; Hon. Case Broderick, of Kansas, and Hon.
Ezra B. Taylor, of Ohio, this day met in the city of Pittsburg, at 7:30
p. m., for the purpose of taking testimony.

All the members of the committee were present.

TESTIMONY OF H. C. FRICK.

H. C. FRICK sworn and examined.

By the CHAIRMAN:

Q. Give your name to the stenographer; also your residence and business.—A. H. C. Frick; residence, Pittsburg; chairman of the Carnegie
Steel Company, Limited.

Q. Mr. Frick, who compose that company of which you are chairman?—
A. It is not a company, sir; it is an association; a limited partnership
association, composed of Andrew Carnegie, Henry Phipps, jr., George
Lauter, H. M. Curry, W. L. Abbott, John G. A. Leischman, P. F. Lovejoy, Otis H. Childs; and a number of other gentlemen hold small interests and whom I can not name at present. I can probably give you a
few more.

Q. Well, that will answer.—A. And myself. I am a member.

Q. I understand you to say it is an association, not an incorporated
company?—A. Not an incorporated company; formed under the limited
laws of Pennsylvania—the limited partnership law of Pennsylvania.

Q. In what business, Mr. Frick, is that company engaged? I do not
mean to go into particulars but the general scope and character of the
business it is engaged in?—A. Well, they are the owners of the Edgar
Thompson Furnaces, at Bessemer; Edgar Thompson Steel Works, at
the same place—that is, Bessemer is near Braddock; the Duquesne Steel
Works at Duquesne, Pa., on the same side of the river as the Homestead Works, and about 3 miles south from Homestead; the Homestead
Steel Works, the Lucy Furnaces, located in the city of Pittsburg; the
Keystone Bridge Works, located in the city of Pittsburg; the Upper
Union Mills and the Lower Union Mills, located in the city of Pittsburg; Beaver Falls Mills, located at Beaver Falls, Beaver County,
Pa.; the Scotia Ore Mines, located, I think, in Center County; the
Larimer Coke Works, located in Westmoreland County, on the Pennsylvania Railroad; the Allegheny Coke Works, in Westmoreland
County, on the Pittsburg, McKeesport and Youghiogheny Railroad. I
could give you the number of men employed, if you would like.

Q. Yes, I will be glad if you will do so?—A. As near as possible I
should say we employ at those several works about 13,000 men.

Q. That is in the aggregate?—A. Yes, sir.

Q. Now, what business is done, the extent of it, at the works of the
company, and what is the number of men employed at the works of
the company near Homestead?—A. About 3,800.

Q. Employed there?—A. Yes, sir.

Q. In what business were they employed in the past?—In the manufacture of structural materials, used largely in fireproof buildings, such
as beams, channels, etc., in the manufacture of armor plate, and in the
manufacture of plate of all kinds.

Q. Armor plate for war vessels?—A. Yes, sir; they do a miscellaneous business; or rather, we do a miscellaneous business at the Homestead Steel Works.

Q. Your company manufactures there armor to be used upon war

vessels being constructed by the Government of the United States?—
A. Yes, sir.

Q. Have you a contract with the Government for that work?—A.
We have.

Q. Will you either produce the contract or give the substance of it,
so we can understand it?—A. I will be very glad to produce a copy of
the contract; I have it not with me. It is for about 6,000 tons of
armor plate ranging in thickness from 4 inches to 20 inches, I believe.

Q. Is it specified in the contract for what vessels it is to be used?—
A. I could not name the vessels.

Q. The contract will show?—A. Yes, sir.

Q. Will you state, Mr. Frick, the different classes of workmen, skilled
laborers, and the wages paid them by you for the different classes
of work. I suppose there are a number of men engaged in the different
classes of work?—A. Yes, sir. Would you like me to state particularly
just whom the new scale affected on July 1?

Q. I would prefer that you state, if you can, the different classes of
workmen and the amounts paid them, and then we may go on with the
other.—A. I think I can get at that better, if you will allow me, by
taking up one department. I have before me a statement of the earnings for the month of May, 1892, for the workmen employed at the 119-
inch plate mill. The statement gives the name of each man, his position, the number of days he worked during the month of May, and his
earnings. There are so many rollers, I will just take one of them. So
many screwmen, I will just take one and give his earnings.

Q. Yes, and state how many it applies to.—A. Thomas Williams,
roller, worked 24 days, 8-hour days, in the month of May, and earned
$259.05; there were 2 rollers employed on that mill in addition to Mr.
Williams, and the earnings of both of them were higher than his. I
have the figures here if you wish them.

Q. State them.—A. H. McCrovy worked 22 days and earned $278.50;
R. Hotchkiss worked 23 days and earned $279.30. The next is what
we call screwdowns: H. Lank worked 22 days and earned $177.35,
William McQuaid worked 23 days and earned $214.05, F. Pifer worked
24 days and earned $211.55. The next I come to are 3 tablemen. The
first worked 24 days and earned $168.85. The next worked 22 days
and earned $179.55. The next worked 22 days and earned $167.30.
Then I come to what are called hookers. There are 6 hookers. The
first worked 24 days and earned $143.80; the next worked 24 days
and earned $143.80; the next worked 23 days and earned $153.65; the
next worked 22 days and earned $153.55; the next worked 23 days
and earned $150.55; the next worked 23 days and earned $153.25.
Then I come to front sweepers. There are 3 of those. The first
worked 22 days and earned $111.40. The next worked 23 days and
earned $109. The next worked 24 days and earned $101.85. Then
there are 3 back sweepers. The first worked 25 days and earned
$97.60. The next worked 23 days and earned $100.20. The next
worked 20 days and earned $95.60. Then I come to the first shearman.
There are 3 of those. The first worked 24 days and earned $216.40.
The second worked 22 days and earned $230.45. The next worked 24
days and earned $217.50. Then I come to second shearmen. There
are 3 of those. The first worked 24 days and earned $141.55. The
second worked 21 days and earned $143.15. The next worked 24 days
and earned $142.25. Then I come to what are called leaders. The
first worked 23 days and earned $121.95. The next worked 22 days
and earned $138.10. The third worked 24 days and earned $129.65.
Then we come to second leaders. There are 3 of those. The first

worked 18 days and earned $93.20. The second worked 22 days and
earned $129.05. The third worked 24 days and earned $121.40. Then
I come to shear helpers. There are 31 shear helpers. I can probably shorten this a little for you. The average number of days'
work by all those shear helpers was about 22 days and their average
earnings was, I should say, at least $95 each, for 8 hours per day. The
next are the heaters. There are 6 of those. The first worked 24 days
and earned $190.40. The second worked 23 days and earned $185.45.
The third worked 22 days and earned $191.30. The fourth worked 23
days and earned $195.55. The fifth worked 21 days and earned $178.
The sixth worked 23 days and earned $199.10. Then comes the heaters'
helpers. There are 5 of those. Their average was about 22 days, 23
days I should say, and their average earnings were about $135 per
month. Then we come to what are called first cranemen. There are
3 of those, averaging about 25 days each; average earnings to each
about $120 for the month. Next are second cranemen; 3 of those.

Q. That is the average earning per man?—A. Yes, sir, the average
per man. Three of those worked on an average of 25 days each,
and the average earnings per man were over $97 each. Then we come
to pull-ups. They are boys, and work by the day. Four of them averaged about 23 days work, average earnings about $40 each per month.
They work 12 hours. Then we come to the head shearers. They work
12 hours.

Q. Per day?—A. Yes, sir. There are 5 of those. The first worked 17
days, earning $112.05. The next worked 23 days, earning $130.75. The
next worked 24 days, earning $90.80. The next worked 23 days, earn-
ing $170.90. The next worked 23 days, earning $110.50. The next
worked 23 days, earning $79.80. Then come the foremen of the mark-
ing gang. They work by the day. There are 2 of those. The first
worked 27 days and earned $85. The next worked 25 days and earned
$85. Now there are a variety of men here, gaugers, stampers, paint-
ers, helpers, table helpers, inspectors, weigh masters, recorders, test
wheelers, millwrights, machinists, knife-grinder, carpenter, greaser, hydraulic man, 3 table men, table engineer, stationery engineers, 4 machinists at planers, shaper, traveling craneman, scale craneman, train
boys, roll engineers, whose average days work I suppose I might say
was 26 days, and average earnings I should say $70 per month. Then
we come to the ordinary laborers in this same department, messenger
boys—well, I suppose 30 of those. The lowest-priced labor at our
works is the ordinary day laborers. We pay 14 cents per hour. They
usually work 10 hours. We have others, though, that we class as
laborers to whom we pay higher wages. I notice one here $1.70 per
day, and others at the same rate. By ordinary labor we mean yard
labor. In that one department alone I see the pay roll for the month
of May was $20,202.95. The number of men I have not footed up, but
the statements will show.

Q. That is the amount paid the men employed by your company at
the Homestead Works in May?—A. Yes, sir; in the 119-inch plate
mill, one department of those works.

Q. How many departments are in the works there?—A. I have them
here; I can read them off to you. I think twelve departments. I will
be able to give you that exactly, however, presently.

Q. In the Homestead mills?—A. Yes, sir. The following is a list of
the departments at the Homestead Works, with the number of men
employed in each during the month of May. Some of the men are
not employed all the time. Some counted as men are boys:

Earnings at Homestead Steel Works for May, 1892.

119-INCH PLATE MILL.

Name.	Position.	Time.	Earnings. Actual, $25 base.	Minimum, new scale, $23 base.
		Days.		
Thomas Williams	Roller	24	$259.05	$160.32
H. McCrory	do	22	278.50	146.96
R. Hotchkiss	do	23	279.30	153.64
H. Lank	Screw down	22	177.35	115.50
William McQuade	do	23	214.05	120.75
F. Pifer	do	24	211.55	126.00
Jake Bletch	Tableman	24	168.85	91.68
O. Colfiesh	do	22	170.55	84.04
J. W. Watson	do	22	167.30	84.04
H. Baynes	Hooker	24	143.80	80.16
John I. Kane	do	24	143.80	80.16
P. S. Collins	do	22	153.65	73.48
C. Colfiesh	do	22	153.65	73.48
James Carley	do	23	150.55	76.82
W. F. Botts	do	23	153.25	76.82
W. Shea	Front sweeper	22	111.40	52.14
J. E. Williams	do	23	109.00	54.51
Joe Steff	do	24	101.85	56.88
Fred Kuhl	Back sweeper	25	97.60	59.75
Dan Kinney	do	23	100.20	54.97
Andy Senn	do	20	95.60	47.80
J. H. Miller	First shearman	24	218.40	126.00
Jno. Klein	do	22	230.45	115.50
Geo. H. Phillips	do	24	217.50	126.00
M. McMillin	Second shearman	24	141.55	91.68
John Martin	do	21	143.15	80.22
Lou. Suter	do	24	142.25	91.68
William Wilson	First leader	23	121.05	65.78
Nick Heusler	do	22	138.10	62.92
Thomas Boyd	do	24	129.65	68.64
E. J. Grove	Second leader	18	93.20	43.02
Con Strott	do	22	129.05	52.58
J. M. Brown	do	24	121.40	57.36
E. Routh	Shear helpers	22	83.25	42.02
H. Wilson	do	23	89.55	43.93
J. Muldoon	do	24	100.20	45.84
N. Stein	do	20½	78.75	39.16
P. Delaney	do	24	91.60	45.84
F. Hillman	do	24	91.60	45.84
J. Reed	do	23½	80.40	44.80
F. Flaherty	do	21	82.80	40.11
Jacob Rushe	do	22	83.25	42.02
William Barclay	do	24	91.60	45.84
A. Haller	do	22	90.10	42.02
F. Zern	do	22	97.55	42.02
William Wilson	do	22	97.55	42.02
A. Redpath	do	22	97.55	42.02
F. Smith	do	22	97.55	42.02
W. Dryburg	do	22	97.55	42.02
J. Potter	do	22	97.55	42.02
Tim Colter	do	22	97.55	42.02
Ed. McNallny	do	21	94.00	40.11
L. P. Shaw	do	21	93.45	40.11
Thos. Evans	do	24	92.10	45.84
Mike Smith	do	24	92.10	45.84
Dan J. Carr	do	24	92.10	45.84
Dan Bonner	do	24	92.10	45.84
Jas. Farquhar	do	24	87.70	45.84
F. Milliken	do	24	87.40	45.84
Robt. Hamilton	do	24	92.10	45.84
Jas. Hurley	do	26	99.15	49.66
H. A. Lash	do	24	92.10	45.84
Jno. Mullen	do	26	103.20	49.66
Jno. Gormley	do	8	24.40	15.28
Owen Carrell	Heater	24	190.40	126.00
Ed. Burke	do	23	185.45	120.75
Jas. Collin	do	22	191.30	115.50
J. H. Bost	do	23	195.55	120.75
Geo. Reylands	do	21	178.00	110.25
Hugh O'Donnell	do	23	199.10	120.75
J. Clifford	Shear helper	24	131.85	68.64
F. S. Artman	do	24	133.05	68.64
W. A. Greig	do	23	141.00	65.78
Henry Flech	do	21	125.40	60.06

Earnings at Homestead Steel Works for May, 1892—Continued.

119-INCH PLATE MILL—Continued.

Name.	Position.	Time.	Earnings. Actual, $25 base.	Minimum, new scale, $23 base.
		Days.		
Wm. Gaches	Shear helper	23	$134.75	$65.78
Wm. Kane	do	23	134.05	65.78
Ed. Barrett	First craneman	25	114.25	65.75
Wm. Watts	do	25	123.25	65.75
Chas. Watts	do	20	122.40	68.38
Ad. Pifer	Second craneman	27	103.10	71.01
Lewis Bost	do	24	97.65	63.12
Wm. Bennett	do	25	97.06	65.75
Dan Gartland	Pull-ups	24	*40.35	40.35
Wm. Hennesy	do	20	*33.30	33.30
Pat Bonner	do	23	*40.75	40.75
Thos. McDonough	do	21	*35.25	35.25
John Durline	Head shears	17	*112.05	112.05
Jas. Cosgrove	do	23	*130.75	130.75
Wm. Herald	do	24	*90.80	90.80
C. Demmell	do	23	*171.00	171.00
John Kinnally	do	23	*110.50	110.50
Wm. Jones	do	23	*79.80	79.80

* Unchanged by new scale.

[Unchanged by new scale.]

Name.	Position.	Time.	Salary, actual, $25 base.
		Days.	
F. P. Carroll	Foreman marking gang	27	$85.00
R. E. Spears	do	25	85.00
E. T. Mailley	Ganger	27	78.75
John Brown	do	25	73.75
Thos. Brown	Stamper	27	62.85
Wm. Hoffman	do	24	56.40
John Carroll	Painter	27	51.95
Ignatius Brown	do	25	49.25
Pat. Ward	Helper	27	44.10
Peter McCoy	do	25	38.25
H. C. Brown	do	25	41.30
John Cronin	Table helper	27	44.10
Wm. F. Brown	Inspector	28	75.00
John Ward	do	27	62.90
C. P. Mills	do	23	59.15
A. K. Mitchell	Weighmaster	25	58.75
H. L. Culp	do	25	61.00
Geo. Ward	Recorder	26	54.55
Jos. Speers	do	25	56.60
Ned Rolfe	Test wheeler	25	41.30
Nic. Farrell	Millwright	28	122.50
C. C. Jackson	do	28	116.15
Walter Sellers	Wheelwright helper	26	62.45
Paul Wilmot	do	27	63.20
Jas. Smith	Machinist	29	59.95
C. E. Dible	Knife grinder	9	16.50
Wm. Reed	Carpenter	26	45.65
Ed. Kitzing	Greaser	31	62.65
Jas. Lamont	Knife grinder	15	25.50
Sam Brown	Hydraulic man	30	110.80
Wm. Redman	Tableman	29	81.50
Thos. Lowry	do	28	58.00
Geo. Worley	do	16	49.60
Aden Shoemaker	Table engineer	24	44.70
Thos. Morris	do	27	49.50
Peter Percival	Engineer, stationary	32	64.00
Chas. Hoffman	do	30	60.00
Mike Miller	Machinist at planer	32	86.40
Angy Lamont	do	31	72.80
Julius Huber	do	28	72.00
Egnatr Miller	do	28	64.85
Lewis Weber	Shaper	11	21.35
Fred Buck, jr	Traveling craneman	26	50.55
Fred Buck, sr	Scale craneman	26	40.60
John Drummond	Scale crane boy	26	29.00

*Earnings at Homestead Steel Works for May, 1892—*Continued.

119-INCH PLATE MILL—Continued.

[Unchanged by new scale.]

Name.	Position.	Time.	Salary, actual, $25 base.
		Days.	
Frank McCune	Scale crane boy	27	$31.40
John Jones, sr	...do	21	33.85
D. L. James	Roll engineer	28½	101.70
Geo. Loveday	...do	30	107.70
Mike Barry	Shear engineer	26½	63.60
Geo. Collins	...do	28½	68.40
Wm. Livingstone	Pressure pumps	31	69.75
Chas. Adams	...do	30	67.50
Thos. Harkness	Tending boilers	33	83.00
J. G. Sellinger	...do	30	75.00
Ambrose Lees	Boiler-cleaner	32	53.85
Wm. Menke	Foreman scale gang	26	74.50
Andy Schwartz	Laborer	24	38.35
Geo. Repko	...do	15	25.10
John Kushma	...do	12	19.45
Geo. Wagner	...do	22	34.35
Mike Matia	...do	16	25.60
Joe Billick	...do	16	31.70
Jno. Halibuta	...do	20	41.85
Geo. Samen	...do	12	21.15
Andy Tomko	...do	12	21.60
Geo. Hatcher	Foreman scales gang	24	70.00
Andy Stopko	Laborer	25	42.00
Jno. Mikula	...do	25	42.00
Mike Elko	...do	25½	43.70
Jno. Goga	...do	16	26.20
Joe Keish	...do	25	42.10
Joe Parlotski	...do	10	16.40
Paul Mikula	...do	15	24.50
Mike Yapanitzki	...do	11	19.05
Jas. Torgoage	...do	1	1.40
Mike Kohute	...do	3	4.65
M Kropps	...do	1	1.70
L. Chortas	...do	3	4.80
Jno. Sesoock	...do	1	1.70
Geo. Perch	...do	1	1.70
Geo. Uskat	...do	1	1.70
Mike Sarron	...do	1	1.70
Frank Dukoste	...do	2	2.40
Jno. Vislic	...do	4	9.35
Mike Dudash	...do	1	1.75
Jno. Weldon	Crane boy	25	32.45
Jno. Morgan	...do	23	29.30
Chas. Shaw	...do	9	10.30
Mike Vitro	Scrap gang	11	21.00
Joe Topko	...do	23½	54.05
Nick Kohutz	...do	25	55.20
Jno. Doroako	...do	25	58.00
Steve Bukosku	...do	22½	56.95
Jno. Kustro	...do	24	60.10
Andy Parlotski	...do	23	57.15
Joe Beresok	...do	24	60.10
Frank Cramer	Water carrier	26	43.40
Andy Gladish	...do	31	41.85
Mike Lyden	Yard-crane engineer	31	67.90
Dennis O'Sullivan	Yard-crane helper	26	47.70
Mike McGregor	Repairing buggies	26	65.00
		Months.	
Henry Jackson	Loader, shipping department	1	70.00
Norman Whitten	...do	1	60.00
C. S. Capohart	...do	1	75.00
M. A. Morgan	Clerk, shipping department	1	65.00
C. W. Streveant	...do	1	55.00
		Days.	
J. J Gilliland	Loader, shipping department	6	16.70
Reese Hughs	Messenger, shipping department	28	21.00
Fred Heige	Crane boy, shipping department	26	26.00
Al. Blumston	...do	1	1.20
W. Stewart	...do	27	27.20
Dennis Ward	...do	27	28.10
John Schinally	Laborer, shipping department	10	13.30
Steve Bonjou	...do	26	36.40
Peter Pido	...do	26	36.40
John Bukoski	...do	10	23.65
Andy Kossun	...do	27	29.50

Earnings at Homestead Steel Works for May, 1892— Continued.

119-INCH PLATE MILL—Continued.

[Unchanged by new scale.]

Name.	Position.	Time.	Salary, actual, $25 base.
		Days.	
Joe Raowell	Labor, shipping department	27	$39.50
H. Brozinaki	do	27	39.50
Joe Biggins	do	27	39.50
Mike Cargo	do	27	39.50
Pete Choushda	do	27	39.30
John Hollar	do	7	9.50
John Sato	do	27	39.30
Sig. Barra	do	21	31.20
		Months.	
W. H. Packer	Clerk, plate-mill office	1	100.00
H. D. Barnhardt	do	1	85.00
Geo. L. Glunt	Clerk, 320-mill office	1	75.00
W. L. Bassinger	do	1	75.00
J. O. Foster	do	1	75.00
Jas. Peterson	do	1	75.00
L. Y. Woodward	do	1	75.00
W. E. Crouch	do	1	60.00
C. B. McCurdy	Clerk	1	60.00
W. T. Oakin	do	1	70.00
J. B. Kenyon	do	1	70.00
T. Coorey	do	1	75.00
J. H. Risher	do	1	65.00
W. E. Bullock	Timekeeper	½	30.00
J. G. Wallace	do	½	27.50
Frank Poup	do	1	60.00
Richard Reeves	Janitor	1	49.50
C. C. Seldon	Clerk (special work)	1	30.80
		Days.	
David Carataira	Office boy	26	18.75
E. Sarner	do	26	18.30
J. Cavanaugh	do	26	16.90
John Bills	Rigger	29	59.50
John Masher	Clean-up	25	36.70
John Close, sr	do	25	33.90
Charles Slelcor	Cartman	25	35.00
		Month.	
W. W. Mechling	General foreman laborers	1	125.00
		Days.	
W. L. Leadbeater	Laborer foreman, 119"-32"	34	104.50
John Stevens	Laborer	20	42.85
Mike Mulhern	do	25	42.00
Mike Beres	do	31	46.75
John Popp	do	25	39.20
Dan Kane	do	15	24.35
Pat Tool	do	28	41.70
John Marko	do	29	44.80
Steve Cornish	do	24	39.30
John Gargo	do	30	47.80
Mike Betco	do	29	46.05
John Banka	do	28	44.35
Thomas Trauny	do	20	44.80
John Verotaki	do	22	33.45
John Badura	do	33½	61.30
John Brozinski	do	28	45.05
Emro Krock	do	28	42.70
Andy Sirdy	do	28	46.30
Ned Close	do	28	51.50
Steve Thomas	do	28	50.40
Paul Hudock	Laborer and greaser	31	55.85
Ralph Welch	Laborer and stand turns	34½	73.50
Sam Wampler	Laborer	20	61.55
Mike Surdy	do	¼	.40
Thomas Cameron	do	1½	1.40
Mike Webber	do	2¼	3.55
George Thomas	do	31	52.60
George Cornish	do	24	40.00
Richard Snelden	do	27	63.50
Peter Weber	do	29	47.25
John Hudock	do	5	8.70
Total			20,202.95

Earnings at Homestead Steel Works for May, 1892—Continued.

32-INCH SLABBING MILL.

Name.	Position.	Time.	Earnings.	
			Actual, $25 base.	Mini-mum, new scale, $23 base.
		Days.		
O. S. Seawright	Screwman	23	$195.75	$166.67
Reid Kennedy	......do	23	201.10	166.67
W. R. Vogle	Heater	26	211.30	182.26
Dennis Kelly	......do	26	224.15	182.26
W. T. Roberts	Heater, first helper	23	137.55	79.58
W. R. Carrick	......do	22	132.40	76.12
John Firbrick	Heater, second helper	24	83.00	57.60
Abe Worman	......do	25	90.85	60.00
John Buck	Craneman	23	93.20	49.68
George Harkins	......do	22	96.05	47.52
Pat Tierny	Cinder tapper	23	68.05	33.58
Mike Mahoney	......do	24	68.50	35.04
Ed Richrads	Roll engineer	29	118.85	94.25
C. Massy	......do	29	118.85	94.25
C. H. Richards	......do	26	118.00	84.50
W. McLaughlin	......do	25	114.60	81.25
J. Bulace	Roll-engineer helper	27	*54.00	....
F. McLaughlin	......do	26	*52.00	....
P. McHenry	......do	27	*54.00	....
F. Cristaner	Roll tableman	24	118.50	62.40
T. R. Davis	......do	25	124.60	65.00
C. P. Clark	Greaser	25	59.25	47.50
E. Donahue	......do	27	67.40	51.30
S. Reid	Sweeper	24	67.90	46.80
R. Dalton	......do	24	68.10	46.80
J. Deitzer	......do	20	57.70	39.00
W. A. Rhotrauff	......do	22	66.75	42.90
Harry Queck	Shearman	24	108.80	96.00
R. Haighey	......do	24	111.50	96.00
Charles Scheif	Shearman, tableman	24	74.95	57.60
B. F. Ross	......do	23	70.55	52.80
Alex. Witherspoon	Table engineer	27	54.00	54.00
J Shallenberger	......do	26	52.00	52.00
J. S. Reed	Shear tongsman	22	61.25	44.88
Pat Mullen	......do	24	66.70	48.96
R. O'Neil	......do	22½	62.60	46.41
P. Dougherty	......do	24	68.50	48.96
M. Goga	......do	31	66.20	63.24
S. Brown	......do	31	52.30	63.24
J. Durori	......do	30	51.10	61.20
P. Giles	......do	24	68.50	48.96
W. Herron	Gauger	23	64.05	64.05
W. F. McConegly	......do	23	67.25	67.25
W. E. Woodside	Stamper	24	60.70	51.84
R. McLaughlin	......do	23	60.45	49.68
W. Naughton	Regulator	24	41.85	35.04
A. J. Hunter	......do	24	46.00	35.04
D. O'Donnell	......do	24	43.00	35.04
W. Patterson	......do	24	41.85	35.04
W. Cristaner	Bottom-maker	5	20.90	15.05
R. M. McCornish	......do	29	73.50	87.29
J. Sellinger	Tongs at pits	21½	47.35	41.93
R. Steveson	......do	31	64.15	60.45
B. S. Straney	Press-pump engineer	31	69.75	60.45
J. W. Shallenberger	......do	27	67.50	52.65
J. P. Blackmore	Tongs at pit	14	40.10	27.30
F. S. Turner	......do	25	58.40	48.75

* Unchanged by new scale.

*Earnings at Homestead Steel Works for May, 1892—*Continued.

32-INCH SLABBING MILL—Continued.

[Unchanged by new scale.]

Name.	Position.	Time.	Salary, actual, $25 base.
		Days.	
J. Horner	Hydraulic man	30	$90.70
H. McMinn	T. craneman	14	50.40
H. Hallsall	do	23	75.10
A. Crum	Standing turn	4	16.35
R. Welsh	do	1	1.65
P. Webber	do	1	2.60
S. Davis	do	1	3.45
P. Bates	Locomotive-crane engineer	28	61.60
A. Matsro	do	2	4.40
W. Stiner	do	29	63.80
N. Rusho	Yard-crane engineer	31	68.20
M. Rogan	do	14½	31.35
E. Dotrosch	Locomotive engineer	28	61.60
N. Clark	Locomotive hook-on	10	22.40
A. Frank	Slab-marker	28	67.20
S. Winer	do	3	7.20
M. Webber	Rigger	3	6.10
W. Hillman	do	24	42.00
G. Davis	Water-tender	30	75.00
J. C. Miller	do	33	82.50
P. Dalton	Boiler-cleaner	31	52.00
J. Raybone	Scrap foreman	26	54.75
N. Miller	Scrap laborer	26	46.35
M. Kush	do	22	40.45
A. Tueck	Scrap craneman	21	21.10
A. Mecshick	Laborer	29	52.35
A. Gatyell	do	30	48.45
T. Desmond	do	31	55.75
P. Maurer	Water-carrier	23	35.45
J. Barrett	do	14	21.70
J. Gilhooley	Shipping foreman	27	50.00
J. McNight	Engineer's helper	26	52.00
W. Harkins	Stocking gang	22	62.85
J S. Smith	do	24	60.70
A. Negran	do	20½	58.80
M. Johnson	do	24	68.50
M. Amond	do	24	68.50
J. Hultee	do	24	68.50
C. Barrett	do	18	52.75
R. Dodge	do	23	64.65
J. Jeffries	Machinist	29	103.95
S. McKnight	do	29	103.95
M. Hatfield	Machinist helper	27	54.50
C. Laird	do	27	51.30
C. Peterson	do	29	56.70
B. Rowan	do	20	57.40
M. Hide	Weighmaster	24	60.00
W. Eyman	do	24	60.00
R. Stevenson	do	24	60.00
J. Thomas	do	24	60.00
W. Spires	Locomotive engineer	28	61.60
J. Ackman	do	26 *	57.20
J. Dodge, sr	do	28	61.60
D. Hillman	do	29½	64.90
J. Ruch	do	13	28.60
J. Migley	Hook-on	18½	27.50
O. Moore	do	25	35.00
H. Dodger	do	26	36.40
F. Milligan	do	28	39.20
J. Dugan	do	24	46.70
W. Brown	do	21	29.40
R. Abbott	do	3	4.20
J. Donahue	do	7½	10.50
G. Aton	Shipping G. laborers	23	33.70
A. Anton	do	20	28.10
A. Sench	do	26	20.20
G. Basak	do	28	40.45
M. Plapopen	do	28	41.40
J. Pedo	do	27	40.70
A. Solvitz	do	3	2.10
J. Frankaritch	do	23	31.90
G. Curitz	do	3	2.10
P. Kushner	do	2	1.40
F. Gilhooley	do	27	36.55
J. Phalson	do	9	9.95
F. Babo	do	7	6.95
J. Koonos	do	7	6.95

*Earnings at Homestead Steel Works for May, 1892—*Continued.

32-INCH SLABBING MILL—Continued.

[Unchanged by new scale.]

Name.	Position.	Time.	Salary, actual, $25 base.
		Days.	
J. Cabouch	Shipping G. laborers	7	$9.95
G. Carnelgh	do	7	9.10
S. Kuku	do	7	9.95
J. Stam	do	2	2.80
J. Ryan	Laborer	29	52.50
J. Volenski	do	27	50.75
J. Damyel	do	31	51.25
J. Korcko	do	30	55.75
H. McBraney	do	25	42.00
M. Firbarak	do	27	47.05
M. Partrick	do	28	48.15
M. Bille	do	24	43.90
A. Koropo	do	4	7.15
M. Daryel	do	4	6.45
P. Durkin	do	1	1.40
T. Williams	do	6	0.65
T. Pitchford	do	3	4.20
P. Baker	Messenger	20	16.60
J. Bonner	do	25	19.75
William Glunt	do	23	17.25
G. Martz	do	1	.75
J. Clouen	do	22	16.50
A. Huston	do	3	2.25
H. Darney	do	6	4.50
W. H. Blakely	do	3	2.25
Total			8,010.20

OPEN HEARTH, No. 1.

Name.	Position.	Time.	Earnings.	
			Actual, $25 base.	Minimum, new scale, $23 base.
		Days.		
J. Nagle	Melter	26	$156.00	$156.00
T. Black	do	24¼	145.50	145.50
T. Hunter	do	28	168.00	168.00
F. Pinder	do	24	144.00	144.00
F. J. Willman	do	18½	111.00	111.00
F. Janero	do	26	156.00	156.00
J. Spoier	do	21	126.00	126.00
C. O. Hoffman	do	25	150.00	150.00
T. Thomas	Melter, 1st helper	12	44.00	35.04
J. Murray	do	27	100.30	78.84
H. Lowe	do	29	107.10	84.68
P. McGrath	do	31	132.35	90.52
T. Bowen	do	26	81.00	75.92
G. Smith	do	31	126.30	90.52
H. Boltz	do	27	101.90	78.84
G. Johnston	do	31	109.35	90.52
J. P. Daily	Melter, 2d helper	26	84.40	61.62
T. Clifford	do	25	77.70	59.25
P. Cameron	do	26	71.40	61.62
J. Eicher	do	24	80.10	56.88
C. Schoup	do	24	56.35	56.88
M. McCann	do	27	93.50	63.99
Ed. Kautz	do	24	85.90	56.88
N. Duffy	do	23	76.85	54.51
A. King	Charger	31	60.40	67.89
D. E. Wilding	do	25	71.75	54.75
D. Evans	do	25	71.75	54.75
T. Hartland, sr.	do	26	77.55	56.94
F Sample	do	24	71.55	52.56
F. Hammell	do	26	62.10	56.94
P. O'Rourke	do	23	62.75	50.37
Wm. Taylor	do	24	71.55	52.56
H. B. Dale	do	26	93.00	56.94

Earnings at Homestead Steel Works for May, 1892—Continued.

OPEN HEARTH No. 1—Continued.

Time.	Position.	Time.	Earnings. Actual, $25 base.	Earnings. Minimum, new scale, $23 base.
		Days.		
T. Floid	Charger	26	$93.00	$56.94
A. Asson	do	20	93.00	56.94
Wm. Molzer	do	26	89.75	56.94
Thos. Kelly	do	20	65.05	43.80
Wm. R. Williams	do	25	79.15	54.75
J. Eighnott	do	27	85.45	59.13
Francis Taylor	do	26	84.70	56.94
M. Franion	do	27	92.95	59.13
R. Farrer	do	26	89.75	56.04
J. K. Halny	do	25	81.30	54.75
D. McGrath	do	26	82.35	56.94
J. Madden	Ladleman	26	84.40	70.98
P. Fagan	do	27	87.95	73.71
T. Smith	do	13	35.75	35.49
J. Dalton	do	26	70.75	70.98
T. Quinn	do	27	96.05	73.71
J. Murphy	do	27	99.60	73.71
M. Gray	do	26	113.30	76.44
J. Gustafson	do	29	113.30	79.17
J. Grocock	Ladleman helper	24	70.80	56.88
J. Ackerman	do	24	67.15	56.88
D. Dunbarr	do	29	83.30	68.73
J. Quinn	do	26	76.95	61.62
O. C. Christy	do	27	78.00	63.99
W. Coley	do	21	73.10	49.77
T. Crowley	Pitman	27	87.90	73.71
J. Hicks	do	25	80.65	68.25
G. Eighnott	do	25	67.70	64.25
J. Davis	do	24	60.00	65.52
P. Morgan	do	23	84.60	62.79
Wm. Sweeney	do	25	101.40	68.25
J. Thomas	do	24	85.20	65.52
J. Sullivan	do	27	105.40	73.71
J. S. Reily	Pitman, first helper	22	61.05	48.18
E. G. Stokes	do	20	65.35	43.80
M. Kosack	do	24	53.40	52.56
J. Zerco	do	24	54.00	52.56
G. Ackerman	do	26	80.50	56.94
H. Schoup	do	24	77.20	52.56
P. O'Brien	do	16	51.60	35.04
D. Creeven	do	25	77.30	54.75
J. Dalton	Pitman, second helper	26	83.35	52.00
T. Stanton	do	24	80.05	48.00
P. Biggins	do	12	36.75	24.00
P. Morris	do	26	82.75	52.00
P. Fares	do	24	71.35	48.00
J. Morris	Craneman	26	60.60	47.32
H. Thomas	do	23	61.30	41.86
H. Clark	do	28	80.55	50.96
G. Crouch	do	25	83.35	45.50

[Unchanged by new scale.]

Name.	Position.	Time.	Salary.
		Days.	
T. Harton, jr	Pull-up boy	27	$31.05
J. Gray	do	26	29.00
A. Close	do	27	31.05
J. Murray	do	26	29.90
Wm. Martin	do	26	29.90
O. Thomas	do	27	31.05
H. Pierce	Weighmaster	26	46.80
J. J. Gilland	do	12	21.05
E. Sill	do	4	7.20
J. S. Kingan	do	27	48.60
R. J. Diabler	do	28	50.40
J. R. Oakley	Foreman, foundry	*1	100.00
J. Donnavon	Molder	26	83.05
J. A. Campbell	do	20	61.30
W. Stranning	do	26	79.80

* Month.

Earnings at Homestead Steel Works for May, 1892—Continued.

OPEN HEARTH No. 1—Continued.

[Unchanged by new scale.]

Name.	Position.	Time.	Salary.
		Days.	
R. Hettrick	Molder	26	$83.05
T. Kaye	do	25	80.30
R. Wotherspoon	do	25	85.25
R. W. Livingston	do	25	80.30
G. F. Bailey	Molder helper	25	40.60
J. Close, jr	do	25	39.05
B. R. Nevile	do	14	23.85
A. Barthol	do	26	42.50
F. Geron	do	20	37.10
R. Colclaser	do	31	55.45
J. Piokar	do	20	31.50
P. McCann	do	25	45.30
A. Barthol	do	26	41.45
M. Dunlap	Standing turns	25	60.45
D. Morluck	do	8	25.00
Pat Hayes	do	3	8.50
J. Welsh	do	2	5.05
J. O'Neil	do	10	57.95
J. J. Davis	do	18	57.90
M. O'Donnell	do	21	59.95
J. Clark	do	3	9.05
C. Eichler	do	15	48.80
J. Gustafson	do	18	52.55
J. Farquhar	do	1	6.00
J. Watts	do	2	5.50
W. Schultz	do	26	73.15
C. Boyles	do	12½	39.25
A. Sauhaurating	Laborer	26	44.75
F. Shauriba	do	26	45.35
R. Streigle	do	17	26.05
J. Dixon	do	2	3.35
P. Gavin	do	12	19.30
C. Schinally	do	27	46.55
J. Buchda	do	26	43.65
M. Wallrich	do	1	1.70
M. Sabo	do	6	9.95
Ed. Toparezer	do	27	46.35
G. Hopsey	do	2	3.35
N. Maures	do	6	10.10
J. Palszo	do	1	1.05
M. Kandlo	do	24	41.85
M. Dyerko	do	26	45.35
A. Dyerko	do	26	43.65
M. Brozinsky	Laborer	27	45.65
A. Yosroe	do	26	43.65
M. Motto	do	26	44.85
J. Ludick	do	24	47.40
J. Trout	do	27	45.35
A. Bollon	do	27	45.40
A. Topreser	do	29	49.80
S. Ballock	do	26	49.05
T. Alexander, sr	do	26	43.65
J. F. Forrester	Laborer foreman	16	40.00
C. W. Creeps	do	*1	64.50
C. Haws	Locomotive engineer	29	63.80
M. Walch	do	28	61.60
R. Jury	Locomotive hook-on (boy)	27	37.80
W. Spires	do	20	28.00
J. Omgler	do	1	1.20
J. Gustapon	Water-carrier	27	30.75
J. McMichaels	Water-carrier (boy)	27	22.40
W. O'Forbe	do	24	20.40
J. W. Thurber	Record clerk	*1	65.00
W. Clint	Foreman metal gang	3	7.50
M. Laskames	do	7	17.50
J. J. Ferick	Laborer metal gang	12	27.25
J. Beacon	do	15	33.30
S. Phœnix	do	15	33.30
G. Coscoe	do	15	33.00
P. Soxkna	do	16	33.90
A. Kansner	do	1	.60
Mike Rogan	do	15	33.30
J. Donahue	Hook-on	5	7.20
Total pay roll, open hearth, No. 1, for May			10,591.05

* Month.

Earnings at Homestead Steel Works for May, 1892—Continued.

OPEN HEARTH, No. 2.

Name.	Position.	Time.	Actual, $25 base.	Minimum, new scale, $23 base.
		Days.		
Jake Stiner	Melter	23	$138.00	$138.00
Wm. Levy	do	27	162.00	162.00
Richard Durham	do	18	108.00	108.00
Joe Gallup	do	26	156.00	156.00
W. C. Wolf	do	26	156.00	156.00
Wm. Williams	do	27	162.00	162.00
Peter Steiner	do	28	168.00	168.00
James Hopkins	do	22	132.00	132.00
Peter Moran	do	27	162.00	162.00
Frank Thomas	do	26	156.00	156.00
Joseph Williams	do	22½	133.50	133.50
Wm. Loadman	do	23	138.00	138.00
Harry Shaw	do	26	156.00	156.00
Jos. Frey	do	18	108.00	108.00
Jake Schoerr	do	26	156.00	156.00
Wm. F. Reese	do	24	144.00	144.00
Jno. Stiner	Melters' first help	29	115.10	84.68
Chas. Fagart	do	26	101.00	75.92
Jno. F. Wood	do	29	119.55	84.68
Wm. White	do	28½	140.90	83.22
Nick Schoerr	do	28	105.00	81.76
Jesse Lautz	do	27	107.15	78.84
Jas. W. Martin	do	5	18.15	14.60
Robt. Cain	do	27	107.45	78.84
Oliver Antiss	do	27	120.45	78.84
Isaac Gray	do	29	113.00	84.68
Mike McNaughton	do	29	119.40	84.68
Andy Stimer	do	29	122.90	84.68
Wm. Ferguson	do	27	109.20	78.84
Wm. Abbott	do	28	103.50	81.76
Sam Worton	do	29	121.70	84.68
C. S. Farquhar	do	29	119.75	84.68
Geo. Bell	Melter's second help	26	86.30	61.62
Jno. Bridges	do	15	50.10	35.55
Thos. Davis	do	27	92.95	63.99
Owen Quinn	do	26½	83.25	62.81
Jno. Bradford	do	26	79.50	61.62
Lawrence Schopp	do	22	86.95	52.14
Elijah Bell	do	25	86.40	59.25
Geo. Larner	do	27	90.10	63.99
Jno. Hines	do	20	87.70	47.40
William Altman	do	22	70.90	52.14
Thos. Wilson	do	25	89.80	59.25
Jos. Macinath	do	25	91.05	59.25
Wm. M. Combs	do	25½	83.40	59.84
Jos. Fish	do	24	74.75	56.88
Henry Knuben	do	26	81.45	61.62
Wm. Worton	do	26	91.00	61.62
Nick Foust	Melter's third help	22	56.85	44.00
Jno. O'Brien	do	20	57.50	40.00
Thos. Beatty	do	23	65.45	46.00
Jos. Allen	do	21	57.70	42.00
Dennis Murphy	do	27	77.40	54.00
David Stevens	do	27	71.45	54.00
Daniel Harris	do	24½	58.85	49.00
Jno. F. Durkin	do	24	65.60	48.00
Rich. Loadman	do	18	48.15	36.00
Jos. Kelly	do	26	65.55	52.00
Lawrence Murphy	do	26	61.40	52.00
Rich. Wood	do	23	57.55	46.00
Anthony Soulier	do	11	30.55	22.00
Grant West	do	19	47.20	38.00
Frank Simrock	do	26	61.45	52.00
Jno. Blakely	do	25	67.15	50.00
Andy Carson	First pitman	24	67.90	70.08
Wm. Espy	do	23	79.55	67.16
Reynold Deemer	do	24	91.80	70.08
Jos. Atwood	do	10	68.35	55.48
Jas. Morris	Second pitman	27	84.10	68.99
Nick Stanford	do	26	76.70	61.62
Jas. J. Duffy	do	26	83.45	61.62
Wm. Guard	do	25	78.65	59.25
Pat Davin	Third pitman	26	73.80	56.94
Samuel Motter	do	26	70.70	56.94

Earnings at Homestead Steel Works for May, 1892—Continued.

OPEN HEARTH, No. 2—Continued.

Name.	Position.	Time.	Earnings. Actual, $25 base.	Minimum, new scale, $23 base.
		Days.		
Wm. Caldwell	Third pitman	26	$76.00	$56.94
David Jones	do	26	74.35	56.94
Geo. Stewart	First ladleman	21	76.75	61.32
Jas. Frew	do	28	100.65	81.76
Mathew Thompson	do	20	75.95	58.40
John McGovern	do	28	100.65	81.76
William Carson	Second ladleman	24	72.50	56.88
John Bartles	do	27	87.15	63.39
G. P. Radcliff	do	28	93.75	66.36
George Champeno	do	26	76.90	61.62
John S. Murphy	Third ladleman	28	88.25	66.36
William Evans	do	28	88.25	66.36
Fred. Bell	do	28	82.85	66.36
George Barker	do	23½	66.80	55.00
Jas. Saulters	Ladle craneman	28	82.30	71.40
J. Watkins	do	26	79.40	66.30
Chas. A. Hillman	Ingot craneman	25	75.75	63.75
Frank Akerman	do	28	79.90	71.40
Al. Scrivener	do	27	77.05	68.85
Paul Russell	do	26	81.95	66.30
Wm. H. Shorts	do	21	62.25	53.55
Wm. Fisher	do	26	77.05	66.30
Martin Davis	Stockers	21	58.20	53.55
Jas. Watson	do	19½	50.25	42.71
Wm. Diamond	do	27	73.15	59.13
Jno. Compton	do	25	68.10	54.75
Jno. Swarts	do	15	30.95	32.85
Roman Urban	do	26	66.20	50.94
Geo. Cain	do	27	68.80	59.13
Jno. Paine	do	14½	26.85	31.70
Jno. Marto	do	23	64.60	50.37
Casper Doran	do	24	67.35	52.56
Mike Soapor	do	24	67.45	52.56
Mike Myrosho	do	26	73.15	56.94
Nick Hony	do	24	63.55	52.56
Wm. Parfitt	do	22	58.25	48.18
Frank Picton	do	22	63.50	48.18
Levi Thomas	do	26	68.80	56.94
Jno. McFarlne	Engineer charging machine	27¾	93.20	70.76
Wm. Drake	do	24½	77.85	61.84
Wm. Malloy	do	26½	92.40	67.58
Jas. Cain	do	26½	80.00	67.58

[Unchanged by new scale.]

Name.	Position.	Time.	Salary.
		Days.	
Sm. Davis	Engineer, press pumps	30	$68.50
Isaac Kenvin	do	32	72.00
Wm. X. Williams	Engineer, locomotive	29	63.80
Jas. Thomas	do	29	63.80
Wm. McClelland	do	28	61.60
Wm. Collins	do	30	66.00
C. M. Cline	do	28	61.60
Geo. Brenn	do	29½	65.45
Hugh M. Wilson	do	29	63.80
Pat. Morning	Engineer, mixing house	31	62.00
Jno. W. Close	do	29	58.00
Dan Dugan	Engineer, hook-on	26½	37.45
Gus. Broadright	do	25	35.00
Wm. X. Thomas	Hydraulic man	24½	75.80
Robt. Doughty	do	31	74.50
Chas. Moore	Hook-on	27	38.50
Wm. Rushton	do	21	29.40
Jno. McDougle	do	27	37.80
Jno. Donahue	do	1	1.40
Thos. Jones	do	21	29.40
Mike Clerk	do	3	4.20
Jas. Adams	do	27	37.80
Robt. Morgan	do	27	37.80

Earnings at Homestead Steel Works for May, 1892—Continued.

OPEN HEARTH, No. 2—Continued.

[Unchanged by new scale.]

Name.	Position.	Time.	Salary.
		Days.	
Jno. Quigley	Hook-on	3	$4.20
R. W. Abbott	do	4	5.60
Jas. Wilding	do	1	1.40
E. W. Morrison	Locomotive engineer	1	2.20
Thos. Kenvin	do	28	61.60
James Redshaw	Water-carrier	27	47.85
John Ewing	do	26	43.05
George Phelps	Bottom-maker	27	64.80
Henry Trautman	do	34½	58.80
Robert Radcliff	do	26	62.40
Andy Bosh	do	27	64.80
James Rushton	Blacksmith	26	80.05
Charles Emery	Blacksmiths' helper	26	54.00
T. P. Jones	do	23	36.80
R. E. Roberts	do	2	3.20
Geo. Rayburn	do	23	37.60
Stephen Pyers	Fireman boilers	14½	29.60
Andy Rogan	do	10	18.60
Wm. H. Smith	do	4	8.15
Thos. Pyers	do	2	4.10
Geo. Kelsey	Coal-pourer	10½	17.65
Dan Boelig	do	2	3.35
Mike Smith	do	5	8.40
David Antiss	Tool man	20	33.60
Sherman Jones	Inspector	28	58.80
H. L. Kirkwood	do	25	50.00
W. L. Forster	Weighmaster	29	58.00
Stewart Depuey	do	27	48.00
David T. Lloyd	do	23	46.00
H. M. Blakely	do	26	47.00
Geo. B. Forster	Record clerk	*1	85.00
Jas. A. Thompson	Timekeeper	*1	55.00
C. M. Loomis	do	*1	60.00
M. L. Price	Foreman, mixing house	30	72.00
Jas. McCracken	do	29	69.60
Jno F. Scott	Foreman laborers	27½	82.50
Jos. Redshaw	do	30	90.00
Ed. Pearson	Standing turns	31	63.75
Jno. Davin	do	27	52.95
Jno. F. Maley	Messenger	26	19.50
Jno. Karney	Laborer, mixing house	27	49.95
Jo. Zolta	do	26	46.20
Juo Timko	do	27	54.35
Mike Houyack	do	27	49.15
Jos. L. Dakosh	do	23	40.75
Jos. Kundash	do	27	48.70
Geo. Corless	do	19	32.35
Jacob Miller	do	27	43.65
Chas. Gehen	do	19	36.15
Mike Dobson	do	26	46.45
Wm. Dee	do	9	17.10
John Varnis	do	25	43.65
William Jenkins	do	16	28.55
George Zohn	do	18	31.50
Steve Fargosh	do	26	51.25
Mike Golden	do	26	36.40
Joe Dukosh	do	17	48.70
Fally Salatiel	do	17	36.00
Sam. Barkley	Laborer, skull cracker	24	64.55
Steve Enner	do	24	64.55
Jule Barghol	do	23	64.55
Mike Daniel	do	23	61.95
Frank Downey	do	24	64.55
Amon Kettering	do	23	61.95
John Fullard	do	25	66.35
John W. O'Brien	do	28	73.75
O. R. Munhall	Unloader	29	62.00
Andy Dudash	do	19	54.45
Joseph Mozek	do	12	33.05
Joe. Fordorkok	do	12	33.05
Geo. Seenic	do	24	72.25
Andy Houyack	do	25	75.45
Jno. Konute	do	26	77.55
Jno. Hurra	do	27	81.65

*Month.

Earnings at Homestead Steel Works for May, 1892—Continued.

OPEN HEARTH, No. 2—Continued.

[Unchanged by new scale.]

Name.	Position.	Time.	Salary, actual, $25 base.
		Days.	
Jno. Hotalhan	Unloader	25	$74.35
Jno. Bushka	do	26	76.70
Gross Ditromazo	do	27	61.75
Jos. Crouch	do	23	67.35
Jas. Miller	do	11	28.15
Jno. Kovosh	do	26	71.05
Geo. Huston	do	16	35.10
Geo. Treko	do	29	82.50
Mike Lucas	Laborer	28	50.85
Geo. Borris	do	28	50.85
Jno. Corless	do	27	49.15
Andy Recto	do	28	50.85
Thos. Baten	do	20	55.35
Geo. Colly	do	8	16.15
Chas. Bateman	do	27	49.45
Geo. Riley	do	26	47.85
Geo. Colwell	do	24	49.70
Wm. Redshaw	do	24	54.05
Larry Partland	do	21	48.90
Andy Kolts	do	27	45.35
Chas. Bostard	do	27	62.90
Wm. Lowe	do	6	10.10
Jas. Morgan	do	26	43.65
Wm. Oakes	do	24	40.30
Dennis McCarthy	do	26	43.65
Jno. Margo	do	25½	65.65
Pat. Morris	do	2	5.30
Wm. Walker	do	28	58.45
Wm. B. Stranger	do	26	56.80
Geo. Dukosh	do	3	6.25
Jno. Ballok	do	1	2.05
Nick Konuto	do	2	4.05
Jenkin Reese	do	27	43.65
Edwin Rowe	do	27	45.35
Dan McShane	do	27	43.65
Joe. Frow	do	27	44.35
Thos. Antias	do	27	43.65
Martin Roach	do	27	43.65
Emmett Riley	do	25½	58.70
Ed. Melvin	do	24½	46.75
Jno. Jenkins	do	25	61.80
Joe. Collns	do	21	39.60
Wm. Winchester	do	25	42.95
James Watts	do	25	58.20
Wm. Rowell	do	25	48.50
Ed. McIntyre	do	27	67.05
Geo. Ewing	do	26	43.65
Peter Crawford	do	15	27.75
Geo. Myroshe	do	17	28.60
Jno. Saulters	do	21½	43.35
Jno. Skinter	do	19	31.00
Geo. S. Diehold	do	20	34.55
Francis McConnell	do	24	60.90
George Kline	do	1	2.75
Joe White	do	1	2.75
Matt Schoerr	do	26	54.05
Amos Cakosh	do	27	51.25
Thomas Shultz	do	21	36.05
David R. Thomas	do	18	31.50
Anthony Patrasavitch	do	17	29.80
E. F. Farquhar	do	20	31.90
Mike Surdy	do	1	1.55
Wm. I. Smith	do	24½	57.30
David Kerr	do	27	52.80
Wm. Stevens	do	26	44.15
Chas. Graham	do	10	35.00
F. C. Williams	do	3	4.80
Mike Rogan	do	2	3.90
Geo. Byers	do	3	5.05
Jno. Hanmahan	do	1	1.70
Geo. Vamist	do	2	3.35
Paul Barlow	do	1	1.70
Jno. Sunco	do	1	1.70
Mike Finco	do	1	1.70
Jno. Barlow	do	1	1.70

H. Mis. 335——2

Earnings at Homestead Steel Works for May, 1892—Continued.

OPEN HEARTH, No. 2—Continued.

[Unchanged by new scale.]

Name.	Position.	Time.	Salary actual, $25 base.
		Days.	
Jno. Forish	Laborer	2	$3.35
Geo. Porish	do	2	3.35
Mike Frank	do	2	3.35
Geo. Mortiss	do	3	4.80
Mike Houshaw	do	3	5.05
Mike Hurra	do	2	2.80
Jno. Troth	do	2	3.10
Mike Hunehar	do	2	3.10
Total pay roll, open hearth, No. 2, for month of May			17,742.55

Q. Now, you have spoken of the earnings of several skilled laborers, specifying the number of days they labored in the month of May and the aggregate amount paid them. Upon what basis or contract did they earn that pay?—A. On the contract made by them, a certain part of the men, in the month of July, 1889, which was to run for three years, terminating on the 30th of June of this year.

Q. Have you that contract in writing?—A. Yes, sir.

Q. You can state what it is, Mr. Frick, and then introduce the paper?—A. Well, it is as follows:

Memorandum of agreement between Carnegie, Phipps & Company, Limited, and the Amalgamated Association of Iron and Steel Workers, covering the Homestead Steel Works, made this 15th day of July, A. D. 1889.

First. The period of time agreed to: For the coming three years, from July 1, 1889, to July 1, 1892.

Second. On the sliding scale system the rate mentioned in the $27.50 column to be transferred to the $26.50 column.

The rates, when agreed to, to obtain for six months, from July 1, 1889, to January 1, 1890, and the average selling price of said six months to be the basis upon whic wages shall be paid for the next three months. The rate to change every three months thereafter, based upon the average selling price of the preceding three months. The standard grade 4 by 4 Bessemer billets to be the basis of price.

A committee shall be appointed consisting of three members of the Amalgamated Association officers and three members of the firm to determine the average selling price for each period; and in the event of these 6 men not agreeing a seventh disinterested party to be chosen by them, whose decision shall be final.

All day labor, except common labor, to be paid the same rates as were paid prior to July 1, 1889, and not to be included in the sliding scale.

The following classes of labor to be included in the three years' agreement at existing wages for the whole term, viz:

All engineers, all water-tenders, pressure-pump men, traveling cranes, narrow-gauge locomotive engineers, river-pump men, millwrights, gas-tenders, stocking gang for blooming mill.

The wages scales for the different departments having been considered and agreed upon, copies of the same are furnished herewith to each party.

The foot-notes on last year's scales are to be applied to the new scales.

(Here follow 58 pages giving details.)

Then the agreement goes on—it is a very lengthy one—reciting details. I have copies of the scale here as presented to the men, as now proposed.

Q. From time to time?—A. No, the new scale.

Q. Take some particular department and explain to the committee the sliding scale in a practical way, illustrating how it works?—A. Yes, very well. I might say I could do that in this way: In the agreement we proposed to make for this new term, commencing July 1, 1892——

Q. Let's not speak of that yet.—A. Very well; I could explain that better in this way: This sliding scale was based on billets at $26.50.

Q. Now, do I understand by that that you are paying the laborers in accordance with that price?—A. Yes, sir. That is to say, their wages were based on the billets at $26.50.

Q. Twenty-six dollars and fifty cents, for what?—A. Per ton. Now, in case the price of billets should drop to $25.50, the wages of the men—

Q. When the price was $26.50, what were the wages paid to the men?—A. Well, I have to refer to this scale to answer that. Take a man, for instance, who was earning $250, and billets $26.50. If the price of billets should drop to $25.50, his wages would be reduced about 3.78 per cent for each decline of $1 per ton in the price of billets down to $25, and after that there was no reduction.

Q. Where do you get the $26 per ton; what was paid for the production of that?—A. The tonnage, you mean? I have the scales here, if you will allow me to look at that and show you that—we will take the $26.50 basis, the rate per 100 tons for the heater's first helper was $3.07. His daily earnings on that basis was $4.53. That was in the 1889–'92 scale. Now, by the proposed 1892–'93 scale on the same basis, I see, his rate was not changed, but the tonnage of the mill was increased, so that on the output, as it now is, his earnings would be $5.47 per day. And the minimum, say that he would work on a $23 basis for billets, his earnings would be $4.75 per day; that will show you the difference.

Q. Well, I confess it is not clear to my mind yet. Mr. Frick, explain that again to us as plainly as you can.—A. Well, colonel, if you will permit me, I will have my assistant, after you are through with me, explain this part of the business—he understands it better than I do—the portion of this scale. I would like at this place to put this paper and statement in evidence.

[From the American Manufacturer and Iron World, July 1, 1892.]

THE HOMESTEAD LABOR DIFFICULTY.

It is with unmeasured regret that we hear that all hope of a peaceful settlement of the labor differences at Homestead has been abandoned and that a strike seems inevitable. This means, if all of the workmen follow the lead of the Amalgamated Association, and most of them must for a while at least, as the works can not be kept in operation while the places of the Amalgamated workmen are unfilled, that 3.800 men will be idle at Homestead before this paper finds its readers to-morrow, and that the $200,000 that are monthly distributed will be unearned for a time at least.

It is possible that the controversy at Homestead would have been settled had it not been that just at this time the general rolling-mill scales are also under discussion, and that it was feared by the Amalgamated Association that any concessions at Homestead might weaken them in their contest with the iron mills. The practice of having all wages settlements at one time in June has much in its favor from the workmen's standpoint, but there are elements of no little weakness in this rule and possibilities of contests that would not arise if scales as diverse as those of the iron mills and mills similar to Homestead were settled at different times, as are the scales at the Edgar Thomson Works.

As we understand the situation at Homestead three questions are involved:

First. A reduction in the minimum of the scale from $25 to $23 for 4 by 4 Bessemer billets.

Second. A change in the date of the expiration of the scale from June 30 to December 31.

Third. A reduction of tonnage rates at those furnaces and mills where important improvements have been made and new machinery has been added that has greatly increased their output and consequently the earnings of the workmen. Where no such improvements or additions have been made no reduction in tonnage rates are asked.

As to the first question. It may be well to point out to those who do not understand the methods of payment that skilled labor about the mills and furnaces is paid on a sliding scale based on the selling price of steel billets, which are one of the products of the Homestead mill. As the price of billets advance tonnage wages or the wages paid per ton advance without limit. As the price falls wages fall down to a certain point called the minimum. Any decline in selling price below this minimum brings no reduction in wages. This minimum has been $25. It is proposed by the company to make it $23. The claim is that if wages are based on selling price that the workmen must be willing to follow that price down at least to a reasonable minimum, and that in view of selling prices $23 is now a fair minimum. It may be stated that the contract now in force provides that the weekly quotations in the market column of the American Manufacturer shall be accepted as the selling prices of billets. There certainly is force in the claim of the manufacturers that if the men demand that they be paid on a sliding scale that the wages shall follow the selling price down as well as up, that they must take the bad with the good; that if the rule applies to high-selling prices when the manufacturer can afford to pay high wages, much more should it apply in times of low-selling prices, where he is less able to pay.

As to the second point, the change of dates of the expiration of the scale. There is argument on both sides. It is well that a manufacturer should know, especially one making the forms of steel made at Homestead, what wages he must pay during the year, so that he can make his contracts for the year accordingly; but, on the other hand, if a contest must come it is better for the workmen that it should be in summer than in winter.

But after all, the important question at issue is the third. The reduction in tonnage rates.

There is a decided misunderstanding in the public mind as to what is covered by this proposed reduction, how many are affected and what the effect of the proposed reduction will be on earnings.

The proposed reduction in tonnage rates apply only to three departments in the works, viz, 32-inch slabbing mill, 119-inch plate mill, and open-hearth furnaces.

Of the 3,800 employed at the works only some 280 men are affected by these tonnage reductions, and the total number of employés who are affected both by the reduction in tonnage rates and in the scale minimum, including the 280, is less than 325, not 10 per cent of the employés. There is, as is stated above, no reduction proposed at any mill or furnace at which the output has not been very greatly increased since the 1889-'92 scale went into effect; and further, at the proposed reduction in tonnage rates, the earnings will in almost every case be greater than the earnings at the time the 1889 scale went into effect, and even on the $23 minimum of the new scale the earnings will in many cases be higher than at the $26.50 rate in force, when the 1889 scale took effect.

For the first five months of the Homestead Steel Works wages scale, which expires June 30, 1892—that is to say, from August to December inclusive, 1889—the average monthly products of the departments for which a new scale, from July 1, 1892, was presented by the Carnegie Steel Company, Limited, to the Amalgamated Association, were as follows:

	Tons.
32-inch slabbing mill	7,681
119-inch plate mill	3,458
Open-hearth furnaces (per turn)	20

While the tonnages for May, 1892, were:

	Tons.
32-inch slabbing mill	9,265
119-inch plate mill	5,268
Open-hearth furnaces (per turn)	23¼

Showing a tonnage increase in—

	Per cent.
32-inch slabbing mill of	20.6
119-inch plate mill of	52.3
Open-hearth furnaces of	17.5

A comparison of the wages paid in representative positions at the beginning of the 1889-'92 scale with those which would be earned under the proposed 1892-'93 scale, shows as follows:

	1889-'92 scale, $26.50 basis.		Proposed 1892-'93 scale.		
			$26.50 basis.		Minimum, $23 basis.
	Rate 100 tons.	Daily earnings.	Rate 100 tons.	Daily earnings.	
32-inch slabbing mill (12 hours).					
Heater...	$4.31	$6.37	$4.31	$7.68	$6.67
Screwman.....................................	4.01	6.81			6.41
Heater, first helper..........................	3.07	4.53	3.07	5.47	4.75
Heater, second helper......................	1.73	2.56	1.47	2.62	2.27
Craneman.....................................	2.23	3.29	1.33	2.37	2.06
Roll engineer.................................	2.50	3.60			3.24
Roll tableman................................	2.50	3.69	1.60	2.85	2.47
Sweepers......................................	1.54	2.27	1.20	2.14	1.86
Shear tongsman.............................	1.54	2.27	1.25	2.23	1.94
Stamper.......................................	1.40	2.07	1.32	2.37	2.06
Shearman.....................................	2.50	3.09			4.00
Shear tableman..............................	1.73	2.56	1.47	2.62	2.27
Buggyman....................................	1.54	2.27	1.25	2.23	1.94
119-inch plate mill.	12 hours.		8 hours.		
Roller...	14.00	9.31	14.00	9.45	8.20
Screwman....................................	11.50	7.66	11.00	7.43	6.45
Tableman.....................................	10.00	6.65	8.00	5.40	4.60
Hooker..	8.50	5.66	7.00	4.73	4.11
Sweeper, front...............................	6.00	4.50	5.00	3.38	2.93
Sweeper, back................................	5.50	3.66	5.00	3.38	2.93
Shearman, 1st................................	13.00	8.66	11.00	7.43	6.45
Shearman, 2d................................	8.50	5.66	8.00	5.40	4.60
Leader, 1st	7.75	5.16	6.00	4.05	3.52
Leader, 2d	7.25	4.83	5.00	3.38	2.93
Heater..	22.00	14.66	11.00	7.43	6.45
Heater's helper..............................	15.00	10.00	6.00	4.05	3.52
Open-hearth furnaces.					
Melter's helpers, 1..........................	18.00	3.60	16.00	3.76	3.26
Melter's helpers, 2..........................	15.00	3.00	13.00	3.06	2.66
Charging machine...........................	15.00	3.00	14.00	3.29	2.86
Ladleman, 1..................................	17.00	3.40	16.00	3.76	3.26
Ladleman, 2..................................	14.00	2.80	13.00	3.06	2.66
Pitman, 1.....................................	17.00	3.40	16.00	3.76	3.26
Pitman, 2	14.50	2.90	13.00	3.06	2.66
Pitman, 3.....................................	13.50	2.70	12.00	2.83	2.45

These statements need but little comment; they cover all the mills and furnaces at which reductions are proposed, and fully justify the statements made above as to increase of output and equality of earnings under the new scale. The reduction in hours at the 119-inch mill should be noted in comparing these tables.

Regarding prices: Since the scale of 1889 went into effect there has been a decided drop in prices. In July, 1889, the American Manufacturer's quotations on billets, which, as is stated above, are taken under the contract, as the ruling rates, were $27. The price gradually increased during 1889 until at the close of the year the quotations were $36. There was a gradual decline in 1890 until at its close quotations were $25.75. In 1891 the highest quotation was $26.50, the lowest $25.25. For these two and a half years, therefore, the quotations were never below the minimum of the old scale. Immediately after the close of 1891 they began to drop, and quotations for 1892 have been as follows:

Prices of Bessemer steel at Pittsburg, January to June, 1892.

January 1 to February 5.. $25.00
February 12 .... 24.50
February 19 .... 24.00
February 26 .... 23.50
March 4 .... 23.25
March 11 to April 1 .... 23.00
April 8 to 22 .... 23.25

April 29	$23.00
May 6 to 13	22.75
May 20 to 27	22.50
June 3	22.40
June 10	22.50
June 17	22.75
June 24	23.75

The increase in quotations at the close of June is due to the prospect of the Homestead strike.

Beams, another product at Homestead, have fallen since January 1 of this year from 3.10 cents a pound to 2 cents or less, that is 33½ per cent. Plates have dropped 20 per cent to 25 per cent in price.

The reasons, therefore, that have led to this demand for a reduction in tonnage rates are:

(1) That as these rates are based on selling prices, the old minimum of $25 is too high in view of the reduction in prices.

(2) That there has been such an increase in output as to justify a reduction and still leave the earnings of the workmen practically unchanged, or in some cases but slightly reduced, even at the reduced minimum, and further that in the near future these earnings will be greatly increased.

If the claims made as to increased output are true, and that they are, the above statement taken from the Homestead books abundantly proves, it seems to us that the Carnegie Steel Company are justified in asking for a reduction. The reduction in selling price to $2 below the minimum adds to this justification. As to what this reduction should be, that is a question of earnings. If there is any justice in the sliding-scale principle scales should not remain at the same rates of wages, when the billets on which the scales are based sell at $23, as when they sell at $25.

By the CHAIRMAN:

Q. Now, Mr. Frick, will you state what scale was proposed by your company to these laborers which they rejected?—A. Well, if you will permit me, I would like to say that in January last we tried to take up the question with the Amalgamated Association at Homestead, to arrange for a new scale to take the place of the one expiring on the 30th of June of this year. We had some difficulty in getting them to take the question up, and did not succeed in getting them to do so until March. They then presented a scale——

Q. Let me interrupt you there. You say that you mean all the workmen?—A. The Amalgamated men at Homestead.

Q. What is the name?—A. The Amalgamated Association of Iron and Steel Workers.

Q. To them you made the proposition?—A. Yes, sir. They, in March, presented a scale covering almost all the departments at Homestead, and in almost every instance it called for an advance in wages. We had several conferences with them there at that time, and up until about the 30th of May, not being able to reach any understanding, when we prepared the scales covering four departments at those works, wherein we asked——

Q. Mention those departments?—A. That is to say, the open-hearth plant No. 1, open hearth plant No. 2, 119-inch plate mill, the 32-inch slabbing mill. I will hand the stenographer copies of those. Those being the same departments whose earnings in the month of May I have given you a statement of, and the only departments wherein we ask for a reduction or change in the wages. They embrace about 325 men out of the 3,800 men employed at Homestead. The wages of 280 of these only are affected by a change in the tonnage rates, while 325, including the 283, are affected by a change in the minimum that we desire to make; that is to say, in the minimum price of billets.

Q. Now, will you explain that change you proposed to make?—A. Under the agreement expiring June 30, it was understood that if billets sold below $25 per ton that the wages would not go any lower. They would not slide below that figure. There was no maximum. We proposed in the new proposition, so far as it related to those four departments of those works, that the minimum should be $22 in place of $25. We proposed also that the termination of this scale should be at the end of the year in place of the middle of it. These scales we sent to our superintendent at Homestead with the following letter, shall I read it?

Q. That is, those scales were a proposition from the company to these men?—A. Yes, sir.

Q. Read your letter.

THE CARNEGIE STEEL COMPANY, LIMITED,
Pittsburg, Pa., May 30, 1892.

DEAR SIR: Referring to my visit to the works this morning—
I now hand you herewith Homestead Steel Works' wages scales for the open hearth plants, and No. 32 and 119 inch mills, which you will please present immediately to the joint committee, with the request that its decision be given thereon not later than June 24, 1892.

These scales have had most careful consideration, with a desire to act toward our employés in the most liberal manner. A number of rates have been advanced upon your recommendation, and the wages which will be earned thereunder are considerably in advance of those received by the employés of any of our competitors in the same lines. You can say to the committee that these scales are in all respects the most liberal that can be offered. We do not care whether a man belongs to a union or not, nor do we wish to interfere. He may belong to as many unions or organizations as he chooses, but we think our employés at Homestead Steel Works would fare much better working under the system in vogue at Edgar Thomson and Duquesne.

Yours truly,

H. C. FRICK,
Chairman.

Mr. J. A. POTTER,
Superintendent Homestead Steel Works, Munhall, Pa.

Sliding scale, proposed by the Carnegie Steel Company, Limited, for the 119-inch plate mill, Homestead Steel Works.

[To take effect July 1, 1892, and to continue in force until January 1, 1894, and thereafter until terminated at the end of any calendar year by three months' notice, which may be given in writing by either party, provided it be accepted before June 24, 1892. Basis, $26.50 billets; minimum, $22 billets. This scale to be subject to revision in the event of the introduction of new methods or appliances. All extras to be discontinued unless otherwise provided for.]

Men.	Positions.	Hours per turn.	Basis rate per 100 tons.	Men.	Positions.	Hours per turn.	Basis rate per 100 tons.
1	Roller	8	$14.00	2	Cranemen	8	$5.50
1	Screwman	8	11.00	2	Pull-ups	12	2.06
1	Tableman	8	8.00	1	Marker	12	4.24
2	Hookers	8	7.00	1	Gauger	12	3.00
1	Front sweeper	8	5.00	1	Stamper	12	2.50
1	Back sweeper	8	5.00	1	Painter	12	2.18
1	First shearman	8	11.00	2	Line drawers	12	2.00
1	Second shearman	8	8.00	6	Helpers at scales	12	2.06
1	First leader	8	6.00	2	Cranemen	12	2.06
1	Second leader	8	5.00	4	Scrap crew	12	2.50
2	Levermen	8	4.55	1	Millwright	12	4.00
6	Shear helpers	8	4.00	1	Millwright helper	12	2.50
2	Heaters	8	11.00	1	Greaser	12	2.06
2	Heaters' helpers	8	6.00				

Sliding scale proposed by the Carnegie Steel Company, limited, for the 32-inch slabbing mill, Homestead Steel Works.

[To take effect July 1, 1892, and to continue in force until January 1, 1894, and thereafter until terminated at the end of any calendar year by three months' notice, which may be given in writing by either party, provided it be accepted before June 24, 1892. Basis, $26.50 billets; minimum, $22 billets. This scale to be subject to revision in the event of the introduction of new methods or appliances. All extras to be discontinued unless otherwise provided for.]

Men.	Positions.	Hours per turn.	Basis rate per 100 tons.	Men.	Positions.	Hours per turn.	Basis rate per 100 tons.
1	Heater	12	$4.31	6	Shear tongs and cranemen.	12	$1.25
1	Heater's first helper *	12	2.13	1	Buggyman	12	1.25
1	Heater's second helper	12	1.47	1	Stamper	12	1.33
1	Craneman	12	1.33	2	Regulators	12	.89
1	Bottom maker	12	1.85		Day rates, not on sliding scale:		
2	Tongsmen, at pits	12	1.20				
1	Roll tableman	12	1.60	2	Roll engineers	12	† .27
2	Greasers	12	1.17	1	Roll engineers' helper.	12	† .21
2	Sweepers	12	1.20	1	Table and pump engineer	12	† .21
1	Shear tableman	12	1.47				

* When outside pits are on, the heater's first helper to be paid $3.07 per 100 tons.
† Per hour.

Sliding scale, proposed by the Carnegie Steel Company, Limited, for the open hearth furnaces, Plant No. 2, Homestead Steel Works.

[To take effect July 1, 1892, and to continue in force until January 1, 1894, and thereafter until terminated at the end of any calendar year by three months' notice, which may be given in writing by either party, provided it be accepted before June 24, 1892. Basis, $26.50 billets; minimum, $22.00 billets. This scale to be subject to revision in the event of the introduction of new methods or appliances. All extras to be discontinued unless otherwise provided for.]

Positions.	Hours per turn.	Basis rate per 100 tons.	Positions.	Hours per turn.	Basis rate per 100 tons.
Melters' first helpers	12	$16.00	Third ladlemen	12	$11.00
Melters' second helpers	12	13.00	First pitmen	12	16.00
Melters' third helpers	12	11.00	Second pitmen	12	13.00
Stockers	12	12.00	Third pitmen	12	12.00
Charging machine men	12	14.00	Fourth pitmen	12	12.00
First ladlemen	12	16.00	Ingot cranemen	12	14.00
Second ladlemen	12	13.00	Ladle cranemen	12	14.00

Sliding scale proposed by the Carnegie Steel Company, Limited, for the open hearth furnaces, Plant No. 1, Homestead Steel Works.

[To take effect July 1, 1892, and to continue in force until January 1, 1894, and thereafter until terminated at the end of any calendar year by three months' notice, which may be given in writing by either party, provided that it be accepted before June 24, 1892. Basis, $26.50 billets; minimum, $22.00 billets. This scale to be subject to revision in the event of the introduction of new methods or appliances. All extras to be discontinued unless otherwise provided for.]

Positions.	Hours per turn.	Basis rate per 100 tons.	Positions.	Hours per turn.	Basis rate per 100 tons.
Melters' first helpers	12	$16.00	Second pitmen	12	$12.00
Melters' second helpers	12	13.00	Third pitmen	12	11.00
Chargers	12	12.00	Fourth pitmen	12	11.00
Ladlemen	12	15.00	Cranemen	12	10.00
Ladlemen helpers	12	13.00	Pull-ups	12	6.00
First pitmen	12	15.00			

NOTE 1.—Ladleman and one helper are to handle the product of two furnaces.
NOTE 2.—These rates apply to all furnaces except No. 8, whose crew is to work at the day rates now in force; with the exception of the change with ladleman and his helper noted above.

The WITNESS. We gave the men from the 30th of May to the 24th of June to consider and answer us. If you will permit me, colonel, in that connection I would like to give you the price of the product ruling July 1, 1889, and July 1, 1892, of the material we make there, to show——

Q. Very well. Each year, if you see proper.—A. Tank steel plates, July 1, 1889, were selling at 2.15 cents per pound. July 1, 1892, they were selling at 1.7 cents per pound, a reduction of 21 per cent. Flange steel plates, on July 1, 1889, were selling at 2¾ per pound; July 1, 1892, at 2¼ per pound, a reduction of 18 per cent. Universal Mill plates, steel, on July 1, 1889, were selling at 2.1 per pound; on July 1, 1892, at 1.7 per pound, a reduction of 19 per cent. Angles, steel, were selling July 1, 1889, at 2.2 per pound; on July 1, 1892, at 1.7 per pound, a reduction of 22 per cent. Beams and channels, which are a large part of the products of these works, on July 1, 1889, were selling at 3.1 per pound; July 1, 1892, at 1.9 per pound, a reduction of 39 per cent. Steel billets, on July 1, 1889, were selling at from $27 to $27.50 per gross ton, while on July 1, 1892, they were selling at $22.75 and $23 per ton, a reduction of 16 per cent. Wire rods, on July 1, 1889, were selling at $39 per gross ton; on July 1, 1892, at $31.50 per gross ton, a reduction of 19 per cent. Nails, on July 1, 1889, $2.20 per keg base, against $1.50 per base, a reduction of 33 per cent, which was because of the great uction of the price we were getting for our material—that is one of causes that we asked for a reduction of the wages.

Q. What per cent of reduction of wages did your proposition involve?—A. In those four departments about 15 per cent.

Q. An average of 15 per cent?—A. Yes, sir; in tonnage rates; but the reduction was a little more than that, because the price of billets was below the $25 minimum which prevailed in the old scale. Billets at this time, I suppose, if the wages would be adjusted on the new scale, after July the price would be found to be probably about $24, so that would mean a further reduction of about 3.7 per cent.

Q. On the old scale?—A. Yes, sir.

Q. How do you account for the fluctuation in the market and the tendency downward of these same products?—A. By overproduction.

Q. Overproduction?—A. Yes, sir. The demand not keeping up to the supply, which affects the price, as you know. I might say in this connection that the tariff was reduced on all this material under the McKinley act, and I have a memorandum here showing the reduction.

Q. Very well, state it if you desire.

	Old tariff.	New tariff (McKinley).
Beams, girders, channels, etc	1¼ cents	.9 cent.
Plates	1¼ cents	.8 cent.
Billets	45 per cent, about .6 cent	.4 cent.
Steel ingots	45 per cent, about .6 cent	.4 cent.
Pig metal	.3 cent	.3 cent.
Rails	$17 or about .8 cent	.6 cent.
Wire nails	4 cents	2 cents.
Rods	.6 cent	.6 cent.
Splice bars	1¼ cents	1 cent.
Round iron	1.2 cents	1.1 cents.
Bar iron	1.8 cents	.8 cent.
Wire	1½ cents	1¼ cents.

Mr. BOATNER. Do you come in competition with any imported product?

A. Yes, sir; beams, we do.

By the CHAIRMAN:

Q. Can you give us an approximate statement of increased production in these lines in which these employés were engaged in the United States within the last three years, beginning at the time that contract was made? You stated awhile ago the reduction in price was due to overproduction. Can you state whether there has been a great increase in production in this country, and if so, what per cent within that period?—A. There has been very great increase in production. I can not furnish you with that percentage just now. I can furnish it to-morrow.

Q. Has there been any increase in importation from abroad of these articles upon which these laborers were employed within the last year or so since the McKinley act was passed?—A. No, sir; I think not.

Q. There has not been an increased importation?

Mr. BYNUM. On the articles in which these men were engaged there was a reduction or increase in the tariff?

A. A reduction, I have just read you.

Q. You have read of billets and ingots, but on the plate?—A. I read a list of about all the material we manufacture at Homestead.

Q. How is it on the manufactured article?—A. Well, these are manufactured articles.

Q. Ingots, of course, are manufactured, but when you put them in a higher process of manufacture, how is the duty upon the higher grades? I do not mean to include wire nails and wire rod, which are made of course of billets.—A. I have given you there a list of the articles we manufacture at these works.

Q. Steel plates?—A. Yes, sir; showing the old tariff and new tariff rates.

Q. Can you give the labor cost of a ton of billets that you manufacture?—A. I could not now.

Q. Do you know the difference in the labor cost in European mills and American mills?—A. Not exactly.

Q. Can you approximate it?—A. I could not at present.

Q. Or on steel rails either?—A. I could not on steel rails.

Q. Is it exceeding three-and-one-half on steel rails?—A. I could not answer.

Q. Have you ever examined Mr. Wright's tables on that?—A. No, sir.

By the CHAIRMAN:

Q. Mr. Frick, you state that there has not been an increase of importation since the McKinley act went into operation in these particular lines which your laborers were engaged in producing, but there has been a very large increase in the amount of American production?—A. Yes, sir.

Q. Then you do not attribute to the operations of the tariff the necessities which you claim on the part of the company for a reduction in the wages?—A. No, sir.

Q. Well, what response did the workmen make to your proposition?—A. I will read you. On the 22d of June, 1892, I addressed Mr. Weihe, president of the Amalgamated Association, the following letter:

THE CARNEGIE STEEL COMPANY, LIMITED,
Pittsburg, Pa., June 22, 1892.

DEAR SIR: Our superintendent at Homestead, Mr. Potter, advises that a committee from your association waited on him last night and asked for a conference to-morrow at 10 o'clock, and that, if satisfactory to us, to advise you to-day. We beg to say that we will be glad to meet you and a committee with full power to act for those of our Homestead employés who are members of your association to-morrow at this office at 10 o'clock.

Yours, very truly,

H. C. FRICK,
Chairman.

Mr. WM. WEIHE,
President Amalgamated Association of I. & S. W., Pittsburg, Pa.

This is signed by myself as chairman. That was the first word that we got that they desired to meet us or would confer with us in regard to this scale after the scale was submitted about the 30th of May.

Q. Well, what next?—A. A committee, said to be from our Homestead Steel Works, about 25 in number, with Mr. Weihe at their head, called at our office at 10 o'clock on the 23d of June. We opened the discussion first by asking them what they had to say. We then discussed the minimum, the proposed change in the minimum, that is, in the price of billets. They argued that there should be no reduction in that minimum. They could not agree to accept anything below $25. I told them that I did not see why there should be any minimum, as there was no maximum. We were willing to pay as they went up; they ought to be willing to accept a reduction as they declined, for the reason that when billets got down to 21 and 22 there was no money in it to us, and we would only be operating the mill in order to keep up our organization and give employment to our workmen.

After considerable discussion we left that point and went to the change in the termination of the scale. For some time past the arrangement has been to terminate all agreements on the 30th of June each year. We desired to have that changed to the 31st of December of each year, for the reason that we desired to know on what to base our calculations for materials which we have to sell for the whole year, and also for the reason that as we are largely engaged at Homestead in the manufacture of beams and material that enters into the construction of fire-proof buildings, July and August and the summer months are the times when the building season is most active, and it is very much against our interest to have our operations interrupted in those months. In the latter part of December and the first of January business operations are not so brisk and it suits us, and I think it would suit the workmen very much better in case we had to have a stoppage, to have it then when there would be less business doing. We could not agree on that point. And we, of course, have to make repairs yearly, and it suits us very much better to make the repairs when business is slack. That was another reason why we desired the scale to terminate at the end of the year.

We then discussed the wages of various men. I had before me the earnings of the men for the month of May. There was not very much discussion about that, and I stated to the committee that there was so many of them and the committee was so large that it was unwieldy. That I would like them, if it were possible, to reduce the committee, so we could get around a table and come close to each other and discuss this matter. Mr. Weihe I think rather favored that. Some of the committee, however, did not. I saw we were not making much progress and told them that they knew what we desired and we would retire and let them discuss the matter among themselves and, when they were ready, to send for us. We left the room and in about an hour and three-quarters we were sent for. On entering Mr. Weihe read us their proposition. I do not remember exactly what that was except some of the principal points—the two principal points. They were willing to reduce the minimum price of billets from twenty-five to twenty-four per ton. They were willing that any scale we might make should extend until the first of July, 1895, and the balance of that report I do not remember. I told them that that was not satisfactory to us and we could not agree to it.

I left the room. Mr. Potter, our general superintendent, remained behind, and, as I learned afterwards, invited Mr. Weihe and some of the committee to remain, and discussed the matter with them for awhile, and said that he would endeavor to persuade us to increase the minimum that we had offered $1 per ton, making 23. They agreed to let him come and see me and see what we would agree to, which he did, and I told him that we did not want to be arbitrary; we wanted to be liberal and we would agree to that—to increase the minimum to 23, asking only a reduction of $2 from the minimum of the previous scale. Those of the committee who had remained left Mr. Potter and said they would go and see their men and call at a later hour and give their report. They called at a later hour and said their men would not agree to it. That is the only conference we have had.

Q. What followed that?—A. The works continued in operation until, I think, the 29th or 30th, when they were closed down.

Q. The 29th or 30th of June?—A. Yes, sir.

By Mr. TAYLOR:

Q. You state that the reduction proposed in this scale of wages applied to 325 men, or 335?—A. About 325, I think.

Q. What reduction was proposed for the rest of your employés?—A. There was no reduction proposed whatever to any of the tonnage men at the other mills until such time as we would put in new improvements which we have in contemplation and were going in.

Q. That is, improvements that would increase production?—A. Yes, sir.

Q. And secondly increase wages?—A. Yes, sir.

Q. You say that in reference to the mill at Homestead?—A. Yes, sir.

Q. There was no change, then, in regard to any of the others at this mill, either way?—A. Yes, sir; that is right, and I might add that we did not propose to change the wages of the various mechanical departments of the Homestead Steel Works; that is to say, the machinists, blacksmiths, blacksmiths' helpers, boiler makers, carpenters, pattern makers, pipe fitters, millwrites, foundry men, riggers, tinners, and painters. In fact our general superintendent on the 20th of June made an agreement with the committee representing all of these men, which is as follows: The committee signed the agreement—

First, wages should not be reduced below those in force at the present date. Second, hours and rules governing overtime shall remain as at present. Third, this agreement to take effect to-day, June 20, 1892, and continue three years from date, or until June 20, 1895.

This is another agreement made with the stationary engineers, water tenders, pressure pump and pressure men, of the Homestead Steel Works, made on the 22d of June, 1892:

First, wages shall not be reduced below those in force at the present date; hours and rules governing overtime shall remain as at present. Second, this agreement is to take effect to-day, June 22, 1892, and continue in force for three years, or to June 22, 1895.

This is another agreement made on the 22d of June with the trans portation department of the Homestead Steel Works, including the following—conductors, brakemen, engineers, and firemen:

First, wages, hours, and extras to remain as at present, Second, this agreement is to take effect to-day, June 22, 1892, and continue in force for three years, or to June 22, 1895.

Mr. BRODERICK. How do the new improvements that you speak of being put in affect the labor; does it make it harder or easier for a man to produce a given amount?—A. It makes it easier, and requires the employment of less men.

The CHAIRMAN. You mean to produce the same quantity?—A. Yes, sir.

Mr. TAYLOR. And those improvements were to be put in four departments only?—A. Yes, sir; that is to say, the improvements in one of the four departments affected; a certain other department, as you will understand. If you will permit me, I will explain. When scales of wages were made in 1889 for the 119-inch plate mill it was based on rolling direct from ingots, the tonnage being about 2,500 tons per month. The tonnage on the mill has since been doubled; that is to say, 5,000 tons on account of change in practice, namely, the ingot is now taken to what is known as the 32-inch slabbing mill, where more than half the work is done. That is one of the mills in one of these departments. By rolling the ingot into a slab, which is taken direct to the 119-inch plate mill to be finished there, and notwithstanding the fact that more than half the work originally done on the plate mill is now done on the slabbing mill, the same wages are demanded for rolling plates from slabs that was originally paid for rolling plates direct from ingots. In other words, besides not deriving any benefit from increased investment, we are compelled to pay the additional labor in the slabbing mill. Then I might say in reference to open-hearth plant No. 1—this is the oldest open-hearth plant—the open-hearth business is, of course, a comparatively new business, and we are gradually learning how to improve it in its operation. The change that we made there is one which will increase the tonnage of that department, and that is the reason that we ask for some change in wages, as the casting of large-sized ingots got out a larger tonnage on that account.

By the CHAIRMAN:

Q. Mr. Frick, not counting anything by way of interest on the plant, what is the cost of the production of a ton of steel billets at your works at Homestead?—A. I hardly think that is quite a fair question; I do not know that you ought to ask us to give that.

Q. Well, I do not know that it is unfair.—A. That is a question I don't think you ought to ask me to go into.

The CHAIRMAN. As you object to answering that I will reserve it for consultation with the committee.

Mr. TAYLOR. In that connection, Mr. Frick, would you have any objection to answer the cost of a ton of steel including all expenses, the salaries and dead work, and all that?

The WITNESS. Yes, sir; I would have the same objection to answering that.

Mr. BOATNER. You do not feel disposed to give away any secrets of the trade.

A. I should have said to you that the principal reason for not answering your question is that we have competitors in business and it would hardly be fair to us that they should know what our cost is as we do not know what it costs them.

By the CHAIRMAN:

Q. Well, will you state the labor cost?—A. That would be about the same.

Q. There are other materials entering into the cost?—A. That is very true, but for that reason I would not like to go into the question of cost at all.

Q. We will not press that question now. Now, in consequence of the disagreement which you have described, what resulted, did the laborers quit work?—A. I would like to submit as an answer to that the following extract from a newspaper.

The CHAIRMAN: Well you can put it in as part of your testimony.

[Pittsburg Post, July 8.]

In an interview yesterday afternoon with Mr. George N. McCain, correspondent of the Philadelphia Press, Mr. H. C. Frick, chairman of the Carnegie Steel Company, Limited, said:

"The question at issue is a very grave one. It is whether the Carnegie Company or the Amalgamated Association shall have absolute control of our plant and business at Homestead. We have decided, after numerous fruitless conferences with the Amalgamated officials in the attempt to amicably adjust the existing difficulties, to operate the plant ourselves. I can say with the greatest emphasis that under no circumstances will we have any further dealings with the Amalgamated Association as an organization. This is final. The Edgar Thomson Works and our establishment at Duquesne are both operated by workmen who are not members of the Amalgamated Association with the greatest satisfaction to ourselves and to the unquestioned advantage of our employés. At both of these plants the work in every department goes on uninterrupted; the men are not harassed by the interference of trade union officials, and the best evidence that their wages are satisfactory is shown in the fact that we have never had a strike there since they began working under our system of management.

What was the basis of the differences existing at present between the Carnegie company and their men, Mr. Frick?"

FIRST POINT AT ISSUE.

"There were three points upon which we differed. The skilled workmen in the Amalgamated Association work under what is known as a sliding scale. As the price of steel advances the earnings of the men advance; as the prices fall their earnings decrease in proportion. While there is no limit to an advance of earnings on the scale, there is a point at which the decline stops. It is known as the minimum, and the figure heretofore has been $25 per ton for 4 by 4 Bessemer billets. We believe that if earnings based on the selling price of steel can advance without limit the workmen should be willing to follow the selling price down to a reasonable minimum, and so this figure was finally fixed by the Carnegie Company at the rate of $23 instead of $25. The reason for asking this upon our part was that the Carnegie Company has spent large sums of money in the introduction of new machinery in its Homestead plant, by means of which the workmen were enabled to increase their daily output, thereby increasing the amount of their own earnings. We had originally asked a reduction to $22, but subsequently agreed to compromise the rate at $23. The Amalgamated Association was unwilling to consider a reduction below $24 on steel billets, notwithstanding the fact that the improved machinery would enable their members, even at $23, to earn more than is paid in other Amalgamated mills. This was the first point at issue.

OTHER STUMBLING BLOCKS.

Under the present Amalgamated system the date of the expiration of the sliding scale is June 30, annually. We asked that this date be changed to December 31 (same as at Edgar Thomson), for the reason that the change would permit us to take our estimate upon the wages that we must pay during the year, beginning on January 1, so that we would be enabled to make contracts for the year accordingly. This point the Amalgamated Association refused to accede and demanded the old date. The third proposition was the reduction in tonnage rates in those departments in the mills where the improvements I have spoken of have been made and which enable the workingmen to increase the output and consequently their earnings. Where no such improvements had been made there was no request upon our part for a reduction in tonnage rates. In other words, we asked no reduction in any department of which the output had not been greatly increased by reason of our expensive improvements since the scale of 1889 went into effect. We are prepared to show that in nearly every department, under our proposed reduction in the tonnage rates, the skilled workmen would make more money than they did when the scale of 1889 went into effect.

As a rule the men who were making the largest wages in the Homestead mill were the ones who most bitterly denounced the proposed revision of the scale, for out of the 3,800 men employed in every department only 325 were directly affected by this reduction.

WORKMEN HELD SWAY.

"Finding that it was impossible to arrive at any agreement with the Amalgamated officials, we decided to close our works at Homestead. Immediately the town was taken possession of by the workmen. An advisory committee of 50 took upon itself the direction of the affairs of the place; the streets were patrolled by men appointed by this committee, and every stranger entering the town became an object of surveillance, was closely questioned, and if there was the slightest reason to suspect him he was ordered to leave the place instantly under the threat of bodily harm. Guards were stationed at every approach to Homestead by the self-organized local government. Our employés were prohibited from going to the mills, and we, as owners of the property, were compelled to stand by powerless to conduct the affairs of our business or direct its management. This condition of affairs lasted until Tuesday, when I appealed to the sheriff of Allegheny County, stating the facts as I have outlined them. The sheriff visited Homestead and talked with the advisory committee. Its members asked that they be permitted to appoint men from their own number to act as deputy sheriffs; in other words, the men who were interfering with the exercise of our corporate rights, preventing us from conducting our business affairs, requested that they be clothed with the authority of deputy sheriffs to take charge of our plant. The sheriff declined their proposition, and the advisory committee disbanded. The rest of the story is a familiar one; the handful of deputies sent up by the Sheriff McCleary were surrounded by the mob and forced to leave the town, and then the watchmen were sent up to be landed on our own property for the protection of our plant.

"Why did the Carnegie Company call upon the Pinkertons for watchmen to protect their property.

"We did not see how else we would have protection. We only wanted them for watchmen to protect our property and see that workmen we would take to Homestead—and we have had applications from many men to go there to work—were not interfered with.

DOUBTED THE SHERIFF'S POWER.

"Did you doubt the ability of the sheriff to enforce order at Homestead and protect your property?

"Yes, sir; with local deputies.

"Why?

"For the reason that three years ago our concern had an experience similar to this. We felt the necessity of a change at the works; that a scale should be adopted based on the sliding price of billets, and we asked the county authorities for protection. The workmen began tactics similar to those employed in the present troubles. The sheriff assured the members of the firm that there would be no difficulty, that he would give them ample protection and see that men who were willing to work were not interfered with. What was the result? The posse taken up by the sheriff—something over 100 men—were not permitted to land on our property; were driven off with threats of bodily harm, and it looked as if there was going to be great destruction of life and property. That frightened our people. Mr. Abbott was then in charge of the Carnegie, Phipps & Co. business, and was asked by the Amalgamated officials for a conference, which he agreed to, fearful if he did not do so there might be loss of life and destruction of property. Under that stress, in fear of the Amalgamated Association, an agreement was made and work was resumed. We did not propose this time to be placed in that position.

"The Pinkerton men, as generally understood, had been summoned and all arrangements made with them to be on hand in case of failure by the sheriff to afford protection. Is that a fact or not?

"The facts concerning the engagement of the Pinkerton men are these: From past experience, not only with the present sheriff but with all others, we have found that he has been unable to furnish us with a sufficient number of deputies to guard our property and protect the men who were anxious to work on our terms. As the Amalgamated men from the 1st of July had surrounded our works, placed guards at all the entrances, and at all avenues or roads leading to our establishment and for miles distant therefrom, we felt that for the safety of our property, and in order to protect our workmen, it was necessary for us to secure our own watchmen to assist the sheriff, and we knew of no other source from which to obtain them than from Pinkerton agencies, and to them we applied.

TRIED TO AVOID TROUBLE.

"We brought the watchmen here as quietly as possible; had them taken to Homestead at an hour of the night when we hoped to have them enter our works without any interference whatever and without meeting anybody. We proposed to land them on our own property, and all our efforts were to prevent the possibilities of a collision between our former workmen and our watchmen. We are to-day barred out of our property at Homestead, and have been since the 1st of July. There is nobody in the mills up there now; they are standing a silent mass of machinery with nobody to look after them. They are in the hands of our former workmen.

"Have the men made overtures for a settlement of the difficulties since this trouble commenced?

"Yes, sir. A leading ex-official in the Amalgamated Association yesterday, when this rioting was going on, called on the sheriff and I am informed asked him to come down to see me, stating that if he could get a promise that we would confer with the representatives of the Amalgamated Association looking toward an adjustment of this trouble, that he would go to Homestead and try and stop the rioting."

"Did you consider his proposal?

"No, sir. I told the gentleman who called that we could not confer with the Amalgamated Association officials. That it was their followers who were rioting and destroying our property, and we would not accept his proposition. At the same time this representative of our former workmen said that they were willing to accept the terms offered, and concede everything we asked except the date of the termination of the scale, which they insisted should be June 30 in place of December 31.

FUTURE OF IT ALL.

"What of the future of this difficulty?

"It is in the hands of the authorities of Allegheny County. If they are unable to cope with it, it is certainly the duty of the governor of the State to see that we are permitted to operate our establishment unmolested. The men engaged by us through the Pinkerton agencies were sent up to Homestead with the full knowledge of the sheriff and by him placed in charge of his chief deputy, Col. Gray, and, as we know, with instructions to deputize them in case it became necessary. We have made an impartial investigation and are satisfied beyond doubt that the watchmen employed by us were fired upon by our former workmen and their friends for twenty-five minutes before they reached our property, and were fired upon after they had reached our property. That they did not return the fire until after the boats had touched the shore, and after three of the watchmen had been wounded, one fatally. After a number of the watchmen were wounded, and Capt. Rodgers, in charge of the towboat, at their request, had taken the injured away, leaving the barges at our works unprotected, our former workmen refused to allow Capt. Rodgers to return to the barges that he might remove them from our property, but fired at him and fatally wounded one of the crew.

"You doubtless are aware, Mr. Frick, that the troubles at the Homestead mill have invited widespread attention, and as a result Congress proposes to investigate the trouble, as well as the employment of Pinkerton detectives?

"I am aware of the fact, sir. While nobody could regret the occurrences of the last few days more than myself, yet it is my duty, as the executive head of the Carnegie Company, to protect the interests of the association. We desire to, and will, protect our property at all hazards. So far as Congressional investigation is concerned, I can say with the utmost candor that we welcome the investigation proposed. We are prepared to submit facts and figures which will convince unprejudiced men of the equity of our position. More than this, I believe that when all of the facts are known revelations will be made which will emphasize the justice of all our claims."

AS TO POLITICS.

"How do you regard the present troubles at Homestead from a political standpoint? What effect will it have as a tariff issue in the political campaign of the coming fall?

"We have never given a thought as to what effect our affairs might have on either of the political parties. We can not afford to run our business and run politics at the same time. It would prove very unprofitable if we were to trim our sails to meet political issues. At the same time I may say that it is not a matter in which the protective tariff is involved, and every intelligent man, whether he be a manufacturer or employé, is aware of the fact. It is, however, a question as to whether or not the proprietors or its workmen will manage the works.

"We did not propose to reduce the earnings of our employés below those of other Amalgamated men in other mills. As I have said, we have put in improved machinery which other mills do not possess; increased our output and increased the earnings of our men. We asked that a reduction be made in these departments so that the earnings of our employés would be on a par with other workmen in other Amalgamated mills. It is not a question of starvation wages, for you will please bear in mind the fact that the proposed equalization of earnings affects only about 325 men out of 3,800, and they are the ones who earn the most money in our establishment. It has no effect upon the wages of more than 15,000 other employés engaged in our establishments at Duquesne, Braddock, Pittsburg, Beaver Falls, and in the coke region."

Q. Mr. Frick, you stated that after the sheriff had gone out with a small posse that you then employed these Pinkertons because you knew of no other way of procuring a guard for your property. Did you make any effort? Did the sheriff make any application to the governor of the State for troops to enable him to restore possession of your property to you?—A. That is before we brought those guards.

Q. Before?—A. I will tell you how those guards happened to be brought; that is what you want.

Q. Yes, sir.—A. As I stated in my interview, the experience of three years ago convinced us beyond a doubt that the sheriff of this county was powerless to give us the protection which we should have; so we concluded that we would obtain watchmen of our own, pay them ourselves, put them on our own property, have them remain on our own property, not to go outside of it or off of it. I then had the preliminary arrangements made for these men with an agent of Mr. Pinkerton, that is to say, an understanding what we were to pay for these men.

Q. You may state that if there is no objection?—A. Well $5 a day per man.

Q. How many men?—A. Three hundred; that is to say, I di ln't know how many we would want or whether we would want them at all when I had this preliminary talk, but after the 24th of June, when these workmen refused to make terms with us, we concluded it would be necessary to protect our own property and secure new workmen, whom we had plenty of applications from.

Q. Non-union men you mean?—A. We did not care whether they were union or non-union, but we wanted men with whom we could deal individually. We did not propose to deal with the Amalgamated Association after that date as we had plainly told them. So on the 25th of June, 1892, I wrote Mr. Pinkerton, of New York City, the following letter. Shall I read it?

The CHAIRMAN. Read it.

THE CARNEGIE STEEL COMPANY, LIMITED,
Pittsburg, Pa., June 25, 1892.

DEAR SIR: I am in receipt of your favor of the 22d.

We will want 300 guards for service at our Homestead mills as a measure of precaution against interference with our plan to start the operation of the works on July 6, 1892.

The only trouble we anticipate is that an attempt will be made to prevent such of our men with whom we will by that time have made satisfactory arrangements from going to work. and possibly some demonstration of violence upon the part of those whose places have been filled, or most likely by an element which usually is attracted to such scenes for the purpose of stirring up trouble.

We are not desirous that the men you send shall be armed unless the occasion properly calls for such a measure later on for the protection of our employés or property.

H. Mis. 335——3

We shall wish these guards to be placed upon our property and there to remain unless called into other service by the civil authorities to meet an emergency that is not likely to arise.

These guards should be assembled at Ashtabula, Ohio, not'later than the morning of July 5, when they may be taken by train to McKees Rocks, or some other point upon the Ohio River below Pittsburg, where they can be transferred to boats and landed within the inclosures of our premises at Homestead. We think absolute secrecy essential in the movement of these men so that no demonstration can be made while they are en route.

Specific arrangements for movement of trains and connection with boats will be made as soon as we hear from you as to the certainty of having the men at Ashtabula at the time indicated.

As soon as your men are upon the premises we will notify the sheriff and ask that they be deputized either at once or immediately upon an outbreak of such a character as to render such a step desirable.

Yours very truly,

H. C. FRICK,
Chairman.

ROBERT A. PINKERTON, esq.,
New York City, N. Y.

Mr. BOATNER. That letter was dated on the 24th of June?

The WITNESS. The 25th.

The CHAIRMAN. That was before the works were closed down—they were closed down when—the 29th or 30th?

A. Partly the 29th and partly the 30th. But the men were not to be sent here until the 6th of July.

Q. Did you have any further communication with Robert A. Pinkerton?—A. The communication was made through our agent, Mr. Schoonmaker.

Q. These men were sent and rendezvoused at Ashtabula, Ohio, before any hostile demonstration was made?—A. No, sir; they were not. The hostile demonstrations were made on the 1st of July, our works were surrounded, as I said in my interview, by a mob. Guards were placed and an advisory committee was appointed and notice served—if you will permit me I will just read——

Q. Your letter of the 25th anticipated it and asked for them to be assembled there on the 25th?—A. Yes, sir; that's correct.

Q. You were anticipating trouble?—A. Yes, sir; judging from the experience we had three years ago.

By Mr. BOATNER:

Q. What notice had you at the time you wrote the letter that there would be any attempt by the Amalgamated Association or the men at Homestead to prevent you from operating your property in your own way?—A. The experience we had three years ago. And these men were subject to recall at any time if we found they were not needed.

Q. Had anything been said or done by your employés at Homestead, which notified you of their intention to forcibly prevent you from operating the mills at the time you wrote that letter?—A. I can not say that there was anything special except that we knew their tactics.

By the CHAIRMAN: After shutting down your mills did you have a plank stockade erected around your property?

A. We had the works fenced in; that has been going on for over a month past; and something we have had in contemplation for a long while.

Q. Was it in contemplation of trouble you might have with the workmen?—A. That had something to do with it; yes, sir.

Q. Was it not done for the purpose of putting the property in a position that it could be more easily defended against an assault?—A. Yes, sir; that is correct.

Q. Mr. Frick, did you not, or the company, make other preparations for landing these men there and for securing them, in the way of barges which were lined to protect them from fire?—**A.** We arranged with Capt. Rogers for the barges and the boats. We told him how many men we would likely want him to transport by water to the works. We thought we could land the men by taking them up by water so that they would not pass along any railroad, through any streets, but would be landed right on our property from the river, so as not to interfere with anybody.

Q. Well, in anticipation of trouble or of an attack made upon them, were not the barges lined internally with iron?—**A.** No, sir.

Q. Or externally?—**A.** No, sir; they were not. You were asking me whether these men were not brought in before there was any trouble.

Q. I recollect your statement.—**A.** But I would like to substantiate that statement by notice served on our assistant superintendent at Homestead by this self-styled advisory committee of the Amalgamated Association at Homestead. Here is a copy of it; shall I read it?

Q. Yes, sir; read it.

[Headquarters Advisory Committee, A. A. of I. and S. W., Homestead lodges, third floor Boat Building cor. Eighth ave. and Heisel st.]

HOMESTEAD, PA., *June 2,"* 1892.

Mr. E. F. WOOD,
     Asst. Supt. :

It has been noticed that the gas is burning in two limestone furnaces in No. 2 O. H. dept. This action has greatly excited a number of our men, and there is a large number who, on account of its being pay day, can not be held in check.

If the gas is not shut off, we can not be held responsible for any act that may be committed.

Respectfully submitted,

ADVISORY COMMITTEE.

This is a correct copy of the original letter.

GEO. B. MOTHERAL.

The WITNESS. This notice was served two days before any of these watchmen started from Chicago or New York.

Q. What did they mean by shutting off the gas?—**A.** Well, we use natural gas largely in our works at Homestead, and gas—that was the fuel. It would make smoke.

Mr. BOATNER. Furnaces were at work?

A. It would indicate that operations were being resumed there.

By the CHAIRMAN:

Q. You put that in to show as an additional reason for your apprehension of the use of violence against your employing other men?—**A.** Yes, sir; in connection with the roadways being guarded.

Q. I say as an additional reason?—**A.** Yes, sir; as an additional reason.

Q. In your letter you stated that you did not wish these guards to come armed, but intimated that only in a contingency they might be armed. What was that contingency?—**A.** May I ask you to repeat that?

Q. When and how were the Pinkerton men armed, if they were, in fact?—**A.** The arms and uniforms of these guards were shipped by rail to this city and taken by Capt. Rogers to his steamboat landing in Al-

---

* This should be July 2, as it was served on that date.

legheny, just across the river, and were put on these boats that were to convey these men to Homestead. They were boxed up.

Q. The guns, ammunition, and uniforms?—A. Yes, sir.

Q. Now go ahead.—A. On the 4th of July I served the sheriff with the following notice; shall I read it?

Q. Read it.

PITTSBURG, *July 4, 1892.*

W. H. McCLEARY,
Sheriff of Allegheny County, Pennsylvania:

DEAR SIR: Will you please take notice that at and in the vicinity of our works in Mifflin Township, near Homestead, Allegheny County, Pennsylvania, and upon the highways leading thereto from all directions, bodies of men have collected who assume to and do prevent to our employés access to and egress from our property, and that from threats openly made we have reasonable cause to apprehend that an attempt will be made to collect a mob and to destroy or damage our property aforesaid, and to prevent us from its use and enjoyment? This property consists of mills, buildings, workshops, machinery, and other personal property.

We therefore call upon you, as sheriff of Allegheny County, Pennsylvania, to protect our property from violence, damage, and destruction, and to protect us in its free use and enjoyment.

THE CARNEGIE STEEL CO., LD.,
By H. C. FRICK, *Chairman.*
CARNEGIE, PHIPPS & CO., LD.,
By H. C. FRICK, *Chairman.*

The WITNESS. To show you that it was clearly our intention that these watchmen should be brought to our property as watchmen and employés, we sent our general superintendent who had with him a few of his assistants to meet these men at Ashtabula and accompany them on their way to our property.

By Mr. BOATNER:

Q. Were these men armed at your expense?—A. No. Mr. Pinkerton furnished those. We paid him so much per man and that included their equipment. We hoped that it would not be necessary, but the arms were there in case they were needed.

Q. You had no letter from Pinkerton in reply to your letter to him?—A. We have an office in New York and a long-distance telephone, and most of this preliminary talk was done over the long-distance telephone with our Mr. Schoonmaker.

Q. You have no letter whatever in reply to that letter?—A. I think not; I will examine and see. I would like to submit two letters given Mr. Potter, which I will read; he is our general superintendent.

THE CARNEGIE STEEL COMPANY, LIMITED,
Pittsburg, Pa., July 2, 1892.

MY DEAR SIR: Please note herewith copy of letter written me by our general counsel, Messrs. Knox & Reed.

I have no doubt you fully realize the importance of not doing anything or permitting anything to be done by any of our employés, or any guards we may employ, to protect our property that is not entirely lawful.

Yours, truly,

H. C. FRICK,
Chairman.

Mr. JOHN A. POTTER,
General Superintendent Homestead Steel Works.

KNOX & REED, ATTORNEYS AT LAW,
Pittsburg, Pa., July 2, 1892.

DEAR SIR: Would suggest that you particularly charge Mr. Potter, that no matter what indignities he may be subjected to in the discharge of his duties at Homestead, that neither he nor any of the company's employés should do any act of aggression, but should confine themselves to protecting themselves and the company's property. They should under no circumstances resort to the use of arms, unless it should be for the protection of their lives.

Yours, very truly,

KNOX & REED.

H. C. FRICK, Esq.

Q. Mr. Frick, this letter that you put in is dated on the 25th day of June, I believe. Had you at the time of writing that letter made any application to the sheriff of this county for assistance or protection in your contemplated troubles?—A. No, sir.

Q. Had you any reason to believe that the sheriff of this county could not obtain as many as 300 citizens who would do their duty in protecting you in your property rights?—A. Yes, sir.

Q. You thought that 300 men could not be had in this county who would protect you?—A. I did not think the sheriff would furnish them, judging from the experience we had.

Q. Did you think the sheriff would not or could not furnish them?—A. That he would not furnish them.

Q. The reason of your application, then, to the Pinkertons, was because you did not believe in the sheriff's disposition and willingness to do his duty?—A. I would not like to say that.

Q. It appears to be the necessary inference from what you have said. The question I want an answer to is: Did you believe that the sheriff could not obtain 300 men in this county to do their duty as citizens and protect you in your property rights?—A. I knew that the sheriff in 1889 had failed to do so.

The CHAIRMAN. Was he the same sheriff?

A. No, sir.

By Mr. BOATNER:

Q. Did you believe that the sheriff could furnish the 300 men, citizens of this county of the State of Pennsylvania, if he desired to do so and made an honest effort to do so?—A. I believe he could furnish that number of men, but I don't think he could furnish men—local deputies—who would protect our property.

Q. You did not believe that 300 men could be found in the county of Allegheny who would protect this property?—A. Such as the sheriff would have furnished.

Q. Did you have any reason to believe that the sheriff would select deputies from that class who would not protect you?—A. Only the experience of three years ago when the sheriff took 100 men up into our property and they were not permitted to land at our property. They were driven off, their hats and coats taken from them, and they were driven back to Pittsburg.

Q. And the upshot of that is that because the sheriff failed three years ago you took it for granted that he would fail now?—A. We thought it was better to secure our own watchmen for use inside of our property and we called on the sheriff to furnish deputies to watch outside of our property.

Q. But you had already made arrangements with Pinkerton to furnish men before you applied to the sheriff?—A. Yes, sir; that was not to do sheriff's duty.

Q. But you did not apply to the sheriff until after you had received this notice from the advisory committee?—A. That is right.

Q. Do I understand you to say that the arms which were furnished there were furnished at the expense and cost of the Pinkertons?—A. Yes, sir.

Q. Did you not advance the cost for those guns—those arms?—A. No, sir.

Q. Was any length of time stipulated for the employment of these Pinkerton men?—A. So long as we needed them.

Q. You intended to use them so long as you thought it necessary for protection of such employés as would go into the works under your new schedule?—A. On our property; yes, sir.

Q. When was this new fence constructed?—A. During the last month or six weeks.

Q. Was its construction commenced before or after the negotiations with the Amalgamated Association commenced?—A. It was constructed after the negotiations were commenced.

Q. After the negotiations were commenced?—A. Yes, sir.

Q. I observed to-day in looking at that fence that there are a number of holes. The holes continue up to the point where the fence crosses the line of the old road, holes about 5 inches in diameter and some 25 or 30 feet apart, cut right across the boards, what is the object of those holes being cut there?—A. I saw a statement in the paper that portholes had been cut in the fence, and I inquired of Mr. Potter what the meaning of this was. He said that the holes were merely for looking through in case of necessity to see who was outside.

Q. For observation?—A. Yes, sir; for observation.

Q. Well, Mr. Frick, in your negotiations with Mr. Pinkerton for the use of these men, was there anything said about the men being supplied with arms or the character of the arms with which they were to be supplied?—A. No, sir; no, no; nothing about the character of the arms. That arrangement, as I said, was done by Mr. Schoonmaker, our agent in New York.

Q. Now, then, Mr. Frick, do I understand you as taking this position, that here in this county, with a population somewhere near half a million people, in the great State of Pennsylvania, you anticipated that you could not obtain protection for your property rights from the local authorities?—A. That had been our experience heretofore.

Q. Well, I am not asking you about your experience heretofore, but about your belief and conviction upon which you acted in this emergency. This was the reason you sent for Pinkertons—because you believed that the sheriff of this county could not, or would not, give you protection in your lawful rights, and that he either could not or would not obtain as many men in the county of Allegheny as were necessary to protect you?—A. Yes, sir.

Q. That is the condition of things, is it, in the county of Allegheny?—A. I think that has been pretty well demonstrated since that riot on the 6th.

Q. Do you know what became of the arms which were furnished these parties?—A. Only what I have heard.

Q. These men were massed at a town in Ohio?—A. At Ashtabula, where the roads east and west join and come this way.

Q. They were brought down the river and taken up by boat?—A. They were brought to Youngstown and delivered by the Lake Shore road at Youngstown to the Pennsylvania Company's lines, and by them brought to Bellevue station, below Pittsburg on the Fort Wayne road, near Davis Island dam on the Ohio River.

Q. The citizens of this county are generally law-abiding citizens, are they not?—A. Yes, sir.

Q. To what fact do you attribute the indisposition of the authorities and the people to enforce the law. I understand you to say that you could not rely upon the local authorities for protection. Now, to what do you attribute that extraordinary circumstance?—A. I think it is to the disposition of the sheriff not to exercise the power vested in him to the fullest extent.

Q. You think the people would enforce the law, then, if the sheriff would use his official authority in justifying them in doing so?—A. I think they would; yes, sir.

Q. Do you know what attempt the sheriff made to obtain a posse comitatus—A. Only what I saw in the papers.

Q. You did not give any personal attention to that matter yourself?—A. No, sir.

Q. Did you make any effort to reënforce the sheriff in obtaining forces to protect your property?—A. Yes, sir; in this way. In the way I have just told you—by employing these 300 watchmen.

Q. Did you make any effort to secure the services of the citizens of the county or State to serve in the same direction?—A. We had quite a number of policemen of our own at the works, but they were driven off before we took these watchmen in. They were stopped on this side of the river. Men came to my house and told me they could not get over to watch our property.

Q. I understand, then, the object of bringing these men was in anticipation of resistance by the Homestead people to your employment of nonunion labor?—A. Only to protect our property.

Q. And to protect that labor and your property in event of a resistance?—A. Yes, sir.

Q. Now, Mr. Frick, was there any law in this State that you know of which would authorize you to send out of the State and import as large a body of armed men as that for such a purpose?—A. I could not say.

Q. Were you advised that there was any such statute authorizing any such procedure on your part?—A. Of what?

Q. As bringing in such a large body of armed men?—A. We did not bring in a body of armed men.

Q. Who brought them?—A. They were not armed when they came into the State.

Q. Were not the guns placed upon the boats at the time they were?—A. No, sir.

Q. Where were the guns taken aboard?—A. They were taken at Allegheny, right across the river.

Q. Then the men were brought here, uniformed, and armed after they reached here?—A. I believe they were armed on the way to Homestead, at Lock No. 1, above the city.

Q. On the way to Homestead then?—A. No, sir; the arms were taken on the boat while it was lying at the dock of its owner.

Q. And then the arms were taken down to the point at which the men were embarked and taken on board there?—A. Yes, sir.

Q. And the men were taken on board the boat inside of this State?—A. They were. I would like to say this; that we refused to bring those men in here after we saw evidences of trouble unless they were brought in by the sheriff and we turned the men over to the sheriff. The sheriff's chief deputy went down to Belleview Station and met the men there.

H. Mis. 1——72

The CHAIRMAN. And the sheriff agreed to accept them and use them as a posse?

A. Just let me finish, please. The sheriff's chief deputy went to Bellevue Station, met the men there and accompanied them on the boat up to Homestead. I was advised that they could not bring them up unless that was the case.

Q. Did the sheriff agree with you to accept and use them as a posse?—A. Yes, sir.

At 10 o'clock p. m. the committee adjourned until July 13 at 9 a. m.

PITTSBURG, WEDNESDAY, *July 13, 1892.*

The subcommittee of the Committee on the Judiciary, appointed to investigate the employment of Pinkerton detectives in connection with the labor troubles at Homestead, Pa., this day met, Hon. Wm. C. Oates in the chair.

All the members were present.

TESTIMONY OF H. C. FRICK—Continued.

The CHAIRMAN. Mr. Frick, Mr. Boatner desires to put some other questions on the same line and in the same connection he was questioning you at the time of the close of our session on yesterday.

By Mr. BOATNER:

Q. I was questioning you, Mr. Frick, in regard to the arms and uniforms that you stated had been sent to this place. To whom were they sent?—A. They were sent originally to the Union Supply Company and by that company delivered to Capt. Rodgers at his boat landing.

Q. Can you state when these goods were ordered to be sent here?—A. I could not give you the exact date when they were ordered to be sent, but I think Capt. Rodgers can tell you—and I understand you are going to call him—when these boxes were received at his boat.

Q. Can you state when they reached this place?—A. I could not.

Q. At what time, Mr. Frick, were your arrangements with the Pinkertons completed to obtain these men? As you have a letter dated the 25th of June, I want to know the time you were advised by them or by your agency in New York that the men would be supplied.—A. If we needed them?

Q. Yes.—A. About the 1st of July, I think. Having a long-distance telephone connecting our office with New York, that is, our New York office with our Pittsburg office, we were able to talk any time just as we do in the city, you will understand.

Q. You were of course advised by telephone of the progress of the negotiations for these men?—A. Yes, sir.

Q. And you say you were advised about the 1st of July that the arrangement had been completed?—A. I think that is about the date.

Q. These men, I think you stated, rendezvoused on the 5th of July at Ashtabula, in Ohio?—A. Yes, sir.

Q. At what time did you advise the Pinkertons you would need the men?—A. In my letter of the 25th of June, I think, I stated that we would need them.

Q. But you stated just now that arrangements were finally concluded about the 1st of July for the men if you needed them?—A. Yes, sir.

Q. When did you conclude you needed them absolutely, so as to direct the men to be forwarded?—A. About that time, I think. If you will pardon me, my letter of June 25 ordered the men, and of course they were always subject to recall in case they were not needed. As I understand you now, you want to know when we concluded to have the men come forward?

Q. Yes, sir.—A. I think that was about the 1st of July.

Q. Can you give the date on which these arms were delivered to Capt. Rodgers?—A. I can not.

Q. I asked you last night if you had received any reply from the Pinkertons to your letter of the 25th of June, and you stated you did not know. Will you state this morning whether you received any or not?—A. I was examining my letter file this morning and I could not find anything from Mr. Pinkerton in answer to that.

Q. That letter of June 25 does not refer the Pinkertons to your New York agency.—A. No, sir.

Q. How do you account for the fact no reply was made to the letter?—A. The reply probably was made to our New York agent, to whom I think I talked on the same day over the telephone.

Q. As the letter does not contain any reference to your New York agency, is it likely you by telephone directed your New York house to see and confer with the Pinkertons?—A. It may be likely.

Q. Are you able to state whether you did so as a fact or not?—A. I think I did.

Q. Are you positive that you received no letter from the Pinkertons in reply to the letter of June 25?—A. No; I am not. I had some correspondence with the Pinkertons on other matters not pertaining to this.

Q. Was your contract with the Pinkertons for the supply of these men verbal or in writing?—A. As far as what they were to be paid?

Q. Yes, sir.—A. That was verbal.

Q. The terms and conditions under which the Pinkertons were to furnish the men?—A. As far as paying them, yes, sir; it was verbal.

Q. Well, in any other respect, was there any written agreement between you and the Pinkertons in respect to this subject-matter at all?—A. Nothing except the letters which may have passed between us and the verbal talk with our agent.

Q. My question, Mr. Frick, is this: Have you a written contract—now a written contract may be evidence signed by both parties, or it may be by evidence in a letter making a proposition and a letter accepting that proposition?—A. We have nothing of the kind.

Q. You have no written agreement?—A. No, I think I stated that before—that we had no written agreement.

Q. What I want to get at is this: Is there any letter from the Pinkertons either to you or to your New York house, or anyone representing you, accepting the proposition made in your letter and giving the terms upon which they would furnish the men you desired?—A. Not to my knowledge.

Q. Then, so far as you know the negotiations with the Pinkertons and final agreement were verbal between your New York house and the Pinkertons?—A. As I stated to you last night, the amount we were to pay them was arranged preliminary to this letter of the 25th. I had a talk in which I wanted to know what the charges would be; this was verbal.

Q. How long before the 25th?—A. Well, a few days, I don't know the exact date. That was the only time so far as I know that the question of what we were to give was discussed, and the only mention so far as I remember it.

Q. With which one of the Pinkertons did this conversation occur?—A. The conversation I had was with Capt. Hinde; I did not meet Mr. Pinkerton himself.

Q. Is he a representative of the Pinkertons?—A. Yes, sir.

Q. Where did you meet him?—A. In Pittsburg.

Q. He is their representative here?—A. No, he came out here.

Q. Did he come out at your solicitation?—A. Yes, sir.

Q. Was that solicitation verbal or in writing?—A. I think the request was made through our agent in Philadelphia.

Q. What is his name?—A. Mr. Hoffman.

Q. And Mr. Hinde came here to see you?—A. Yes, sir.

Q. Are you not able to fix the date on which he made his appearance?—A. I am not.

Q. Can you approximate whether it was three, eight, or ten days?—A. It was a few days before the 25th of June, but just the date I could not give you now. I might find it by reference.

Q. It might be a week?—A. It might be.

Q. It might be; well, it certainly was not less than three days previous, was it?—A. I could not answer that; it would only be a guess.

Q. At this conversation were the terms upon which the men were to be furnished agreed upon between you and Mr. Hinde?—A. Yes, sir; that is to say, I asked him the terms and he told me, and nothing further was said about it. I was satisfied.

Q. Do you mean that you did not indicate to him whether you would accept his terms or not?—A. I do not think I accepted any more than not finding any fault with them. They were satisfactory.

Q. Then there was an implied agreement between you and Mr. Hinde when he went away that the men would be furnished if you desired them?—A. Yes, sir—no: I guess I am a little wrong in that. Mr. Hinde had to report to Mr. Pinkerton and he would have to decide.

Q. Did you receive any communication, either verbally or in writing, from the Pinkertons after your interview with Capt. Hinde and before this letter of the 25th of June was written?—A. I do not remember that I did, although as I stated to you before, I had some correspondence with him on some other matters about that time not pertaining to these watchmen we wanted. I have no doubt if you asked him Mr. Pinkerton could furnish you all the correspondence (he has probably copied it) with our New York office, and anything we may have had with him.

Q. Yes, sir; but we have you here and have not Mr. Pinkerton.—A. Certainly, but I understood you to say, or some one to say, that he was willing to appear before you. That being the case, I have no doubt he can give you everything in connection with it more fully than I can, probably, as this was carried on, as I have told you, partly by myself here and partly by our agent in Philadelphia, Mr. Hoffman, and partly by our agent in New York, Mr. Schoonmaker.

The CHAIRMAN. We will have both the Pinkertons called hereafter.

The WITNESS. That is why I make this statement.

By Mr. BOATNER:

Q. It is a matter of some importance, Mr. Frick, and it appears to me you should be able to refresh your recollection upon that point, as to whether you had anything from the Pinkertons, either directly or through your Philadelphia house or New York house or elsewhere, indicating they would furnish the men if you desired them?—A. Well, it is likely I did have something, but I do not remember. As I stated before to you, we had this telephone and we have frequent conversations. I have given you this letter of June 25, which states we did order the men and what we wanted them for.

Q. But your letter of the 25th indicates that was the first negotiation on the subject; it contains no reference whatever to any prior negotiation, and it appears there were prior negotiations, and what I am trying to get at is whether there was any agreement, expressed or implied, between you and the Pinkertons before the date of that letter of the 25th with reference to the use of these men?—A. I believe I have answered that.

Q. Your answer is that you do not know; that you can not recollect.—A. I think there was some conversation, but what it was I do not remember.

Q. Do you know whether during that conversation anything was said about the necessity of providing arms?—A. I do not.

Q. When was it that the Pinkertons were requested, or advised it would be necessary to supply their men with arms?—A. I could not tell you when.

Q. Do you know who it was who directed the supply of the arms?— A. It was probably done by Mr. Schoonmaker, our agent in New York.

Q. It was not done by you?—A. Not directly. I may have had some communication with Mr. Schoonmaker in reference to that.

Q. Will you be kind enough to state what the communication was?— A. I say "I may have." I will not be positive as to that.

Q. Will you please state whether you did or did not have? because you are the person who knows.—A. I have answered you by stating I may have, and it is likely I did have.

Q. The question is, do you know whether you did or did not?—A. I have replied to that, I think.

Q. Well, I submit to the chairman that you have not.

The CHAIRMAN. I think he has. He has stated that he had some communication.

The WITNESS. As far as I recollect, I answered it. I think I did have, I say.

By Mr. BOATNER:

Q. Now, Mr. Frick, please state whether or not at any time before the receipt of the arms which came here for the use of the Pinkertons you, or any of your firm, advised the Pinkertons that it would be necessary for them to furnish their men with arms?—A. I think I have answered that question to the best of my knowledge.

Q. You have merely stated that you think it may be that you have had some communication with Mr. Schoonmaker, but you have not stated that you *had* any communication from Mr. Schoonmaker or what the purport of it was, and what I want to get at is the fact. If you know it and if you do not know it, it is sufficient for you to state so.— A. Yes, sir; I think I answered that question before to the best of my ability.

By Mr. TAYLOR: ˙

Q. You mean you have answered it before this morning or that it was answered last night?—A. I mean this morning.

Q. There may be an uncertainty, which is this: When you say "I may have," that may mean one of two things. It may mean it is so or it is not so, and I will not tell you, or it may mean I do not remember.— A. I do not want to be construed that way. I think I did have some conversation with Mr. Schoonmaker.

By Mr. BOATNER:

Q. Is it your recollection that you did?—A. That is my best recollection.

Q. Have you any reason to doubt the accuracy of your recollection?—
Well, I am a very busy man.   I have a great many things to look after,
but that is my recollection.

Q. Then, if you have no doubt of the accuracy of your recollection,
why do you say "I think I did" instead of stating positively whether
you did or did not?—A. Well, I did not want to give an unqualified
reply, because I am not positive.   If I were, I should have done it by
saying "yes" or "no."

The CHAIRMAN. I understand the substance of Mr. Frick's testimony
on this point to be—if I quote you wrongly, correct me—that you negotiated with the Pinkertons for the 300 men to be sent here, and also
for arms to be used in the event they were necessary, and that you
take all the responsibility for the employment of them to go to Homestead, as you state, to get possession of your property.

Mr. BOATNER. I did not understand the statement that he negotiated for the arms.

The CHARMAN. He stated there was a contingency——

The WITNESS. The letter states our position so far as these watchmen are concerned, and it is just as fully as I could possibly give it set
forth in the letter of the 25th of June.

Mr. BOATNER. I want to ask Mr. Frick this question: In the employment of these men was it stipulated that they should be armed?

The WITNESS. A. I think not.   In fact, I may state it was not so
stipulated.

By the CHAIRMAN:

Q. Mr. Frick, in your examination last evening, the committee did
not get a clear idea of the compensation of your employés on the sliding scale.   Are you prepared this morning to give a fuller explanation
of that?—A. Yes, sir; I think I can, and I would say the purpose and
effect of the sliding system is to have wages change and adjust themselves with the market price of the article on which the wages are
based.   For instance, with the Homestead Works the wages are based
upon the selling price of steel billets and advance or decline in accordance with the market for billets.   With the Homestead scale there is
no limitation upon the advancement of price, but a guaranty that wages
shall not decline below a certain point.   The sliding scale also presents
an advantage or benefit of running over an extended period, and not
being subject to adjustment yearly.

Now, in order that you may fully understand how this scale operates,
I have and will give you the sliding scale worked out by each department.   For instance, here is the scale of the Homestead Steel Works
governing and fixing the wages in the 119-inch plate mill; secondly,
the wages for each 100 tons to be paid under an agreement of July 15,
1889.   This line [referring to papers in his hand] gives the price of billets, starting with $25, which was the minimum under that agreement,
and advancing 25 cents every line—the second line, for instance, 25¼—
and on up until it reaches $40 billets.   It shows, for instance, that a
roller who earned in the plate mill in the month of May, by working 24
days, $259.05, was paid on the $25 minimum, and paid at the rate of
$13.21 for each 100 tons.   That made his wages for the month, based
on $25 billets, $259.05; that was owing to the amount he handled.
The next roller, however, worked a less number of days—22 days—and

made $278.50. He was paid the same rate per 100 tons, but evidently handled a little more tonnage. The next roller worked 23 days and was paid the same rate per ton and made $279.30. This statement goes on to show what wages this roller would make as the price of billets advanced above $25 per ton. For insrance, at $25 per ton he was paid $13.21 per 100 tons. At $25.25 per ton he would have been paid $13.34 per ton, and so on up until he reaches, we will say, $30 billets. At that price he would have been paid $15.85 for each 100 tons. If billets should reach the price of $40 per ton he would have been paid $21.13 for each 100 tons. By this you can follow all the men, and taking these wage scales in connection with the statement of the four departments which I handed to you with the earnings of the men for the month of May, you can analyze them and they can be easily understood.

By Mr. BYNUM:

Q. What I want to know is what regulates the $13.21 when billets are $25?—A. That was agreed on in the negotiation.

Q. That is the rate paid for 100 tons?—A. Yes, sir; when billets sell at $25 per ton.

Q. Is that arbitrarily fixed?—A. I think I stated, if not, I would like to, that the May wages earned by the men as furnished you in the four departments, are based on the $25 per ton minimum. In regard to your asking whether that price was arbitrary, I would say, of course that was a matter of agreement reached.

Q. Of course we understand it was not fixed in relation to anything else except the $25, and of course if that is agreed upon it works out then on the basis you give?—A. Yes, sir.

By the CHAIRMAN:

Q. Now I asked you about a contract you had with the Government for furnishing plates for naval vessels on yesterday evening?—A. Yes, sir; and I beg to submit that.

Q. This is the agreement you have?—A. Yes, sir; a copy of it.

Q. It explains itself?—A. It does.

Contract for steel armor-plates and appurtenances.

This contract, of two parts, made and concluded this twentieth day of November, A. D. 1890, by and between Carnegie, Phipps & Company (Limited), a limited partnership association, organized under the laws of the State of Pennsylvania, and doing business in the county of Allegheny, in said State, represented by William L. Abbott, chairman, and Henry M. Curry, a manager, and John G. A. Leishman, a manager, of said association, party of the first part, and the United States, represented by the Secretary of the Navy, party of the second part: Witnesseth, That for, and in consideration of, the payments hereinafter specified, the party of the first part, for itself, and its successors, heirs and assigns, and its legal representatives, does hereby covenant and agree to and with the United States, as follows, that is to say:

First. The party of the first part will, at its own risk and expense, manufacture and deliver to the Navy Department, in the manner, within the periods prescribed, and according to the conditions stated herein and in the printed circular (including the drawings appended to and forming part thereof) approved by the Secretary of the Navy, February 12, 1887, and the addenda thereto approved by the Secretary of the Navy, March 11, 1887, and November 20, 1890, which circular and addenda, hereto annexed, shall be deemed and taken as forming part of this contract, with the like operation and effect as if the same were incorporated herein, except as hereinafter provided, six thousand (6,000) tons of steel armor-plates and appurtenances, the armor-plates to be of thicknesses from four to twenty inches, both inclusive, at the prices per ton for the different exhibits as stated in the second clause of this contract, free on board cars at the works of the party of the first part.

Such armor-plates and appurtenances to be of domestic manufacture, and to conform to and with all the details, requirements, and stipulations relating to material, manufacture, tests, inspection, and delivery, and in all respects to the conditions stated in the aforesaid circular and addenda thereto, except as hereinafter provided, it being expressly understood, covenanted, and agreed, by and between the parties to this contract, that deliveries thereunder shall be commenced by the delivery of not less than three hundred (300) tons on or before July 1, 1891, and shall be continued thereafter at the rate of not less than five hundred (500) tons per month, until the delivery of the six thousand (6,000) tons aforementioned is completed, which shall be within eleven months and fifteen days from the date last mentioned.

Second. It is further mutually understood, covenanted, and agreed that the party of the second part shall, from time to time, order from the party of the first part, and furnish such description and drawings thereof as may be necessary, such quantities of armor plates and appurtenances as shall be required, so that the aggregate of such orders shall equal the amount of armor plates and appurtenances herein contracted for, to wit, six thousand (6,000) tons, and such orders shall be given from time to time, but for each of such orders given after June 1, 1891, the party of the first part will be allowed ninety (90) days from the date of said order in which to commence deliveries thereunder.

The prices per ton to be paid to the party of the first part for the armor plates and appurtenances above mentioned shall be the different prices per ton that would be paid therefor under the provisions of a certain contract for armor plates and appurtenances, made and concluded the first day of June, A. D. 1887, by and between the Bethlehem Iron Company, of South Bethlehem, Pennsylvania and the Secretary of the Navy; and the prices per ton above mentioned, which shall be paid for the armor plates and appurtenances ordered under this contract, shall be determined as follows:

When an order is given to the party of the first part for armor plates for appurtenances, the Secretary of the Navy will cause a board of naval officers, appointed by the Secretary of the Navy, to determine under which exhibit or exhibits of the said contract with the Bethlehem Iron Company the articles thus ordered should be classed, and the said board shall assign the articles thus ordered to "Exhibits," in such a way that the prices per ton to be paid to the party of the first part, by reason of such assignment, shall be the prices per ton that would be paid therefor under the said contract with the Bethlehem Iron Company for the articles ordered as aforesaid. If any articles are ordered which, in the opinion of the board, can not be assigned as aforesaid, it will so state.

The prices per ton, determined as above mentioned, will be stated by the Department at the time of giving said orders to the party of the first part. If the party of the first part considers that the armor plates and appurtenances thus ordered have been incorrectly assigned to the different exhibits, and that consequently the prices as stated by the Department are incorrect, it will so inform the Department in writing, within ten days of the date of receipt of said order, and before the manufacture of the articles in question begins. In this case the matter will be promptly referred by the Secretary of the Navy to the board which made the assignment thus objected to by the party of the first part, or to another board, similarly constituted, which board will finally determine under which exhibit or exhibits the said armor plates and appurtenances shall be classed.

Third. It is further mutually understood, covenanted, and agreed that the ballistic test for acceptance under this contract for armor plates under six (6) inches in thickness, and for those over thirteen (13) inches in thickness, shall be fixed and determined by a board of naval officers, to be appointed by the Secretary of the Navy, in such a manner that the ballistic test thus determined shall be, as far as practicable, of the same relative severity for the plates of the thicknesses above mentioned, as is required in the aforesaid contract with the Bethlehem Iron Company for plates of thicknesses between six (6) and thirteen (13) inches, both inclusive.

Fourth. It is further mutually understood, covenanted, and agreed, by and between the parties to this contract, that the Secretary of the Navy may require all or part of the armor-plates and appurtenances herein contracted for, to be made of ordinary steel or of nickel-steel. If nickel-steel armor-plates or appurtenances are thus furnished, the prices per ton that shall be paid therefor, shall be the prices per ton before mentioned for similar articles of ordinary steel, made in accordance with the requirements of the circular and addenda thereto, which form part of this contract, said prices being increased or diminished by the greater or less cost of labor and materials only to the party of the first part in the production of the nickel-steel armor-plates and appurtenances ordered, as compared with the cost of labor and materials only to the party of the first part in the production of similar articles made of ordinary steel, as above mentioned; the intention being that while the party of the second part shall have the fullest power to vary the requirements of this contract from ordinary steel armor-plates and appurtenances, such as are herein specified, to nickel-steel armor-plates and appurtenances, either in whole or in part, this contract shall, nevertheless, continue to exist on the basis of ordinary steel armor-plates and appurtenances as aforementioned, modified only in this respect, viz, that additional cost and expense, as aforesaid, occasioned to the party of the first part by such modification, shall be paid to the party of the first part, and that any saving, as aforesaid, thereby occasioned, shall be deducted from the contract price, so that in the end the party of the first part shall be neither advantaged nor disadvantaged, as aforesaid, under this contract, by the ordering of said nickel-steel armor-plates or appurtenances, instead of said ordinary steel armor-plates or appurtenances; but the cost above mentioned shall not be construed to include the cost of such armor-plates and appurtenances as fail to pass the ballistic and other tests and inspections, under the rules that may be established by the boards herein provided for, or that may not be presented for such tests and inspections.

The amount of increased or diminished compensation, as aforesaid, if any, that the party of the first part shall be entitled to receive for furnishing nickel-steel armor-plates and appurtenances, as compared with that which would be paid for similar articles made of ordinary steel under the provisions of this contract, shall be ascertained, estimated, and determined, by a board of naval officers, to be appointed by the Secretary of the Navy. Every facility will be given by the party of the first part to the aforesaid board, or to other persons appointed by the Secretary of the Navy for the purpose, in obtaining all necessary information as to the comparative cost only above mentioned. All information thus obtained will be considered strictly confidential.

In case any charges on account of royalties, guarantees, etc., are included in the cost of manufacture of the nickel-steel armor-plates and appurtenances aforementioned, the agreements of the party of the first part, in consequence of which the said charges are made, must be first approved by the Secretary of the Navy.

Whereas certain patentees claim by reason of their inventions to control the right to make armor plate containing nickel; and

Whereas the party of the second part declines to recognize the claims of said patentees, and to pay the royalty demanded by them, said royalty being two (2) cents per pound upon finished armor plates and appurtenances:

Therefore, for the protection of the party of the first part, there shall be added to the cost of the said nickel-steel armor plates and appurtenances, when computed as aforesaid, the sum of two (2) cents per pound to cover said claims, which sum the party of the second part agrees to pay from time to time, as the payments for said nickel-steel armor plates and appurtenances are made, according to this contract. Said sums as paid are to be deposited by the party of the first part in such depositories of the United States as the Secretary of the Navy may designate.

Should it finally be decided by the courts of competent jurisdiction that the said patents are invalid or that there is no valid claim against either of the parties hereto, their agents or employés, said fund shall be promptly paid over by the party of the first part to the Secretary of the Treasury, after deducting therefrom such reasona₂ ble counsel fees and expenses, if any, as may be approved by the Secretary of the Navy, incurred by the party of the first part in defense of such litigation; or in case of amicable settlement between the parties hereto and said patentees, the balance remaining after such settlement and payment of expenses as aforesaid, which may have been necessarily incurred by the party of the first part, shall be paid over to said Secretary of the Treasury.

In case of a final judgment in favor of said patentees, the said fund shall be used, so far as necessary, for the payment of said judgment, and costs and expenses approved as aforesaid, including reasonable attorneys' fees, but in case all of said fund shall be required for the payment of said judgment, then the party of the second part shall pay such expenses as shall have been properly incurred by the party of the first part, after approval as aforesaid, including reasonable attorney's fees, in the defense of any such suits.

It shall be the further duty of said board, or of a board similarly constituted, to determine and fix the physical, chemical, and other tests and requirements for said nickel-steel armor plates and appurtenances, and the preliminary and final ballistic tests for acceptance therefor, and also the rights to earn premiums for ballistic resistance in excess of that required by said ballistic tests for acceptance.

The party of the first part shall have the right to appeal from the finding of the said board with reference to the tests for acceptance of nickel-steel armor plates and appurtenances, and also with reference to the said premiums, to another board composed of three persons and constituted as follows, viz: One member to be nominated by each of the parties to this contract and the third member to be chosen by the two first mentioned.

The finding of the board last mentioned, or of a majority thereof, shall govern, subject to appeal as hereinafter provided.

Fifth. It is further mutually understood, covenanted, and agreed, by and between the parties to this contract, that in case the United States incurs expenses in the purchase, from the party of the first part, of plates and bolts, or either, for experimental purposes in connection with the development of said nickel-steel armor plates or appurtenances, that the cost of said plates and bolts shall be deducted from any premiums that the party of the first part may earn on nickel-steel armor plates, as stated in the preceding clause, for ballistic resistance.

Sixth. It is further mutually understood, covenanted, and agreed, by and between the parties to this contract, that changes in the conditions or requirements of the circular and addenna, hereinbefore referred to, and which form a part of this contract, may be made by and with the mutual consent of the parties hereto, and that, if changes are thus made, the actual cost thereof, and the damage, if any, caused thereby, and the amount of the increased or diminished compensation which the party of the first part shall be entitled to receive, if any, in consequence of such change or changes, shall be ascertained, estimated, and determined, by a board of naval officers to be appointed by the Secretary of the Navy.

Seventh. Both the parties to this contract shall have the right to appear before the board or boards herein provided for, either in person or by representatives, and to make such statements, written or oral, as they may see fit concerning the matters with which said board or boards may be charged, and said board or boards will duly consider such statements. In each case a decision of a majority of the board shall govern, and both parties to this contract hereby expressly covenant and agree to abide by said decision, subject, however, to appeal to the President of the United States, and his decision shall control.

Eighth. It is further mutually understood, covenanted, and agreed, by and between the parties to this contract, that every reasonable consideration shall be extended to the party of the first part, in case of unavoidable delay in the manufacture and delivery of the armor plates and appurtenances aforesaid, provided it shall appear that said party has assumed the obligations of this contract in good faith, and that it is prosecuting the work under the same with due diligence, in which case reasonable extensions of the periods prescribed for deliveries of the armor plates and appurtenances required under this contract shall be granted. In case any delay shall arise in the prosecution of the work required under this contract or any part thereof, or in case any question shall arise under the provisions hereof concerning premiums, such questions, with all the facts relating thereto, shall be submitted to the Secretary of the Navy for consideration, and his decision thereon shall be conclusive and binding upon the parties to this contract.

Ninth. It is further mutually understood, covenanted, and agreed, that if, at any stage of the work prior to the final completion of said armor plates and appurtenances, the Secretary of the Navy shall find that the party of the first part is unable to proceed with, and make satisfactory progress in, the manufacture and delivery of the armor plates and appurtenances required, and within the periods prescribed, as aforesaid, including such extension or extensions thereof, if any, as may have been granted under the eighth clause of this contract, then and in such case it shall be optional with the Secretary of the Navy to declare this contract forfeited on the part of the party of the first part; and in case the Secretary of the Navy shall, under the provisions of this clause, declare this contract forfeited, such forfeiture shall not affect the right of the United States to recover for defaults which may have occurred under this contract, and as liquidating damages, a sum of money equal to the penalty of the bond accompanying the same.

Tenth. The party of the first part, in consideration of the premises, hereby covenants and agrees to hold and save the United States harmless from and against all and every demand or demands of any nature or kind, for, or on account of, the adoption of any plan, model, design, or suggestion, or for, or on account of, the use of any patented invention, article, or appliance, which has been or may be adopted or used in or about the manufacture or production of said armor plates or appurtenances, or any part thereof, under this contract, by the party of the first part, and to protect and discharge the United States from any liability on account thereof, or on account of the use thereof, by proper releases from patentees or otherwise, and to the satisfaction of the Secretary of the Navy, before final payment under this contract shall be made; except patents as to nickel-steel armor plates and appurtenances, which are specially provided for in the fourth clause of this contract.

Eleventh. It is further mutually understood, covenanted, and agreed, by and between the respective parties hereto, that this contract shall not, nor shall any interest herein, be transferred by the party of the first part to any other person or persons, and that any such transfer shall cause the annulment of this contract so far as the United States are concerned; and that all rights of action to recover for any breach of this contract by the party of the first part are reserved to the United States.

Twelfth. It is hereby mutually and expressly covenanted and agreed, and this contract is upon the express condition, that no Member of or Delegate to Congress, officer of the Navy, nor any person holding any office or appointment under the Navy Department, shall be admitted to any share or part of this contract, or to any benefit to arise therefrom.

Thirteenth. The United States, in consideration of the premises, do hereby contract, promise, and engage to and with the party of the first part, as follows :

1. The contract prices to be paid by the United States to the said party of the first part for armor plates and appurtenances manufactured and delivered under this contract, shall be the prices per ton determined as provided for in the second or in the fourth clause of this contract.

2. Payments under this contract shall be regulated and made in accordance with the provisions contained in this contract and in the circular and addenda aforesaid.

3. There shall be a reservation of 10 per cent on each payment made under this contract, until the aggregate of such reservations shall reach the sum of one hundred thousand dollars ($100,000), when such reservations, so far as subsequent payments are concerned, shall cease, and the sum last mentioned shall be held as a special reserve under the conditions hereinafter stated.

4. No payment shall be made except upon bills, in triplicate, certified by the inspector, in such manner as shall be directed by the Secretary of the Navy, whose final approval of all bills thus certified shall be necessary before payment thereof.

5. All warrants for payments under this contract shall be made payable to the party of the first part or its order.

6. The special reserve aforesaid shall be retained until all the armor plates and appurtenances furnished under this contract shall have successfully met the requirements of paragraph 155 of the circular and addenda aforesaid, and subsequent modifications thereof, if any; but for the purpose of such responsibility, the party of the second part agrees that after eighteen months from the delivery of any plate, if notification of failure of such plate as referred to in said paragraph shall not have been served on the party of the first part, the responsibility of the party of the first part for defects shall cease as to such delivery, and no portion of said reserve shall thereafter be held for such delivery.

7. When all the conditions, covenants, and provisions of this contract shall have been performed and fulfilled by and on the part of the party of the first part, said party shall be entitled, within ten days after the filing and acceptance of its claim, to receive the said special reserve, or so much thereof as it may be entitled to, on the execution of a final release to the United States, in such form as shall be approved by the Secretary of the Navy, of all claims of any kind or description, under or by virtue of this contract.

Fourteenth. If any doubts or disputes arise as to the meaning of anything in the circular and addenda aforesaid, or if any discrepancy appear between the same and this contract, the matter shall be at once referred to the Secretary of the Navy for determination, and the party of the first part hereby binds itself, and its successors, heirs, and assigns, and its legal representatives, to abide by his decision in the premises. If, however, the party of the first part shall feel aggrieved at any decision of the Secretary of the Navy, it shall have the right to submit the same to the President of the United States, and his decision shall control.

In witness whereof the respective parties have hereunto set their hands and seals, the day and year first above written.

[Seal of Carnegie, Phipps & Co., Limited.]   CARNEGIE, PHIPPS & Co. (Limited),
                         By WM. L. ABBOTT, *Chairman.*
                         H. M. CURRY, *Manager.*
                         JOHN G. A. LEISHMAN, *Manager.*
                         THE UNITED STATES,

[Seal of Navy Department.]   By B. F. TRACY, *as Secretary of the Navy.*

Signed and sealed in the presence of—
     OTIS H. CHILDS, *Sec'y.*
     WM. B. REMEY,
          Judge Advocate General,
As to B. F. TRACY,
          Secretary of the Navy.

By Mr. BRODERICK:

Q. Will you take the paper which you submitted last evening giving us the wages of these different classes of men, and state from that briefly, in order that we may get it into the record, the character of the work each class performs?—A. Well, I do not believe I am competent to describe that to you so you will understand it; I do not pretend to be a practical steel man.

Q. Is some one here who can?—A. Yes, sir.

Q. You may state, if you know, how these men were paid with reference to payments made in other mills in this country for the same character of work?—A. To some extent I can. We can furnish a gentleman who is thoroughly familiar with that, and his testimony on that point will be certainly much more satisfactory to you. I may say, though, that from all the information I have and have been able to get, the wages paid at our works are, if anything, higher than those paid at almost any other works in the country, particularly much higher than in the eastern part of the State; and from the best information I can get, I am justified, I think, in saying they are almost 40 per cent higher in almost every particular than they are in the Eastern mills.

Q. The scale was fixed in 1889 as I understand?—A. In 1889; yes, sir.

Q. When that was fixed, was there an increase or a decrease in the wages they had been receiving?—A. I think in some cases an increase, and in others a decrease, but I am not very familiar with that, as I was not then——

Q. From that time were the men satisfied until the recent proposition to change the scale?—A. So far as I know, yes.

Q. After the conflict between the Pinkertons and your men, did you join the sheriff in a request to the governor to send troops?—A. I did not until on Sunday evening last, when I sent to the governor a telegram urging the importance as I thought of his supporting the sheriff by the military, but that was not in conjunction with the sheriff, however, and the sheriff knew nothing of my telegram.

Q. Did you have a personal interview with the governor? A. No, sir.

By Mr. Boatner:

Q. Will you be kind enough to furnish the committee with a list of the classes of men who would be affected by this proposed change of the scale of wages?—A. I have done so.

Q. But what I want to get at is this: I want the paper to show how much wages they were receiving under the old scale and what they would receive under the new scale; an estimated statement?—A. I will have that furnished. [See same on list already in evidence.]

Q. As to the class of labor to which you referred in your testimony yesterday, receiving, I think, the lowest one $250, and two I think something over $270?—A. Yes, sir.

Q. Will you please state whether these men were required to employ any assistants in making that money?—A. They were not.

Q. That was for their own individual labor?—A. For their own individual labor in all of the cases that I have cited, with the number of days these men worked and the amounts they received monthly. There has not been one instance where they were required to pay to my knowledge, and I think I know, one cent to anybody else out of the amount paid them.

Q. They are not required to pay help?—A. They are not required to pay help.

By Mr. Bynum:

Q. I understood your answer to Judge Oates to be that you think the reduction of wages as proposed by the scale would be about 15 per cent?—A. The reduction in these four departments in the tonnage rates would be about an average of 15 per cent.

Q. Then I understood you in addition to say that they would still receive enough to make more wages than they were able to make when this schedule was first entered into, before new machinery was introduced?—A. As we get the mills in operation month after month they will be able to increase the output, and I am satisfied the wages they earned in the month of May under the old scale would have been far exceeded in the next May, that is, May 1893, under the new scale.

Q. That is, you think after the machinery is introduced it would decrease the labor cost 15 per cent.—A. It would.

Q. It would be 15 per cent and whatever they earned over what they had previously earned?—A. Yes, sir.

Q. You manufacture billets in one of your establishments?—A. Yes, sir.

Q. Which one of them?—A. We manufacture billets at these works.

Q. Any others?—A. At the Duquesne Steel Works.

Q. When did you purchase the Duquesne Steel Works?—A. Last November a year, or, in other words, November, 1890, I believe.

Q. Since the agreement was entered into in the year 1889?—A. Yes, sir.

Q. In the statement of wages paid in the month of May do these men in these departments do steady work, or do they work more some months than others?—A. They work more some months than others.

Q. When is the largest amount of work done?—A. In the summer months.

Q. During the winter months the number of days they are able to put in is much less than it is in summer?—A. Well, not very much less. It depends a great deal on the condition of business.

Q. Well, the condition of business is naturally better during the summer season?—A. Yes, sir.

Q. Do you know how much on an average—and can you give an estimate—these men worked during the winter months, say January or February?—A. I think that the average number of days worked a year would be about 270.

Q. During the whole year?—A. Yes, sir; I could not say positively, but I think that is correct. Of course in some departments it may not have been so many days as that, while in others it may have been more.

Q. Can you give a statement of the price of billets for the last ten years?—A. I think so. I can not do it at present, but I can get it for you.

The CHAIRMAN. Then furnish that when we recall you.

The WITNESS. Very well.

The CHAIRMAN. We will not examine you any further now, Mr. Frick.

TESTIMONY OF WILLIAM B. RODGERS.

WILLIAM B. RODGERS sworn and examined.

By the CHAIRMAN:

Q. What is your business?—A. I am in the coal business and general steamboat business.

Q. You run a boat on the river?—A. Yes, sir; I have three boats.

Q. What do you know about transportation up the river to the Homestead works of men known as Pinkerton detectives?—A. I can answer you better if you will allow me to place in evidence a statement which I gave to the Pittsburg Post last Saturday, July 9, and which was printed in that paper on July 11, Monday.

Q. You can read that as your evidence.—A. I will be very much pleased to do so.

On the day after the Homestead rioting Capt. W. B. Rodgers made a statement in the Post of his connection with the ill-fated expedition up the Monongahela. The following more detailed account will be read with interest, having just been made by him:

"On the 25th of June Mr. H. C. Frick sent for me and made arrangements for the transportation, on a date to be thereafter given, of 300 or more men, with their subsistence, from a point not then determined on the river to the Carnegie works at Homestead. He said they were to act as watchmen in the works and that they would be under the direction of the sheriff of the county. He said nothing about any apprehended trouble. I proceeded at once to fit up the barges for the accommodation of this number of men, by making berths and putting on provisions. Mr. Frick said he intended to house the men on the boats and make them a hotel or boarding house. He also arranged with a supply house adjacent to my office to take such supplies on my boats to the men as necessity required.

"On Tuesday, July 5, early in the day, I got orders from Mr. Frick to send my boats to Davis Island Dam to meet a train that would arrive there between 10 and 11 o'clock with these men on board. I was also notified from Mr. Frick that a deputy sheriff would meet me at the dam to take charge of the expedition.

"EX-SHERIFF GRAY'S PART.

"I went down with our two small towboats, each in charge of a barge, and arrived at the dam about 10 o'clock. Was there met by Mr. Joseph H. Gray, who had a letter of introduction to me, stating he was to accompany me as a deputy sheriff. We had to wait half an hour for the arrival of the train on the Fort Wayne road with the men on board. I did not count them, but was told by those in charge there were 300. They seemed to be a nice-looking set of men and intelligent, well dressed, and behaved. They seemed to be under the charge of four men who acted as captains. The men talked freely of going to Carnegie's to act as watchmen and seemed to have no idea of being engaged in a work of danger. On the way up from Davis Island Dam they seemed more intent on getting something to eat and bunking than anything else. Two-thirds of the men were asleep until the firing on the boats commenced near Homestead.

"I was on the *Little Bill*, and when we got near the lock, the barge in fact being in the lock, we heard a distress signal from the *Tide*, and I directed the *Little Bill* to go back and ascertain what was the matter. When we got to the railroad bridge we found the *Tide's* machinery disabled so she could not proceed. We then took her barge in tow and proceeded to Homestead with both in tow of the *Little Bill*.

"ALL QUIET AT THE LOCK.

"Everything was quiet at the lock, and nothing occurred of an unusual character until we were within about 2 miles of Homestead, when, we heard many whistles blowing, which impressed us with the idea we were expected. As we neared Homestead, daylight was breaking and we could see the crowd gathering on the Homestead shore. When within 1 mile of Homestead and until we reached the landing they were firing into us, the balls striking the pilot house and chimneys, but hurting no one up to that time. We proceeded to land, just above the railroad bridge, on the property of the Carnegie Steel Company, which was fenced in. We went right on against the shore and were there met by an armed mob, I think about 50 to 100, whose numbers were being reënforced by the crowd on the river bank following the boat, until there were probably a thousand there within five minutes after we made the landing.

"The first crowd attacked and tried to stop our tying up and putting out a stage plank. As they came it was something like a charge over the river bank, with the evident intent to get on the barges. They got on the stage and were met by the Pinkerton men. One young man threw himself flat on the stage, when Capt. Hines, of the Pinkerton corps, went forward to push him off. His lying there looked like a piece of bravado, and the others were trying to crowd in over and pass him. While another Pinkerton man was endeavoring to keep the crowd back with an oar, the man lying on the landing stage fired the first shot at the captain—I mean the first shot that did any damage—wounding him in the thigh.

"THE FIRING FROM THE BANK.

"Immediately the crowd began firing from the bank, as well as on the river's edge near the barge. Two men of the Pinkertons were shot at this time at the head of the barge, and one was reported to me to have been shot at the stern of the boat. All this occurred before the Pinkerton men fired, but immediately upon it they fired a general volley, that is about 20 at the head of the boat with revolvers principally, and the crowd retreated behind the intrenchments which they had provided of pig iron and iron plate.

"We then put out our stage and the firing ceased, with the exception of an occasional shot, until we left to go to Port Perry with the wounded. Our time and theirs the next two hours was spent in taking care of the wounded.

"The arms that the Pinkerton men had were sent in advance, and were put on the boats with other stores before they arrived. On the way up, after the firing commenced, they unpacked the arms, and were engaged in it during the firing.

"About our going to Port Perry, owing to the condition of Capt. Hines, who would have bled to death, and others of the wounded, it was thought we should take them where they could get medical aid. The captain is an intelligent, cool and courageous man, and it would have been better all around had he not been stricken down. He merely said to me, 'I don't feel like lying here and bleeding to death.' There were five others beside the captain, one of whom died before he got to the hospital.

"WHO WERE ON THE BOAT.

"After we had put them on the train at Port Perry and made arrangements for them at the hospital, we stayed at that place two hours and for breakfast. There were at that time on the boat, when we started back, a crew of six men, Col. Gray, one Pinkerton man and myself. We went back with the intent to land with the barges and stay with them, or go on to town for further commissary supplies which had been left behind. In anticipation we would be fired on we determined to fight under the colors, and so ran up two flags, one at each end. When we attempted to land alongside the barge we were met with heavy volleys from both sides of the river, particularly the Homestead side, and from behind intrenchments. The firing was so heavy the pilot and engineer were compelled to leave their posts and we were compelled to stop the boat, which drifted around at the mercy of the mob, which continued firing. This lasted until we drifted away from the point and to some extent out of the range of the guns. The shore was lined with thousands on the Homestead side, and a good number on the opposite side, all of whom seemed bent on destroying our lives and our boat. Holes in the boat show missiles were fired from artillery. This firing gradually died away until we were 1¼ miles from Homestead, when it ceased.

"When we were opposite the barges our watchman, John McCurry, was dangerously wounded by a shot in the groin and is now in the Allegheny Hospital.

"I can only say, in conclusion, that I have never heard or read of any such inhuman action as that of this mob, or a part of it, in shooting at wounded men, and doing it with fiendish delight.

"When we were drifting to the point, in point-blank range of the mob, and only 30 or 40 feet away, our destruction would have been inevitable had we not used means of defense we found on the boat. We did this with such effect that the mob scattered and we were enabled to put the pilot and engineer at their posts and so get away."

Q. You give that as your testimony?—A. Yes, sir.

Q. You state that Mr. Gray came to you with a letter of introduction?—A. Yes, sir.

Q. From whom was that letter?—A. From Carnegie's attorneys.

Q. Name them.—A. Knox & Reed.

Q. Does that state all the facts within your knowledge?—A. In reference to Col. Gray, I stated to Knox & Reed that I did not know him, and that some one must give him a letter of introduction, otherwise I could not take him up.

Q. That was before he came?—A. Yes, sir. I did not quite catch your question.

Q. I asked you if that embodies all the facts which you know in this connection?—A. As near as I recollect. I was careful to give the facts at the time, and I have nothing further to add.

Mr. BOATNER. You say that these arms were loaded on your boats with the supplies. Are you able to state on what date they were loaded?

A. With relation to the arms, I did not know they were arms when they were loaded on the boat, but of course that fact was patent to me when they were unloaded. They came with a lot of general groceries and stuff, and they were just packed in ordinary boxes the same as dry goods.

The CHAIRMAN. Groceries and supplies, etc.

The WITNESS. Yes, sir; there was nothing to indicate they were arms until they were unpacked.

By Mr. BOATNER:

Q. What I want to get at is the date when they were put on the boat?—A. Somewhere between the 1st and 2d—Sunday was the 3d and Monday was the 4th—probably the 1st or 2d.

Q. The 1st or 2d of July?—A. Yes, sir.

Q. And they came with promiscuous supplies which were sent for the use of these men who were to go on the barges?—A. Yes, sir.

Q. By whom were they delivered to you?—A. Well, they were just sent down to be loaded by Mr. Frick who was going to send some stuff, and this stuff came along with it and was unloaded on the beach and we loaded whatever came.

Q. Did you receipt for it?—A. I did not receipt for it in that way. In fact I was not at my boat at all times, and I told them whatever came marked to me was to be loaded on.

Q. We noticed in looking at the works yesterday the remains of a car, the wheels and iron of a flat car which appeared to have been burnt. Were you there when that was burnt?—A. Yes, sir; it was burning when we came past it about 11 o'clock.

Q. It was not burning when you reached there in the morning?—A. No, sir.

Q. You did not see it fired?—A. No, sir; it was burning and making a blaze when we came past.

Q. You do not know who fired it?—A. No, sir.

Q. Had the arms been unpacked when you reached the landing?—A. Not all of them, no, sir. I really do not know how many, but they were unpacking them when they were landing, or, rather, working then at that.

By Mr. TAYLOR:

Q. Were these barges prepared by a sheet-iron lining, or anything of that sort?—A. No, sir; nothing of that sort.

Q. Was any such lining in them for any purpose?—A. In all freight boats there is a lining running up 5 or 6 feet, about as high as that [illustrating], merely to make a place to store goods, and these were lined in the usual way.

Q. There was no preparation for defense?—No, sir. As I say, this is true with that class of barges.

The CHAIRMAN. That lining is a wooden lining?

A. Yes, sir.

Mr. BRODERICK. I do not understand whether there was firing before you reached the landing or not.

A. Yes, sir; for twenty-five minutes before we reached the landing.

Q. What distance were you from the landing when the firing commenced?—A. About a mile and a half would be my judgment.

Q. When was the first return fire?—A. After we were in against the shore these men were being shot at on the head of the barge.

Q. What were they doing while going that mile and a half?—A. I think they were running along following us.

Q. I mean what were the men on the barge doing?—A. I say they began to awake to the situation and began to get out their arms and get ready.

The CHAIRMAN. Did the Pinkerton men use any rifles?

The WITNESS. The first firing on the barge next to the shore, I think, was done by revolvers principally, and then, I think, the firing was with rifles on the other barge.

TESTIMONY OF WM. H. M'CLEARY.

WM. H. MCCLEARY sworn and examined.

By the CHAIRMAN:

What official position do you hold?—A. Sheriff of Allegheny County.

Q. State what you know in reference to what is popularly known as the strike at Homestead and what efforts, if any, you made in connection with that as sheriff.—A. I was notified by Mr. Knox, the attorney——

Q. On what date?—A. That I could not tell, sir, but I judge it was a week before the men went out—that there was liable to be a strike there. He stated that they were going to put 300 watchmen in the works and asked me the question would I deputize them. He told me they were Pinkerton men. I told him I thought, in my judgment, it would be well if they got the watchmen here about the city, got some from a detective agency instead of employing those men, and he said they had made an arrangement to employ these other people. He then asked me if I would deputize them. I told him I could not answer at the present, but would have to see my attorney, Mr. Petty, about it. I did not know whether I had the authority to deputize these people. I went after Mr. Petty and told him of my conversation with Mr. Knox. I told Mr. Petty that he could say to Mr. Knox if these men were watchmen in the mill and the mill was attacked and there was liable to be a destruction of property or loss of life to them that I would deputize them, but the contingency would remain in my hands and that the time I thought that should be done would be entirely optional with me. That is the extent of that matter as far as it went. On last Monday, the 4th of July, they served a notice on me that there was a strike going on there and they feared destruction of property and notified me they wanted me to protect their property. That being the 4th and a holiday——

Q. Who gave you that notice?—A. It was served by the attorneys of the company. On Tuesday morning we started out to see if we could get up deputies. I have only 17 people in the office force, clerks, and all in the office, and I was unable to procure any deputies except two to go up there outside of my regular office force. I sent them up on Tuesday afternoon—12 of them. They were not permitted to enter the works. They were driven away. I had been to Homestead myself that day and went to see some gentlemen connected with the locked-out workmen and had a talk with them for an hour and a half or two hours, trying to make an arrangement to allow me to put watchmen in for the protection of those works. When I came back there was no question I should put them in, although I thought at the time if I did not send up more than 50 men they would permit them to go in, but I had no understanding that they should be allowed to go in.

Q. You tried to have an understanding?—A. Yes, sir; that they should be permitted to go in. Two years ago there was a strike in that neighborhood and there were 150 deputy sheriffs sent up there and they were driven away and not permitted to enter the works.

Q. Whom did you see and talk with in reference to putting deputies in charge of the work?—A. I saw several gentlemen there; I saw Mr. O'Donnell, Mr. Lynch, and several members of the advisory committee.

Q. What did they say about it?—A. Well, they said this. They wanted to know how many men I would put in and I said 50 if I could get them. They said there was no necessity for watchmen there, that it was not required, and that there was no danger of that property being destroyed. I explained to them that I was not the judge of that and that this firm had notified me to that effect and under the law I was compelled to protect their property.

Q. So you came away; what did you do next?—A. Then I came down to town and went out to try and get some deputies to go up there; but I could not get any person to go there. Every person refused to go except two parties, two outside parties. Those I sent with 10 of my regular force to Homestead.

Q. That was the second time that you sent up?—A. No, that was the first time. I said I was there first myself.

Q. That was the force you sent there which was turned away?—A. Yes, sir.

Q. Well, did you make any further efforts to impress men and get a sufficient force to take possession of the works or not?—A. That was at 4 o'clock when they went up, and these people did not get back until half past 7 o'clock and I did not do anything further that night, and when this trouble occurred the next day I issued a proclamation and sent a proclamation up by a bill-poster.

Q. Was that on the 4th or 5th of the month?—A. On the 5th.

Q. What did you proclaim, what did you set forth?—A. I set forth that there was trouble at the works of Carnegie & Co.

Q. Have you a copy?—A. No, sir, I have not, but I can get a copy though. There were six of these bills posted and this man was turned away where he was posting them around the works

A PROCLAMATION.

To whom it may concern:

Whereas it has come to my knowledge that certain persons have congregated and assembled at and near the works of the Carnegie Steel Company, Lim., in Mifflin Township, Allegheny County, Pennsylvania, and upon the roads and highways leading to the same, and that such persons have interfered with workmen employed in said works obtaining access to the same, and that certain persons have made threats of injury to employees going to and from said works, and have threatened that if the owners of said works attempt to run the same the property will be injured and destroyed:

Now, I, William H. McCleary, high sheriff of said county, do hereby notify and warn all persons that all the acts enumerated are unlawful and that all persons en-gaged in the same in any way are liable to arrest and punishment.

And I further command all persons to abstain from assembling or congregating as aforesaid, and from interfering with the workmen, business, or the operation of said works, and in all respects to preserve the peace and to retire to their respective homes or places of residence, as the rights of the workmen to work and the right of the owners to operate their works will be fully protected, and in case of failure to observe these instructions all persons offending will be dealt with according to law.

WILLIAM H. McCLEARY,
High Sheriff of Allegheny County.

SHERIFF'S OFFICE, *Pittsburg, July 5, 1892.*

Q. Now, what effort did you make—just describe the extent of it—to obtain from citizens a force to go up there?—A. I sent out some 400 notices to citizens asking them to report to the sheriff's office on Thursday morning at 9 o'clock for duty at Homestead as a posse comitatus and to furnish their own arms and subsistence, as that is what the law requires. The law does not allow me to furnish arms and subsistence or anything of that kind.

Q. I am not familiar with your statute. Does the statute make it their duty to obey the sheriff; is there any penalty for disobedience?—A. It is a misdemeanor.

Q. To refuse the command of the sheriff?—A. Yes, sir.

Q. Did any report to you?—A. There were about 23 reported on Thursday and 29 on Friday morning.

Q. What did you do?—A. On Friday morning I told the gentlemen I would not take them up to Homestead on Friday, but to hold themselves in readiness and I would see if any more persons reported, and they should hold themselves in readiness to go at any time that I called upon them, and that I would give them notice.

Mr. BOATNER. You did not think it was safe to go there with 52 men?

The WITNESS. No, sir, I knew it was not.

By the CHAIRMAN:

Q. Did you make any further efforts to augment your force with others?—A. Not from that time, except to try and get the persons whom I had notified to come; every person just point blank refused to come.

Q. They refused?—A. Yes, sir.

Q. Were they notified by your deputies?—A. Yes, sir, with a written notice, too.

Q. What did you do then, Mr. Sheriff?—A. Then I called on the governor for assistance.

Q. What did you state to the governor?—I stated I was unable to obtain a sufficient force to quell the trouble at Homestead, and in my opinion the military would have to be called out for that purpose, as I could not get a sufficient force.

Q. What was the governor's reply to you?—A. I telegraphed to the governor on Wednesday, the day of this trouble there, and he answered me he did not think that civil authority had been exhausted. Then I went to work and issued these notices I told you for a posse comitatus

Mr. BRODERICK. Would it not be well to have copies of the correspondence between the sheriff and the governor?

The WITNESS. I can give you a copy of the correspondence between the governor and myself from the commencement to the finish.

No. 1.

JULY 6, 1892.

ROBERT E. PATTISON,
    Governor of Pennsylvania, Harrisburg, Pa.:

Situation at Homestead is very grave. My deputies were driven from the ground and watchmen sent by mill owners attacked. Shots were exchanged and some men killed and wounded. Unless prompt measures are taken to prevent it further bloodshed and great destruction of property may be expected.

The striking workmen and their friends on the ground number at least 5,000, and the civil authorities are utterly unable to cope with them. Wish you would send representative at once.

WM. H. McCLEARY,
    Sheriff.

No. 2.

JULY 6, 1892.

ROBERT E. PATTISON,
    Governor of Pennsylvania, Harrisburg, Pa.:

The works at Homestead are in possession of an armed mob; they number thousands. The mill owners this morning attempted to land a number of watchmen, when an attack was made on boats and 6 men on boats were badly wounded, a number of men on shore were killed and wounded; how many can not say. The boat later came down and was fired on from the shore and pilot compelled to abandon pilot house. I have no means at my command to meet emergency; a large armed force will be required; any delay may lead to further bloodshed and great destruction of property. You are, therefore, urged to act at once.

WM. H. McCLEARY,
    Sheriff.

No. 3.

JULY 6, 1892.

ROBERT E. PATTISON,
   Governor of Pennsylvania, Harrisburg, Pa.:

After personal visit to the Homestead works yesterday morning and careful inquiry as to surroundings, I endeavored to gather a force to guard works, but was unable to obtain any. I then sent twelve deputies (almost my entire regular force) to Homestead, but they were driven from the grounds. The mill owners early this morning sent an armed guard of 300 men by river. Boats containing this guard were fired on while on their way up the river, and when they attempted to land at company's ground were met by an armed mob, which had broken down company's fences and taken possession of the landing. An encounter ensued, in which a number were wounded on both sides; several are reported dead. The coroner has just informed me that one of the guards has just died. The guards have not been able to land, and the works are in possession of the mob, who are armed with rifles and pistols and are reported to have one cannon. The guards remain on the barges near landing, having been abandoned by the steamer which towed them there. The civil authorities here are powerless to meet the situation. An armed and disciplined force is needed at once to prevent further loss of life. I therefore urge immediate action on your part.

WM. H. MCCLEARY, *Sheriff*

No. 4.

JULY 7, 1892.

ROBERT E. PATTISON,
   Governor of Pennsylvania, Harrisburg, Pa.:

Last night I went to Homestead accompanied by officials of Amalgamated Association and succeeded in bringing away guards sent by river who had surrendered to the rioters. The arms of the guards, who numbered about 300, are all in possession of the rioters. To-day everything is quiet; the works are in possession of a large force of strikers. Any attempt on the part of the civil authorities to disperse them will be met with resistance. Last evening I issued a general summons to citizens to attend this morning at 9 o'clock to aid in restoring order, and I also issued a large number of notices to individuals. The result is that up to noon to-day 32 persons have reported, all without arms. They have been notified to appear to-morrow morning at 9 o'clock, and I have issued several hundred additional notices to individuals summoning them to appear at the same time. These notices will be served to-day. I am satisfied from present indications that I will be unable to obtain any considerable force, and the force thus gathered, without discipline and arms, will be of no use whatever. As soon as any effort is made to take possession of the property another outbreak will occur.

WM. H. MCCLEARY, *Sheriff.*

No. 5.

JULY 10, 1892.

ROBERT E. PATTISON,
   Governor of Pennsylvania, Harrisburg, Pa.:

The situation at Homestead has not improved, while all is quiet there. The strikers are in control, and openly express to me and to the public their determination that the works shall not be operated unless by themselves. After making all efforts in my power I have failed to secure a posse respectable enough in numbers to accomplish anything, and I am satisfied that no posse raised by civil authority can do anything to change the condition of affairs, and that any attempt by an inadequate force to restore the right of law will only result in further armed resistance and consequent loss of life. Only a large military force will enable me to control matters. I believe if such force is sent the disorderly element will be overawed and order will be restored. I therefore call upon you to furnish me such assistance.

WM. H. MCCLEARY,
Sheriff.

No. 6.

JULY 10, 1892.

ROBERT E. PATTISON,
  Governor of Pennsylvania, Harrisburg, Pa.:
  Your telegram notifying me that the division of the National Guard under command of Maj. Gen. George R. Snowden had been ordered to my support has been received. Pursuant to your direction I have telegraphed Maj. Gen. Snowden at Harrisburg and Philadelphia requesting that he should advise me of movement of his division of the National Guard and probable time of arrival of troops here and such other information as he might deem advisable.

WM. H. McCLEARY,
Sheriff.

No. 1.

HARRISBURG, *July 6, 1892.*

W. H. McCLEARY, *Sheriff, Pittsburg:*
  Local authorities must exhaust every means at their command for the preservation of peace.

ROBERT E. PATTISON.

No. 2.

HARRISBURG, *July 6, 1892.*

W. H. McCLEARY, *Sheriff, Pittsburg:*
  How many deputies have you sworn in and what measures have you taken to enforce order and protect property?

ROBERT E. PATTISON.

No. 3.

HARRISBURG, *July 6, 1892.*

W. H. McCLEARY, *Sheriff, Pittsburg:*
  How many deputies have you sworn in and what measures have you taken to enforce order and protect property? The county authorities must exhaust every means to preserve peace.

ROBERT E. PATTISON.

No. 3.

HARRISBURG, *July 6, 1892.*

W. H. McCLEARY, *Sheriff, Pittsburg:*
  Your telegram indicates that you have not made any attempt to execute the law to enforce order, and I must insist upon you calling upon all citizens for an adequate number of deputies.

ROBERT E. PATTISON.

No. 4.

HARRISBURG, *July 10, 1892.*

WILLIAM H. McCLEARY,
  Sheriff of Allegheny County, Pa., Pittsburg, Pa.:
  Have ordered Maj. Gen. George R. Snowden with the division of the National Guards of Pennsylvania to your support at once. Put yourself in communication with him. Communicate further particulars.

ROBT. E. PATTISON,
Governor.

No. 5.

HARRISBURG, *July 11, 1892.*

WILLIAM H. McCLEARY,
  Sheriff of Allegheny County, Pittsburg:
  In reply to your dispatch I have issued orders for the movement of the troops and will communicate with you to-morrow.

GEORGE R. SNOWDEN,
Major General, Commanding.

No. 6.

HARRISBURG, PA., *July 11, 1892.*

W. H. McCLEARY, Esq..
High Sheriff of Allegheny County, Pittsburgh:

I expect to reach Blairsville Junction sometime this afternoon, and desire to meet you there. I will inform you of the hour in ample time.

GEORGE R. SNOWDEN,
Major-General, Commanding.

———

No. 7.

DUNCANNON, PA.

W. H. McCLEARY,
High Sheriff Allegheny County, Pittsburgh:

I expect to be at Blairsville intersection at 10 o'clock p. m. I would like to see you there and then.

GEORGE R. SNOWDEN,
Major-General, Commanding.

———

RYDE, *July 11, 1892.*

WM. H. McCLEARY,
Sheriff Allegheny County:

I will arrive at Radebaugh at 9:45 this p. m. Please meet me there at that time instead of, as wired heretofore, at Blairsville intersection.

GEORGE R. SNOWDEN,
Major-General, Commanding.

———

RYDE, *July 11, 1892.*

WM. H. McCLEARY,
High Sheriff Allegheny County, Pittsburg:

I will arrive at Radebaugh at 9:45 this p. m. Please meet me there at that time instead of, as wired heretofore at Blairsville intersection.

GEO. R. SNOWDEN,
Major-General, Commander.

. By the CHAIRMAN:

Q. Then what did you do, Mr. Sheriff?—A. I do not understand your question.

Q. What did you do next—what was the next step you took? The governor declined, you say, until you had exhausted all sources of civil authority.—A. When I could get no more persons on Friday to go we just let the thing remain quiet, and on Sunday I telegraphed the governor again my inability to get a proper posse sufficient in number to be of any benefit in protecting the works at Homestead.

Q. What was the response to that?—A. I received a telegram from him at 10 o'clock, stating he had called out the militia and for me to enter into correspondence with Maj. Gen. Snowden.

Q. The militia came?—A. Yes, sir. I might state there was a list of business people handed me by some gentleman living in Homestead, of parties living there who would serve as a *posse comitatus*, and there were sixteen names on that list, and I sent to Homestead and sent for those gentlemen and six of them came. They all refused to serve. The balance never reported at all.

Q. Six of the sixteen came?—A. Six reported, but they refused to serve.

Q. Was there any offer by them to furnish a guard for the works? —A. From the workmen? Yes, sir.

Q. What was the proposition?—A. They said they would furnish 500 to guard the works, 100 or 500.

Q. Did you decline?—A. Yes, sir, I did.

Q. Why did you decline the services of those men?—A. Well, I did not think I was putting those people in a proper position, they being locked out, with the owners of the mill, to put them there to guard the property.

Mr. BOATNER. Did not you think it would be a safe guard, that they would keep everybody out of the property?

The WITNESS. Yes, sir, I was satisfied they would keep everybody out and I was satisfied they would protect the property, and I was also satisfied they would not permit anybody to come in except they saw proper.

By the CHAIRMAN:

Q. But they would keep out the owners; that was the reason you rejected them?—A. Yes, sir, because I did not think it was a proper thing to do in the line of my duty.

Q. You conceived it to be your duty to put the owners in possession of their own property?—A. Yes, sir; and to put people in who I knew would assist me if I needed them; that is, to put men in who would assist me if I could get them in.

Q. Is Mr. Gray a deputy of yours?—A. I appointed him as deputy during this time.

Q. What do you know with reference to the actual employment of Pinkerton men to be sent there?—A. As I told you, Mr. Knox came to me and told me they were going to send 300 Pinkerton men as watchmen. I told you about that; and I will now tell you about the time I came down from the Homestead works. Mr. Knox and Mr. Reed, the attorneys of the company, they have done the business for us along with my own solicitor; they came over and said they were going to send these men that night. I told them, being at Homestead that day, that I advised them against sending them there, and I told them I did not think it was a proper thing to do or the proper time to send them that night. They then wanted me to send Colonel Gray with them. That I first objected to doing. Mr. Knox said, "You have some one of your own people there and they may assist in preserving the peace." I finally consented, and I instructed Colonel Gray to go up with that force and if there was liable to be a breach of the peace in the landing or any conflict between the people on the shore and the boat, and if the boat could not be landed at the Carnegie property, for him to use his discretion in taking them away, getting them to come away. Those were my instructions to Colonel Gray.

Mr. BOATNER. Use his discretion in telling whom to come away, the Pinkerton men or the rioters?

The WITNESS: I say if they could not land peacefully to advise the parties having the Pinkerton men in charge to take them away.

By the CHAIRMAN:

Q. He went along as a deputy sheriff in charge of the Pinkerton men for that purpose?—A. I did not so consider him in charge of them. I sent him there for the purpose of preserving the peace. That if there should be a collision on the arrival of the boat at Homestead—and in my own mind, I rather thought there might be, and that is the reason I advised against sending those men up that night.

Q. And you sent this deputy along to try to prevent any conflict between them?—A. Yes, sir, the locked-out men and the Pinkertons.

Q. Did you do anything further towards employing them as a *posse comitatus*?—A. No. sir.

Q. You sent your deputy, you say, with qualified instructions?—A. Yes, sir.

By Mr. BOATNER:

Q. Was the deputy sheriff authorized under any contingency to make deputy sheriffs of these Pinkerton men?—A. No, sir, not at all, sir. The only talk of making them deputy sheriffs was the time I first spoke of, when Mr. Knox came to me a week beforehand.

Q. You say you anticipated there would be trouble?—A. Yes, sir; I rather thought there would be trouble.

Q. A collision between the forces? As the first peace officer of the county, did not you consider it was your duty to be present on that occasion?—A. I was staying in town for the purpose of trying to gather up additional people myself, and I sent Mr. Gray, who was the former sheriff of this county, in charge of these men.

Q. Were you trying on that day to obtain additional men to go up, the day the difficulty occurred?—A. Not that day. That day we spent most of the time trying to get the Pinkerton men out of the position they were in. That afternoon I got these notices printed and served them that evening and night.

Q. That was after the difficulty had occurred?—A. Yes, sir.

Q. Did the Carnegie people ever call on you to furnish protection by a posse comitatus until after this difficulty occurred?—A. Yes, sir; they notified me that they feared the destruction of their property and they gave me a written notice to that effect on the 4th of July.

Q. Was that the first demand they made on you for the protection of their property?—A. Yes, sir; the first written demand.

Q. Had not they advised you before that time that they proposed to introduce 300 Pinkerton men for watchmen?—A. Yes, sir.

Q. But At that time they stated that to you verbally?—A. Yes, sir.

Q. Did they at that time ask you to summon a *posse comitatus* or to take any action in your official capacity for their protection?—A. Not at that time.

Q. Then they did not send to you for a *posse comitatus* until the day this difficulty occurred?—A. No, sir, on the 4th of July, when they gave me written notice. I considered from that time I was bound to get any person I could to act as a watchman of the property.

Q. You say the people here absolutely refused to serve? On what grounds?—A. The majority of them said they would not go up there and take the chances of being killed.

Q. The warlike feeling does not appear to be very strong in this county, does it? Now, Mr. Sheriff, did you give Mr. Gray instructions of any kind to take charge in the event there was any difficulty there?—A. No, sir; I did not.

Q. Then, what was Mr. Gray along for?—A. I sent him for the purpose of trying to preserve the peace.

Q. Do you mean by persuasion or how?—A. Yes, sir. By trying to get these people away from there, if there was going to be a conflict between them.

Q. You say now that Mr. Gray was not authorized to deputize these people?—A. No, sir.

Q. And neither was he authorized to take command in the event of trouble, and that he was sent along for the purpose of preserving the peace. Do you mean just by his own individual efforts?—A. As deputy sheriff.

Q. To command the peace in the event of a riot?—A. Yes, sir. Mr. Knox had a note of introduction for Col. Gray to the captain of this boat—Capt. Rogers, I think his name is—and when I objected to putting anybody on board that boat at all, we arrived at the conclusion I would send Col. Gray there for the purpose I have stated that of protecting the peace, and if there was liable to be such a collision as I have described before that boat could be landed on the property of Carnegie, Phipps & Co. that he would then have the power to instruct them to back out and leave.

Q. Was that letter written by your authority?—A. The first part of it was not, but the latter part was.

Q. Do you mean that you authorized a part of the letter and did not authorize the balance?—A. I mean this : Mr. Knox had that letter written when he came to my office—that is, the first part was—and the latter part was written afterwards.

Q. What part did you authorize?—A. The latter part.

Q. Did you make any actual attempt to put the company back in possession of its workmen?—A. I was unable to.

Q. You did not go there with those twelve deputies?—A. No, sir.

Q. Do you know whether they met with any physical resistance?—A. No, they did not so report to me. There were just 1,500 or 2,000 people who just crowded them away and who would not permit them to enter the works.

Q. They just shoved them out of town?—A. Yes, sir.

Q. Is it your opinion if you had gone there with the majesty and power of the law behind you with any number of men and informed these men that you came there to take possession of those works in the name of the law, do you think you would have met with any physical armed resistance; in other words, that you or the posse would have been killed?—A. I think I would have met with such a resistance I would not have been able to do anything.

Q. If you go to arrest a man and he says, "Oh, no, I do not care about being arrested," do you go back and leave him alone? Do you as sheriff have criminal jurisdiction?—A. No, sir.

Q. The sheriff does not serve warrants for the arrest of people?—A. Not without an injunction from the court. I do not serve warrants.

Q. You then give it as your opinion, if you had gone there and undertaken to forcibly execute the law, that you and your posse would have been killed if you had persisted in it; is that your opinion?—A. I do not say that we would have been killed, but we would have been driven away; I am satisfied of that.

Q. How could a man be driven away if he would not go?—A. I thought if I could not get a sufficient force there was no use in going.

By Mr. BRODERICK:

Q. Were you in the mill that day?—A. Yes, sir; the day I went up, and had a conversation with the gentlemen. I went through the works that day.

Q. Did you notify them you were there to take possession?—A. Yes, sir.

Q. What did they say in answer to that?—A. I told them I was going to send men that afternoon to take possession and put in watchmen as deputy sheriffs to guard the works.

Q. What was their reply?—A. They wanted to know how many and I told them probably fifty if I could get them. After coming back from the works I went up to their headquarters again and I and the gentlemen there had a consultation and they said if I decided to send men up there that they had made up their minds to dissolve the advisory committee.

Q. Then how many did you say you sent?—A. Twelve.

Q. Did they give the men to understand what they were there for?—A. I suppose so; yes, sir, they were instructed to. The gentleman who had them in charge is Mr. Cluley, who is here.

Q. You were not sheriff three years ago, when that strike occurred?—A. No, sir.

Q. Do you know how many men were sent there then?—A. Nothing but by report, sir.

Q. Well, about how many?—A. I understood there were about 100 or 150.

Q. Were they deputies selected in this county?—A. That I can not tell you, as I was not connected with the sheriff's office at all.

Q. When you were there with your deputies and demanded possession, did the men offer to furnish guards to guard the property?—A. Yes, sir; I answered that to the chairman of the committee.

Q. That has been answered fully before?—A. Yes, sir; I answered that.

Q. Did they say what number they would furnish?—A. They said they would furnish 100, and I think some gentleman spoke after we came back and said they would furnish 100 or 500.

By the CHAIRMAN:

Q. Did Messrs. Knox & Reed write in your office or in your presence to Mr. Potter with reference to sending Mr. Gray as a deputy sheriff, or did they show you that note, and was that sent with your sanction [handing note]?—A. Yes, sir; that was sent with my sanction.

Q. Who was Mr. Potter?—A. I believe he was the superintendent of the works; but I do not know, as I never saw him.

Q. This paper reads:

JULY 5, 1892.

JOHN A. POTTER, Esq.:
  DEAR SIR: This will introduce Col. Joseph H. Gray, deputy sheriff.
    Yours, truly,
                                                KNOX & REED.

You will understand that Col. Gray, as the representative of the sheriff, is to have control of all action in case of trouble.
                                                KNOX & REED.

This is a correct copy of the original letter.
                                                GEO. B. MOTHERAL.

Mr. BOATNER. You meant by that he should have the right to withdraw the men in case of trouble?

The WITNESS. Yes, sir. I think Mr. Knox and Mr. Petty, my own solicitor will say the same thing.

By Mr. TAYLOR:

Q. You say the addition to that letter was put on by your direction and sanction?—A. Yes, sir.

Q. It was added for the purpose of giving Mr. Gray command of the expedition.—A. It was given for the purpose of giving Col. Gray authority in case of trouble to take these men away.

Q. Giving him control of them?—A. Yes, sir.

Mr. BOATNER. In other words to retreat.

. The WITNESS. Yes, sir; I did not agree with their taking Pinkerton men there myself, at all.

By Mr. BYNUM:

Q. You did not accompany the party, I understand?—A. No, sir.

Q. When did you first hear during that day there was any difficulty up there?—A. On Wednesday.

Q. The day of the trouble?—A. The trouble occurred Wednesday morning. I heard it about half past 8 or 9 o'clock.

Q. Did you go up there during that day?—A. I went up there that night.

Q. But it was some six or seven hours after you heard there was serious trouble and loss of life before you went up?—A. Yes, sir.

Q. You made no effort to suppress it or quell it?—A. I made an effort to get a posse and was unable to do so.

Q. During that day?—A. No, sir.

Q. You would not go without a posse?—A. No, sir.

Q. What time did you go up there?—A. Twelve o'clock at night, I think it was when I got there.

Q. Where were the Pinkerton men at that time?—A. They were in the rink.

Q. Who had charge of them?—A. The people at Homestead.

Q. Did you bring them away?—A. Yes, sir.

Q. Did you have any trouble in bringing them away?—A. None at all.

Q. How many deputies did you have at that time?—A. I did not have any deputies. Mr. Weihe and several members of the Amalgamated Association and Mr. Brennen were there and——

Q. Where did you bring them to?—A. I brought them to the Union Depot.

Q. Who came for you to get you to go up there—who sent you word?— A. Well, on Wednesday about half past 12 o'clock—Mr. Weihe had been up to see me in the forenoon and he had just left my office a short time—I sent for him to get him to go up and use his influence to stop the trouble, and he went up and came back at 6 o'clock, and just shortly after he came in my office I received a telegram from Homestead that these people had surrendered and were under arrest.

Q. And you thought it was safe to go up?—A. And then they telephoned for me to get a special train and come up and take them away; that if I did not there was liable to be more lives lost that night.

By Mr. BOATNER:

Q. Why didn't you go up that day as soon as you heard of this trouble?—A. I could not get assistance to go there that would be sufficient to stop anything.

Q. Did not you think your presence as sheriff of the county, as the officer who has jurisdiction to quell disturbances might have some influence in quelling that disturbance?—A. Not at all, without I had assistance of the proper number of people, too.

Q. Did you apprehend personal violence to yourself?—A. No, sir; I did not, as I am acquainted with a great many of those people, and they do not bother me.

The CHAIRMAN. Will you furnish us with copies of your telegrams to the governor and his replies? (See same inserted.)

The WITNESS. Yes, sir. I do not know whether this has been in testimony or not, but here is the letter of Carnegie, Phipps & Co., served on me at the time they served me with a notice. (See same in evidence of Mr. Frick.)

By Mr. BOATNER:

Q. You were served with a copy of that?—A. At the time they served me with the notice.

Q. That was on the 3d of July.—A. The 4th of July.

H. Mis. 335——5

Q. Did you send down your proclamation by a deputy?—A. I sent it with a deputy and bill poster to post it.

Mr. TAYLOR. Col. Gray is still a deputy of yours?

The WITNESS. Yes, sir; and I telegraphed for him and he will be here.

TESTIMONY OF SAMUEL B. CLULEY.

SAMUEL B. CLULEY sworn and examined.

The WITNESS. I will state that on the 4th of July Sheriff McCleary sent for me to come over to see him, that he wanted to see me. This was after dinner. I went over and he told me he had received notice from the owners of the mill at Homestead to take charge of that mill in his official capacity of sheriff; that they were afraid of its being destroyed by the men on the lockout, and he asked me if I would go as one of the special deputies, and I told him I would; and he asked me to meet him at the train the next day and go to Homestead with him. I went with him.

Q. You went with him? A. I went with the sheriff. We went there and met the advisory committee and they talked over the matter and they talked about putting in special deputies, or at least people to guard the works. The sheriff said he had no doubt at all but what they would guard the works, but it was his place to put in special deputies to take charge of it and that he would have to do. Then we were asked if we would visit the mill and see if it was all right and properly cared for. We visited the mill and found everything in excellent order. There were some men outside and some watchmen inside. The watchmen, as I understood, belonged to the company. We then came back to the advisory committee and talked the matter over again. Some gentlemen there volunteered to act as special watchmen and they then offered to give bail that they would do their duty correctly, but the sheriff insisted that he could not do that; that he would be compelled to put men of his own choosing in there. The advisory committee then asked us to retire from the room, which we did, and when we came back they said they would disband and he could put in his deputies; and they asked him how many he would put in, and he said he thought he would put in 50. That being over we crossed the river to the Baltimore and Ohio road and returned to town and came to the sheriff's office, and he asked me then if I would take the deputies up to the mill and place them in the mill, and I said that I would if I could. "Well," he says, "you will have no trouble, I think, from what the advisory committee says." I said, "That is all right; I will go." I think the force all came out of the office with the exception of 2, and that made 12 with myself.

Q. Eleven beside yourself?—A. Yes, sir.

Q. With that force did you go up there?—A. I went up.

Q. At what time?—A. We took the half-past 4 train and got there a little after 5.

Q. It was past 5?—A. Yes, sir, when we landed at the station, right at the works, and I stepped off the train, and the deputies with me; and when we came down from the platform some of the men came up to us, and one in particular, acting as spokesman, said "What do you fellows want here?" I said, "I am a special officer representing the sheriff of Allegheny County to put deputies in this mill to act as a guard and to protect the property for the company." He said, "No deputy will ever go in there alive." By this time—in the first place the crowd had augmented to probably 500 or 1,000 men, and they kept crowding around me, and they said, "Men, we tell you you can not get into that mill." We were going down to the gate toward Homestead, and I saw it was a matter of impossibility for me to get to that gate, because we were crowded so we could not do anything.

Q. You had your eleven men with you?—A. Yes, sir; and I said to them, "Boys, you keep close to me." I said in going up on the train that if any of them said anything not to answer and I would act as spokesman. They crowded around me and kept crowding the men so that we could not get to the mill and they said, "Men, you can not get to that mill." I said, "We are going in there with the consent of the advisory committee." One man said, "The advisory committee has nothing to do with that. If you get in there they have got to call a meeting of all the locked-out men of Homestead before you can get any body in there." I saw it was utter nonsense for me to attempt to put that body of men in the mill, so I said to them, "Come with me and possibly we will get to some of the advisory committee." I went a short distance and we met Mr. O'Donnell, the chairman of the advisory committee. I said to him "I am here in a tight fix." He said "Yes, what are you going to do?" I said "It is a matter of impossibility for me to put these deputies in here. I can not do it and we will go down to the hall." Mr. O'Donnell waved back the men to keep them away from us and we went to the hall and talked the matter over there and he asked me what I expected to do and I said I would return to the city and report to the sheriff. We went to the little boat, the *Edna*, and came over to Greenwood and we took the street cars there and came home.

Q. Did you ask Mr. O'Donnell to aid you?—A. I said to Mr. O'Donnell—when we met there I turned to these men and said: "Mr. O'Donnell, did not the sheriff get the consent of the advisory committee to put these men in the mill?" He said: "You have, but you see it is impossible to do it." I returned to the city and so reported to the sheriff.

Q. Did you see anything of the trouble there on the 6th?—A. No, sir. I went up on Friday with the sheriff to take the posse that had been tendered him, as I understood him, by the citizens of Homestead, and I went to take that posse into the mill, but it was impossible to get one of them. They answered that they would not go.

Q. How many came?—A. I think there were six, and the others refused to come. One of them said he would not (there was a big table standing there); that if I would stack as much money on that table as would reach to the ceiling he would not go. The other fellow said he would rather go to jail, because he would know where he was then and he would be safe.

By Mr. BOATNER:

Q. Were these men armed when they crowded around you and insisted that you could not get in the works?—A. The men, not all of them, had clubs; a good many of them had; the leaders had. I saw one gentleman patting a shotgun very affectionately.

Q. Was your force armed?—A. No, sir.

Q. None of the deputies were armed?—A. I do not think they were. I did not arm any, as I thought it had been amicably arranged and there would be no trouble.

Q. Did they impress you as being entirely in earnest?—A. They told me that no deputy should be put in there alive. They said that they were put in there to protest nonunion men and that none of them should go in.

By Mr. BYNUM:

Q. You stated in a conversation there with the men they refused to go into the mill; did not some of them make a proposition that they would go in if Mr. Frick would go?—A. At Homestead that day?

Q. Yes.—A. No, no, there was nothing of that kind; they did not want to go. There was one gentleman, the doctor up there, Dr. Gladden, who was one of the parties given to the sheriff as a man who would act as a deputy, and he said this. He said he knew nearly every man connected with the lockout, and he said, "I would not go there, because I know they would take my life as quickly as anybody else; I would be afraid of my life to go near that mill."

TESTIMONY OF WM. B. RODGERS—Recalled.

WM. B. RODGERS recalled and examined.

By the CHAIRMAN:

Q. What became of the barges you towed up there and landed?—A. They were burned up.

Q. Did you see any effort made by anyone to burn the barges or boats?—A. They were making an effort to burn them by the use of oil when we came past them.

Q. When was that?—A. About 11 o'clock.

Q. You left them?—A. We left them and went up the river a short distance to put the wounded men on the train, and when we came back and passed the barges they were endeavoring to burn them up by pouring oil and running it down the bank in a drain towards them and setting the oil on fire.

Q. Running it down to the river?—A. Above the head of the boats, as it were.

Q. Did they succeed in burning anything?—A. It seems as though the wind was blowing the flames from the barges, and as far as I could see they had not succeeded in setting the barges on fire.

Q. What became of Mr. Gray?—A. He remained with me on the boat and came to Pittsburg.

Q. Did you see him attempt to take any official control or any official action as deputy sheriff?—A. Yes, sir; I understood thoroughly he was the officer in charge and we all looked to him for advice, and there was a conversation between him and Mr. Potter directly as to what we should do, more particularly when going towards the landing.

Q. Did he give an order or exercise any authority; if so, state what?—A. Mr. Potter asked, "In the event of danger, what will we do?" He said: "Protect yourselves; keep them off."

Q. Mr. Potter asked that?—A. He asked that question.

Q. Was he the superintendent of the works?—A. Yes, sir.

Q. He was on the boat with you?—A. Yes, sir.

Q. Why did Mr. Gray leave with you; those men were still there?—A. He never went off the steamboat, to my knowledge, from the time we went there until we came back to the wharf. We asked him if what had been done was justifiable, and he said certainly; that what had been done was justifiable on the part of the Pinkerton men; that they had been attacked and that they had only defended themselves.

Q. He was not on the barges?—A. The boat was between the barges, one boat on each side.

Q. And he was on the boat?—A. Yes, sir.

Q. And when you left the barges and steamed off he remained on the boat?—A. Yes, sir; and when we came down the firing was so heavy it seemed impossible to land, but still we were rather trying to devise ways and means to get in, and he came to me at that time and ordered me to take the boat to Pittsburg and he said he would report to the sheriff and get a sufficient force to put down the mob.

Q. You were trying to take the barges away?—A. No, sir; we went away from the barges to take the wounded men over and we intended to return to them and lie with them, or come to Pittsburg, as the case might be, if there was no further riot, and take up the balance of the stores which had been left behind.

By Mr. BOATNER:

Q. How is it that Col. Gray did not stay there in charge of the force instead of coming away with you on the boat?—A. Indeed I can not answer that.

Q. The captain was shot down and that left these people practically without anybody in command.—A. I would say there were two or three other captains, you know—well, two captains there, I suppose.

Q. What is the name of the captain who was shot down?—A. Hinde, I think.

Q. He was the leader?—A. Yes, sir.

Q. Was the firing going on at the time you and Col. Gray went away?—A. Oh, no, an occasional shot, nothing of any consequence since the early engagement. We went away probably two hours after the morning engagement.

Q. How was it when you came back?—A. Whether they fired still while we were away I am unable to state, but there was probably a lull of two hours after the first firing until we went away.

Q. Were you under the impression when you went away that the fight was over?—A. Of course I could not tell anything about that, but there was a lull there. I did not know whether there would be a repetition or whether there would not. Crowds were gathering from both sides of the river from this neighborhood, and as we were coming down the river we met them coming in all directions armed, and they kept up a firing on us until we were a mile and a half below.

The CHAIRMAN. Do you know how many Pinkerton men were killed or have died since from their wounds?

The WITNESS. In the first engagement six were wounded, one of whom died, and I have no further knowledge. I was told (of course the captain was wounded) by a captain that the balance were wounded in the surrender; but that is principally report.

By Mr. BOATNER:

Q. Is that Captain Hinde?—A. Yes, sir.

Q. He is in the hospital?—A. Yes, sir.

Q. He was not present when they surrendered?—A. No, sir; but the captain left in charge made the report to me.

Q. Where is that captain?—A. I do not know; I suppose he has gone back home.

Q. What is his name?—A. I do not know; I am not acquainted with him.

By the CHAIRMAN:

Q. Are any of them here?—A. Four to my knowledge.

Q. None except the wounded men?—A. No, I think not.

By Mr. BOATNER:

Q. Are they men wounded in the engagement or wounded after the surrender?—A. Wounded in the engagement.

By Mr. BYNUM:

Q. When you employed your boat crew to go there did you tell them where you were going?—A. I told them that as a rule I was not at liberty to do so; but before we started from Davis Island dam I said that any who had any objection to going could get off at Lock No. 1, and all who objected to going got off.

Q. Where were the Pinkertons when you and Col. Gray left the barges?—A. In the barges.

Q. There was a large crowd congregated on the shore and there had been skirmishing and the men had been preparing better fortifications on the shore at the time?—A. That appeared to be the case; yes, sir.

Q. And you can not say there was any appearance of a cessation of hostilities when you went away?—A. With the exception there was no firing.

Q. But the excitement was great?—A. I suppose there was a great deal; there was certainly a great deal of noise, I know.

Q. A larger crowd coming and all coming armed?—A. Yes, sir.

By Mr. BRODERICK:

Q. You spoke of some men going off?—A. Some of the crew.

Q. About how many?—A. There were some four, I think, got off the two boats; four or five probably.

Q. Do you know whether the Pinkerton men all understood where they were going or do you know anything about that?—A. I did not have any reason to doubt it. They talked freely of Homestead and asked where it was.

Q. Did any of them want to get off?—A. No, sir; they asked where the place was and how long it would be before we got there, and such questions as would naturally arise with strangers coming into a place.

Q. Did they know what they were going for?—A. To act as watchmen.

Q. Did they know before the firing commenced the arms were there?—A. I presume they did, as they were unpacking them and getting them out. They were unpacking some arms all the way from the the Lock up; uniforms or blouses they had, but I did not pay much attention to it.

Q. They were uniformed on the way up?—A. These men seemed to have uniforms; they all had whatever belonged to them. Each man knew his own suit, or at least I presume so, or at least every man seemed to have some equipments which he was looking for.

The CHAIRMAN. Did they put them on before they landed?—A. Some of them did, but a great many of them were asleep until the firing began and they seemed—I will state the boats were furnished very conveniently, and they laid down on the beds and quite a number were asleep there until the firing began during the first engagement, when they had on citizen clothes.

Mr. BOATNER. I understand these barges had been fixed up by a carpenter for the men to eat and sleep in while they should be engaged at Homestead.

The WITNESS. Yes, sir; one barge was arranged for eating and one for sleeping. One accommodated 400 for sleeping, and of course you can accommodate more men for eating than sleeping.

TESTIMONY OF WM. WEIHE.

WILLIAM WEIHE sworn and examined.

By the CHAIRMAN:

Q. Where do you reside?—A. Pittsburg.

Q. What official position do you hold or have you held in connection with the skilled workmen at Homestead?—A. I am president of the Amalgamated Association of Iron and Steel Workers.

Q. How long have you been connected with them or held that position?—A. As president 9 years, or nearly 9 years; not quite that. My term will expire on the 1st of next November.

Q. You are familiar with the work that has been carried on in the Homestead Iron and Steel Works there?—A. To a certain extent, in the way of regulating wages.

Q. You are familiar, are you not, with this sliding scale of wages that has been spoken of by Mr. Frick?—A. Yes, sir.

Q. Will you explain that to the committee?—A. That is from the time it was adopted in 1889?

Q. Yes.—A. Well, in 1889 there was a scale adopted, known as the sliding scale, but previous to that time the men had been working on a scale that was signed yearly; that ran from July to July.

Q. But in 1889 there was an agreement made for three years, was it?—A. A sliding scale; yes, sir.

Q. Now, explain that.—A. Well, at that time the basis of the scale had been permanent; there was no slide. In 1889 the scale was based on four-by-four steel billets, which was the most stable article in a steel mill. The company at that time had likewise made a proposition to the men which they did not feel like accepting, but it was based upon the sliding system. The men then agreed to take the sliding scale, but it was not satisfactory to the men in the rates they had proposed. The first thing taken into consideration was the minimum upon which the scale should be based. It was first suggested by the men to make it $27, the firm's proposition was $25, and finally the men arrived at the conclusion to take a minimum of $25 as a basis of rate; that is, the amount which the workman was to receive for his work was to be based upon a $25 minimum.

Q. This $25 is a minimum?—A. Yes, sir; of four-by-four steel billets.

Q. And if the price should fall below $25 they should still receive wages on the basis of $25?—A. Yes, sir; but at that time the quotations showed that four-by-four billets were quoted at $27.25.

Q. In 1889, at the time this agreement was made?—A. Yes, sir; and when we arrived at a basis the wages were based on $26.50, although the minimum was $25, and there were quite a number of men or situations reduced. It affected the entire mill at that time which was working on the tonnage system. There were a few departments there were great reductions in before reaching the minimum as agreed upon. The 23-inch mill, the 33-inch mill, likewise the 119-inch mill, the armor-plate mill, had been working, I believe, by the day up to that time. It was a new mill, but there was a tonnage rate at that time adopted. The blooming mill and converting mill had been working under the permanent scale. Likewise the 23-inch and the 33-inch mill. I mean by permanent, signed year by year. The method then of sliding as arranged by the committee which met in joint session with Carnegie, Phipps & Co. representatives was agreed upon in this way for the first six months. The rates as agreed upon on July the 15th should be permanent.

Q. For what year?—A. Eighteen hundred and eighty-nine, and at that time, or at the expiration of that time, the average selling price of four-by-four billets should be the basis upon which the wages should be based for the next three months.

Q. Well, that continued during the contract?—A. Yes, sir.

Q. Now, what was the proposition made by the company, and which I understand was rejected by the workmen, for the new contract running three years again for the present year?—A. You mean for the present year?

Q. Oh, yes. You have spoken of a contract begun in 1889 which ran about three years?—A. Yes, sir.

Q. That is an executed contract, and we only speak of it by way of explanation. Now, there was an effort made to make a new contract?— A. Yes, sir.

Q. And the company made you another proposition. State what it was and how it was received and all about it.—A. The proposition I think was made to the men some time in March.

Q. Of this year?—A. Yes, sir; I was not present at any of their conferences at that time. Just exactly what the propositions were I could not say, but they were reductions offered to the men.

Q. I do not want you to state anything which did not come within your knowledge. Go to the point where this proposition did come to your knowledge as president of the Amalgamated Association of Iron and Steel Workers.—A. At the time the convention was in session in June that was the time we received the scales with the firm proposition as well as the men's. Before getting at that we have had a rule or law of the organization that all changes desired in the scales that have been signed shall be taken up in the month of February or March by the men. They discuss them and see what changes they desire. After they have gone through the scales they have been working on and considered the changes desired, they then send them to the general office. They are printed in a pamphlet and each sublodge in the organization gets a copy of all of those pamphlets. When the delegates come there that programme then is gone through. There are two committees, an iron-wage committee and a steel-wage committee. All suggestions pertaining to the steel department are referred to the steel committee and all suggestions pertaining to the iron department are submitted to the iron-wage committee. Both of these committees meet some three or four days previous to the meeting of the general convention. A programme is formed by those committees and it is reported back to the convention.

After these scales have been formed by the committee and reported they are then brought up seriatim; that is, each scale is brought up separately; each steel mill in the association has their own scale. It is not like an iron scale. The iron scales are general and the steel scales are what we call local. The reason of that is each steel mill is different in its system of work on account of improved machinery and other methods, and for that reason there must be separate scales for those mills. Among them were the Homestead, or the Carnegie-Phipps scales for its department. In fact, there were only four departments at that time, if these scales were to be changed, that would be affected. There were other departments which were to continue on at work not affected at the time on account of the proposition made; they were to continue on. When these scales came up in the convention the Homestead scale was referred locally to the men at Homestead—the proposition of the firm I have not got with me.

Q. Do you recollect and know what they were?—A. There was quite a number of figures on them, and I could not recollect all of them,

Q. Can you tell us just what the facts were?—A. Well, reductions were made in almost every department.

Q. That is, proposed reductions?—A. Yes, sir; proposed reductions, but in some departments it operated more than others.

Q. That is, the four departments affected?—A. Yes, sir.

Q. How many men work in those departments who would be affected by that proposition?—A. That I could not exactly state, as I do not know the number of men affected.

Q. Go on and state your understanding of what the proposition amounted to?—A. The question came up for a conference, and the men requested a conference with the committee to discuss the matter of scales. I believe they informed the firm to that effect, and the next day afterwards there was a conference held, on the 23d day of June. These scales are all based on 2,240 pounds per ton in all departments. That is one of the old customs that has been in vogue in iron and steel mills, I suppose, ever since they have been working on tonnage rates. The reason the men objected to accepting the proposition of the firm was, they did not believe it was necessary to effect any reduction as proposed, and also that it was necessary to have the scales expire on the 31st of December instead of on the 30th of June.

Q. What was the minimum basis proposed by the company?—A. Their proposition was $22.

Q. Instead of $25 as formerly?—A. Yes, sir.

Q. Did their proposition embrace a sliding scale above that according to the market as before?—A. I presume it did. It was to be worked upon the same principle as you saw on those sheets. I presume it was to slide in the same way from $22 upwards as the percentage should be agreed upon.

Q. Will you state what reduction that would effect if it had been accepted and gone into operation on the wages of these men in these departments?—A. Well, it varied in different departments. It ran, I believe, from 10 to 25 or 30 per cent.

Q. You heard Mr. Frick's testimony in which he estimated the average reduction at 15 per cent?—A. Yes, sir.

Q. What do you say to that?—A. The information I received from the men who had calculated it was that it would run 18 per cent.

Q. You did not calculate it yourself?—A. No, sir.

Q. You are a skilled workman and know all about these things, do you not?—A. I have worked in the mill up to the time I took hold of this position.

Q. But you never have made the exact figures on that basis to see what would be the probable reduction and to find the average?—A. No, sir.

Q. You can not say of your own knowledge?—A. That is, I could not state just exactly what the average reduction would be.

Q. Well, the men declined the proposition?—A. What I was going to state in regard to the date of the expiration of the scale is that that is a vital matter for all iron and steel workers in the country; that is, the date of the expiration of the scale.

Q. Why?—A. During the summer months, which are the most heated terms of the year, the men would prefer to be idle rather than work if there must be any repair work done or any idleness of any kind. It has been in vogue for a number of years to have these scales expire on the last day of June. The first attempt which was made in regulating these scales was way back in 1875 or 1876. Ever since that time they have expired in iron mills and in steel mills, excepting rail mills, on the 30 th of June of each year.

Q. Now, let me see if I understand you just there. The company insisted upon making the term of expiration the close of the year, as they say, because business in their line is duller then than at other times, and the workmen wanted to retain it at the close of June, in the summer months, because it is the most convenient time for them to take their vacation or to do less work than at any other time of the year?— A. Yes, sir; on account of the heated term.

Q. Now, was that the point of difference in respect to the term of expiration?—A. That was one point.

Q. What was the other?—A. The minimum.

Q. I say in respect to the term of expiration, that was the trouble, was it not?—A. Yes, sir.

Q. Now, the other point of disagreement was in lowering of the minimum?—A. Yes, sir.

Q. Did the proposition of the company affect the workmen at all in respect to that sliding scale except the reduction of the minimum from $25 to $22?—A. Oh, yes.

Q. State wherein?—A. There were certain jobs where the men were reduced before they reached the minimum.

Q. Can you name those jobs?—A. I could not as I have not got the scales present, but I think they will be presented here. They were reduced to a certain extent, and then they would take another reduction from $25 to $22 as a minimum. In other words, there were some jobs where the men, for instance—say there was a crew, perhaps, of 9 or 10 men at the shears, and in addition to the shearers' helpers, whatever they may have been there—there were men taken out of the scales that had been enumerated, and the remainder would be requested and asked to do that work without these other men who had been taken out of the scales.

Q. Was not this presented to the workmen by the company, and urged as a reason why they would not be injured, that additional improved machinery would be put in there by which the same number of men could produce a greater output, and in that way they could still make as high or higher wages even if the minimum was reduced?— A. That was an argument presented by the company, and the men did not agree to that.

Q. Do you know what kind of machinery they proposed to put in there?—A. No, sir. There are always improvements made right along. The organization never objects to improvements and makes allowances in every particular where there are improvements, and in steel mills there are special clauses, and whenever there is an improvement made by which certain men will be done away with, then their jobs will be done away with. There is no objection.

Q. Can you state to the committee the approximate or exact labor cost of the production of a ton of steel at these mills?—A. We have calculated and can give an estimate as near as we can get at it, but it is very hard to get at it exactly.

Q. Well, give it as you understand it.—A. You mean in all departments, the wages of these four which are affected?

Q. Well, the four affected, or any others you may illustrate.—A. The only way we can arrive at our estimate is the number of men that are employed and enumerated in the scale; the others that are not enumerated we can not reach, but estimate them.

Q. Give us the nearest and best statement you can of the exact figures?—A. Now, at Homestead in the converting and blooming mill, as near as we can estimate, it runs about $1.55 per ton, or $155 per 100 tons. That is as near as we can estimate and figure on the blooming and converting mills.

Q. One hundred and fifty-five dollars?—A. One dollar and fifty-five cents per ton is the labor cost of production, as near as we can figure it, and that is for four by-four billets.

By Mr. BYNUM:

Q. That is, you take the work from the billets to the plates?—A. That is from the time the metal is placed in the cupola until it is a finished billet of four by four.

Q. That is in making the ingot and finishing it up to the billet?—A. Yes, sir, that is for the labor cost on the scale; there is other labor not enumerated.

By the CHAIRMAN:

Q. You do not include that?—A. No, sir.

Q. Do you know what it is? A. Well, I could not state that. Of course there are men with different rates, and we could not get at that.

Q. Can you state it in another department?—A. We only calculate on the four-by-four billets, because that is where the entire scale is based upon. The other departments make the finished product except ing the slabbing mill or armor-plate mill.

Q. How about the armor-plate mill, can you state that?—A. No, sir; that is a scale that I think will come up here when these other gentlemen come here.

Q. Can you state about the product of steel rails?—A. There are no steel rails made at that mill.

Q. Who are the persons you referred to a moment ago?—A. Persons employed in those departments.

Q. Can you give any names of the people?—A. In the armor-plate mill?

Q. In any of these departments?—A. Mr. Roberts, Mr. Donegal—I do not remember all the names, but I should say, Mr. Colflesh and others.

Q. Were you at Homestead on the 5th or 6th?—A. I was at home on the 5th—no, on the 6th.

Q. You were not there?—A. I was there on the 6th.

Q. Were you there in the morning when this fight occurred at the landing with the Pinkerton force?—A. No, sir.

Q. You did not see that and do not know anything of your own knowledge about that?—A. No, sir.

Q. Is there anything else connected with this investigation you wish to state?—A. I wish to state and to impress the committee with this fact. I will state I was on the afternoon of the 6th at Homestead at the request of the sheriff. Now, in regard to the scales, the men, as I have already stated, have their wages based upon the tonnage rate of 2,240 pounds. They reason they did not feel like accepting the proposition made by the company on the $22 basis was that billets at that time were being quoted at $24. The arrangement previous to that was that the average quotation of thirteen weeks in the quarter was taken and 50 cents taken off as a basis upon which wages were to be regulated for the next three months. I will say the men did not desire, if it was possible to avoid it, to have any trouble at Homestead. I am speaking of the conversation which took place that day.

Q. What time do you mean?—A. The 23d day of June. The men thought it best to offer a compromise, and they then changed their opinion from $25 and made it $24, which was to be the minimum.

When they came to discuss it, Mr. Frick suggested in regard to the expiration of the scales, and the men offered the other scale. They made the proposition, which is as follows:

The scale to be in force from July 1, 1892, and to remain so until June 30, 1895. Either party desiring to change the scale shall give three months' notice previous to July 1, 1895, otherwise the scale shall continue in force from said date for one more year.

The reason of that was in case either party desired any change, and notice was not given three months previous to July 1, 1895, there would be no rearrangement of the scale for that year, and that would continue through just the same as it had previously for one year longer. The reason, I say, the men preferred to have the scale expire on the 30th of June was that if one firm would get that privilege in a mill of that kind all the other firms would want the same terms, and that is a vital point for all iron and steel workers; but rather than have a difficulty they made this proposition so there would be no changes made.

Q. What became of that proposition?—A. After it was read to Mr. Frick, he stated that they had gone over their scales carefully and they could not accept it.

Q. Then what followed?—A. When we were going out Mr. Potter was there, and I think he stopped one or two of the men, and I was with them, and we began negotiating with him, and he finally said he believed he could persuade the company to make the minimum $23. We retired, but came back in the afternoon, later, and the manager, Mr. Potter, and Mr. Childs were there. I do not remember just who were there in the room, but I remember Mr. Frick was not there, and he then said the company would make the minimum $23, but the other change, that is, the change in the date of the scale, they could not recede from and would not recede from.

Q. Then what did your people say to that?—A. That ended the conference.

Q. There was no agreement?—A. No, sir; there was no agreement.

Q. When did the work cease there?—A. I think on the night of June 29, or June 30 in the morning; I am not exactly certain about that.

Q. How did it end; who directed it?—A. The firm, at the conference which was held, or rather Mr. Frick, said the mill would run up to July 1, but it stopped one day previous to July 1, and the men looked upon it as a lockout.

Q. Did the men give notice to the company that if their terms were not agreed to they would not continue longer at work?—A. That was understood by the scale.

Q. It was understood under the agreement that if a new agreement was not signed they would cease to work for the company on that day?—A. Yes, sir.

Q. And the 30th was the last day?—A. Yes, sir.

Q. That being the expiration of the contract?—A. Yes, sir; and previous to that the company had made a proposition to the men stating that, if they did not agree to the proposition as submitted by the firm on or before June 24, then there would be no more conferences, and each man would have to come and make application for a job individually.

Q. They stated they would decline to negotiate with your association after the 24th?—A. Yes, sir.

Q. But that they would negotiate with the employés as individuals?—A. As individuals.

Q. Whether they belonged to the association or not; on their own responsibility?—A. Yes, sir.

Q. That is the substance of it?—A. Yes, sir.

Q. What is the extent of the Amalgamated Association of Iron and Steel Workers; what are their numbers and what is the extent of that organization?—A. It goes all over the United States.

Q. All iron and steel workers?—A. Yes, sir; they are not all organized, but they are generally governed by the wages adopted by this association.

Q. You do not mean to say all skilled laborers belong to that association, but part of them throughout the United States?—A. No, sir; I would say the great majority of them.

Q. Do you know the number belonging to the association in the United States?—A. The exact number I could not just state.

Q, Well, about?—A. Between 24,000 and 25,000 of the skilled workmen.

Q. About what per cent of the laborers in the works of this company at Homestead belong to that association?—A. The number I could not state. There are eight lodges. Each department has a lodge of its own, and the number of men belonging there I could not just state.

Q. You do not know the number of men; can you tell us about the number?—A. Well, I perhaps could, but I could not give it now.

Q. Do you know the number employed by this company in the Homestead works who were not members of that association?—A. No, sir.

Q. There were some employed there?—A. Oh, yes; quite a number. There are departments not eligible to the association, such as machinists, blacksmiths, carpenters, and other grades.

Q. They are not eligible?—A. No, sir; they have an organization of their own.

Q. They, therefore, had nothing to do with the negotiations?—A. Not with the tonnage rates.

Q. It was only the members of this association who were affected by the proposition of the company who tried to negotiate?—A. Yes, sir.

Q. Do you know what number there were in those four departments belonging to that association who were affected?—A. No, sir; I have no knowledge, only I saw what the firm gave out, 325.

Q. What is your best impression about that as to whether it is correct or not?—A. They are running three turns in some departments and twelve hours in others, and I would not like to make an estimate.

Q. Were all the men employed in those four departments members of your organization?—A. I do not think all were, and I do not believe all were.

Q. What benefit or supposed benefit results to those laborers from that organization?—A. To obtain a fair remuneration for their labor; that is, by watching the market as closely as they can and to be ready and prepared to meet the firm upon issues of that kind if there are changes to be made in the scales, so there will be no advantage taken of them in getting a greater reduction than necessary.

Q. It is to secure a uniformity of price?—A. That is the object where the job and work is similar.

Q. Now, take two men belonging to that association. Suppose one has greater skill and productive capacity than the other. Does it equalize them in their remuneration or would the one with greater skill get more?—A. Well, to illustrate that, suppose here is a heater working one train and there are four furnaces in the train, or three furnaces, or two, as the case may be. Each heater gets the same rate. There may be some a little more skillful than others, but the rate for the job is the same.

Q. And so, for a particular class, if one is a better workman than the other he would have no advantage in compensation?—A. No, sir; all have the same rates.

By Mr. TAYLOR:

Q. Where do you reside?—A. Pittsburg.

Q. How long have you been connected officially with this association?—A. I was president for nearly nine years. I had been previous to that, I mean officially.

Q. The Amalgamated Association of Iron and Steel Workers extends throughout the United States?—A. Yes, sir.

Q. Wherever there are iron and steel establishments?—A. Yes, sir.

Q. Do the Mahoning and Shendoah Valley workmen belong to this association or have they their own association?—A. They belong to the Amalgamated Association of Iron and Steel Workers.

Q. Considering the importance of the steel and iron business, as I understand it, there has been but little collision between this association and the manufacturers heretofore?—A. Not for a number of years. There have been no local difficulties.

Q. I say considering the importance and the extent of the whole business there has not been a very great deal of that clashing of interests; there has been a watchfulness on both sides and care taken?—A. There have been cases where there has been some discussion in regard to it and perhaps idleness for a few weeks.

Q. You understand, as I believe I do, that the association is quite a conservative association, and, in a general way, tries to be fair all around?—A. It does.

Q. Well, now, you speak about the labor cost on a certain kind of steel?—A. Four-by-four billets.

Q. That labor cost, you say, is $1.55 per ton?—A. That is for the labor enumerated in the scale.

Q. That does not include, by a large consideration, the entire labor cost?—A. No, there is other labor outside that is not in it.

Q. It does not include the expenses of the manufacturer in salaries in general or office rent and other agencies, etc. ?—A. No, sir.

Q. So it would be but really a slight approximation of the real cost?—A. I say it is an estimate.

Q. When you approximate that cost it does not include all the conditions?—A. No, sir.

Q. Are you well acquainted at Homestead with the people and with the plant there?—A. I could not say well acquainted. I have been there quite a number of times, but not much lately.

Q. You have met the workmen who have worked there in the mill?—A. Yes, sir.

Q. How long has that plant been in existence there?—A. Since 1882, I think.

Q. Has there been much change in workmen?—A. No, not very much.

Q. It has been pretty steady; how much of a town is it—what population is it—some 12,000?—A. Well, I could not say. I never heard what the population was.

Q. Do you judge it was about that? I was so informed of that yesterday.—A. Yes, sir.

Q. Do you know who owns those houses and dwelling houses in the town?—A. I think the workmen do.

Q. They and their families comprise substantially the population of the town?—A. Of those employed in the mill, yes, sir.

Q. Do you know about the nationality of the workmen there in a general way, whether they are of all nationalities, Americans and others?—A. I believe they are mostly Americans; I believe it runs that way.

Q. I so understood, but not wholly so?—A. Not altogether.

Q. Now, there is one thing about this investigation which I do not know is particularly legitimate, but it is one I wish to talk to you about because I thought you would be able to tell me more than most other men, and that is, I would desire to get the workingman's idea of the situation, of the whys and wherefores. I can understand why the workmen should oppose the introduction of a foreign force armed, and I can understand why they should be so much prejudiced against watchmen or anybody else called Pinkertons, or call them what you please. I think I understand that, but there is another branch of it that I do not understand and that is their views in regard to their right to take possession of the mill. Now, I want to get at that. I understand that about the 1st of July it was understood that if the new scale was not signed, or a new contract in some form made, there was to be no more work in that plant; that was correct?—A. As I stated before, that is the rule in all agreements where the scale is not signed.

Q. It is necessarily so, because when a contract ceases the parties cease working until they make a new arrangement?—A. Yes, sir.

Q. Well, on the 1st of July, or the day before, the mill ceased working?—A. The day before.

Q. Now, it seems that the workmen conceived an idea it was their duty and right to take possession of that mill; that the sheriff or deputy sheriff, or officers, had some difficulty in taking possession; in fact, they were refused possession. There has been a controversy which we know about, and the mill yet, as far as I know, is in possession of the workingmen, not claiming it as their property, not claiming that they have any title or any part in it; and now I would like to get at their ideas about it, as to why they think they are justified in doing that.—A. There may be some who think that, but I do not know that it is the sentiment of those who are members of the association. There may be some that think that. Some may do so, but they are not authorized, nor does the association teach anything of the kind.

Q. I understand that most thoroughly; that is, I supposed that was so; but what I want to get at is to put myself and yourself in the place of these men who really did this—took possession of the plant—of those men who thought they ought to take possession; and I want to ask you if you can help me in regard to an explanation of that. Now, it seems one class of men thought they had a right to take possession and another part does not think so, and of course the party who does not think so will not have anything to do with taking forcible possession, or if he does he will be conscious at the time he does it that he is doing wrong. I want to get at that class. Now, here is a mill which does not belong to him; there are millions of dollars invested there, or suppose it is a small bit of property, no matter which, and say that the owner of that property and I disagree about something that is valuable to me; have I the right to take possession of that property and hold it against all comers or any comer? I want to know how their minds work and what they think about it.—A. Well, it is pretty hard to answer that question as to what they think about it. All I know is they ceased working.

Q. You know more than that; you know in this particular case they took possession of it.—A. I heard so; that it was done by certain parties, that is, by a certain class, but I do not know who did it.

Q. Are you so acquainted with the working of the minds of these men that you could give me any more information than I have already? I have none and it has been a mystery to me and one I wanted to solve.—A. No, I could not give you any information on that.

Q. Well, there has been another thing stated, that at a certain time the deputy sheriff went with a certain number of deputies to take possession and watch the property; that these workingmen, some of them, that is, those who were present, said, " No, we will do this; we will give bonds that this property shall be protected; we will furnish 100 or 500 men to protect the property and we will give bonds that no injury shall be done." Now, can you tell me what their idea was about that; were they to take possession of this property so the owners could not work it?—A. I only saw what the papers stated.

Q. You have heard it stated here to-day?—A. Yes, sir.

Q. What would you state? Do they say, "We will do this out of regard for the benefit of the company" or do they do it saying that there shall be no labor employed there unless they are employed to do it?—A. If they were thinking men it would be that there should be no advantage taken to destroy the property and I believe the men would assist the firm to prevent the property from being destroyed.

Q. I have no doubt that would be so; there is no question in my mind about that, but the point with me is different and this is a new matter to me. It is like something I never heard very much of. The point seems to be that for the mere safety of the building standing there it would be just as well that the workmen should occupy it as anybody else, but if the property was to be owned by the owners and used by the owners the possession and watchfulness of the workmen would have two effects: one would be to keep it safely and the other would be to keep it safely away from the owners.

By the Chairman:

Q. Judge, let me help you there; was not the object of these laboring men in fighting the Pinkertons away and resisting the sheriff in taking that property to prevent the owners from putting nonunion men in there and working it by nonunion labor?—A. That might have been their idea.

Q. That is your understanding of it. Do you know that from mixing with them and from their talk whether that is the object or not?—A. They believe they have the right to speak to men if they should come there. The workingmen believe that they have the right to see them and explain their position as to why they are not at work and why they are locked out.

By Mr. Taylor:

Q. Do you think that fully covers the case. They have the right to speak to them, but do they not go further than that and say that they have no right to go in the mills?—A. I say that individuals may sometimes say that.

Q. Then you understand the workmen claim no right to take possession of the mill or to keep it away from the owners?—A. Not that I know of.

Q. And if anybody did that they did it outside of the advice of your association and outside of the proprieties of law and order of the country?—A. They have tried, as far as I have been informed, to keep the peace and prevent disorder, but in regard to leaving any one in the mill to prevent any one from coming in there, I could not say anything about that.

Q. I did not make any point in regard to keeping the peace, but I did really want to know in regard to the other, and perhaps I will find some workmen who will know more about it and know how they really thought upon it.

Mr. BOATNER. Their idea of the best way to keep the peace was to stop the row before it got started?

The WITNESS. Yes, sir.

By Mr. BRODERICK:

Q. You spoke of a convention here; was that a local convention or a national convention?—A. It was a national convention.

Q. When there is a difference between the employers and the men and they contemplate force or resistance of any kind, to whom is that matter submitted—to what tribunal is that submitted?—A. They first try to remedy it themselves.

Q. But when they contemplate resistance in an effort to change the workmen on the part of employers, to whom is that question submitted?—A. To change workmen?

Q. Where employers contemplate changing workmen, as it is suspected they did in this case, and get in nonunion men, and there is a difference of opinion between the employés and the employers, to whom in your order is that question of whether they will use physical force or not submitted; to an advisory council?—A. No, sir. There is no executive board or anything else that takes charge of anything of that kind.

Q. Are these matters of physical resistance, when they occur, determined entirely by the local organization at the mills or are they determined in any way by the national organization?—A. Well, in steel mills the wage-question is local; each steel mill regulates its own affairs.

Q. Are you acquainted with the wages paid men throughout the country for this class of work?—A. Yes, in the converting and blooming mills. There are two departments in this dispute. I do not believe there is another mill in the country like it. The armor mill and the 119-inch mill are both modern mills, and in regard to the slabbing mill I do not believe there is another mill in the country of its character.

Q. You said something about two departments.—A. They are both open hearths. There are open-hearth departments elsewhere, but those are constructed upon a different system, with larger furnaces and more methods of improved machinery in use there than in any other place.

Q. Do you know how the wages paid there will compare with the wages paid in mills elsewhere in this country?—A. Well, in the open-hearth department, I will state this. If the tonnage rates were given to the men at Homestead as paid in other places which work similar per ton—there are places that pay $9, $10, and $12 per ton for the open-hearth department, and sometimes $15 to $20—if these men got the same rates per ton they would make more money at Homestead than elsewhere, yet at the same time the rates per ton in other mills costs more than it does at Homestead. The tonnage cost at other mills is above those of the open-hearth department at Homestead.

Mr. BYNUM. He is speaking of the average wages throughout the country.

The WITNESS. The tonnage is very low at other places and they have to have a higher rate.

By Mr. BRODERICK:

Q. I believe you stated you did not know about these improvements, or do you know about the improvements to be put in?—A. No, sir; I could not say about those they are going to put in.

Q. Or those already in?—A. Of course the scale was regulated in respect to them.

By Mr. BYNUM:

Q. Were there ever any offers from your association to the company for an arbitration?—A. No, sir; on the day that this occurred when I came to the city and saw what happened I at first intended to go and see Mr. Frick, but when I saw the papers I saw it was placed in the hands of the sheriff and I went to see him.

Q. Are you willing that disinterested parties shall arbitrate the difference?—A. Well, if the men at Homestead are willing, the association will not object.

Q. Are you willing that Congress shall pass an arbitration bill, so that all these matters could be arbitrated?—A. I could not speak for the association; I could only speak for myself. I am only an individual member of it.

Q. What would be your idea, that that would be a settlement of the dangers of strikes and contentions?—A. From the experience we have had with arbitration it seems it is almost always against the workman. You take the English system, which has always been a compromise or nearly so.

Q. All law suits are compromises in one sense of the word?—A. I will say nearly all of them.

By Mr. BOATNER:

Q. I suppose that the idea or principle upon which the organization of labor is based is that organization is necessary to prevent the oppression and tyranny of capital?—A. That is the object and intention of all labor organization.

Q. Organized labor, however, does not go to the extent of asking that it be given the ultimate decision of questions which affect its own interests; in other words they do not claim to be the judge of their own cases?—A. No, sir. But suppose there is a mill here with one thousand or twelve hundred men and they would desire to do a certain thing which they ask through their lodge, but they must continue on at work; they can not stop until it is investigated and——   .

Q. If you stopped or limited your demand to the right of stopping work and not preventing any one else from working who wanted to, of course their position would be unassailable, but I understand that organized labor not only insists upon the right to withdraw and not work but to prevent the owners of that plant from employing any other employés; if they did not the strike would be of no account. The point I want to get at is this, that your contention is that organized capital would oppress labor unless labor organized for the protection of its rights. Then there is a conflict, a conflict of effort so to speak. The owner of the mill claims that he has a right to operate his mill as he pleases under the law, and that is unquestionably his legal right. Organized labor claims that they must stop it in some way in order to prevent capital from employing unorganized labor and reducing it to the condition such as they want. Now, in your judgment, as a representative of an organization of labor, would there be any valid objection to a tribunal which would have the authority to ascertain the merits of a question and to render a decision which would be binding on both parties?—A. Well, I believe, that may eventually be the result; I think organized labor will come to that.

Q. For instance in this case here are a highly protected set of manufacturers; these iron manufacturers have been protected for twenty years upon the plea that by this protection they were enabled to pay their laborers a rate of wages unknown in the Old World, which would afford them a comfortable income. Now, then, is it considered by organized labor that they have any rights to the benefit of this protection by law created nominally in their interests?—A. Yes, sir; they think they are entitled to a share in it.

Q. Do you think they are entitled though to know what their profits are?—A. Well, we try to estimate what the profits are and to regulate wages by that. They know the manufacturer must make some profit.

There is one thing I would like to speak of. Yesterday evening Mr. Frick read off some agreements which were signed by some workmen at Homestead and it appears he objected to signing the scale for the tonnage workmen to expire on the 1st of July or the last day of June, and that these agreements were signed on June 20 to expire about a year hence or two years, I do not just remember which. Why should there be any objection to the tonnage men having the same privilege as those other men have?

Q. I want to call your attention as the representative of a very large class in the United States of skilled labor to the question of compulsory arbitration. In your opinion is it desirable or not to establish compulsory arbitration?—A. There is a law in this State in regard to a volunteer trades tribunal, but it is not satisfactory, and if it was made compulsory I do not know whether it would be satisfactory. We have what is called "the trades tribunal," which is voluntary; we have a law to that effect. It has been tried on two or three occasions, but it has not been satisfactory.

Q. But there are no compulsory features in that?—A. No, sir; it is voluntary.

Q. Now I am speaking of arbitration with compulsory features. Take the case under consideration. Mr. Frick is right or the Amalgamated Association of Iron and Steel Workers is right; one or the other must be right or wrong in this contention. Can you see any objection to a tribunal which shall have jurisdiction in the matter to decide which is right?—A. No; I do not think——

Q. And to enforce its decrees?—A. In regard to the enforcement part, whether the firm or the men would be satisfied after it I could not say, but I doubt it.

Q. You never saw a man who was satisfied with a judgment rendered against him. I never saw a case of that kind; it is always so that one party or the other would be dissatisfied; but do not you consider that in the interest of the general welfare that it would be better that some tribunal should be organized which would have the authority to decide, say that either Mr. Frick was wrong or that the contention of the men was wrong?—A. I believe rather than to have strikes there should be something done to prevent them. We have come to that point that there should be some authority, but the question in my mind is, how are you going to reach it just right on the question of wages unless we can find exactly what the profits of the firm are. If we are going to have compulsory regulation of wage matters, then the books and everything should be shown to see what the profits are. Otherwise I do not believe it would be proper. All parties should be compelled to show what their profits were so they could reach something that would be satisfactory.

By Mr. BRODERICK:

Q. Has your association, as an association, ever considered the matter of such a law?—A. Not for years. They did at one time, but that has been years ago, and they did not favor it then.

Q. In view of the fact that all the settlements of disputes are compromises largely—a jury trial is simply an arbitration in one sense and a compromise—do not you think it would be better to have compulsory arbitration?—A. I do not know whether it would be better; of course I could not speak in regard to that. What I was going to say is this, if you compel either side to do a thing that they do not wish to do, it certainly would not be satisfactory to them. Let me make a statement now. There are so many different things connected with iron and steel that disinterested parties do not understand, and the workmen believe that if they can go to the manufacturers and talk matters over with them they will understand their own affairs better than strangers, because you folks are not so familiar with mill work. You will find, perhaps, one hundred things in a mill an outside party would hardly understand if explained to him, and the men think if they can talk with their own firm in regard to the matter that they will agree upon something satisfactory to both.

By Mr. BOATNER:

Q. Well, it seems they can not agree until after a whole lot of people are killed?—A. Well, there is—the men claim that they were entitled to have the minimum price of $24. Now the reason for the minimum was that if the workmen had no minimum in the scales the manufacturers could go out and sell the product upon which wages are based at very low figures and take contracts at that, and what would the final result be? The market would be low, and the manufacturer having a large capacity could go into the market and cut rates, knowing the workmen would have to follow that. That is one of the reasons why the workmen claim they should have a minimum.

Q. They could go into the market and buy their own products?—A. Well, I do not say they do that, but it might be done.

The CHAIRMAN. That is speculative, of course.

By Mr. BYNUM:

Q. Of course I can readily see the difficulty in compulsory arbitration, because it is trespassing on private rights, but suppose a law was enacted by which one party or another could propose arbitration, and if it was accepted that there should be a compulsory power to enforce it after they had voluntarily entered into it?—A. Well, if it was a law certainly they would have to accept it.

Q. But suppose it would be a voluntary matter whether they would go into it or not, but after they had gone into it that they would have the power to compel both parties to stand by it?—A. If they entered into it voluntarily, certainly.

Q. Do you think the workmen would object to a thing of that kind?—A. No; if it was voluntary for them to enter into it I do not see any reason why they should object.

Q. It would simply throw the responsibility upon one side or the other of proposing arbitration. Of course if the workmen on one side or the mill on the other refuse to arbitrate the matter it would place them, as far as public sentiment was concerned, in the wrong. That would be the advantage of a system of that kind, and to that extent of course it would influence the mind of the public.—A. Well, if both parties entered into it——

Q. What I mean is if there should be a law giving the power of either side to voluntarily propose arbitration, but that arbitration after being entered upon should be enforced by the statute; do you think the workmen would generally indorse a law of that kind?—A. Certainly, if that was the law we could not do otherwise.

Q. Now in regard to this reduction of wages, I want to find out something about that. Can you give the classes in which the reductions would have been made; that is, the different classes?—A. They are made in the armor-plate mill——

Q. What workmen are designated; what would you call them?—A. They were men around the rolls, furnances, and at the shears, and some on the 119-inch mill, also on the open hearth.

Q. This is a class of men getting the highest wages, so far as Mr. Frick's testimony was concerned?—A. Some of them; yes, sir.

Q. Now the price of billets is fixed on the Bessemer billets?—A. Yes, sir.

Q. The Bessemer is less than the open hearth?—A. Yes, sir.

Q. What is the difference between the Bessemer and the open hearth?—A. The open hearth are never quoted.

Q. The Bessemer billet is the standard?—A. Yes, sir; it is the standard billet.

By the CHAIRMAN:

Q. Is it not the practice of the Amalgamated Association whenever they enter into a contract to carry it out for the period or term agreed upon?—A. As far as wages are concerned, yes.

Q. Are you not aware that the employés in another mill here belonging to the Amalgamated Association entered into contract two weeks ago with this company and have served notice on them that unless they renew or make a contract satisfactory to the Amalgamated people at Homestead that they, the mill here, will break with them?—A. I heard that this morning or last night; that they would cease work providing there was no conference brought about.

Q. Do they operate in that way wherever they are employed, bringing that kind of influence to bear in favor of each other?—A. That I could not say. I was here yesterday afternoon and morning, and I only heard last night when I was leaving here of what was done and from what the papers gave this morning.

Q. You have no knowledge except from rumor and report?—A. No, sir.

Mr. BYNUM. There is this fact, the Amalgamated Association stands as a whole does it; where there is a controversy with one branch of it the others are deemed to be parties to that controversy?

The WITNESS. Certainly; that is a rule of the association.

The CHAIRMAN. While they make their own contract with each particular mill where employed, they aid each other?

The WITNESS. The contract is signed for wages, nothing further.

TESTIMONY OF HUGH O'DONNELL.

HUGH O'DONNELL sworn and examined.

By the CHAIRMAN:

Q. I do not assume that you have had connection with any illegal transaction at all, but I want to say to you in advance that if any question which we propound to you should call for an answer which in your opinion would subject you to a prosecution or anything of that kind you need not answer it. I do not assume you have of course, but I just give you that precaution, which is but right.—A. I am not afraid of that at all.

Q. What position do you hold in connection with the skilled laborers formerly employed at Homestead in this State, if any?—A. I am simply a member of W. T. Robers Lodge, No. 125, Amalgamated Association of Iron and Steel Workers.

Q. Have you been a worker yourself in Homestead?—A. Yes, sir; for the last six years nearly.

Q. Have you recently held some other position in connection with the troubles which have occurred there?—A. Yes, sir; chairman of the advisory committee.

Q. Who compose that committee?—A. Members of the eight amalgamated lodges, representing so many departments.

Q. Do you know the membership of the eight lodges; if so, how many?—A. I could not say positively.

Q. Well, about?—A. No, I could not estimate. I could not approximate it as there have been so many changes there. There is a mechanical lodge, and the plant has been growing so in the last three years that I have paid very little attention to it.

Q. Were you one of the committee or have anything to do with the proposition submitted to you by the company in whose employ you have been with reference to the scale of wages on the 23d of June?—A. I was one of the committee who was called into the office last January, when they made a proposition to us in a formulated scale.

Q. Did you have any connection with any proposition in June?—A. Not in connection with the scale. I was one of the committee who was called in by the general manager of the Homestead Steel Works with the privilege upon us to lay before the lodges to have the scale discussed so as to have it signed by the 24th—that is, to accept the scale proposed by the firm on the 24th of June. That is the only connection I had with the scale. When we formulated the scale—it is provided in the laws that at a certain time—that is, in January, February, March, and along there—we gather up all the data possible in regard to the market, such as we can, and it is discussed in lodge. There is a wage committee appointed, and it is then submitted to the national lodge, and it is printed in a programme, and submitted to the convention; and there ends our responsibility for the scale.

Q. The convention of the Amalgamated Association?—A. Yes, sir; the national convention.

Q. You took that course with the proposition made to the company?—A. Yes, sir.

Q. Did you have any personal knowledge whether negotiations continued, or did your connection with it terminate there?—A. It terminated there.

Q. What work have you been performing?—A. Heater in the 119-inch plate mill.

Q. What is the extent of your experience in that kind of work in that mill?—A. In that mill I have been a millworker since I have been 17 years of age. I commenced in the sheet mill.

Q. How long have you been engaged in it?—A. I have been engaged in that mill for five and a half years, or about that time.

Q. In that mill up there?—A. Yes, sir; I commenced in that mill when the mill first started and grew up with it.

Q. Do you know the departments up there that would be affected by the new scale proposed?—A. Yes, sir; the departments are the 119-inch plate mill, and the armor mill, and the open hearth departments Nos 1 and 2.

Q. Do you know the labor cost of producing a ton of steel?—A. No, sir.

Q. You do not profess to know that?—A. No, sir; I could not get at that at all. There is no possible chance to approximate it at all.

Mr. BOATNER. That is a secret, is it not?

The WITNESS. It is.

By the CHAIRMAN:

Q. You have heard the testimony of Mr. Weihe with respect to the difference between the company and your association in respect to the new scale. Does your knowledge of that difference correspond with his?—A. What I heard of it. I did not hear all of Mr. Weihe's testimony.

Q. He stated there were two points: one, the time when the contract would terminate, the company proposed to make it the last of the year and the workmen wanted it the last of June; and the other was, he stated, to make the basis or minimum $22 instead of $25 per ton, with the same sliding scale as heretofore. Were those the points of difference?—A. Yes, sir; exactly.

Q. Do you know what new machinery the company proposed to put in there?—A. No, sir; the mill I am working in has not had any improvements made in it since the mill was constructed.

Q. You do not know what they propose to put in or what effect that would have?—A. I do not know that I could answer the question. Mr. Frick is here and other members of the firm.

Q. You started to state something about the improvements where they worked?—A. I said there were no improvements in our mill; that is, the 119-inch mill, but it stands intact to-day as it did when it was first built.

Q. Well, in regard to this proposition, do you know what effect it would have if accepted upon your wages?—A. In regard to my wages, I am one of the high-priced people. My wages were not reduced.

Q. They would not have been reduced?—A. They would if the $22 minimum should obtain; then it would be affected about 12 per cent.

Q. But suppose it would go to $23 or $24 only and $22 was the minimum, how would that affect you?—A. It would not affect me very much, a very small percentage of reduction.

Q. Five or six per cent, about that?—A. About 6.

Mr. BOATNER. One-third of 12 would be 4 per cent?

The WITNESS. Yes, sir; 4 per cent.

By the CHAIRMAN:

Q. There was no agreement between the association and the company and the mill shut down on the 30th of June?—A. So we were instructed in our lodges.

Q. Was there any order of the lodges or of your association to quit work on the 30th, or with the expiration of the 30th, in consequence of this disagreement?—A. I think our department shut down on the 28th. I think ours was the first department closed down—no, the open-hearth closed down first; I think that was on the 28th of June.

Q. Did the Amalgamated Association through your lodges give instructions that if the terms were not complied with you should quit work?—A. That was all understood. Every man was supposed to be instructed that way in the event of a disagreement, and they would remain out until such a time as there was an agreement.

Q. After the shut down of the mills did the workmen who had been employed theretofore exercise any controlover them in respect to keeping anybody out and looking after the property or any sort of supervision, and, if so, to what extent within your observation?—A. To this extent, that there was a mass meeting held, and there was quite a large number there. For instance there is a mechanical department there, that is, mechanics, blacksmiths, and others who are purely incidental to the production of a ton of steel, and we called a mass meeting.

Q. They were not affected by this?—A. No; they were not affected by the scale at all. We called a mass meeting and we considered the matter, and a resolution was passed there that they remain out with us until such time as we arrived at an agreement with the firm. Immediately after the mass meeting all the lodges—the meetings are secret to a certain extent, as all business transactions are mostly—the eight lodges had a joint meeting and they deliberated upon the crisis at hand and they there elected a certain number from each lodge—assuming they had the responsibility, each of the eight lodges was empowered to appoint five members of an advisory committee. That was a committee constituted an advisory committee. Then this action was taken. Members were appointed to this committee by each lodge. I was appointed by our president, with several others, and we organized ourselves into an advisory committee and I was elected chairman of that. This advisory committee got headquarters. We knew if we went on strike there we had quite a number of irresponsible people and there would be others coming from a distance, and we appointed subcommittees and we placed men around the works to guard them; not around the fence, but on the outside to keep outsiders, wholly irresponsible people, from doing any damage.

Q. You placed them outside of the fence which had been placed around the works of the company?—A. Yes, sir.

Q. When was that done, on what date?—A. I do not remember the date but I think it must have been on the 30th of June or on the 1st of July. The 1st of July, I think it was, that the mass meeting was called and that committee was organized, but these men were fully instructed they should simply use moral suasion, and that nobody should be threatened, that there should be no violent language. We did that because we assumed we had the moral responsibility and each man pledged himself. The best men, in my estimate, composed that advi-

Q. Nonunion men?—A. Yes, sir.

Q. They were there to use moral suasion with such people who came to keep them from going into the works in the employ of the company?—A. Yes, sir.

Q. And they were not there for the purpose of using any violence?—A. No, sir; their methods were peaceable.

Q. Did you see the sheriff of this county when he went there?—A. Yes, sir; he called at headquarters and we invited him in.

Q. On what date?—A. Well, I have lost all track of time, but I think it was on the 5th of July. He was accompanied by Mr. Cluley, the deputy and ex-Sheriff Gray.

Q. Did he demand possession of the works for the company?—A. I do not think he did; we were not in possession of the works; their own watchmen were in there. I will answer it in this way. The day the Congressional committee arrived in Homestead, last Wednesday, we would have encountered the same difficulty of obtaining admission to the works then as on yesterday, because their own watchmen were in possession.

Q. Did you see the deputy sheriff on the second trip?—A. I saw a crowd—I was standing at headquarters and I saw a crowd congregating on the railroad track and on the hills and on the hilltops, and they looked to be a large crowd, and I saw them moving towards Homestead and I walked down Eighth avenue and I met Mr. Cluley, the deputy sheriff, and he offered his hand—I had met him in the forenoon—and he said, "Mr. O'Donnell, we claim your protection." I said, "You certainly shall have it, but you do not need it; you shall have protection and nobody shall molest you." I offered him my arm and invited all the deputies to the committee room, and they met several members of the advisory committee. I asked him what they would do, and they replied in the face of circumstances they thought they had better retire to Pittsburg, and he did not ask for any protection any further than to give him a safe pass through the streets. That was all of that. I myself went down towards the crowd to disperse them.

Q. Did he make any application to you to get possession of the works?—A. No, sir, I did not have the power to give it to him nor the advisory committee. I will say we disbanded the advisory committee. We explained to him our position, that we had a patrol which went around the works to guard it and keep men away from the fence, and I will say that on one occasion, in regard to the pipe which runs around the fence, there was a man who rushed to headquarters and informed me the gas was escaping and that somebody threatened to ignite it. I took two members of the advisory committee and we went down to investigate. It seemed a valve had been left open on the inside and we placed a guard over it; we went up to the station and got a guard of about four and we told them to protect it with their lives and allow no man to ignite that gas. Two days afterwards some one came into headquarters and said the gas was escaping right opposite the main office near the company house and I think he said he had requested the management to have it turned off. While that gas was turned off I went down and investigated it about an hour afterwards and the leak was repaired. I do not know whether it was a leak or whether it was an open valve; I could not say. I offer this to prove to you that our methods were to protect the property. I will say for myself and nearly every member of the advisory committee that we were around personally seeing that no violence was offered and to keep the crowds away.

Q. On the morning of the 6th did you see anything of the Pinkerton guards who were carried up there on a boat and barges? And, if so, where did you first see them and what do you know about it?—A. Am I compelled to give evidence about that here?

Q. Not of any participation.

Mr. TAYLOR. I would suggest this, that if he answers at all in regard to the matter, according to the law in every case he will be obliged to answer fully, would he not?

The CHAIRMAN. I think not.

Mr. TAYLOR. If he says he does not care to answer that, I do not think he ought to be made to do it.

The WITNESS. I am not afraid to answer any question in connection with it fully as far as cross-examination is concerned, and I will state that I went there accompanied by Capt. O. O. Coon and he gave me the privilege of mentioning his name. He was with me and we went there as peaceable citizens and we were unarmed. I do not think I ought to be asked to give evidence in connection with that affair, as I did not participate in it at all.

By the CHAIRMAN:

Q. If you were there and saw it we would like to hear you, as you are an intelligent man?—A. Thank you.

Q. We would like to hear from you because you can give the details probably much better than some other witnesses can?—A. Well, I am going to make a brief statement in regard to the matter. I could not say the exact hour, but I think the alarm came up about 2 o'clock or 3 that two barges loaded with Pinkertons were coming up the river. That was the alarm spread out which aroused the entire population. I, with others, got out of bed and with Capt. Coon, who was a near neighbor of mine, we both went down to the river bank and there had already assembled a very large crowd of people—men, women, and children. There were a lot of half-grown boys and there were Slavs, Hungarians, and others who were firing pistols in the air. They must have been firing in the air because Capt. Coon and another man were passing along the crowd and were admonishing the crowd to stop this firing of pistols and put them back in their pockets. We were going along with the crowd, following the crowd, and there had been a few random shots, but whether they were fired at the boat or not I could not say. I was on the edge of the river bank and I had my hands up advising the men not to fire, but who they were I could not answer. It was dusky and there was a fog on the river.

Q. It was early in the morning?—A. Yes, sir; I with others followed the crowd up the river to the landing. They had broken down some boards, that is, the fence belonging to the boundary limits of the city farm, the borough limits, and pulled down several boards, I do not know how many, and we passed through there and went to the river bank and saw them land. Capt. Coon and I and another friend who accompanied us went down close to the beach, and there was quite an excited crowd standing around there and they were hallooing to the captain to pull back and not to land. I do not know how it came about, but there was some scuffle around the gang plank; I stood with my back to the beach about 40 feet, as I showed you yesterday, and there was some firing. I did not see any rifles in the congregation on the river bank and I saw no one, but I think I heard a rifle shot and then a regular volley at that. I was still addressing the crowd. One ball crossed my thumb [holding up same]—it is nearly well now—and struck another man in the head and I crawled up the bank and got behind a sewer trap until the firing ceased, which I should say was about five minutes' duration.

Q. Do you know what direction the ball came from which struck your finger?—A. Certainly; I was standing with my back to the barges.

Q. Did it come from there or from the front?—A. It came from the barges.

Q. You were between the parties who were firing?—A. Yes, sir; I believe that is the way I attracted their notice, because I was at an exposed point.

Q. Do you know whether the parties on shore fired first or the parties on the boats or barges? You say shots were being fired as they came up the river.—A. Those were fired as an alarm. That is, their object was, as I understand it, to give an alarm.

Q. Could you state whether shots were fired from the people on shore at the men on the barges or boats first or did the men on the barges and boats fire first?—A. I can not answer that question. That is, when they were coming along the river?

Q. Or when they attempted to land?—A. I do not think there was a shot fired from the crowd until they fired into it, but there was one rifle shot and a volley, but where that came from I do not know. I was informed there was a man attempting to move the gang plank there, at whom it was fired.

Q. You need not state that, but just what you saw and know of your own knowledge. How long did the fight continue; you came out of that sewer trap after awhile?—A. Yes, sir, after they ceased firing.

Q. About what time after they ceased firing did you come out?—A. I said the firing ceased after about five minutes' duration.

Q. Not more than five minutes?—A. I do not think it was more than five minutes.

Mr. BOATNER. Five minutes is a terribly long time under those circumstances.

By the CHAIRMAN:

Q. You came out of the trap soon after the firing ceased?—A. Yes, sir.

Q. When you came out what was the situation in respect to the parties?—A. They congregated on the banks and held them at bay.

Q. You say they held them at bay; whom do you mean they held at bay?—A. The people on the boats.

Q. Did you see anybody on the boats or barges?—A. Yes, sir; I saw uniformed men on the boats. I saw, I think, the captain of them; I think I could recognize him. I saw him standing on the bridge or deck. It is very uncertain though, as it was about half past 4 o'clock, and it may not have been so late, but I think I saw the captain or some one whom I supposed was the captain standing on the bridge by himself or on the deck.

Q. What was the crowd on shore doing at that time?—A. They were not doing anything that I know of. They were excited of course.

Q. How were they disposed?—A. They were crowded together almost in a solid mass in some places and scattered here and there.

Q. Were they occupying any defenses or arranging any defenses?—A. Not at that time; they were simply trying to prevail upon the captain to pull out.

Q. They were talking?—A. Yes, sir; they were very much excited.

Q. They were talking to the people on the boats?—A. Yes, sir.

Q. What was the nature of the colloquy going on; what were they saying back and forth?—A. It was very indistinct to me, for I was very much occupied at the time.

Q. How long was it before the steamer pulled away from there?—A. I could not say; I left there and went to the telegraph office to telegraph to the West End and Southside Hospitals for ambulances and to give some attention to the wounded.

Q. How many people were killed on shore or died of their wounds subsequently?—A. Five or six, I believe; possibly somebody here could answer better.

Q. Was there any more firing than you saw?—A. I saw firing, but I could not say who was firing. They were all ambushed and I could not say where the shots came from though. I did not return there. I went back to headquarters, and I came back in the afternoon about, I think it was, 4 o'clock, when President Weihe came up there.

Q. Did you see the oil turned into the river and set on fire or anything of that kind?—A. I decline to answer that.

Q. What became of the barges, if you know?—A. About 5 o'clock, after President Weihe and Garland and several officers of the association had called an assemblage and addressed them and prevailed upon them to let the barges go and to cease the firing, I, with the advice of friends, mounted the side of a bin of beam metal of the open-hearth furnaces, and I got an American flag to show it was appointed for an assembly to congregate, and I addressed them. I tried to prevail upon them, in the interest of humanity, to cease firing, and I said that I had not the slightest doubt that if they would raise a flag of truce that those people would surrender. They objected to that, and I replied to that and told them a flag of truce was simply for a parley. The men finally agreed to it, and I asked them to appoint a committee, and they said I would do myself. I declined it, but they insisted that I make the parley for them. I told them I would not do it unless they pledged themselves to a man in the event of the Pinkerton men surrendering that they would go unharmed and in peace. They pledged themselves with a cheer. I got a handkerchief and I took the rifle from one man there and I tied the handkerchief to the end of the barrel and I raised it and waved it.

Then there were a number congregated around me and told me not to raise the white flag, so I pulled the flag down, and at the risk of having my hand shot off I put it through one of the beams and continued to wave it until the commander or some one responsible to the men on board the barge responded. I saw him crawling on his hands and knees and waving his handkerchief, and I got one of our men to tell him in the event any man on the barge exposed himself to fire from the beach, that one of our men would expose himself. One of the men jumped aside and said that he would expose himself also, and we jumped from behind the beams. I will say that the Pinkerton man came to the bow first and he exposed himself and waved a handkerchief, and some other man with him. Seeing this we immediately went down to the boat and parleyed. I made the remark, "Are not you sick of this firing?" and he said, "Yes; heartily sick of it." "Now," I said, "what are the conditions on which you will surrender?" He said, "We are willing to surrender on a pledge from you and your people that you will pack our arms in boxes, and we will first unload them." I do not know the technical expression for it. "We will pack them in boxes, and you will give us safe passage from Homestead." I flattered myself I had sufficient control over our own people to do that, but I did not consider at the time that half the people who had congregated there were from various points in the vicinity of Homestead. I then placed a guard over the gang plank and told them to allow no one to enter. We got some of our best men and placed them, and appointed a committee of other men, and they commenced to unload the rifles.

Afterwards, when I went to see them unloading the rifles, I spoke to one man in charge and requested him to allow me to have one loaded rifle to prevent the looting of the barges, for, as I said, we had a mob outside of wholly irresponsible parties, and I mounted the table—they had a table running the full length of the barge—I got on that table, and I superintended the unloading of those rifles. I will state that I had lost my voice, but in fact I admonished the people not to loot anything, as we were responsible for it. The men changed their uniforms, etc., and started out. Before they started out they were formed into companies. I had asked men who had marched men, to form them into companies, and to assume command, and to guarantee these people safe protection to the railroad station. When all was ready I gave the order and they marched out, and I remained on the boat until the last man. I will state by this time people were coming up, down, and across the river, and that the barges were in the hands of the rabble. I left the boat and they were marched to the rink, and the people formed on either side—men, women, and children—and I must say they were subjected to very inhuman treatment, which our men were powe 'e s to protect them from, and I know that many of our men have received scars and bruises in their endeavor to protect the Pinkertons. We took them to the rink, and that night we sent them off.

Q. Were any of the Pinkertons wounded?—A. Yes, sir; quite a number were wounded—do you mean at first?

Q. After they had surrendered a d while they were being taken to the rink were any of them wounded on the way?—A. Well, now, I am not prepared to say, as that is only rumor, and I did not see any of that. I brought up the rear with a loaded rifle, and none of my men were injured. One man, from Chicago, had two valises, and one was from a dead friend which he wanted to take home to his wife. This friend was killed before that. His valises were taken from him, and I had them restored to him. We assembled at the rink, and got all the medical force of Homestead and had their wounds dressed, and we swore in some deputies and extra policemen of the parish to take charge of them, and we arranged that they should be protected until the train should arrive that night and that we would see them safe on board, and the special train arrived at about 1 o'clock in the morning. I will say one thing, it was not our people who gave them such treatment as they received, but it was from irresponsible people, and in the passage from the hall, which is a distance of about six squares, there was not an angry word and not a threat made; this was on the way to the station. I went out to President Weihe, and I requested him to address the people. I addressed them myself, and told them he would address them, and I do not think there was an angry word spoken, although at the station there was a large crowd.

Q. Did anyone say anything about throwing them into the river?—A. Not a word that I heard.

Q. That was after they were taken out of the rink and when they were carried to the train at 1 o'clock at night?—A. Yes, sir. There were three cheers sent up when they started, and that is all I know about it.

By Mr. BYNUM:

Q. You say the alarm was given some time during the early morning that the Pinkertons were coming. Do you know how the news was communicated and brought to Homestead?—A. Well, the chairman has instructed me that I should only answer what I know.

Q. Certainly.—A. If I should answer that it would be only the rumor of others.

Q. I wanted to know if you knew of your own knowledge.—A. No, sir; I do not know anything about it.

Q. When they first landed the boat was there an effort made to put out a gang plank?—A. I saw them working at a gang plank, but I could not recognize anybody owing to the darkness.

Q. Were not the parties attempting to put it out assailed at that time by those on the shore?—A. That I could not say; I did not see them.

Q. Were not they assailed with stones and driven back?—A. I did not see that.

Q. They did not succeed in getting it out the first effort?—A. I could not say.

Q. How long after that time before you say there was a volley fired?—A. I say about ten minutes after the landing—no, I could not say as to the time; I could not give that truthfully.

Q. Were not the men on the boat attempting to come ashore when the first fire was opened?—A. I did not see that, I was at the lower end of the boat, what you might call the stern of the boat.

Q. I understood you to say the first shot, you think, came behind you as you were standing with your back to the boat?—A. Yes, sir.

Q. And you think your wound was caused by a bullet coming from behind you?—A. Yes, sir.

Q. When was that, after the firing had been carried on for awhile?—A. No, the first volley.

Q. What were the men on the boat attempting to do at this time—were they trying to come ashore from the boat?—A. No; I could not say they were. In regard to that gang-plank incident, I did not see that at all; I heard it.

Q. How could you tell that shot came from the rear instead of the front?—A. I do not know, but I do not see how there could be any possible doubt.

Q. It seems to me it might have come from the front as well as from the other. Was there any sensation or anything by which you can tell which way it came except by the sound?—A. That is all; the sensation and the sound, of course.

By Mr. BOATNER:

Q. Your instinct was that it came from behind?—A. Yes, sir.

Q. I suppose you are one of the skilled laborers in these works?—A. These jobs are skilled jobs.

Q. You said awhile ago you were one of the high-priced men. About what is the average wages that you earned under the old schedule?—A. I think about $144 a month on an average. That is the average price paid for such class of work.

Q. What were the hours of work at that mill?—A. Eight hours.

By Mr. BRODERICK:

Q. How many years have you been in the steel and iron work altogether?—A. In Carnegie's works about five and a half years.

Q. How long have you worked on those lines altogether?—A. Nearly all my life.

Q. You have had occasion to observe what effect that sort of work has upon the health as compared with manual labor in other lines of work?—A. Yes, sir; and I say that in the 119-inch plate mill, the peculiar construction of the furnaces is such that a man can not stand it very long, and it is necessary for him in the summer months to retire and get a breath of fresh air.

Q. Are there any elderly men working on those jobs?—A. Very few.

Q. Have those few been working all their lives?—A. They have worked in steel mills all their lives; that is, most of them.

Q. You have lived in Homestead, I understand, about five years?—A. Yes, sir.

Q. Do a large per cent of those workmen own their own homes?—A. Yes, sir.

Q. How are they—good, average homes?—A. Yes, sir; they are all very good homes; above the average, in fact.

Q. And the people live fairly well?—A. Yes, sir; they live very well.

Q. Is there much extreme poverty and dissatisfaction there?—A. Only the result of misfortune and accident in the mill; there is a great deal of that, as a great many accidents occur.

Q. That is, injuries?—A. Yes, sir; injuries.

Q. Aside from that there is no extreme poverty?—A. No; not to my knowledge.

By Mr. TAYLOR:

Q. You went down the river that morning after you heard the alarm; how far did you go?—A. I went down and turned to the right——

Q. I understand the location, but how far down, in yards or measures of a mile, did you proceed before you met the boat?—A. The boat was nearly opposite the river bank when I got there, and a big crowd had already assembled half a mile long.

Q. Where had you been the morning before that?—A. At headquarters.

Q. How far is that from the landing place where the boats landed?—A. I should say fully half a mile.

Q. Of course you did not know what had taken place before you went down?—A. No, sir.

Q. You did not know what firing had transpired, whether it was from the boat or not, while the barge was landing?—A. No, sir.

Q. In reference to this working in the mill, I suppose there is a good deal of danger in that kind of labor?—A. Yes, sir.

Q. Aside from the air of which you speak and liability to accidents of which you speak, are those men who have the higher wages more liable to be injured than those who have less?—A. No; there are men working, even foremen; I think we have had one or two foremen who were injured there.

Q. So far as the air is concerned I take it that all in the mill would be exposed to that, but as far as the accidents are concerned, I did not know how that was, and I did not know whether the men who were paid the higher wages were paid them because of their dangerous position, or because of their skill?—A. I beg your pardon, I wish to be distinctly understood that this is confined to one department and that is on account of the peculiar construction of the furnaces. I think even there there is good ventilation in winter, but it is only during the heated months when it is so severe, extremely so.

Q. Then it is true that the mills, organized as they are, are healthy?—A. Yes, sir; very healthy work.

Q. And the accidents are accidents which occur simply because of the handling of such large machinery and such heavy goods?—A. There are accidents owing to the rush and push of a mill, you know.

Q. After the Pinkertons surrendered, you say they were treated badly by outsiders; were many of them injured?—A. Yes.

Q. Were most of them or all of them struck and bruised?—A. Oh, no; there were quite a number not injured at all. I conversed with them all and remained with them until I saw them safely off on the train.

Q. You spoke in reference to a disagreement between the men and the manufacturers in regard to the time of signing this scale, and you gave some reason why the men did not want it; but does this reason exist also, that the men fear, if the scale is to be signed in the winter time at the end of the year, on the first of January, that there will be more delay in getting to an agreement because there is less pressure of business at that time?—A. That is the general feeling.

Q. That is the feeling why they do not wish it?—A. Yes, sir.

Q. I suppose it would be better for them if they could work then and not work in midsummer and that one of the reasons the men object is they are fearful they will be idle longer if they waited until that time?—A. Yes, sir.

By the CHAIRMAN:

Q. Do you know whether a majority of the laborers down there owned their own homes before the Carnegie Company erected their works or not?—A. Well, you know the town is a new town. It was built up with the works.

Q. You are very well acquainted and speak about the parties that you first saw along the river banks, some of them boys and Slavs and some others who were firing. Do you know what proportion of the population down there are aliens or are native born?—A. I could only approximate it, but I should say that about 40 per cent were American born. I, however, leave that to Burgess McLuckie.

Q. Of course that is an estimate of yours?—A. That is purely an estimate.

Q. How would you say in regard to the other 60 per cent, what nationalities do they represent?—A. I should say Slavs and Hungarians, not many Hungarians, a great many Slavs, Irish, English, Welsh, and German.

Q. What is the nationality of the men who would be affected by the price proposed in those four departments; are they mostly American born or foreign born?—A. Mostly all are American born.

Q. Nearly all are American born?—A. A large proportion of them. I do not know exactly whether I could answer that accurately or not.

Q. I am not calling for perfect accuracy.—A. I think they are, though.

Q. It is not so very important, only the committee desired to know something about it. Now, from your witnessing this scene of violence and hearing the expressions as you must have done, will you state to the committee what was the cause of the great antipathy of these people to the Pinkertons, and what was their object in fighting them and keeping them from landing? If you have gathered it from hearing from all these sources, just state what your impression was and the reason why they were so much opposed to their landing?—A. Of course you know the laboring class have a natural antipathy to that class of men; I suppose that will about answer that.

Q. It is a general one to Pinkerton's detectives, or guards, as they may be called?—A. Yes, sir.

Q. Why is it the working people generally are so much opposed to them?—A. In that particular instance, in regard to the Pinkertons leaving the barge—which has been referred to in the newspapers afterwards as running the gauntlet—it might be owing to the fact that in the town there were then lying dead 5 men who had been shot to death and more wounded.

Q. And that is one reason of the maltreatment after they surrendered?—A. Yes, sir.

Q. What was the motive that you gathered, from mixing with the crowd, as to their resisting the landing?—A. Well, we looked upon the Pinkertons as armed invaders—men who are thoroughly antagonistic to all laboring interests and allies of the capitalists.

Q. Did the people on shore, as you gathered, have an apprehension that if the Pinkertons got possession of the property of the company that the company would employ nonunion men to run the works?—A. Yes, that was the impression.

Q. And they did not wish that to occur?—A. Yes, sir.

By Mr. TAYLOR:

Q. That was the real matter of difference, I suppose?—A. Yes, sir.

Q. Now, you have stated those men who mistreated these parties were not citizens of Homestead?—A. I will not say that; did I say that?

Q. Well, not of your association then?—A. We assumed no further responsibility; we placed our men in charge of them and they fought all along the line when they were running the gauntlet. They were women who did the most of it?

Q. Wives of the workmen there?—A. And friends of the injured people.

Q. I got the impression that it was the people who came from around there who assaulted the Pinkertons, but when you suggested that the knowledge of the dying and wounded there might have infuriated the people, it occurred to me it might have been those connected with those killed and wounded who did that. My understanding of the facts is, the real objection to the Pinkertons was that they were trying to dispossess you people of what you wanted?—A. I have no desire to be unfair in any statement I make; I wish to be frank, and I do not wish to inject any coloring in any of my evidence at all. I wish to saddle the responsibility on outsiders who——

By the CHAIRMAN:

Q. See if this is right: I gather from what you say, Mr. O'Donnell, that the parties who maltreated the Pinkerton men after their surrender were those you and your assistants could not control?—A. That is it exactly.

Q. There may have been some belonging to your association, and others not, but they were simply people you could not control?—A. That explains it.

Mr. BOATNER. There was no objection to the militia.

The WITNESS. None at all.

Thereupon the committee took a recess until 4 p. m.

H. Mis. 335——7

AFTER THE RECESS.

TESTIMONY OF JOHN McLUCKIE.

JOHN McLUCKIE sworn and examined.

By the CHAIRMAN:

Q. Where do you live?—A. Homestead.

Q. Do you hold any official position there?—A. I am burgess of that borough.

Q. How long have you held that position?—A. This is my second term, this year, 1892.

Q. How long have you lived in Homestead, Pa.?—A. Over five years.

Q. What business have you have been engaged in?—A. I am a steel worker.

Q. Do you mean you worked in the mills of Carnegie, Phipps & Co., at Homestead?—A. Yes, sir.

Q. What particular kind of work did you do?—A. In the converting department.

Q. How long have you worked there?—A. Ever since I came to Homestead, five years ago last May.

Q. Do you belong to the Amalgamated Association of Iron and Steel Workers?—A. I do, sir.

Q. About what wages have you earned and received for the work you have been doing there?—A. I can not say, but I suppose it would average, probably, $2.25.

Q. About how much per month?—A. Perhaps $55.

Q. Do you know anything about the contract under which skilled workmen have been working for that company for some considerable time past?—A. The late steel contract?

Q. Yes.—A. I know it is based on the $25 minimum and was supposed to be a sliding scale, and did slide, too.

Q. Do you know anything about the company proposing a different scale this year, and if so when and what was it?—A. Not of my own knowledge. Our committees so reported it.

Q. You do not know of your own knowledge and it came to you through the committees of the organization to which you belong?—A. Yes, sir.

Q. Did you hear the testimony of Mr. Frick about that contract?—A. I did not, sir.

Q. What points were involved in the proposition wherein it differed from the contract under which you were at work?—A. From what information I received from the sources I have mentioned I think that there were three points involved; that is what I understood from our committee. One is the change in the minimum; another is the change of the time for the expiration of the scale, and another is a reduction in wages.

Q. Do you know about the time when the mills were shut down?—A. Yes, sir.

Q. When was that?—A. We shut down on the 29th of June; that is, the converting department.

Q. The one in which you worked shut down on the 29th of June?—A. Yes, sir.

Q. That was in consequence of a disagreement between the company and certain employés?—A. I so understood.

Q. Do you know anything of any trouble which resulted subsequently from attempts to put Pinkerton guards in possession of the mill?—A. I heard there was some trouble.

Q. You did not witness any?—A. No, sir; I am burgess of that borough, I am the peace officer.

Q. Were you there on the morning of the 6th of July when this trouble or this fight occurred?—A. At Homestead?

Q. Yes, sir.—A. Yes, sir.

Q. Did you see anything or know anything of it of your own knowledge?—A. I saw them carrying the dead and wounded back into the town and I supposed that there might be a conflict about the mill or somewhere else. I could not locate it at the time.

Q. You did not see anything of that?—A. Not of the conflict; no, sir.

Q. Is there anything else you wish to state of your own knowledge?—A. I do not know——

Q. Connected with this trouble between the company and the employés?—A. I do not know that there is anything that would be of interest to this committee. I should prefer the committee ask me anything they think proper. However, I want to go on record to this effect, that I think it was a gigantic conspiracy on the part of this company and their representatives, assisted, aided, and abetted by vicious legislation, to deprive the workmen of their right under the Constitution which this Government guarantees, the right of life and liberty in pursuit of happiness. I think that is a fact and if the opportunity was afforded I suppose we could establish that.

Q. That is your opinion?—A. That is my opinion based on my observations of the preparations and acts, consequences and results, of H. C. Frick and——

Q. Will you state some of those facts?—A. Three years ago—I do not need to go into details about that—we had trouble of a similar character when we got our scale signed three years ago, and it has been already stated that there were 150 or 200 deputies came up there to take possession of the place.

Q. This same place?—A. This same place. The management of the plant were afraid their property would be destroyed and all that sort of thing, and these people came upon one train and went home on another. They did not meet with violence there, but were simply induced to leave.

By Mr. BOATNER:

Q. By the force of moral suasion?—A. Yes, sir; by the force of moral suasion. After considerable trouble of that description the scale was signed and our wages were based on 4 by 4 inch billets. That proposition was made and examined by the officials of the association of which I have the honor of being a member and we concluded it was safe to base the wages on that as on anything in the list. The productive capacities of the mills of the United States at that time were quite limited, and it was protected by the tariff as well as any other article. After going to work feeling assured we had a safe basis upon which we could depend, the McKinley bill came in and reduced—as you will discover by an examination—the tariff upon that identical article upon which our wages were based and raised the tariff on every other article, such as plates, beams, and structural iron. It increased the protection as far as other products, plate, etc., was concerned and decreased the tariff on the identical article on which our wages were based, and that is the reason I say it is a gigantic conspiracy assisted by vicious legislation to wrong the workman of what he is entitled to, a fair day's pay for a fair day's work. That is all I have to say on that point.

Q. You occupied a position at Homestead corresponding to what is generally known as the mayor of a town?—A. Yes, sir.

Q. It was stated by a witness here this morning that most of the people working in that mill owned comfortable homes in the town of Homestead?—A. That is not true.

Q. You say that is not true?—A. That is not true.

Q. If you know, state what is the financial condition of those who do own homes with reference to mortgages, etc?—A. I could not state positively in regard to that, because I am not in that business, but I think H. C. Frick & Co. could more likely furnish considerable data.

Q. Do you know to what extent, if any, Frick & Co. hold mortgages on the homes?—A. I have understood they do.

Q. To any considerable extent?—A. To quite a considerable extent.

Q. Do you know to what extent the employés have money on deposit with the company, if any?—A. There are employés who have money on deposit; I have understood that, but from the limited amount of wages I have made you would not expect me to know very much about mortgages or money on deposit.

Q. You are not one of the high-priced men?—A. No, sir; I am on the other end of it.

Q. The people at that town appear to have a great aversion to the Pinkertons?—A. Yes, sir.

Q. To what is known as the Pinkerton police or detectives?—A. Yes, sir.

Q. What is the reason for that hatred or aversion which they manifested on the 6th?—A. I could not speak from personal experience because I have never hired any of those people, nor have I ever worked where they were hired, nor camped with them. Personally I can not speak myself, but our people as a general thing think they are a horde of cut-throats, thieves, and murderers and are in the employ of unscrupulous capital for the oppression of honest labor.

Q. Do you think there would have been any resistance to any constituted authorities of the State of Pennsylvania?—A. There has not been nor would have been.

Q. Has there been any occasion any time recently when the use of Pinkerton police has caused the loss of life?—A. Yes, sir.

Q. When and where?—A. In the coke regions, so I understand.

Mr. TAYLOR. I would rather object to a sweeping declaration of historical facts by this witness.

The CHAIRMAN. You only heard about it in the coke regions?

The WITNESS. Yes, sir; I never employed any of them and was never where any of them were employed.

By Mr. BOATNER:

Q. Your idea is that the company, after having obtained a scale of wages based upon the market value of steel billets caused the duty on steel billets to be reduced?—A. That is my idea and I further offer this in evidence to show they were active to reduce the only article our wages were based on. The Duquesne mill after our scale was signed was turned from its original product—that is, a mixed product—to a billet mill in order to flood the market and reduce the value upon the identical article upon which our wages were based.

Q. This Duquesne mill produces billets largely?—A. Almost exclusively billets.

Q. Do you know whether or not this company is the largest producer of billets in the United States?—A. I believe the Amalgamated officials would know.

Mr. TAYLOR. Would not that necessarily be a matter of opinion?

Mr. BOATNER. That is what I do not know; do you know?

Mr. TAYLOR. No.

The WITNESS. I can say this, that they produce more billets than any other mill in the United States.

By Mr. TAYLOR:

Q. McLuckie is your name?—A. Yes, sir.

Q. You probably involved in your last answer a matter not from your own information. You do not know personally about it?—A. No, sir; I did not want to go on record that way.

Q. You have been speaking quite largely in your statements from information and reports of other people to you?—A. That is as far as the scale and this question is concerned.

Q. In regard to everything except your opinion upon one or two points. Is not that so? Will you state any fact in your testimony of your own knowledge, any one?—A. I have read the McKinley bill, and I have discovered that the identical article our wages were based on three years ago was one of the articles in the steel list which was reduced, and the other articles we produced at Homestead, such as plates, beams, and structural iron were increased.

Q. Is your memory correct on that?—A. I think so.

Q. Is it not a fact it was decreased on the others also?—A. No, sir.

Q. I have the bill, I believe, in my room. Now, you think that the reduction upon that particular article you produced was by conspiracy?—A. I do.

Q. You think that the less the tariff the less the wages?—A. You are cross examining me, and you are a judge and lawyer and——

Q. No, I am simply a man and a member of this committee. I understood you to say the conspiracy consisted in the McKinley bill reducing the duty upon this particular article of steel, and that that depressed wages?—A. It did.

Q. So, then, it would be true——A. I said it did on this particular article.

Q. Why did it on this particular article?—A. Because it was part of this conspiracy to furnish material——.

Q. How could a conspiracy reduce the price of an article of that sort; a conspiracy of Maj. McKinley and Mr. Frick, I suppose?—A. To reduce our wages.

Q. For that reason the higher the tariff upon an article which you make the better your wages?—A. Not always, sir.

Q. Well, in this case?—A. Look here, we did not get anything——

Q. But in this case you regarded the law to be a conspiracy to reduce your wages by reducing the tariff?—A. Simply because our wages were regulated by the selling price of that article, and by their reducing the value of the article it reduced our wages.

Q. You understand by reducing the tariff you were paid less wages directly or indirectly?—A. In this case lower wages were paid.

Mr. BOATNER. It gave them an excuse to do it.

The WITNESS. It was to their interest at the time.

By Mr. TAYLOR:

Q. Now, have you any other information upon that subject as to the purpose of that act?—A. I do not think of it now.

Q. You do not think of it now, do you?—A. I believe I do not.

Q. Now, if it should turn out that all the other articles produced at that plant were substantially reduced by that same tariff then you would think the conspiracy was more extended than to your line of work?—A. It was not.

Q. I heard a man state once that you could not be so sure of a thing that you might not be a little surer.—A. When you strike the pocket we feel them.

Q. You do not strike the pocket when you look at a law book.—A. You strike some pocket, somebody's.

Q. Well, if you looked at that book again and if you saw it was not so, how would you adjust your opinion?—A. I am not supposed to discuss that.

Q. Then we will leave that.

By the CHAIRMAN:

Q. I understand you to give an opinion, and you base your opinion as to the causes of the reduction in the selling price of billets on the reduction of the duty thereon and the increased product by this company?—A. That is the idea.

Q. That is the idea upon which you based your opinion?—A. Yes, sir.

By Mr. TAYLOR:

Q. Upon that, how could this company make more money by selling their steel at a less price?—A. Simply because the billets were a very small item in the productive capacities of their mill.

Q. You say the Duquesne mill makes nothing else; do you know how many tons they make, or not?—A. I am not in that department and I do not keep any account of that.

Q. The Duquesne mills are almost exclusively devoted to that business?—A. Yes, sir.

Q. Can you tell me how they would make money even then by selling their goods at a less cost than before?—A. The Duquesne mill is not a union mill and does not pay union wages to the people at Duquesne.

Q. No matter about that——?—A. You asked a question, and if you will please excuse me I am going to complete that answer. The Duquesne mill is not a union mill and they have no scale for the price of wages. At any time this company sees fit to reduce those men they have no possible defense, and they can run billets down to almost any price and compel those people to come down with them, and by doing that bring the entire Homestead plant down.

Q. After all they do not make billets at the Homestead plant?—A. They do, some.

Q. Not much?—A. Not a great deal.

Q. Can you tell me again—no matter how little it costs to make billets, suppose they could grow billets in the garden—how can they make money by selling them at $20 instead of $25?—A. I answered that question.

Q. I did not hear you.—A. I said that billets was a small item in the productive capacity of these mills; that while we made possibly 100 tons of billets we made 5,000 tons of beams and plates and structural iron.

Q. Very well. Then another question: What do they want a tariff reduction for if it would be of slight moment to them in order to justify reducing the price of billets?—A. Simply because every article of steel we produce, beams, structural iron and plate, is all based on this 4-inch billet; that is, the wages.

Q. I do not see that that is an answer.—A. Then I will answer better.

Q. I do not know that you can. This is the point: I understand you to say they could make money by putting billets low because it was but a small matter in comparison with the rest of the matter?—A. That is correct.

Q. Why could not they do that without any tariff as well as with?—A. On this 4-inch?

Q. On the billet?—A. They could if they had the scales signed and our wages based on it.

Q. If they can make at the Duquesne mill by selling low why can not they do it regardless of any tariff?—A. Here is the idea. I answered that. I stated if they had our scales signed based on the selling price of these billets then they could do it better than if they had no tariff at all, because it would be that much cheaper.

Q. That is, much cheaper there?—A. They have got to get the minimum basis of our scale low enough which would pay them to take the tariff off.

Q. Do you know the difference between the price of billets here and in England?—A. I have understood it was about $7 a ton difference.

Q. You have understood that?—A. Yes, sir.

Q. I was trying to get at this: If they had the whole control of the matter by reason of just fixing the wages as they pleased, how could they make more money by selling cheap and why would anybody want to enter into a conspiracy so as to get a chance to sell cheap?—A. You have been answered, sir.

Q. You need not answer again unless you wish.—A. I will take pleasure in trying to clear the matter up for you. I said the scale was signed for three years and this was a conspiracy on the part of this company to do by legislation what they had not succeeded in doing with the deputies three years ago.

Q. That scale was good, then, at the time that law was passed for two years more; so they had that. They had two years on that scale from 1890, when the law was passed, and I do not see well why they could not have sold the billets if it was a matter of any consequence what the cost of billets was—but no matter.—A. They were not working two years ago when this Duquesne mill was turned—

Q. I do not know anything about that. Let me get a further idea. You thought a conspiracy existed; of whom did that conspiracy exist; who were the parties to that conspiracy in your judgment?—A. I think the Pacific Railroad people were connected with it.

Q. Who else?—A. The Carnegie and H. C. Frick interest.

Q. Who else?—A. I do not know; it is a pretty hard question.

Q. It must have been the majority in Congress also.

Mr. BOATNER. There is no doubt about that.

The CHAIRMAN. It certainly took a majority to pass the bill.

By Mr. TAYLOR:

Q. So, in your judgment, it would involve Congress as well?—A. I have not said so and I do not wish to insult this committee, and I am not here for that purpose.

Q. You said that was a moving part in the matter, and Congress had something to do with it. Now, you stated that three years ago there was some trouble there on the re-signing of the scale on the last of June or the first of July?—A. Yes, sir.

Q. Who was sheriff of the county then?—A. Mr. McCandlish.

Q. Is he a resident of the city now?—A. Not to my knowledge; I do not believe he is.

Q. You say there was a number of people went up there then?—A. Yes, sir.

Q. Under his protection?—A. Yes, sir.

Q. About how many?—A. I believe 150 or 200.

Q. Were you there?—A. I was at Homestead.

Q. You saw them?—A. Yes, sir; I saw them go up and come back.

Q. How long did they stay?—A. Oh, they stayed a couple of hours.

Q. They were induced to retire?—A. Yes, sir.

Q. Do you mean us to understand that nothing but, as suggested to you, moral suasion was the inducement for them to retire?—A. That is all I heard.

Q. Do you include in moral suasion threats or something of that sort?—A. Oh, no.

Q. Who had possession of the mill then?—A. Mr. Schwab.

Q. Who was he, a workman?—A. No, the general superintendent.

Q. Did he then have actual control of the mill?—A. As far as I know.

Q. Or had it been taken possession of by anybody else?—A. Not to my knowledge.

Q. And there was no difficulty of any access to the mill, to your knowledge?—A. Not to my knowledge.

Q. They returned, and afterwards the scale was signed?—A. Yes, sir.

Q. That is the scale we have last been talking about.—A. Yes, sir.

Q. Now, in reference to the Pinkerton people, you think they were regarded as bad people?—A. Yes, sir; very bad.

Q. Are they regarded as being the same individuals in each case?—A. Oh, no; you know there is an exception to all rules.

Q. You did not understand my question. My idea is, I do not know I am correct, that if there was need of Pinkertons at New York, or in Chicago, or anywhere else, that it would not be the same persons who would go to watch to each of those places, but it would be anybody who would enlist or be hired for that purpose; am I correct about it?—A. I do not know much about the operation.

Q. In other words, it is not a permanent standing party; that the individuals in it vary and change from time to time as occasions require?—A. No, sir; we do not so understand it at all.

Q. Do you understand it to be the same men?—A. It is an organization that is owned and operated, so I understand, by unscrupulous capital.

Q. Unscrupulous capital; is there any difference in capital; is some scrupulous and some unscrupulous?—A. Yes, sir.

Q. So you would give the attribute of conscience to capital?—A. Yes, sir.

Q. Regardless of the owner?—A. There are capitalists who are unscrupulous in the employment of labor, and there are other capitalists who are not, but employ justly and fairly.

Q. Very well; I do not know but what you are right about the Pinkertons, but my idea is the Pinkertons are men hired as they were called for in an emergency. They may be bad men, I do not know anything about it. I have no sympathy with them in any form.

The CHAIRMAN. You mean to characterize them simply as a class?

Mr. TAYLOR. I understand him to think it is a continuing organization.

The WITNESS. In regard to giving you a better idea of the Pinkertons I do not wish this little affair at Homestead to be considered a war between labor and capital. That was a war, if it could be so styled, between laboring men because these Pinkertons and their associates were there under a consideration; they were there under pay, and the person who employed that force was safely placed away by the money that he has wrung from the sweat of the men employed in that mill, employing in their stead workmen to go there and kill the men who made his money.

Q. You did not see who began the shooting?—A. No, sir.

Q. Did you have any experience, or ever meet the Pinkertons anywhere?—A. Not to my knowledge.

Q. Was this a matter of general information which you have received from various sources. In regard to this Homestead population there, you being the magistrate probably will know what others do not know; do you know what is the population of the little city?—A. To some extent; yes, sir.

Q. How much?—A. Between 11,000 and 12,000 within the corporate limits.

Q. Composed mostly of laboring men?—A. Workingmen.

Q. I mean workingmen; I speak of that in its technical meaning.—A. Yes, sir.

Q. You were not there when the town was born, so to speak?—A. I was just across the river at Braddock.

Q. How long ago was that?—A. Nine years ago.

Q. It grew up under the plant, under the works; there was not much of a town before that!—A. I would say it was twelve years ago, I made a mistake in that.

Q. Now, it appeared to me, that those houses, as I looked at them yesterday, were very comfortable, and rather more so than I ordinarily find in towns taking them as a class; they were well painted and looked as if they were large; that is true, is it not?—A. Let me ask you a question—but you are not on the stand.

Q. Well, I will go on the stand.—A. Do you think they are too comfortable?

Q. I do not; not half comfortable enough for any workingman.—A. Thank you.

Q. They pleased me because I saw they looked bright and cheerful, and looked as though they would be comfortable for any family; but not too much so, I assure you.—A. Thank you.

Q. Are they owned by the working people?—A. To some extent.

Q. In a general way?—A. No, sir.

Q. Who does own them?—A. There are people there who have quite a number of houses, and there are others who have not any at all.

Q. Are those people who have a number of houses workmen?—A. They either are or have been; that is, there are not many of our mill men who have large houses.

Q. Those are actual workingmen?—A. They have been. They have been in business, probably, for a number of years.

Q. Do these men who own the property rent the houses or do they sell them?—A. They sell them sometimes and sometimes rent them.

Q. You do not know to what extent, as you stated, houses are mortgaged?—A. No, sir.

Q. Or to what extent the citizens or workmen have deposited their money?—A. No, sir.

Q. But you know this, that there is a bright, beautiful town there?—
A. Happy and prosperous before this horde came there.

Q. I hope it will become so again, Mr. McLuckie.

By Mr. BOATNER:

Q. Were your wages affected, or would have been affected by the proposed change in the schedule?—A. There was no scale submitted to our department.

Q. But under the scale that was submitted upon which the disagreement arose would your wages have been affected?—A. Not that I know of, but I am complaining about what it has done.

TESTIMONY OF W. T. ROBERTS.

W. T. ROBERTS sworn and examined.

By the CHAIRMAN:

Q. Where do you live?—A. I live in Pittsburg.

Q. Are you well acquainted with Homestead?—A. Yes, sir.

Q. Do you work at the Carnegie works there?—A. Yes, sir; I worked there.

Q. How long have you worked there?—A. I will be up there two years next September.

Q. In what department? —A. In the armor plate department.

Q. You are familiar with the terms of the scale of compensation under which workmen were employed in those different departments up there, particularly in four departments, as I understand it, who would be affected by the proposed new scale?—A. Somewhat; yes.

Q. The basis was $25.—A. We are based on $26.50, that is, our wages were based on that three years ago, with a minimum of $25.

Q. Did you have anything to do with the proposition which was submitted by that company to the workmen for a new scale or a new contract during the present year?—A. Yes, sir.

Q. In what capacity did you act, individually, or as a representative of the Amalgamated Association?—A. As a representative of the Amalgamated Association.

Q. Well, state now what that connection was.—A. I will state that on or about January or February, I am not sure about the date, the firm asked the men at Homestead to present their scale. All of these departments up there, and I am not sure, but I believe six departments not now mentioned in the controversy also presented their scale at that time. At least the four departments did, and the one I am engaged in, the 119-inch mill, open hearth No. 1 and open hearth No. 2 presented ours. We presented our scale, and I believe it was two weeks after our committee was sent for to the office and I thought we were going up there to talk over our scale. When we got to the office we were presented with another scale by the representatives of the firm, Mr. Potter, Mr. Childs, Mr. Martin, and somebody else, I think were there. They asked me if I would present their proposition to our people and I told them I would do it providing they would give me a reason why they had demanded such a reduction in the scale submitted by us. They did not seem disposed to talk the matter over and said they had not given it that much thought.

I told them that seemed rather strange to me and asked them to present their side of the question so that we could give some reasons and explain to the men why it was necessary in the first place to make this reduction. Manager Potter then stated it became necessary to make these reductions from the fact that the heaters, for instance, had been making so much money that the firm had come to the conclusion that there must be a reduction made in some of their jobs in that mill. I then said to Mr. Potter: "It seems to me you are very inconsistent from the fact you are not asking reductions from the men who receive this large amount of money; you are asking reductions of men who have been receiving for this last eight weeks not averaging more than $1.50 a day, and the men you claim have been receiving a vast amount of money are not touched by this new proposition." I had been somewhat accustomed to talk of the scales with the manufacturers and from all the experience I had had in that position in the Amalgamated Association, I proposed then and there to go into an argument on the proposition, and I think I told them I thought the first comer ought to be the first served. I took up their scale and asked the reason for making these reductions, commencing at my own job first, being it was first on the scale reduced. I found the heater had suffered no reduction.

Q. Right there just state what your "job," as you term it, was paying you and how the proposition that was made, if it had been accepted, would have affected you.—A. My position on there is first helper. Under the scale that was just expiring, I was receiving $3.07 for 100 tons, when billets were selling at $26.50. Up to the time of the termination of our scale I was receiving 2.90 for 100 tons. The firm proposed to give me 2.13 for 100 tons and we took up that part of it. The heater remained on the proposition they had made, as on the old arrangement, $4.31. I took up that part of the proposition and I said to the gentlemen representing the firm, "Why have you reduced this position," and after considerable talk about this position they allowed that probably it was a mistake made in that particular position; that they had probably not known as much about it as they ought to have known, and then the question was if they did not know that whether they would revoke it if a mistake had been made. Consequently when the ultimatum came out on the 30th day of May, I think, they put at the foot of the scale a clause which put me back again from 2.13 to 3.07. We talked the matter over for some time and we could finally come to no conclusion. Mr. Potter claimed it was necessary to talk this matter over with a committee who had some power. "Now," he said, "I understand your people's position; you have no power to act in the matter; whatever might be done here is subject to alterations."

I then said this, that if we went on talking that scale over and an agreement was arrived at that would be satisfactory to the firm and the men, they need not be a particle afraid of the convention making any alterations in that scale or anybody else making alterations in it. That did not seem to be satisfactory to the representatives of the firm and probably a week after that the superintendent of our department came to me and said, "Billy, I do not like to see this thing kept off. It looks like we were shutting off negotiations." I said, " I have no power in regard to it." He said, "If you could only come back with some power to make concession, some power to settle this, I think the trouble is now over." Knowing, as I knew, the firm had been making preparations for three or four months back—for what I did not know, but they looked suspicious to me, however—I said nothing to him. I knew they had been building this fence around the mill and I thought we might expect trouble in July from the fact that one of the superintendents up there said to me, " Wait until July comes and you will not

get paid for that gold mine of yours," meaning our jobs down there.
I went to the men and told them that things looked in that kind of
condition that if they could give any power to make the best arrangements possible I thought it would be best for them. After considerable
talk with the men they gave that privilege. I immediately notified
Mr. Hunt to go and notify Mr. Potter that I had a promise from the
men in that department to make any amicable arrangement that could
be made and that we were ready and willing to consult with the firm
with that end in view at any time. He notified Mr. Potter. On that
day, the 30th day of May, I think, when we went in, Mr. Potter read
off the scale and gave the scale proposed for each department. I did
tell Mr. Potter I did not think it was fair after I went to the men and
got the power to make such concessions that the firm should do that.
I did tell him I did not think it was fair to cut off negotiations in that
manner. There it ended until the conference on the 23d day of June
in Mr. Frick's office, when it ended there absolutely. That is all I
know about this thing, only I do know the men in our department have
done everything in their power in order to have this thing adjusted in
a satisfactory manner.

Mr. BOATNER. Your opinion is that if the matter could have been
kept open a few days it could have been amicably adjusted.

The WITNESS. That was my opinion at that time; yes, sir.

By the CHAIRMAN:

Q. What did they pay you per month or per day?—A. Well, there
is a curious fact in connection with the pay there. You could hardly
get at it. I know this by the statement that they could make $147 in
twenty some days in May. That may be so, but there are days and
weeks and sometimes months when not one-half of that is made. Some
days I have worked twelve hours a day and earned 98 cents.

Q. To what is that variation attributable?—A. To the want of steel
generally; sometimes to the breakage of the machinery.

Q. From a want of material to operate the mill?—A. Yes, sir; to
operate the mill.

Q. Do you know about what would be the average percentage of the
reduction of the new scale proposed, between that and the old scale?—A.
The average reduction in the armor-plate mill, leaving off the men
they have left off the new scale, would be 18 per cent on the $26.50
basis; besides, if the scale ran down to the minimum they proposed,
that is, $23, there would be another 8 per cent added to that.

Q. Do you know the labor cost of the production of a ton of steel in
the department in which you worked?—A. There is no possible way
for us to find that out any more than what our scale would tell us. I
will state that while up in the office on the first occasion when they
presented this scale to us, I said, "Why do you ask a reduction; you
get your armor plate rolled for less than any plate in the world, not
only in America, but any place in the world; no place in the world rolls
as cheap as we can roll it, and why should you ask it be rolled any
cheaper." Then the remark was made that it was not a question of
tonnage, but it was a question of pay roll. That brought out the discussion in regard to making this reduction on the lower-paid men and
leaving the higher-paid men where they were and not touching them.

By Mr. BYNUM:

Q. State as near as you can the classes in which this reduction would
have operated?—A. The classes of people?

Q. Yes.—A. Well, there is one man there who makes 1.33 a 100 tons. He is a cranesman; that is, by the proposed rate. He is now receiving 2.23 on the $26.50 basis. You will understand here that the heater receives 4.31. He stands no reduction, but the man who received 2.23 is reduced from 2.23 to 1.33 on their proposition. These are the people that have been reduced in the plate mill. Not only that, but in several instances the engineers received even a greater reduction. The firm claims that the improved machinery has increased the output of the mill. Now, there have been two engineers in our mill and if the output has increased their work has correspondingly increased. You can not add an increased output in the armor-plate department that does not increase the labor of the engineer, roller, and furnace men. There can not possibly be any machinery put in there that does not increase their labor also. Now, in regard to the engineers in the armor-plate department, if there were an increased output it would increase their labor twofold, from the fact that the stuff is heavier that they have got to pull through. They have got to take hold of the lever and stand and pull with all their might and keep it open, which necessarily makes the work hard. They propose to reduce those people something like 50 per cent. They proposed to put them back from tonnage rates to day rates, which would give them about 1 cent an hour less than they got when the mill was first put into operation.

Q. The impression was made on my mind that the only reduction of this class was by reason of the reducing of the price of the minimum?—A. No, sir. There is an 18 per cent reduction of this that has not got anything to do with the reduction of the minimum on billets. There is an additional 8 per cent, that is, provided billets run down to $23, which takes place immediately.

By Mr. TAYLOR:

Q. You stated you spoke to one of the company's representatives and asked "How was this?" and he replied, "I am not speaking of tonnage, but it is a question of pay roll," or something to that effect. Who was that man?—A. Mr. Potter; he said it was not a question of tonnage, but a question of pay roll.

Q. What did you understand that to mean, that they would prefer to pay in some other way than by tonnage because that was too large, the pay roll would be too large?—A. I intended to try to demonstrate to that firm that they got a lower tonnage rate than any other mill in the world, because they are not paying in that department one-third they are paying in other mills of similar character. To say they have got mills of the same kind would be saying something that is not true. For instance, heating. Men receive in our mill only 4.07 cents. Our heater finishes the plate for that. There is not another mill that does that.

Q. You are going away from my point. I wanted to get at the idea as to what you understood by Mr. Potter's remark that it was not a question of tonnage but of pay roll?—A. I simply tried to convey to Mr. Potter that they were getting lower tonnage rates.

Q. And his answer was that it was not a question of the tonnage rate but of pay roll?—A. Yes, sir; that is it.

Q. Was that based upon the idea that he claimed that the tonnage was increasing, that the output of tonnage was large, and it made the pay roll larger than anyone else paid if they were paid by the tonnage?—A. That was his idea.

Q. And he wanted to get at some definite way of paying so the pay roll could not be increased in that way?—A. You must understand, also, when he made that remark I called his attention to the fact that the men whom they claimed were drawing too much money were not affected by that scale and that——

Q. I am not making any point as to how much they pay, but I wanted to get at your meaning, as I do not know I understand it rightly. You say there are some people you named, who by this proposed scale get one cent an hour less than when they first went there; what was this class of workmen?—A. Engineers in the armor plate department.

Q. What was their pay then?—A. Their pay was then, when the mill first started, $3.25 per day.

Q. How many hours makes a day?—A. Twelve hours.

Q. They were paid then by tonnage?—A. They were paid the last three years by tonnage.

Q. Were they paid then by tonnage?—A. No, sir.

Q. They were paid so much a day by the day?—A. Yes, sir.

Q. You spoke of the fact that you were idle sometimes by accidents to the machinery, breakage, or by the fact that there was no material; that does not occur very often.—A. Well, it occurred very often during this spring and last winter.

Q. It would hardly be to the interest of the parties to allow the machinery and hands to be idle, so it is simply accidents that might occur?—A. Yes, sir.

By Mr. BOATNER:

Q. Did you understand when the superintendent stated that it was not a question of tonnage but a question of pay roll, that he meant the company was paying the men too much money?—A. I suppose that he meant the men were drawing too much money out of the office to suit them.

Q. The idea was to reduce the pay roll and expenses?—A. The idea I suppose was, from what he said, to reduce the pay roll and expenses.

By the CHAIRMAN:

Q. Were you there when the Pinkertons came?—A. No, sir.

Q. You do not know anything of that of your own knowledge?—A. No, sir.

Q. Are there any facts you wish to state? And, if so, state them.—A. No; not unless the committee wish to ask me further. I heard the question debated here this morning in regard to the expiration of our scale. It seemed to me that almost everyone who talked upon the matter evaded the vital point in the matter. I can state a reason why we object to ending the scale in the winter time, and that is, that the burnt child dreads the fire. We know from past experience—at least, I do—that when winter time comes around and our contract ends in the winter—I do not know that the Carnegie firm would do it, but I know people who have stood just as high in the estimation of the working people of this country who have done it—they take that opportunity at that time of the year to starve us into submission. They have done it on every occasion. We, as working people, have fought for this principle we have got in the organization from the very earliest inception of the organization, until to-day every manufactory in the United States, with the exception probably of one or two, those run by nonunion, are willing at all times to sign our scale from one summer month to another. In the winter time when they throw us idle there is always a class in this country known as "snow birds" who never work in the summer time. They crowd our mills in the winter time, and we are almost crowded out in the winter time by those people whom no manufacturer can employ in the summer, but they are always ready and willing to do this work in the winter time, after we have labored all through the summer, and they ought not to require of us that when we come to the winter months these idlers should drop in there to take our places and then after all the damage has been done and spring comes on and we have been out four or five months that we should be compelled to go back and work for the wages this rabble has made for us.

By Mr. TAYLOR:

Q. These fellows are a sort of tramps?—A. They are tramps or what are called "snow birds."

Q. Snow birds are out of doors in the winter time, but these seem to get in.

By the CHAIRMAN:

Q. The objection to the proposition of the company making the contract terminate at the end of the year was the objection that you have stated, that you would probably have the advantage of the company at the end of June and that they would have the advantage of you if the contract was made terminating at the end of the year?—A. I wish to state that to allay any fear of that the representatives of the firm and Mr. Frick himself came down there and insinuated that they could not have it expire in the summer time, on account of their having the biggest part of their orders to fill in the summer time. We made the proposition that we were willing to make our scales to run three, five, or more years; that we were willing to run them ten years if they saw fit, thereby doing away with that idea, and on the sliding-scale basis, why, we could not possibly get advantage of them any more than they could of us, and we were willing to extend the time of the scale for ten years, to do away with that idea that we were seeking to catch him in the summer time when he was busy.

Q. Some one here was speaking on the proposition that three months notice must be given if there was an intention on the part of the employés to terminate the contract and if that was not done it should continue one year longer; was a proposition of that sort made?—A. Yes, sir; (reading) "To take effect July 1, 1892, and to continue in force until January 1, 1894, and thereafter until terminated at the end of any calendar year by three months' notice given in writing by either party, provided it be accepted before June 24, 1892. Basis, $26.50 billets; minimum, $22 billets. This scale to be subject to revision in the event of the introduction of new methods and appliances. All extras to be discontinued unless otherwise provided for." We took the three months, which was not at all necessary in the first place. We were imitators in that respect.

Mr. BOATNER. Has the Amalgamated Association any agreements expiring in December?

A. Only in one rail mill in South Chicago. That was because—in the first place the Carnegie firm owned the rail mill at Braddock and that scale they have forced upon them expires at the end of the year and people who are willing to be governed and obey the Amalgamated Association rates should not be discriminated against and so their scale was allowed to expire at the same date.

By Mr. BRODERICK:

Q. Have you discussed with the working people the proposition as to having arbitration provided by law for settling these matters?—A. No, sir; I have not.

Q. Have you thought of that subject yourself?—A. I have, yes, sir; considerably.

Q. If you have any ideas about that please state them briefly.—A. In this instance in particular it would work admirably, and it seems we can not get anything else to work. I can not see what else is going to be done for the working people if the working people are to receive the same protection the manufacturers are receiving, and they will certainly have to have some method to compel the manufacturers to submit to a board of arbitration their profits, and if it is a just one I suppose, or should think, that the workingmen will get a just proportion of them, and that is the only solution of the labor problem. That is my idea of it.

Mr. BOATNER. Do you think if the manufacturer is protected to an extent of 50, 75, or 100 per cent, there ought to be some means to compel him to divide it up?

The WITNESS. I certainly do.

Mr. BOATNER. I think so too.

Mr. BYNUM. That would be a division between the laborer and the capitalists and the poor consumer would be left out in the cold. Who would take care of him?

The WITNESS. I understand the laborer is largely the consumer.

By the CHAIRMAN:

Q. I will ask you another question. Are you familiar with the wages paid for similar kinds of work in other mills doing the same or similar work; if so, state it?—A. Yes, sir; I am acquainted with the wages paid in other mills to some extent for similar work in the structural department, and the difference in favor of Carnegie is fully 30 to 40 per cent.

Q. You mean they pay more?—A. I mean they pay less.

Q. To what mills do you allude?—A. I will take first the 23-inch structural iron mill to compare with Jones & Laughlin's Iron Works on the south side, one of their principal competitors. For instance, the roller at Jones & Laughlin's receives 70 cents per ton. The roller on the 23-inch mill in Homestead receives about 22 or 23 cents per ton.

Q. Is there any difference in the productive capacity of the machinery, making it easier to produce more per day or per week in the Carnegie mills than the other?—A. The difference is in favor of Jones & Laughlin's over this 23-inch mill.

Q. With the same exertion of labor, is the difference in the amount produced larger than in the Homestead mill?—A. Jones & Laughlin's mill is a more modern mill—that is, the 18-inch mill—than the Carnegie 23-inch mill, and will do more work a day and easier.

Q. If there is any other comparison you may state it.—A. Yes, sir; in the plate mill. Their plate-mill roller receives 14 cents a ton, and the rollers in the other they pay 70 cents a ton.

Q. Do they compete with Homestead?—A. They have to compete in the market with Carnegie, Phipps & Co.

Q. Is the market for the production the same, or do you know about that?—A. The same product comes from both; that is, a similar product comes from both firms and they go into the same market. As the manufacturers say, they only get what those people can not fill.

Q. Which people?—A. The Carnegie people.

Q. They only get——.—A. They only get from the market what these people can not supply.

Q. I do not know that I understand you?—A. For instance, say here is 100 tons in the market to be sold to-day and Carnegie could not supply 100 tons, these other people would get what they could not supply.

Q. From what does that result; the purchaser generally goes to the market where he can buy the same article cheapest?—A. The result is when times are dull and all the other mills are idle Carnegie is running.

Q. How do you account for that, as I do not quite understand it. If these other mills are producing the same material and the market price of that produced at the Homestead works would be the same, why would they give the preference?—A. You will understand the market price is what these people make it; they make the price in the market.

Q. What people?—A. The Carnegie people.

Q. How can they do that?—A. Because they get a monopoly of it almost.

Q. You speak, however, of another firm in here?—A. I spoke of one of the oldest firms in the United States of America.

Q. Is that owned and controlled by the Carnegie people?—A. No, sir; and as a consequence they have done very little work in that line during the last year.

Q. This is a rival mill?—A. In this structural iron.

Q. That is to say, it is engaged in the same kind of product?—A. In the structural business; yes, sir.

Q. They would have a market for all they could produce, I suppose, on the same terms with Carnegie & Co.?

Mr. TAYLOR. But he says the Carnegie people, by making cheaper, undersell the others.

The CHAIRMAN. I did not understand him to say that.

The WITNESS. I will just call your attention to a fact. When the first six months was by, and we went down to the office to fix the rates for the coming three months on the sliding scale, it was agreed then we were to take them from the quoted price on the market at 50 cents off the lowest quotation. Mr. Abbott at that time said their quotations were an even $2 below the market quotation. That is where I am taking it from.

Q. So that the Carnegie Company, controlling the market to the extent of their ability to supply it, did undersell the other mill?—A. Yes, sir; that is what I meant to say.

By Mr. BYNUM:

Q. Their ability to undersell was caused by low wages?—A. Yes, sir.

Q. I can not understand the immense difference you speak of between the other mill and Carnegie's. You say the roller at Carnegie's gets 14 cents a ton and they get 70 at the other establishment?—A. There is a little difference, but there is not any material difference in the work these people do; but in the Carnegie mill the roller can turn out probably twice or three times what he can at the Oliver mill, for instance; they do not turn out as much in this mill as they do in Carnegie's.

By Mr. BRODERICK:

Q. The impression I got was that this mill does not run all the time; does that have anything to do with their giving higher wages?—A. I do not hardly think that this other mill could run when the market was bad, and there was not a great demand for the stuff in the market; they could not work for nothing.

Q. Does the fact that it does not run and give employment to the men constantly have anything to do with their giving them more when they are employed?—A. They seem satisfied to pay what they are paying; they do not seem to think the men are earning too much.

By Mr. TAYLOR:

Q. Did you ever work for them?—A. I worked for Jones & Laughlin's fourteen years.

Q. When did you quit?—A. Two years ago last April.

Q. And you have been working at Carnegie's works?—A. At Homestead.

Q. What does the roller get now in Carnegie's mill, when he rolls at 23 cents a ton?—A. The roller in the Carnegie mill I do not think can make any more than $10 a day. In these other mills—you see, the only difference in Carnegie's mill is the roller pays no one and in the other mill the roller pays the rougher 30 per cent of his wages, leaving 49 cents clear to himself.

Q. In the first place, the Carnegie output is three or four times over what it is at the other mill?—A. Not in this particular mill.

Q. Which particular mill?—A. The one mentioned, the plate mill. In their plate mill the output is greater than any other plate mill I know of.

Q. In what other mill at Carnegie's do they get 23 cents a ton?—A. Take the 23-inch structural mill.

Q. I understand he gets at the Carnegie mill 23 cents a ton and that he will make not over $10 a day clear to himself; that is, he makes that and has to pay nobody, but in the other mill the roller has to pay his assistant?—A. He gets 49 cents.

Q. He gets 49 cents a ton and has to pay 30 cents out?—A. Not out of that. He gets 70 cents and pays 30 per cent of that to his rougher.

Q. In that mill does he roll as many tons as they do in the Carnegie mill?—A. Yes, sir.

Q. How much would he make a day?—A. In this other mill all the way from $25 to $30 a day.

Q. After paying their assistants?—A. After paying their assistants.

Q. That is a pretty good price.

By Mr. BYNUM:

Q. How many of these rollers are employed in these different mills who get these high wages. You say there is one employed in Jones & Laughlin's now, how many are employed at Carnegie & Co.'s?—A. There are not any at Carnegie's mill who get those wages.

Q. I mean those who get the high wages of $10 a day?—A. There is one in the 23-inch, and one in the 33-inch, and two, or probably three, rollers in the plate mill.

Q. About five you think out of 4,000 employés?—A. That is about all.

By Mr. BOATNER:

Q. Is not there one in the 23-inch mill?—A. I mentioned that.

Q. Are there not two in the 23-inch mill?—A. Yes; they work double turns.

By Mr. BYNUM:

Q. These rollers are responsible for the character and quality of the product turned out?—A. Yes, sir.

Q. Are they held responsible if there is any condemnation of the material?—A. Yes, sir.

By the CHAIRMAN:

Q. How are they held responsible?—A. They are held responsible—in a general way they are held responsible to the firm for the quality of the work they turn out, but of course they are not expected in every instance to pay for it, although in some instances they have to when it is spoiled. It is a very hard matter to get at the spoiling of stuff in a rolling mill. The management may say it is spoiled because the men did not know how to work it, when it is really the material put in the stuff.

Q. How many years have you been engaged in that kind of work?—A. Well, I am now—let me see—I have been engaged in that kind of work since I was a boy of 10 years of age and I am now 36.

Q. Where did you learn your trade?—A. I commenced to work in England.

Q. You are a native of England?—A. Yes, sir.

By Mr. TAYLOR:

Q. How many times during all your life have you known a roller to be obliged to pay for damages for bad work?—A. I never paid any particular attention to that at all, but it came under my notice about four years ago in Pittsburg in the Wayne Iron Works.

Q. Do you know it to be paid there?—A. Yes, sir.

Q. How much?—A. Thirty-odd dollars.

Q. Do you know of any other case in your life where a roller has been obliged to pay for damages on condemnation?—A. These things often take place, and an outsider would not be likely to know.

Q. I am only asking about what you know and if you do not know you can say so.—A. A representative of Jones & Laughlin's says it has been done there.

Q. But I am asking you?—A. I do not know that myself.

TESTIMONY OF JOSEPH H. GRAY.

JOSEPH H. GRAY sworn and examined.

By the CHAIRMAN:

Q. Have you at any time recently acted as deputy sheriff to the sheriff of this county?—A. I have since the 5th day of July up to the present time. I just left Gen. Snowden's headquarters.

Q. You commenced work as deputy sheriff on the 5th of July?—A. Yes, sir.

Q. Will you state to the committee what you did on that day and subsequently?—A. I went with the sheriff to Homestead on the 10:40 train from Pittsburg, and I remained with him until, I think, we left there about 2 o'clock and returned to the city. We looked over the works and we met Mr. O'Donnell and the advisory committee at Homestead, and the sheriff told them that he was going to put some deputies in the mill that afternoon, and asked if he would be permitted to do so without molestation or without violence, and at the first interview there was a disposition shown by them to allow him to take possession.

Q. Who were they?—A. Well, I do not know all the names, but I know Mr. O'Donnell, Mr. Lynch, and I was introduced to several others.

Q. It was some of the officials of the advisory committee of citizens and laborers up there at Homestead?—A. Yes, sir. They invited the sheriff and his deputies to go to the mill to see if there was any disorder, and we were accompanied by a part of the committee down to the gate, and we went through the mill and returned and met those people still waiting at the gate, and they escorted us back to the hall which we had left, and they held another meeting and they invited the sheriff and myself to retire, and afterwards they notified him that they would not be responsible for the admission of any person, and the sheriff left. They escorted us down to the river bank and we took a skiff and came across to the Baltimore and Ohio road, and came to the city. When we came to the city we met at the sheriff's office Mr. Knox, of the firm's attorneys, and Mr. Petty, the sheriff's attorney, and we were informed that there would be some people taken up that night, and the sheriff authorized me to go with that boat.

Q. What people?—A. Well, they were Pinkerton men.

Q. How many of them, and where were they?—A. I met them at Davis Island Dam, below the city. I went aboard the boat when it landed, about 10 o'clock.

Q. Were you authorized by the sheriff to go as deputy sheriff to take charge of those men?—A. No, sir; I was there to protect and preserve the peace.

Q. You were to go with them on the boat?—A. Yes, sir; I was to go with those men to Homestead and preserve the peace if a breach of the peace was threatened.

Q. They were to be put into the Carnegie works?—A. Yes, sir; as watchmen.

Q. Well, what time did you proceed with them on the boat?—A. They arrived at about a quarter of 12, I think, and marched on the boat.

Q. That was on the 5th?—A. On the evening of the 5th.

Q. Do you mean to say it was a quarter to 12 at night?—A. Yes, sir, and the boat, as soon as the men were aboard, cast anchor and started up the river and we passed this place and arrived at Lock No. 1, I think near 1 or 2 o'clock, and there was an accident happened to one of the boats, that is one of the tow boats, which consumed some time, and the tow boat, *Little Bill*, took the two boats and towed them and we proceeded to Homestead.

Q. Where were the Pinkerton men, on the boat or on the barges?— A. They were on the barges.

Q. Were they armed at that time?—A. I did not see any arms at that time.

Q. Well, describe your journey up there.—A. Before we arrived there Mr. Potter, the superintendent of the Carnegie Company, was called into——

Q. Was he on the boat?—A. He was; yes, sir; he was called into the cabin and Capt. Hinde and another Pinkerton officer, and we gave them some instructions that in case of any trouble under no consideration were they to fire their guns unless in self-preservation, and not until some person was wounded or killed of their party. They went back to the barges, and when we came in sight of Homestead whistles began to blow there, some miles away, and some steamboat lying at the wharf, and all through the town, and there was a firing on the wharf, a promiscuous firing of small arms, pistols, etc. We ran on up past the crowd, and there was some fog on the river, but we could see a congregation of people on the river banks, and we were going pretty rapidly. When we got up pretty well and as we were nearing the shore I commenced to hear balls rattle against the boat fired by small-arms, but before we passed into the Carnegie place—there is a fence running down to the river dividing it from the line—there was a ball came through the pilot-house. I examined the glass, and I concluded that that was a rifle ball. Another struck the whistle and another struck the smoke stack, and we had a good deal of firing of that kind. When we got in near the shore these people followed us up pretty rapidly, and when they struck the fence they could not get through, so they tore it down, and therefore we gained on them and were ahead of them all the way to the landing. I could see the crowd coming, and when we reached the landing they came down through the mill property in a large number. When we came to the bank the captain asked Mr. Potter to send a couple of men out to assist them in tying the boat, which he did. Capt. Rodgers came and Mr. Potter and he sent some person out to protect him when he was tying the boat, and immediately upon his going to tie his boat they commenced coming down over the embankment and to the water's edge, and very soon thereafter commenced firing.

Q. Who commenced firing?—A. The mob on the bank.

Q. Had the gang plank been put out?—A. I could not say that. I was on the upper deck of the boat and could not see over the top of the barge, and I could not say what the men were doing on the front of the barge.

Q. Up to that time had any Pinkerton men or any person on the boat or barges fired?—A. Not a gun.

Q. You swear that the firing began from the crowd on the shore?—A. I do most positively. No gun was fired from that boat until after there had been very considerable firing from the front.

Q. What did you, as deputy sheriff, do?—A. There?

Q. Yes; did you give any orders to the crowd?—A. No, sir; I never gave any orders.

Q. You gave no orders to the crowd on shore?—A. They ran away. When that firing ceased there was no person to be seen on the bank, they ran away back.

Q. You did not give any orders to the Pinkerton men there?—A. No, sir. Capt. Hinde came to me and asked me if I would authorize or would swear them in as deputy sheriffs, and I said "No, that there was no necessity for that at that time," and they wanted to know what their legal position was. I stated to them that Mr. Potter was the representative of the company and he had a perfect right to put them on that ground and that they had a perfect right to defend their lives in the prosecution of their duty.

Q. Did any of the Pinkertons get on shore at all?—A. I think not. However, I could not say because I could not see the front end of that boat from where I stood.

Q. It was not a comfortable place to go to see?—A. Not just at that moment; no.

Q. Was that the front end or the bow of the boat where the shooting was the thickest?—A. Yes, sir.

Q. You did not care about going to that end to see what was going on there?—A. Well, sir, I had been there before and I was there afterwards; I mean under fire.

Q. You have been an officer and a soldier?—A. Yes, sir.

Q. And had experience?—A. I have had some experience.

Q. And commanded men?—A. Yes, sir.

Q. Did you hear any command given by the captain of the Pinkertons to fire or to advance or any order to those people on shore to retire?—A. Yes, sir; I heard the Pinkerton men say to those people that they must retire. They came out at the rear of the barges and wanted to make speeches to the crowd on the boat, that is, the Pinkerton men had come outside and there I saw the men armed for the first time, and I do not think I saw more than ten men with arms in their hands.

Q. Did you try to make speeches to the men on shore?—A. No, sir; one of our number warned those people they must go away. It was a very short speech, and, when the firing was over, there was no person there. They ran away, and remained quiet until the time the steamboat left there to take the wounded, which were carried on the steamboat. It was perfectly quiet then.

Q. Did you remain there? If so, how long?—A. I think we were there about an hour after the firing was over.

Q. Did you leave on the boat?—A. I did.

Q. And you carried the wounded up the river?—A. Yes, sir.

Q. Did you return with the boat?—A. I did.

Q. What was the condition of affairs at that time?—A. Well, sir, when we came within gunshot of the works, they opened a very brisk fire on us.

Q. On the boat?—A. Yes, sir; fired on the boat from both sides of the river, so hot that the engineer—especially the pilot—had to leave the wheel and come down to save his life.

Q. Where were the barges then?—A. They were lying at the mill, just where we left them.

Q. Was any fighting going on there then?—A. There was some fighting, I think, but not very much. They turned their batteries on the boat.

Q. Did you notice any firing from the barges at that time?—A. I did not notice any from the barges when we were coming down.

Q. Do you know what became of the barges?—A. Not personally. I came to the city on the boat.

Q. You came on down straight to the city?—A. Yes, sir.

Q. You did not hear any person give any order to the Pinkertons?—A. No, sir.

Q. And you did not see any attempt to land or go on shore?—A. Except the order Mr. Potter gave these two officers of the Pinkertons about preserving the peace.

By Mr. BRODERICK:

Q. In going up there did you give the usual signals going up?—A. Yes, sir; they whistled a good many times. They whistled at the locks and the boat which was disabled whistled a distress signal, whatever it was, for the boat ahead to come to her rescue.

Q. Did they have lights on board?—A. Yes, sir; the boat was lighted up.

Q. How far were you from the landing when you first discovered they were shooting at the boat? A. We probably were a half a mile or more.

Q. The shooting commenced before that, did it not?—A. Yes, sir. I regarded the shooting—I heard of its being a signal to assemble and I never thought they were going to shoot on the boat until they commenced to strike us.

Q. Balls began to strike the boat when you were about half a mile away?—A. Yes, sir; fully half a mile, perhaps more.

Q. Where were you when the firing was first returned from the boat?—A. We were at the landing.

Q. About how rapid did the boat move?—A. We ran up very slowly until we came inside the inclosure of the works, and then we ran up at an increased speed to the landing. I know we kept ahead of the crowd coming up the river bank and we were there before they were.

Q. Now, in regard to the arms which were on the boat, when did they commence opening and getting them out?—A. Well, I do not know that, sir.

Q. Did you have charge or have anything to do with the arms?—A. No, sir.

Q. Do you know under whose control they were?—A. I suppose the Pinkerton people.

Q. You got on the boat here?—A. Yes, sir; below the city several miles.

Q. How far below?—A. It is 5 miles below; I presume 4 or 5 miles.

By the CHAIRMAN:

Q. I will ask you what river that is, so it may go into the record.—A. The Monongahela River.

Q. It is navigable for some distance above Homestead?—A. Yes, sir; slack-water navigation.

Mr. BRODERICK. You knew they were Pinkertons when you went on the boat?

The WITNESS. Yes, sir.

By Mr. BOATNER:

Q. You say you were along for the purpose of preserving the peace?—A. Yes, sir.

Q. Did you do anything toward preserving the peace?—A. Yes, sir; I think I did.

Q. What did you do?—A. I advised Mr. Potter and these Pinkerton officers at the time the trouble was apparent that they had the right only to protect their lives.

Q. When you reached the landing were there some moments before the firing commenced?—A. Well, there were very few.

Q. You said that the people rushed right down to the water's edge?—A. Yes, sir.

Q. Now, at that time did you inform those people in any way that the men there were under the protection of the legal authorities and did you command the peace and order them to disperse and give them information that an officer was present?—A. There was no opportunity to do that in the moment of time between the running into the shore and the firing.

Q. Well, the sheriff swore here this morning that you were along to preserve the peace and to order the men away in the event of a conflict?—A. Yes, sir.

Q. To order the Pinkerton people to withdraw; did you order them to withdraw or take any steps to take them away when you found there was to be an armed resistance to their landing?—A. Well, not at that time, but I intended when we returned. I thought an hour or two hours' time would give the people there an opportunity to consider the situation in which everybody was placed. I thought it would give the advisory committee time to exercise their power. On my return there, there was no person on the boat except the captain and the crew and myself and then I intended to exercise the power vested in me to prevent any further conflict.

Q. You found on your return the conflict was going on at an increased rate?—A. That was the reception we received when we came within gunshot.

Q. So you were compelled to go on by and leave the boat there with those men on it?—A. Yes, sir.

Q. Then there was no exercise of your authority as deputy sheriff on the trip except to advise Mr. Potter and the Pinkerton people that they had no right to do anything except to protect their lives and act in self-defense?—A. I want to say Mr. Potter never for a moment, when I talked to him, in his demeanor thought but what he would get peaceable possession. When we passed Lock No. 1 and there was no congregation of people there he was very much gratified at it. He expected to be met at Lock No. 1 by some of those people, but when we passed that point he was most confident then that he would go on the premises without any molestation except, perhaps, a demonstration.

Q. Well, at the time you left there you to state that the people had all retired and all was quiet?—A. Yes, sir.

Q. Was it the idea of the Pinkerton people at that time that they would go in and take possession without further resistance—I mean when you left there with the wounded?—A. Yes, sir; those men seemed to be very calm, and there was no display on their part when we left there of any intention of fighting except this. There was some men in the pump-house who had their guns there; we could see them, and the Pinkerton men had also sharp-shooters on the boat watching them.

Q. After the firing subsided and the people retired why did not you go out on the bank and inform those people you were there as a representative of the sheriff to put those people in possession of the works and command them in the name of the law to retire and not interfere with their taking possession of this property?—A. There was no person within speaking distance, except one foreigner who came down and undertook to make a speech, and he retired very soon. There were two or three newspaper men sitting on the bank.

Q. What did he say?—A. Well, I did not understand him.

Q. The newspaper men seem to have been in sight all the time.—A. Yes, sir; I think one was sketching the surroundings.

By the CHAIRMAN:

Q. Where was he?—A. He was sitting right out in front of the boat.

Q. Out on the bank?—A. Yes, sir.

Q. He did not seem to be apprehensive of danger?—A. No, sir; there was no person there to disturb him.

By Mr. BOATNER:

Q. To come back to my question, then, the only official act you did in the discharge of the duty imposed upon you to preserve the peace was to give the people the advice to which you have referred?—A. Yes, sir.

Q. There was no opportunity for you to preserve the peace otherwise?—A. No, sir; not with that mob.

Q. What time did you reach Pittsburg on the return trip?—A. I think I reported to the sheriff's office very soon after 12 o'clock.

Q. Was the sheriff advised of the assault which was being made upon the boat and the attempt to burn it with coal oil?—A. Yes, sir; they knew that before we arrived, and I reported to the sheriff that something must be done and that soon; that we had been driven past and not permitted to land and that something must be done and that very soon, or there would be no Pinkerton people left alive there in a short time.

Q. Did the sheriff do anything?—A. Yes, sir.

Q. What did he do?—A. Well, I know he spoke to Mr. Weihe and he was in conference with people in regard to the situation. I do not know what he expected to do, but I know he went away late in the night to bring them away.

Q. He tried to relieve these people by negotiations but he did not call for a posse or go there himself or take active steps to relieve the Pinkertons of the great danger they were in at the time, that you know of?—A. No, sir.

By Mr. BYNUM:

Q. Who was the representative of the firm who was there?—A. Mr. Potter.

Q. Where did Mr. Potter go?—A. Mr. Potter when he left there came to Port Terry and went over to the Bessemer Works at Braddock and reported to the office in Pittsburg the situation of affairs. Mr. Potter said to me "I will not take the responsibility of any more bloodshed."

Q. I am not asking you what he said; then he did not go back to the boat?—A. We did not wait for Mr. Potter.

Q. When you came back was it your intention to take the barges away?—A. Yes, sir.

Q. Was there any appearance of a determination to burn them or destroy them as you came back?—A. Yes, sir; they were accumulating the oil along there when we came past.

Q. Where did you see them accumulating oil?—A. They were rolling something down the bank, but we did not have free access to that side of the boat to observe just what they were doing.

Q. The view was a little obscured then as you passed by?—A. Yes, sir.

Mr. BOATNER. You only caught occasional glimpses?

The WITNESS. Yes, sir.

By Mr. BYNUM:

Q. You landed at 12 o'clock?—A. Yes, sir.

Q. Did the sheriff send anybody up there at all; you did not go yourself?—A. I did not go.

Q. Did you go back there during that day?—A. No, sir; not that day.

Q. Did the Pinkerton men on the boat make any signal for you to come and get them?—A. I do not think so; I think they were pretty well housed up then.

Q. When you first landed there you say there was no firing done by the men on the boat until after there was firing from the crowd on shore; do you know whether any person was hurt on the boat before the firing was begun from the boat?—A. I could not say. They carried one wounded man in very soon; the officer who died afterwards.

Q. Who was that man?—A. Capt. Cline.

Q. Were any other persons there with whom you were personally acquainted?—A. Yes, sir.

Q. State who they were.—A. There was a young fellow, a river man, I can not give his name, who was with me on an expedition at the time of the flood at Johnstown. I took two boats up the Alleghany River to clear out the drift and look for bodies in that flood, and there was one of the crew on this boat who was on this other boat.

Q. He is not a resident here?—A. Yes, sir.

Q. What is his name?—A. Now, I never knew his name, but I knew the man.

Q. Can you find it?—A. Certainly.

Q. He remained there all the time?—A. Yes, sir.

Q. He remained on the barges with the men?—A. Yes, sir; and he did a very heroic thing that night; we had a man to fall overboard and he rescued him.

Q. Was that going up?—A. Yes, sir.

Q. He stayed on the barges all day?—A. Yes, sir; we did not lose any of our crew.

Q. Did he go away with the boat with you and the captain or did he remain with the Pinkertons?—A. Oh, no; he was one of the crew of the boat.

Q. You do not know anybody who remained on the barges?—A. Not personally.

By Mr. BOATNER:

Q. On your return trip did you float by or run by, or how; did the boat drift by or did it come by under steam?—A. The boat drifted by the barges down by the Carnegie property and pretty well through the town before they fired up. We had to go to the pilot house once to turn her out from shore.

Q. Was the wheel going?—A. I did not see the wheel.

Q. Could not you tell whether the wheel was going or not?—A. The boat was running into the shore and we went up into the pilot house and turned her away.

Q. Then you were diverted from going to the relief of those men by the firing and danger which were incurred?—A. Yes, sir; we were being fired upon from both sides of the river by expert marksmen.

Q. Some of them good guns?—A. Some of them .45-caliber.

Q. Winchesters?—A. Winchesters.

Q. Did you have some arms on the boat you were on?—A. There was one Pinkerton man on board who had a navy revolver, a large Colt revolver.

Q. The captain of the boat states in a written interview that the boat drifted into shore at that time, and they used some means which they found to repel the attack which was made and with effect; what was that?—A. Well, I saw the captain come out with his rifle, but that was the only means of defense we had on that boat, one Winchester rifle.

Q. Did he use that rifle at all?—A. I did not see him.

Q. Did you see a gun fired, or do you know if any fire was returned from the boat?—A. I think not.

By Mr. BRODERICK:

Q. You speak about allowing time for the advisory committee to take some action.—A. Well, I thought with a little time this would give the people an opportunity to think.

Q. Were not you there when the advisory committee was disbanded or dissolved a few days before?—A. No, sir.

Q. Did you not know about that?—A. No, sir.

Q. What kind of arms did they have on board; you saw them during the conflict, did you not?—A. The Pinkerton men; they were Winchester rifles, I saw them just a few moments before we arrived at the landing when a man came out of the boat and stood on the——

Q. You spoke of sharpshooters being on board, what do you mean by that and when were they first placed?—A. They were on the barge watching the pump house. The windows were full of men standing behind the jambs of the windows, and they had guns and these Pinkerton men were on the barges watching those windows.

Q. Did the firing commence from the boat by a volley or was there one shot here and there, and then a volley, if you remember?—A. I think perhaps there were several shots fired before there was any continuous firing.

Q. Several shots from the boats?—A. I think so.

Q. Do you know who fired them?—A. No, sir. It was not a volley, it was what you would call a running fire, a firing by file.

By Mr. BOATNER:

Q. You stated from the position you occupied on the steamboat you could not see over the barge?—A. I could not see what was there over the end of the barge.

Q. How could you tell then where the firing commenced, whether from the bank or not. The people had come down close to the edge of the water and how could you ascertain whether the firing came from the boat or the bank?—A. I was watching that end of the boat and I could not see the people over the barge, but the firing began from that bank very suddenly.

Q. The barge was right against the bank?—A. The end was; yes, sir.

Q. I just want to know for information, because that is a very important point, how you could from where you were standing ascertain that fact. A witness has testified that the first firing came from a man who was on the gang plank?—A. Well, sir, I could not tell the individual act of any person on the boat only from that result.

Q. You could not from the position you held tell whether the first firing came from the Pinkerton men or from the people, the Homesteaders?—A. Well, I could tell that the firing came down on that boat from the bank there very suddenly and unexpectedly; that from where I stood it was not possible for any person there to have fired without my seeing the smoke out of their gun and I saw the effect of their firing very quickly, and I believe I am right.

Q. Then it is an inference and impression on your part rather than actual knowledge.—A. They did not fire first.

By the CHAIRMAN:

Q. You are somewhat like myself, you have had experience enough in getting shot and you were seeking to keep out of the range of the balls?—A. No, sir; I was not.

Q. Then we are unlike; I should have kept out of range, as I have had enough of it.—A. If I had had some person to put in the front I would perhaps have done it, but I was there alone, and I stood there by myself.

Q. What is the name of that newspaper man?—A. Well, I did not ascertain his name, but he was a pretty heavy set man.

Thereupon the committee adjourned to meet at 9 a. m. Thursday, July 14, 1892.

PITTSBURG, *Thursday, July 14, 1892.*

The subcommittee of the Committee on the Judiciary, appointed to investigate the employment of Pinkerton detectives in connection with the recent labor troubles at Homestead, Pa., this day met at 9 a. m., Hon. Wm. C. Oates in the chair.

All the members of the committee were present.

TESTIMONY OF JOHN ALFRED POTTER.

JOHN ALFRED POTTER sworn and examined.

By the CHAIRMAN:

Q. Are you a skilled laborer at work in the steel mills at Homestead?—A. Yes, sir.

Q. What position, if any, do you hold or have you held in the past?—A. I am at present general superintendent of the Homestead steel mills.

Q. How long have you held that position?—A. Three and one-half years.

Q. Are you familiar with the work that is done in the four departments there, the laborers in which would have been affected by the new scale proposed by the company?—A. I am.

Q. You know the character of the work done in each of those departments?—A. I do.

. Q. Will you describe to the committee what each class of those workmen do, the methods by which they perform their labor, not in perfect detail, but so as to give us a general idea, beginning, say, with the rollers, and so on through?—A. Well, the rolling at Homestead is different from what it is at any other mill. Our organization at Homestead is made up so that it takes the responsibility from the rollers. In the first place, our rollers are not responsible for the men, as they do no hiring or discharging of men. We have superintendents in each department to attend to those duties. In some other mills the roller has charge of a certain number of men whom he pays out of his salary, but that is not the case at Homestead. We pay each man. The rollers' duties vary on each mill at Homestead. On the plate mill, where the rollers are in question, which is known as the 119-inch mill, there the roller receives the piece of steel on his table in the slab form, probably 4 or 5 inches thick and of different dimensions. He has before him a sheet which tells him the size of the plate which must be made out of that slab. He then manipulates that through the mill, passes it through the rolls different times until he has reduced it to the proper width and proper thickness, and then it goes through a different process of being sheared into the proper dimensions. The roller is responsible for the work done on his mill in this way: he has to gauge that piece of steel to see he gets the proper thickness and that it is also gauged to the proper dimensions.

Q. And a neglect of duty which would spoil the piece, so that it would not conform to the requirements, he would be responsible for?—A. Yes, sir.

Q. How, by a recoupment of his wages?—A. If that piece could not cut to advantage he would not be paid for it.

Q. He would simply lose his compensation?—A. Yes, sir; but there is very little of that. Our work has been very satisfactory in that line.

Q. Well now describe some others so we will have an idea of it?—A. Well in the shearing of the plates the piece is delivered from the rolls and run out on a long line of tables probably 300 feet long, where it is allowed to cool on its journey to the shears. While it is passing to the shearer it is there "laid out." That is to say the sheet is taken and lines drawn on it with what we call a "line drawer" or "layer out." These lines are in chalk, representing where the piece is to be sheared. It then arrives at the shearer where the shearman who is known as first shearman takes it and passes it through the shears with the aid of his helpers; holds it in a certain position where the shears descend and shears off on those lines. It is then placed on the floor ready for inspection by the different inspectors, and, if satisfactory, it is shipped.

In the melting department the raw material, such as pig iron, scrap, etc., is placed in the yard within separate bins, where we have cars run up close to those bins, so as to load them with different qualities of metal for making different grades of steel. It is then taken into the building where the smelting furnaces are located and there it is by a machine dumped into the furnaces to the extent of probably 27 tons. It is then melted, which takes six or eight or ten hours, and boiled, down—meaning that the carbon is taken from it by heat—and it is then recarbonized; that is to say, we will take all the carbon out first and then give it the proper amount of carbon. Then it is put into the ladle and from there poured into the molds, which are called ingot molds, where the steel is allowed to solidify. It is then taken away from there hot and taken over to the soaking pit at the assembling plate mill, known to us as the 32-inch slabbing mill. They are then heated to a proper heat and then laid on the slabbing-mill tables and passed through the large rolls. There we have what is known as the universal mill, which rolls it to a slab, and also on the edge at the same time; that is, as it passes through the mill it is rolled both vertically and horizontally, and it is reduced from a standard ingot 27 inches thick by 54 inches wide, and weighing from $12\frac{1}{2}$ to 13 tons, down to various thicknesses. For ordinary plate-work, it is reduced to perhaps 5 inches thick and 54 inches wide, and any length desired. It is then taken from there to the plate mill, and that is the one I have just been describing to you. It is there heated to a sufficient heat to allow it to be soft enough to be manipulated in the plate mill, and it then goes to the shears.

Q. Is it cut in a hot or cold condition?—A. Cold.

Q. Have you had experience in working in other mills of similar character?—A. Yes, sir.

Q. I mean mills which make similar products?—A. Some of the products of the mills; I never had any experience with plate mills or the open hearth furnaces before I went to Homestead.

Q. The processes are different, I suppose?—A. Yes, sir; my experience heretofore has been in the Bessemer process; we have also that process at Homestead.

Q. How do these mills work, especially in those departments where there is a great deal of skill required, in comparison with other mills with which you have had experience; that is, in which the laborers performing these various duties make better wages?—A. We have at Homestead the finest mills in the world; the best built and the most automatic. We can produce, at least in some of our departments, 50 per cent more with the same amount of hours.

Q. How is it with reference to those four departments in which the proposed reduction in the scale would be effected?—A. In the department known as open hearth No. 2 there is no department in the world that is as well equipped with automatic machinery and appliances. In the slabbing mill, known as the armor plate mill, there is not another mill of that kind in the world that I know of, and I have seen them in England and France. We are head and shoulders ahead of anything of the same nature.

Q. You have had a large experience in connection with these processes?—A. Yes, sir.

Q. How many years?—A. I have been at it since I was 12 years old, and I am now 34.

Q. You are 34 years of age?—A. Yes, sir.

Q. Well, go on and speak of them where I interrupted you.—A. In regard to the plate mill, there is no such mill as that in the city of Pittsburg; not the mill itself, but the facilities connected with it are far superior to any I have ever seen.

Q. What are the advantages of the mills at Homestead over the others, by which one man working in there can make, relatively, more products?—A. Well, the chief are the powerful machinery, working automatically.

Q. You mean that the product turned out is greater in proportion to the force employed?—A. Yes, sir.

Q. The tonnage is greater?—A. Yes, sir; greater.

Q. Can you give about the percentage it is greater than that of other mills?—A. In proportion, our open hearths produce in each furnace more than any other mill that I know of. The slabbing mill, as I say, its product is different from any other mill in this country. You might say there is not any other mill a competitor with it. The plate mill, I think, would produce, with the help of the slabbing mill, 50 per cent more than any other mill, with 50 per cent less labor.

Q. Can you give the committee approximately an idea of the cost of the production of steel in its different forms?—A. I could not, Mr. Oates; I do not know the cost of these different products.

Q. Can you give us an approximate idea of the labor cost?—A. I am not thoroughly conversant with the labor cost. Our system of bookkeeping I do not get to see when it is figured out at the end.

Q. That does not have anything to do with the sale?—A. No, sir; not as far as I am concerned.

Q. We have in evidence the scale upon which these laborers worked for three years beginning in 1889 and the contract terminating the last of last month, June. You are familiar with that?—A. Yes, sir.

Q. Do you know of your own knowledge of the proposition which was made by the company at Homestead with those laborers for a change of compensation?—A. Yes, sir.

Q. Will you explain in what that change consisted, that we may fully understand it?—A. The change, as I understand it, consisted of three different changes; one was in the minimum, meaning we wanted a lower minimum than we had, a difference of from $25 to $23. The other change was the expiration of the scale, that is, instead of its expiring on June the 30th we wanted it to expire the 31st of December of each year. There was also some reduction made in different positions in the mill.

Q. Now, can you give us the percentage of reduction as applicable to the different classes of workmen?—A. As near as I saw it figured out it amounted to from 12 to 13 per cent. In some cases it was only 4 per cent, but it averaged, I should say, 12 per cent.

Q. Do you think that is a high enough average?—A. I think that is a fair average.

Q. Were there any employés there affected by the proposed change except in four departments?—A. No, sir.

Q. How many, if you know, were affected in those four departments by the proposed change?—A. In those four departments there would probably be employed 500 men. Out of that 500 there would be probably 280, or something of that kind, who would be affected by this reduction. Some of those mentioned have been reduced and some reduced have been raised; others remained as they were. It was to equalize the rates.

Q. Do you know the reason why the company proposed and insisted on that new arrangement?—A. Yes, sir.

Q. Please state it.—A. The first reason was, that we were paying much more money than any of our competitors. The next reason was, we had put in new improvements in some departments which increased the output and reduced the work, and we thought we were entitled to some of the benefits.

Q. The impression was that these laboring men were receiving more compensation and a greater share of the profits than they were entitled to?—A. The question was that we were paying more money than our competitors in the same class of work and we had also invested more money in the machinery to do that work than our competitors.

Q. Now, in regard to the income or profits of the company, do you know about that, and do you know whether they are greater than your competitors?—A. I do not.

Q. If these new facilities caused a corresponding increase in the profits of the company, you could well afford to go on paying your laborers much more than any of your competitors, could you not?—A. That would be a question for the company to settle. I know nothing of their profits or losses.

Q. Well, that would be true if those are the facts, would it not?—A. Well, under some circumstances it probably would be.

Q. Well, these men declined; they and the company did not agree to the terms?—A. Yes, sir.

Q. When were these mills shut down?—A. They started to shut down on the 28th of June, and on the morning of the 1st of July we were all through.

Q. All were closed down?—A. Yes, sir; all.

Q. There was a fence put around the works; when was that?—A. We have had a fence around these works for the past three years, and we reënforced that fence. The firm had secured other property which was outside and we fenced it in.

Q. What was the purpose of completing the repairs about that time?—A. The purpose was to thoroughly inclose our works, so the men could not get in from the outside.

Q. To protect the property?—A. Yes; to protect the property.

Q. Did you see or know of some disturbances which occurred there?—A. Yes, sir.

Q. After the shut down?—A. Yes, sir.

Q. Will you tell the committee when you first saw the disturbances?—A. Well, the first disturbance we had probably took place in the mills while the mills were running the last three or four turns Each morning we woke up we would find our effigies hanging through the works.

Q. When you say "our" whom do you mean?—A. Mr. Frick and myself.

Q. They had you hung up in effigy there?—A. Yes, sir. I sent the officers and my private clerk to tear one down which I learned was Mr. Frick's effigy. The mills were still in operation, and as he tore it down and he walked into one department they turned the hose on him and hooted at him.

Q. They washed him down?—A. Yes, sir; washed him·down. The morning ot July 1 as I went to go to work I found the office gate was surrounded by probably 20 or 30 men. I stood and watched the proceedings and saw some of my foremen, none of my superintendents, but all of my foremen were stopped and intimidated or turned back with some little argument. I finally went there and had to walk around several men to get into the gate. That lasted until I received, which was July 2——

Q. Who were they, employés, working in the mill?—A. Yes, sir.

Q. It was only a demonstration and no actual violence?—A. I saw no fire-arms or clubs, but I saw them approach the men and talk to them. I do not know what they stated to them, but the men would turn around and go away.

Q. Arguing with them to keep them out, I suppose?—A. Some of the men stated they were threatened, but I do not know whether they were or not.

Q. A part of your force was willing to go to work?—A. Our superintendents; yes, sir.

Q. Do you know anything of the organization of the Amalgamated Association of Iron and Steel Workers?—A. Yes, sir; I know something of it.

Q. But you do not belong to that association?—A. I do not; no, sir.

Q. Who were these men who were about the gates; did they belong to the Amalgamated Association?—A. I assume they did. I recognized several faces among them who had attended several committee meetings.

Q. That was the 1st day of July?—A. Yes, sir.

Q. Did all the laborers you had in there stop work?—A. Yes, sir.

Q. How many were employed?—A. We employed, I think, about 3,200 men.

Q. And some boys?—A. Thirty-two hundred men and boys. There have been as high as 3,800.

Q. What was the next thing in the shape of a disturbance or trouble which occurred?—A. I left the works on Saturday afternoon at 5 o'clock in company with several of the superintendents——

Q. That was in July?—A. The 2d of July.

Q. When did you return there?—A. I returned there on July 5, or rather the morning of the 6th.

Q. You did not return then until the boat went up with the barges?—A. No, sir; I was on the boat.

Q. Who was on the barges?—A. I do not know who were on the barges, but I know who were on the boats.

Q. Then just answer that.—A. On the boats were Mr. Gray, who was representing the sheriff, several of my assistants and myself, Captain Rogers and his crew, whom I did not know.

Q. By assistants you mean workmen up there?—A. Superintendents of the different departments.

Q. You had along about 300 Pinkerton men?—A. There were 300 men supposed to be watchmen.·

Q. Where were they?—A. On the barges.

Q. Well, now, describe what occurred on the trip up the river.—A. Well, I met the barges at Bellevue, I think that is the place, on the

Ohio River. I went on board the steamboat *Tide*, and there I was met by Mr. Gray, who produced a letter, saying he represented the sheriff and would take charge of the watchmen. I then made it my business to find the heads of the watchmen, who were two, and introduced them to Mr. Gray and told them that he was representing the sheriff. I left them talking with each other and I went into the cabin. The boats parted then and as we got up as far as opposite the depot here, the Baltimore and Ohio depot, one of the boats' engine broke down and it was disabled, the one I was on: The signal was given for the boat with the other barge farther ahead to come back to their assistance. They came back and took in tow the barges and left the disabled steamer lie there, which was proposed to be repaired.

Q. You transferred to the other steamer?—A. I then transferred to the other steamer with my assistants. After we got to the locks the steamer took the two barges and proceeded up the river a short ways, when there was a cry of "a man overboard," and the boat stopped and a skiff was sent out and a man picked up, who proved to be one of the watchmen. We then proceeded on our journey, and as we approached near Homestead we heard the sounds of whistles, and as we drew near, I should judge opposite to Homestead's waterworks, a crowd began gathering on the banks shouting and finally began shooting. Some of the men became uneasy on the barges, on the back end of the barges, and I spoke to Mr. Gray and I said, "There is no necessity for our men getting excited; these shots are landing on the boats, but I do not think they——"

Q. The shots were striking the boat?—A. Yes, sir. I was trying not to have the men commit any overt act. He stepped forward and addressed the men. In the mean time we proceeded up the river. We seemed to be going faster than the men on the land. As we approached the city farm fence the men paused for a moment, and finally one or two got through and more followed, and the whole crowd followed running on the bank.

Q. They broke through the fence?—A. Yes, sir; on the outside of the city farm fence. There was a small fence running down to the river, and that was opened by some means; however I do not know how. As we approached near the pump house I remarked to Mr. Gray that I did not think they would go any farther and that we would have a peaceful landing. I again cautioned him against any overt act that the watchmen might do and asked him to address them again, which he did. The boats proceeded on and the captain asked where we wanted to land. That was while we were below the pump house, that is, the steel-works pump house, and we told him on the steel-works wharf. The boat then turned to the shore, and the firing behind us from parties running up paused for a moment. The boats were then tied, and I understand, but I did not see it, a gangplank was sent out, and as the men went as though to move out the firing suddenly commenced.

Q. Do you know how it commenced?—A. Well, from what I could see and from the bullets which struck around the point I was standing on on the steamer it commenced from the bank, mingled with the throwing of clinkers, etc., and pieces of iron.

Q. Thrown or shot?—A. Thrown. Every once in a while I would hear a heavy thud with the small rattle of revolvers, and afterwards I heard rifle balls. Some of them penetrated through the barge. I then ran to the barge, and as I got there the men had about recovered and got under cover, and I shouted for them to stop firing, which they did.

Q. To whom did you shout?—A. To anybody.

Q. Did you go on shore?—A. No, sir; on the barge.

Q. They had been firing some?—A. They had been retreating and firing, and as they were under cover I shouted for them to stop firing, which they did. The firing lasted, I judge, about two minutes after that from the shore, and then it ceased. It was understood that two or three of our watchmen were lying wounded on the front of the barge. The men pulled them in and carried them over to the other barge, where we began to dress their wounds, and we found that two of them were wounded very badly. One was insensible, having been shot at the top of the head. I noticed then the Pinkerton people or watchmen were beginning to get the firearms out of the boxes—to unpack the boxes.

Q. Did not they have their rifles out before that?—A. I recognized probably eight rifles.

Q. Before?—A. Yes, sir. I recognized them in the front end of the barge as I went forward at the time of the firing. They were the men I hallooed to to stop firing. It was a question then whether we could get into the works by force or whether we should let the thing take its course. Mr. Gray did not feel like taking the responsibility upon himself, and I would not. We held a consultation consisting of Mr. Gray, the ex-sheriff or deputy sheriff, Capt. Rogers, and I think three or five of the leaders of the watchmen. It was decided that the wounded had to be taken care of, and that we would allow the barges to remain where they were, as the crowd seemed to be going away, and we thought in an hour, or two or three hours, there could be a peaceable landing made. Mr. Gray, the deputy, refused to take any action in the matter, and I felt my instructions had been carried out. I had letters on my person at that time that cautioned me against any overt act, and I did not propose to order any charge.

Q. From whom were those letters?—A. From Mr. Frick to me. I have the letters now. He desired I should go with the boat. We took the wounded to Port Perry, and I then reported the case to our people to have them report the case to the sheriff and see what could be done.

Q. Well, what else did you see?—A. I saw nothing else.

Q. You did not see anything that transpired after that?—A. No, sir.

Q. You got off at Port Perry?—A. Yes, sir.

By Mr. BYNUM:

Q. You say that the workmen in that mill can turn out twice the product by reason of the improved machinery?—A. Yes, sir.

Q. Than any other mill in the world?—A. Yes, sir; of the same character.

Q. What do you mean by the same character?—A. The same class of mill.

Q. Well, if there is no mill like it in the world there is no other same class?—A. That is right.

Q. The labor cost of turning out that product at that mill would be one-half what it would be anywhere else where they are paying the same wages?—A. I do not know whether that is so or not.

Q. Does not that follow as a necessary result?—A. Not under our system. We pay two mills for reducing the plate; other mills take the ingot direct and roll it into the plate in one mill. In our case, as I have explained to you, we cast the ingot, 12 tons in weight, and we roll it down on one mill.

Q. Now, you are going away entirely from the question. You stated that with your machinery there the men could turn out twice the product, and I ask the simple question whether, if that is true, the labor-cost of that product would not be one-half of any other mill having the same rate of wages?—A. I do not think it would.

Q. Well, that is all then; that answers the question. What kind of machinery is there which increases the facility of labor?—A. Automatic machinery, hydraulic, etc.

Q. Is that the machinery of which there is no other mill possessed?—A. We use hydraulic machinery to a greater extent than any other mill.

Q. Then the use of machinery actually reduces the cost of the product does it not?—A. Well, it should do it; that is what we want it to do.

By Mr. BRODERICK:

Q. I was going to ask if this machinery is more expensive than is used in other mills?—A. Yes, sir.

Q. By reason of this improved machinery you do not employ so many men and do not need so many men?—A. We do not need so many men; no, sir.

TESTIMONY OF OSCAR COLFRESH

OSCAR COLFRESH, sworn and examined.

By the CHAIRMAN:

Q. Have you been a workman in the Homestead Mills, belonging to Carnegie & Company?—A. Yes, sir.

Q. Were you at work up to the shut down on the last of June?—A. Yes, sir; up to the 29th of June.

Q. In which department did you work?—A. I worked at the rolls in the 119-inch mill, known as the plate mill.

Q. Can you inform the committee of the difference in the proposed new scale of wages and the old; in other words, the reduction which the company proposed and to whom it was applicable. If you can, just proceed to explain that in your own way?—A. Well now, in regard to the reduction I can not state just what the percentage would amount to in the dollar; but I can give you some few facts and figures here in regard to three jobs and to what the difference would amount to in 100 tons between the old rates paid on the $26.50 basis and the proposed scale as proposed by the firm of Carnegie, Phipps & Co. In the principal jobs—that is, we will say heating and rolling—the reduction amounts to only about 8 per cent. Why those jobs were not reduced more I can not tell, as there is a difference of opinion in regard to those jobs among the workmen. The most reduction was made where the hardest work comes in, at the rolls and shears. Now, we will take the job I represent there, known as the tableman's job. On the $26.50 basis it pays at 10 cents per ton; the proposed reduction will bring it down to 6.67 cents per ton making a reduction on a thousand tons from $100 to $67, a reduction in that one job of $33 on 1,000 tons. That job is cut more than any other job at the rolls, and I think it is considered the hardest work at the rolls.

Q. That is, it is cut more by the proposition of the company?—A. Yes, sir; it is cut on the old basis 2 cents per ton. That is, it formerly paid at the basis of $26.50, $10 per ton, but on their proposed scale of $26.50 they propose to pay 8 cents per ton; then they wanted to reduce it to $23, making it 6.67 cents, or a total reduction of 3.33 cents on the ton.

Q. But if the material sold higher than that of course you would get more?—A. Yes, sir; that is the lowest.

Q. That is on the basis of $23?—A. On the basis of $23. Now, to give you an idea of what I could make at those rates, and the reductions at those rates, we will say on 1,500 tons—we have made 1,500 tons in a month—sometimes more and sometimes less, but in a month, say, at the present minimum of $25, I would make $141.45, and at the present rate proposed by the company at the reductions I would make $92; a reduction in a month's work of $49.45. That is as near as I can make it; there may be a few cents more or less.

Mr. BRODERICK. Is that about an average month's wages?

The WITNESS. The average month's wages for last year was $130.

By the CHAIRMAN:

Q. Is there anything else you wish to state in regard to wages, or in regard to the trouble up there?—A. Now, I could tell you something in regard to low price jobs at the shears, known as shear helpers. The present rate at the $25 minimum is 5.19; the proposed scale by the company for such work is 4 cents per ton.

Q. That is the proposed scale?—A. Yes, sir; the proposed scale.

Q. What difference would that make?—A. It would make their rates with the minimum at $23 an average of about $1.85 per day 8 hours work with the average mill, as it is 56 tons per turn of 8 hours.

Q. How much did they make on the old scale?—A. I forget what the average was.

Q. Do you know the cost of producing a ton of steel?—A. That is the labor cost and everything included?

Q. Yes, or any part of it?—A. No, I do not. All I know in regard to the labor cost of a ton of steel is what it takes to heat, roll, and shear a ton of steel in our department. That costs $1.50. The shearer's helper averages $69 according to the company's own statement.

Q. When you say it costs that, you mean that is the amount paid to the laborers for doing that work?—A. Yes, sir; for heating, rolling, and shearing a ton of steel it costs $1.50 according to our scale of contract with the company.

Q. That is in three of those departments?—A. That is for the heating, rolling, and shearing departments.

Mr. BOATNER. That is ready turned out for use?

The WITNESS. From the slab to the finished plate.

The CHAIRMAN. Do you know anything of your own personal knowledge of the landing of the Pinkertons on the morning of the 6th of July?

The WITNESS. I do not; I was not there.

By Mr. TAYLOR:

Q. You say this labor cost is $1.50 a ton; do you take it in the slab or in the ingot?—A. In the slab.

Q. It has been all through the slabbing mill when it comes?—A. It has.

Mr. BRODERICK. That includes skilled labor?

The WITNESS. It does not embrace anything outside of skilled labor.

By Mr. BOATNER:

Q. What is the labor cost behind that that is necessary to be done to it to put it in shape?—A. That is in the slab?

Q. Yes.—A. The labor in the armor-plate mill I am not thoroughly familiar with that. Of course, after it comes into our mill it is handled by the day laborers. I do not know what that amounts to.

TESTIMONY OF JOHN KENNEDY.

JOHN KENNEDY, sworn and examined.

By the CHAIRMAN:

Q. What business were you engaged in or where were you on the 6th of this month?—A. I was on those barges as watchman.

Q. You were watchman on the barges?—A. Yes, sir.

Q. You mean the barges which carried the Pinkerton men up to Homestead?—A. Yes, sir.

Q. How long had you been on the barges?—A. I went there on the 1st of the month.

Q. When did the Pinkerton men arrive on the barges?—A. Well, they arrived on Wednesday night, I believe.

Q. The night before they went up?—A. The same night they went up.

Q. The boats went up the river early in the morning, did they not?—A. It went down in the evening and got them down at Davis Island Dam.

Q. What time was it when they went up?—A. When they passed here I suppose it must have been 2 o'clock or about that time.

Q. Did you remain on the barges during the day until after the trouble was over?—A. Yes, sir; I did.

Q. Well, now, tell about their going up the river, and where you discovered any trouble or any hostile demonstration; just state the whole thing to the committee.

By Mr. BOATNER. Let him commence at the landing, because there is no controversy about what occurred before they got to the landing. Just let us know what occurred from that time on.

The CHAIRMAN. Let him state from the time the boat received the first hostile demonstration. When you got near Homestead what occurred? Tell that.

A. The first we noticed after we went up was just about what is called the glass house there at Homestead, and there were some pickets there in a skiff——

Q. Pickets in a skiff?—A. Yes, sir; I think there were about four of them in a skiff. That was the first report we got. They shot something like a sky rocket out of their guns and gave warning, I suppose, to the Homestead crowd. The first I noticed I was on the hurricane deck at that time, and then I came down on the deck, that is the main deck of the barges.

Q. Well, what else occurred? Describe it.—A. Then the *Edna* there she commenced blowing her whistle, and made a continual blowing of her whistle then.

Q. That was a little steamer lying there?—A. Yes, sir; lying at the wharf at the Homestead works, just above the glass works.

Q. You went right on up?—A. Yes, sir; we went up until we came up and when we got fornenst the fence then there came a big drove of men, women, and children down the street, and they took some stones and mashed the fence down so they could get through and some went through. There was a big crowd of men, women, and children. We went along the shore a little faster than they did, if anything, but they were there by the time we got our lines off the barges and they hollered, "Don't you land," "You must not land," "You shall not land," etc. They called us all kinds of names, of course.

Q. Well, what was said to anybody on the boat?—A. There was not a word said after that; every one was commanded to be quiet.

Q. Had there been any firing?—A. Not yet; not on the boat.

Q. Had there been any firing of any kind?—A. Well, yes, sir; some pistol shots up the shore from the time they came through the fence. I do not know whether it was from men or boys; I could not tell that, as it was just between daylight, early in the morning.

Q. You tied up to the bank?—A. We tied up to the bank; yes, sir.

Q. What else occurred?—A. They came down, that is the strikers came down to the end of the gangway plank and said that we should not come off, that we should not tie up, but we were tied up at that time. We got tied up before they came there; that is, a good many of them. They then commenced shooting down the bank at the barges and——

Q. The lower bank or upper bank?—A. Down the lower part of the bank; there is a railroad there on the shore, and there is where they commenced shooting.

Q. They commenced shooting from there?—A. Yes, sir.

Q. Did you see the first shot?—A. That is where I saw the first shot at the barges, at the men. They shot at the men on the barges and I was standing at the lower end of the barges; I was on the inside barge next to the shore, and I could see everything that was going on.

Q. When did the men on the barges fire?—A. Not until after there were several shots fired from the Homestead people, and I think there were one or two crippled before there was a shot fired from our men; I think so.

Q. Did these Pinkerton men try to land and go ashore?—A. There were a few of them did go out on the gangway plank and jumped off the gangway plank on the shore, but I do not think there were more than a dozen or half a dozen. I could not see exactly how many, because it was kind of dusky, and I could not tell exactly how many of our men were there. There were not many shots fired from our men, very few. It was kinder to scare them away, enough to scare them away.

Q. How long did that firing continue?—A. Oh, about three minutes I reckon, I should say that, may be not quite that.

Q. What were the balance of the parties doing?—A. They ran just as fast as they could run, just broke right away for their homes I guess. I do not know where they went off, but they tried to get out of the way of the Pinkerton men.

Q. Did they run up the bank?—A. Yes, sir; up the bank and down the river and in every direction.

Q. Did the Pinkerton men run back into the barges?—A. Yes, sir; they came back to the barges.

Q. It was a sort of mutual running?—A. I do not think they had much running to do; it was a short run for them.

Q. Did the firing cease then?—A. The firing ceased then until, I suppose, half an hour or an hour, or something like that; oh, an hour, I suppose.

Q. What time did the steamer leave you?—A. Well, the steamer laid there I think about an hour or an hour and a half I suppose, and then it left.

Q. It left before there was any further firing?—A. Yes, sir; the men wanted something to eat and I went to work to cook them a lot of coffee and fry them some meat. There were no cooks, but one of the men came to my assistance, and I got a lot of water and put on the coffee boiler and I made some coffee for them. There was no more firing to amount to anything then,

Q. Was there any attempt of the Pinkerton guards to go out and land at this time?—A. No, sir; they did not try to go out. They were too big cowards to go out, I think, most of them. There were some of them brave enough, but in a general way they were very much affected.

Q. They were very much frightened?—A. Yes, sir; they were very much frightened; they were quiet.

Q. I expect they were.—A. There is no doubt of that.

Q. Then there was a renewal of the firing?—A. Yes, sir; I suppose it was about 8 o'clock, or may be later than 8 o'clock.

Q. That was while the boat was going up the river?—A. Yes, sir.

Q. Taking some wounded up the river?—A. Yes, sir; went up the river with the wounded.

Q. Now describe that; where and when did that commence?—A. While the men were eating and drinking their coffee I happened to go out to the stern of the boat and looked up and saw a big crowd coming on the bank, jumping down——

Q. The upper bank?—A. The upper bank, yes, sir; right down from the mill yard. I hallooed, "Here they come again, boys; look out."

Q. Were these people armed?—A. They were all armed, they seemed to have more revolvers than anything else. There were a few guns, some shotguns, as I could hear the shot very distinctly against the side of the barge.

Q. How far did they come there?—A. Well, they came to the wharf; they came down to the railroad. Here is the railroad which comes close to the river, and that is about as close as they got [illustrating].

Q. What did the Pinkerton men do then?—A. Well, at that time they had most fixed up to guard the barges. They had portholes, like what you would call portholes; that is, the doors were kinder opened, and they gave a little volley out of them and that scared them again, and they ran again, and that was the last we saw of them.

Q. That is, the people on shore?—A. They all took away from there.

Q. There was no running among the Pinkertons?—A. No, sir.

Q. There was no chance for them to run?—A. No, sir; they were as far as they could get without jumping off into the river.

Q. When these people ran from the shore they did not try again to take possession of the property?—A. No, sir; they did not go out at all. I said to them, "What in the name of God did you men come here for; now is the time to make a strike!" Well they said, "We did not come here to fight, we only came here as guards."

Mr. BOATNER. Maybe they understood, like the sheriff, that they would leave if there was any objection to their landing?

The WITNESS. I suppose they would have done that, but they could not get away very well.

By the CHAIRMAN:

Q. How long did you remain there with them?—A. I remained with them until 6 o'clock that evening.

Q. That is the time they surrendered?—A. Yes, sir; that is the time we surrendered.

Q. Now, about the firing: About how much firing was done?—A. There was a great deal of firing up the river and down the river, up and across from this side. There was a great deal of firing done, and they had cannons on the hill, but that did not amount to anything, as they did not come near touching the barges. We had the protection of the hill, and they could not hit the barges.

Q. They could not depress them sufficiently to hit you on account of the embankment?—A. Yes, sir.

Q. Was anyone killed or wounded on the barges after the first firing?—A. Yes, sir; there were about 5, I believe, wounded at the second round.

Q. That is when they came back to the attack?—A. Yes, sir; the second attack there were 5 wounded, 3 slightly wounded and 2 pretty badly.

Q. How many were killed altogether?—A. There were not any killed, not a man.

Q. Some died from their wounds?—A. They did when they came to the hospital.

Q. Do you know how many?—A. I do not know how many just only from hearsay, but I heard there were 3; I do not know myself.

Q. Do you know how many were wounded altogether?—A. I think there were 12 wounded altogether.

Q. Did you see any burning there, anything set on fire?—A. I saw them run oil down the hill and try to set it afire, but it did not amount to anything. They threw cans from the hill lit up with fire, but our Pinkerton men knocked them to pieces before they could do any damage. We were outside of some pickets drove there, so that no fire could have gotten to us. I did not consider we were in danger from that at all.

Q. Well, after the surrender, did you go away?—A. Yes sir; I went up the hill.

Q. Do you know what became of the barges?—A. They were burned.

Q. Did you see them burned?—A. I saw them burning, but I did not see them set afire.

Q. Who burned them?—A. It was, it must have been the Homestead men, of course, as our men would not have burned them, I don't think.

Q. One witness said some people came across in boats from the other side?—A. There were some skiffs there from the other side, but they were not burned by those men, because oil had to be poured on top of those barges before they would burn.

Q. They were burned up but you do not know who burned them?—A. They were burned up, and I know that they had to be set afire on top because they could not be set on fire from the bottom.

By Mr. BOATNER:

Q. What class of people did these Pinkertons seem to be; were they reckless, desperate people?—A. No, sir, they were not. They were very calm, very sober, calm men. I suppose from 25 to 50 of them were very firm men who knew what they came there to do. They knew what their business was. Those were the men who stood picket after the second volley. We cut out plank all along the top of the barge next to the roof so if anybody came on the bank we could see them and so our pickets could pick them off. I did not want to be killed there if I could help it, and we were going to protect ourselves, and they stood regular watch and changed the watches every hour, and whenever a man would show from the hill who they thought was pretty close they tried to pick him off.

Q. What did the balance of them do at that time?—A. The balance were lying around on the barge, lying down on the deck and hiding behind the boxes.

Q. Do you know why they did not go out and take possession when the Homestead people ran away?—A. Well, in the first place they did not have any commander who was worth anything .The first com-

mander was shot immediately, and after that they had no commander
who had any control of the men.

Q. Was Mr. Potter there?—A. He was there; he came up with us,
but he went away on the Little Bill.

Q. He never came back any more?—A. No, sir, he did not come
back.

Q. Did you see Deputy Sheriff Gray take any action to stop this
disturbance?—A. Well, I did not see much about him. I think he
was like some of our Pinkertons, I think he was a little cowardly and
I think he held back.

Q. You think he was a little reserved in his remarks that day?—A.
I think he was a little reserved. You know he was a little lame and
he could not run very well and I guess he thought the best plan was
to hold back.

Q. Were you there when this car was set afire and run down on the
railroad track?—A. I did not see any car run down on the railroad
track on fire. There was a car on the railroad track which was set
on fire, or rather it was tried to be set on fire——

Q. Did you see any evidence of where it was set on fire?—A. Yes,
sir, I think there was some oil cans there where they set it on fire.

Q. It seems something was burned near the edge of the water; was
it a house?—A. There was no house burned there while we were there
that I saw and I think I saw all that was going on.

By Mr. BOATNER:

Q. You went with the party up to the round house, I suppose, or the
skating rink.—A. No, sir, I did not go with that party. That was the
last of our party. The first of our party got along without any trouble
at all. They had their own citizen's clothes on, and they went a great
many ahead of me and some behind me, and there was no trouble with
them at all.

Q. You did not see any indignities put upon them?—A. No, sir, I did
not get to see it, but I could see it at a distance. I had no business
with them at all.

Q. What class of people did it appear who were abusing and mal-
treating them?—A. It appeared to be mostly women and boys. There
were some few men, but not many, mostly women and boys whom I
saw; that kind of a crowd.

Q. Did the Homestead men make an effort to stop it?—A. I did not
see any effort at all made to stop it, none at all.

Q. Were any of these Pinkerton men killed or wounded by an accident on the boat by firearms?—A. There were none killed in there.
but two wounded in there by their own men. The last one wounded
—now, there was a great many of those men who did not know how to
load a gun and did not know anything about a gun. They could not
load a gun and they were trying to teach them to load a gun. One of
them, who when the order was given to give up the gun—they were
ordered to unload the guns—and one man went to another man to show
him how to unload the gun and the other one was unwilling and in some
way it was jerked up and it shot off and wounded a man. He was shot
through the shoulder and he was one of the worst wounded men we
had in the whole list.

Q. Do you know whether these Pinkerton men knew what they were
going there for? Was there any expression of surprise at the reception
they met?—A. They understood they were hired to go there as watchmen; they said they were not hired to fight and they said they would
be damned if they would fight.

By Mr. BRODERICK:

Q. Did the men all leave the boat at the same time?—A. No, sir; there are a great many of the men who hung back on the barge, as many of the Pinkerton men wanted to get what they could.

Q. That was after the surrender?—A. After the surrender, yes, sir. A good many of the men had taken off their guard's clothes.

Q. Do you know whether the Homestead people went on board the barges?—A. Yes, sir; it was like a swarm of bees. As quick as the word was given there to come away they came on there like a swarm of bees, and the men could scarcely get out of the barges for the Homestead people.

Q. About how long was it after the men left the boat until you saw the barges on fire?—A. I suppose it was about a half an hour after I left the boat until the barges were set on fire.

Q. Did you see or hear any one of the Homestead people throw himself across the board and say if any one attempted to cross and go ashore he would have to go over his dead body?—A. There was nothing of that kind said while I was there. Everybody apparently passed off peacefully.

Q. I was speaking of before the surrender, when they first landed?—A. I do not think anybody threw themselves across the gangway at all. They were going on down the gangway, but I do not know that anybody threw themselves across it.

Q. Did you hear any language like that, that if anyone crossed it he would have to go over his dead body?—A. They threatened that they had come there to take their places and they would die before they should have their places.

Q. Do you know whether any one of these men who went down first were hurt?—A. After the firing I saw several of them carried away from there, but I could not say how bad they were hurt, but I saw them carry them up the hill.

Q. Where were you when the firing commenced?—A. Right on the after end of the inside barge.

Q. Could you see the men on shore?—A. Yes, sir, I could see everything going on.

Q. Were they down there near the water's edge when the firing commenced?—A. Well, they could not get down to the water's edge on account of the barges being—I say the barges were run against the pickets and the gangway was run from the pickets to the shore.

Q. You say they ran away after the firing had gone on for some little time?—A. Yes, sir.

Q. Do you know whether they went down the river to Homestead or up the river, or back to the breastworks?—A. They went in every direction, I could not tell where they went. They could not go up the river, as they had to go on straight up the hill and the bank being there I could not judge.

TESTIMONY OF A. M. HUFF.

A. M. HUFF sworn and examined.

By the CHAIRMAN:

Q. Were you on the steamboat *Little Bill* on the morning of the 6th of July up at Homestead?—A. I was on the barge; I was not on the steamboat. I was on the *Little Bill* while she laid there.

Q. Did you see the landing of the boats there?—A. Yes, sir.

Q. And the people on the shore? Just tell us what you saw.—A. From the time she got to the shore?

Q. Yes, sir.—A. From the time she got to the shore I saw firing on both sides; firing of guns and revolvers.

Q. Which side began first?—A. I saw the shore side first.

Q. Did you see the Pinkerton men attempt to land?—A. Yes, sir.

Q. Tell about that; how many went out?—A. A few started out, but they did not get any on shore, but I saw them start to go out on the staging, which was launched, and I saw a pile of men on shore meet some of them at the end of the staging——

Q. Was that before or after the shooting?—A. That was before any regular firing, but there had been several shots, and several bullets struck around them barges before we got to the shore.

Q. Did you hear the testimony of Mr. Kennedy?—A. Just the latter part of it, as I just came in about five minutes ago. I am working down there and came from my work.

Q. Did you remain on the barges after the firing?—A. No, sir, I came away on the *Little Bill*, when we brought the first lot of wounded away.

By Mr. BRODERICK:

Q. About the lights, were there any lights on the boat when you went up?—A. Yes, sir.

Q. The usual lights?—A. Well I do not know what you would call usual lights, but there were two or three dozen carbon lamps burning on the barge I was in. That was my business, to watch them lamps.

Q. Inside or outside?—A. None outside, only the regular signals called for, the green and red signals.

Q. Do you know whether any of the crew got off here?—A. Some of them got off at the locks.

Q. Those who did not want to go; did they understand there might be trouble?—A. No, sir, I do not know that they did.

Q. How many got off?—A. I think there were, to the best of my recollection, two or three who got off at the locks.

Q. What induced them to get off?—A. They supposed they were going to Homestead, and they did not want to have anything to do that would hurt the workmen there, I guess, as much as anything else. That is what we understood. I did not want to have anything of that kind to do, either.

Q. Then they had information there was to be trouble of some sort?—A. Not that I know of.

The CHAIRMAN:

Q. They just did not want to take any action against the workmen?—A. Yes, sir.

Q. You say you did not like it yourself?—A. No, sir; and I would not.

TESTIMONY OF WM. L. DANAHEY.

WM. L. DANAHEY, sworn and examined.

By the CHAIRMAN:

Q. Where do you live?—A. Pittsburg.

Q. What business are you in?—A. Reporter.

Q. For what?—A. Pittsburg Leader.

Q. Were you at Homestead on the morning of the 6th of this month?—
A. Yes, sir.

Q. Were you down at the works of Carnegie, Phipps & Co.?—A.
Yes, sir.

Q. What time did you get there?—A. About 8 o'clock in the morning.

Q. You were not there at the time the boat landed?—A. No, sir.

Q. How long did you remain; you say you got there about 8 o'clock
in the morning; how long did you remain?—A. I remained there at
least an hour during the scrimmage.

Q. Well, what was the situation when you were there; what did you
see?—A. When I arrived there at 8 o'clock I saw numbers of men who
were assembled near the bank, or at least as close as I could get to the
bank, who were there with rifles and guns.

Q. The upper bank?—A. Yes, sir; the bank right in the rear of the
mill, this side, where the barges were.

Q. Were they down where the railroad is or on the upper bank?—A.
On the upper bank above the railroad, and there was some shooting going on at that time.

Q. When you arrived?—A. When I arrived; yes, sir.

Q. Who was shooting?—A. I could not say who was doing the shooting.

Q. Was it from the people on the banks?—A. It came from the river
bank; the shots were from the bank. It was a hazardous task to get
anywhere near the barges, because a person's life would be in danger.

Q. Did you see two barges lying there?—A. Yes, sir; I saw two
barges lying there.

Q. Was the shooting in the direction of the barges or in some other
direction?—A. I could not just say in which way the guns were leveled,
but they appeared to be aimed towards the river, apparently towards
the barges.

Q. Was there any shooting from the barges?—A. Now, I could not
see any.

Mr. TAYLOR. You do not mean you could not see, but did not see?

The WITNESS. I did not see any. There might have been, but I was
not in a position to see it.

By the CHAIRMAN:

Q. You remained there, you say, about an hour. Was that all you saw
while you were there?—A. I remained there about an hour and then
went back several times during the morning and also in the afternoon,
and around the entire day there was more or less shooting; at least you
could hear reports from cannon and rifles, and this continued up to
near 5 in the evening, when the surrender was made.

Q. Were you there at the time the surrender was made?—A. No; I
left just as the white flag had been shown.

Q. Well, after the white flag went up and the Pinkertons surrendered and came out, did you see what transpired, and did you see
them march into the rink?—A. No, sir; I was in quite a rush to get
down to the telegraph office, and had my back turned to the scene at
the time, and could not tell what transpired.

TESTIMONY OF WM. WEIHE—Recalled.

WM. WEIHE, recalled and examined.

By the CHAIRMAN:

Q. You stated when you were on the stand before that the membership of the Amalgamated Association of Iron and Steel Workers was from 20,000 to 25,000, about?—A. Probably about that number.

Q. I have been requested to ask you not a very important question, but there is no harm in it that I see, if you know the comparative nationality of the membership of that order?—A. That is, the entire organization?

Q. Yes, sir; the membership of the organization, what proportion of them are native Americans or foreign born, no matter whether they have been naturalized or not?—A. They are composed of different nationalities.

Q. All the nations are practically represented in the membership; we understand from one of the workmen they come from different nations?—A. There are some from England, some from Wales, some from Scotland, and a good many Americans.

Q. Are you a native American?—A. Yes, sir.

Q. Do you know what percentage of them are natives?—A. We have never kept statistics to that extent. There are different nationalities but what the numbers are I could not state.

Q. What are the essentials of eligibility to become a member of that order?—A. Those who work at the furnaces and rolls, at any of those jobs, such as working around the furnaces, helping at the rolls, working with the tongs, or shears—doing duty at the time the rolls and furnaces are in operation.

Q. Is that a copy of the constitution and by-laws [handing pamphlet]?—A. Yes, sir.

By Mr. BOATNER:

Q. There is nothing secret about the organization?—A. No, sir. The password is the only secret we have. We give the managers and mill-owners copies of these every year when they are revised or when there is any change made, so they will be acquainted with what the laws and rules of the association are.

CONSTITUTION AND GENERAL LAWS OF THE NATIONAL AMALGAMATED ASSOCIATION OF IRON AND STEEL WORKERS OF THE UNITED STATES.

[Adopted as amended by the national convention at Pittsburg, Pa., June, 1890, and will remain in force until August 1, 1891.]

PREAMBLE.

"Labor has no protection—the weak are devoured by the strong. All wealth and all power center in the hands of a few, and the many are their victims and their bondsmen."

So says an able writer in a treatise on association, and in studying the history of the past the impartial thinker must be impressed with the truth of the above quotation. In all countries and at all times capital has been used by some possessing it to monopolize particular branches of business until the vast and various industrial pursuits of the world are centralizing under the immediate control of a comparatively small portion of mankind. Although an unequal distribution of the world's wealth, it is perhaps necessary that it should be so.

To attain to the highest degree of success in any undertaking, it is necessary to have the most perfect and systematic arrangement possible; to acquire such a system it requires the management of a business to be placed as nearly as possible under the control of one mind; thus concentration of wealth and business tact conduces to the most perfect working of the vast business machinery of the world. And there is perhaps no other organization of society so well calculated to benefit the laborer and advance the moral and social condition of the mechanic of the country, if those possessed of wealth were all actuated by those pure and philanthropic principles so necessary to the happiness of all. But, alas, for the poor of humanity, such is not the case. " Wealth is power," and practical experience teaches us that it is power too often used to depress and degrade the daily laborer.

Year after year the capital of the country becomes more and more concentrated in the hands of the few; and, in proportion as the wealth of the country becomes centralized, its power increases and the laboring classes are more or less *impoverished*. It therefore becomes us as men who have to battle with the stern realities of life, to look this matter fair in the face. There is no *dodging* the question. Let every man give it a fair, full, and candid consideration, and then act according to his honest convictions. What position are we, the iron and steel workers of America, to hold in society? Are we to receive an equivalent for our labor sufficient to maintain us in comparative independence and respectability, to procure the means with which to educate our children and qualify them to play their part in the world's drama?

"In union there is strength," and in the formation of a national amalgamated association, embracing every iron and steel worker in the country, a union founded upon a basis broad as the land in which we live, lies our only hope. Single-handed we can accomplish nothing, but united there is no power of wrong we may not openly defy.

Let the iron and steel workers of such places as have not already moved in this matter organize as quickly as possible and connect themselves with the national association. Do not be humbugged with the idea that this thing can not succeed. We are not theorists; this is no visionary plan, but one eminently practicable. Nor can injustice be done to anyone; no undue advantage should be taken of any of our employers. There is not, there can not be any good reason why they should not pay us a fair price for our labor, and there is no good reason why we should not receive a fair equivalent therefor.

To rescue our trades from the condition into which they have fallen, and raise ourselves to that condition in society to which we, as mechanics, are justly entitled; to place ourselves on a foundation sufficiently strong to secure us from encroachments; to elevate the moral, social, and intellectual condition of every iron and steel worker in the country, is the object of our national association. And to the consummation of so desirable an object, we, the delegates in convention assembled, do pledge ourselves to unceasing efforts.

CONSTITUTION AND GENERAL LAWS.

ARTICLE I.—*Name and objects.*

SECTION 1. This association shall be known as the National Amalgamated Association of Iron and Steel Workers of the United States, and shall be composed of all men working in and around rolling mills, steel works, nail, tack, spike, bolt, and nut factories, pipe mills, and all works run in connection with the same, except laborers, the latter to be admitted at the discretion of the subordinate lodge to which application is made for membership.

SEC. 2. The objects of this association shall be the elevation of the position of its members, the maintenance of the best interests of the association, and to obtain, by conciliation, or by other means just and legal, a fair remuneration to members for their labor, and to afford mutual protection to members against broken contracts, obnoxious rules, unlawful discharge, or other systems of injustice or oppression.

ARTICLE II.—*National jurisdiction and general office.*

SECTION 1. This association shall have supreme jurisdiction over the United States, in which there are at present or may be hereafter subordinate lodges located, and shall be the highest authority of the order within its jurisdiction, and without its sanction no lodge can exist, or any scale of prices be recognized in any mill except the regular adopted scale of wages of this association.

SEC. 2. The general office of the association shall be located in the city of Pittsburg, Pa., and it shall be required that the president and secretary of the national lodge reside in the city where the general office is located.

ARTICLE III.—*National lodge elective officers and their duties.*

SECTION 1. The elective officers of the national association shall be a president, who shall also be organizer; a secretary; an assistant secretary; a vice-president for each district or division of a district; a treasurer, and three trustees, who shall hold office until their successors are elected or appointed.

SEC. 2. The president shall be elected from among the delegates at convention, or those who have been delegates at any previous convention, or who ever held office in the national association previous to the adoption of this article, and shall be an active member in good standing. He shall appoint an assistant to himself, subject to confirmation by convention, and said assistant shall be a member of the advisory board. He shall instruct all new members in the workings of the association, and superintend the workings of the order throughout the jurisdiction. He shall sign all official documents whenever satisfied of their correctness and authenticity, and appoint vice-presidents or trustees of the national lodge where vacancies occur. He shall have power to visit any sublodge and inspect their proceedings, either personally or by deputy, and require a compliance with the laws, rules, and usages of this association, and if any sublodge shall refuse or neglect to place any of their books, documents, or any information in their possession, into the hands of the president or his deputy, whenever required by either of them, for any information or investigation he may deem necessary, the president may fine or suspend the sublodge immediately and report his action to the secretary of the national lodge, who in turn shall report the same to the vice-president of the district in which the lodge is located, and to all sublodges in the association as soon as possible. He shall submit to the secretary at the end of each month an itemized account of all moneys, traveling and incidental, expended by him in the interest of the association, and at the end of his term of office he shall report his acts and doings to the national convention. He shall preside at all national conventions, preserve order and enforce the laws thereof. He shall have the casting vote when equally divided on any question, but shall not vote at other times, except at election of officers; he shall appoint officers *pro tem.* He shall make out and announce the following committees:

On western scale of wages, consisting of fifteen, six from the forge department, six from the finishing department, and the president, secretary, and treasurer of the national lodge; on steel workers' wages scales, consisting of not less than fifteen, whose reports shall have precedence over all others; on conference with manufacturers; on report of the president and other officers; on ways and means; on auditing; on secret work; on grievances; on claims; on appeals; on constitution and general laws; on general good of the order; on mileage.

He shall be required to devote all his time to the interest of this association; he shall give a bond of five thousand (5,000) dollars for the faithful performance of his duties, and for his services shall receive such sum as the national convention shall determine.

SEC. 3. The secretary shall be elected from among the delegates at convention, or those who have been delegates at any previous convention, or who ever held office in the national association previous to the adoption of this article, and he shall be an active member in good standing. He shall take charge of all books, papers, and effects of the general office. He shall furnish all elective officers with the necessary letter heads and stationery. He shall convene and act as secretary of the national convention, keep all documents, papers, accounts, letters received, and copies of all important letters sent by him on business of the association, in such a manner and place and for such purposes as the national convention shall direct. He shall collect and receive all moneys due the national association, pay the same to the treasurer, taking his receipt therefor. He shall also draw all warrants on the treasurer, which shall be signed by the president. He shall prepare a quarterly report of the financial transactions connected with the national association, and furnish each sublodge with a copy of the same. He shall register the names of members who have received strike or victimized benefits and the amount each member has received. He shall close *all* accounts of the national association on the thirtieth day of April in each year, and *all* moneys received or disbursed after said date shall not be reported in the general balance account at the next national convention. He shall, after the adjournment of each national convention, prepare a general account of all moneys received and disbursed, a copy of which shall be furnished gratis to each subordinate lodge in good standing. He shall give a bond of five thousand (5,000) dollars for the faithful performance of his duties, and for his services shall receive such sum as the national convention shall determine.

SEC. 4. Upon the death, resignation, or removal of the president of the national lodge, the vice-president of the first division of the first district shall immediately assume the duties of the president and notify the different vice-presidents, who shall meet and, in conjunction with the national lodge officers, shall elect a successor for the unexpired term.

SEC. 5. Upon the death, resignation, or removal of the secretary or the treasurer of the national lodge, the president thereof shall immediately take charge of the books, papers, and effects of the general office, and notify the different vice-presidents, who shall meet and, in conjunction with the national lodge officers, shall elect a successor for the unexpired term.

SEC. 6. It shall be the duty of the vice-presidents to act as executives of the several districts or divisions of districts in which they may reside, and render such other assistance to the president as he may require. They shall report their acts and doings for their term of office to the national convention, and such reports shall be referred to the proper committee without being read in open convention. They shall appoint three deputies each to assist them in their duties, the same to report to their respective vice-president every three months. When either or all of the regular deputies can not attend, then the vice-president shall have power to appoint special deputies for that occasion. Vice-presidents shall be delegates at large to the national convention.

SEC. 7. The treasurer shall receive and take charge of all moneys, property, and security of the national association delivered to him by the secretary. He shall deposit all moneys belonging to this association in bank, in his name as treasurer of the Amalgamated Association of Iron and Steel Workers, and before any moneys, thus deposited, can be drawn each check shall be signed by him as treasurer, and countersigned by the president, secretary, and resident trustee of the national lodge. He shall pay, through the secretary, all warrants regularly drawn on him, signed by the president and countersigned by the secretary, as required by this constitution and none others. He shall submit to the national convention a complete statement of all receipts and disbursements during his term of office. He shall be required to attend the sessions of the national association, and at the expiration of his term of office he shall deliver up to his successor all moneys, securities, books, and papers of the national association under his control, and for the faithful performance of his duties he shall give a bond in the sum of ten thousand (10,000) dollars.

SEC. 8. It shall be the duty of the board of trustees to receive and hold the required bonds of the president, secretary, assistant secretary, and treasurer, which shall be five thousand (5,000) dollars each for the president and secretary, two thousand five hundred (2,500) dollars for the assistant secretary, and ten thousand (10,000) dollars for the treasurer. They shall also, in conjuction with the president, secretary, and treasurer, audit all accounts of the national lodge every three months, which settlement shall be final for each quarter. A copy of such settlement shall be sent to each sublodge, by the secretary of the national lodge, in which shall appear the individual expenses of the national lodge officers, including the deputies and members of the executive and conference committees of the several districts, and those settlements shall be referred to the committee on auditing at each national convention. For the faithful performance of their duties the trustees shall give a bond of five thousand (5,000) dollars each, which shall be deposited with the president.

SEC. 9. The trustees and officers of the national lodge, including the assistant to the president, shall also constitute an advisory board to the president of the national lodge, with whom he shall consult at his discretion.

SEC. 10. The national lodge officers, vice-presidents, deputies, executive and conference committees shall, at the end of each quarter, present to the secretary of the national lodge an itemized report of their actual lost time in the mill and all traveling and other necessary expenses incurred by them in the discharge of their duties, which shall be paid by the national association. (See section 8 of this article.)

SEC. 11. The term of office of the president, secretary, treasurer, and trustees of the national lodge, also the vice-presidents of the several districts and divisions, shall not expire untill the first day of October, after a successor to either of them has been elected or appointed, and the salaries of the president and the secretary shall remain as decided upon by each annual convention, and continue in force for one year, commencing October 1, following each annual session.

ARTICLE IV.—*Formation of sublodges and representatives.*

SECTION 1. Any sublodge composed of at least ten practical workmen, as provided in section 1, Article I, who are of good character and not under the age of eighteen years, and who are eligible to membership in this association, shall, after obtaining the approval of the president, be entitled to a charter of the same, upon payment of $25.00. Each member shall sign the constitution and comply with all rules therein contained.

SEC. 2. After receiving said charter, they shall also be entitled to a representation • in the national association as follows: A sublodge with less than one hundred members shall be entitled to one representative. A sublodge with one hundred and twenty-five members shall be entitled to two representatives, and one representative for each additional hundred.

SEC. 3. Each representative to the national convention shall be entitled to one vote, but can not vote unless present at the meeting when a vote is taken.

SEC. 4. Representatives to the national convention shall, after their term of service in that capacity expires, be permanent members of the same so long as they retain their good standing in any sublodge (proof of which they shall present) and said lodge retains its connection with this body. They may discuss any question, and be eligible to any office.

SEC. 5. That one of the representatives shall make out and forward the quarterly report of the lodge which he represents to the secretary of the national lodge, together with all assessments levied by the president of the national lodge, on or before the thirty-first day of October, the thirty-first of January, the thirtieth of April, and the thirty-first of July next succeeding the session of the national convention in which they have last served, and in case neither of the representatives nor the lodge forward their quarterly report for July thirty-first, October thirty-first, or January thirty-first, within six days after the same becomes due, said lodge shall be deprived of all strike benefits and the password during said quarter; and any lodge failing to forward its report for April thirtieth, on or before May tenth, shall be deprived of the strike benefits and the password for said quarter, and shall not be entitled to a seat in the succeeding national convention.

SEC. 6. In order to ensure a duplicate quarterly report the corresponding representative of each sublodge shall send to the general office both the original and duplicate reports, and the latter shall be returned, when corrected (if necessary), to the sublodge.

SEC. 7. All lodges failing to forward reports as above shall be charged with all assessments according to the number of members on the preceding report, and any lodge failing to send in their quarterly report for two successive quarters shall be deprived of strike benefits for six months after they again become in good standing.

SEC. 8. The corresponding representative of each lodge shall send a report to the general office of the association once in each week, stating how the mill is running, the number of men standing turns, etc., the same to be published in the *National Labor Tribune*. And in order to educate our members one of the delegates shall at each regular meeting expound one article of the constitution.

ARTICLE V.—*National Convention.*

SECTION 1. The national convention shall meet annually on the first Tuesday in June, at 10 o'clock, at such place as shall from time to time be designated by the preceding annual convention. A quorum for the transaction of business shall consist of one-fourth of the whole number of representatives elect.

SEC. 2. Prior to the assembling of the convention a programme of business shall be sent to each subordinate lodge by the secretary of the national lodge six weeks prior to the date appointed for the calling of the convention. The programme shall contain any suggested alterations or amendments to the laws, and any alterations or proposed changes in the scale of prices that shall have been sent by sublodges under their seal to the secretary of the national lodge, and any resolutions bearing upon questions of law or prices not contained in the programme shall not be entertained at the convention.

SEC. 3. In order to facilitate the business at convention the names of delegates elect shall be sent to the secretary of the national lodge, who shall enter the same on the roll of delegates for convention, and at the opening thereof shall call the roll, when each shall answer to his name. As the delegates arrive at convention they shall present their credentials to the secretary, who shall examine the same, and at the termination of the calling of the roll he shall state whether all present are entitled to seats. All disputed or contested seats shall be referred to a special committee, who shall proceed to investigate forthwith, but no contest shall be recognized unless those contesting have properly notified the sublodge to which they belong of their intentions, and have properly applied to the secretary of the national lodge, which application shall bear the signature of the recording secretary of the said lodge and the seal thereof. Any delegate to national convention absenting himself (except in case of sickness of self or family) the president shall call upon the alternate-elect to fill unexpired term.

SEC. 4. Should the national convention assemble without a quorum it can transact no business, but may issue an address to the subordinate lodges with a view to secure a full representation at an adjourned meeting or at the next stated meeting of the national association.

SEC. 5. At each of the annual sessions an executive session with closed doors shall be held. The first business at said executive session shall be devoted to the consideration and adoption of a scale of prices, and during such sessions no person shall be present except the representatives to the national convention.

SEC. 6. The elective officers may, at their discretion, call an extra session of the national association: *Provided*, A request to that effect be made by a majority of subordinate lodges.

SEC. 7. Representatives to the annual convention shall be elected by sub-lodges annually, at the last regular meeting in the month of April, and shall hold their offices one year, commencing the first annual session following said election. The written ballot shall be used in balloting, and where but one is to be elected, and should there be no election on the first ballot, all but the two highest shall be dropped. Where two are to be elected, the candidate receiving the lowest number of votes shall be dropped until two have received a majority of votes cast over the third or lowest candidate in nomination. When a sub-lodge is entitled to two or more delegates, and such lodge decides to send them, each ballot shall contain as many of the names of candidates in nomination as the lodge has decided to send; and any ballot containing less names than the number of representatives the lodge has decided to send, the same shall not be counted. They shall also elect alternates to insure a representative of the lodge in case the representative elect fail from any cause whatever to attend.

SEC. 8. To be eligible as representative to the national convention, candidates for the same must be clear on the secretary's books up to and including the night of election; must be fully qualified to perform the functions of the office to the knowledge and satisfaction of the lodge they aspire to represent, and must be working at some of the trades represented in section 1, Article I, and shall have served six months in office in any sub-lodge, either as president, vice-president, recording secretary, financial secretary, treasurer, or corresponding representative. This law, however, does not apply to lodges not organized long enough for the officers named to have served the six months in office.

SEC. 9. All necessary expenses, except mileage, incurred by the representatives to the national convention, including lost time, shall be defrayed by their respective lodges.

SEC. 10. The secretary of the national lodge shall negotiate with the various railroad companies for reduced rates for delegates attending the national convention, and such reduced rates shall be the actual amount that delegates shall receive for their mileage, which shall be paid by the national lodge.

SEC. 11. Any subordinate lodge being in arrears to the national lodge, the same shall be deducted from the mileage of the representatives of such lodge to the national convention.

ARTICLE VI.—*Revenue.*

SECTION 1. The revenue of this association shall be derived as follows:

For organizing a subordinate lodge, the sum of twenty-five ($25.00) dollars shall be charged, said sum to be paid at the time of organization. The supplies to be furnished a newly organized sub-lodge, which the organization fee of twenty-five ($25.00) dollars is intended to cover, shall be: 1 charter, 3 rituals, 25 constitutions, 25 due cards, 10 withdrawal cards, and 8 quarterly report blanks. Additional supplies shall be charged for as follows:

For issuing a duplicate charter (for one destroyed) to a subordinate lodge, $5.00; remodeling an old seal, $4.50; rituals, $1.00 each; constitution and general laws, 10 cents each; quarterly report blanks, 10 cents each; scale of prices, 10 cents each; due and withdrawal cards, 5 cents each.

SEC. 2. In order to create a fund to meet the expenses of the national association it shall be the duty of the president to assess a quarterly or per capita tax on the different subordinate lodges, sufficient to defray the expenses of the national association.

SEC. 3. In order to create a fund for the support of victimized members, or such members as may be engaged in legalized strikes, it shall be required that each member of the association shall pay to his lodge, for the protective fund, the sum of twenty-five (25) cents per month.

SEC. 4. At the last stated meeting in each quarter the financial secretary of each lodge shall report to the lodge the correct number of members on his books taxable to the protective fund for the quarter, when an order shall be drawn on the treasurer for a sum equal to seventy-five (75) cents for every member on the books thus reported by the financial secretary, and the sum thus drawn on the treasurer shall be given to the corresponding representative, who shall, as soon as possible, forward the same to the secretary of the national lodge, who will receipt therefor.

SEC. 5. In order to replenish the protective fund, when it has been depleted by a long and continuous drain thereon, the president of the national lodge shall have discretionary power to levy a special assessment upon each member reported in good standing on the past quarterly report (except members on strike or out of work two weeks), which assessment must be collected by the financial secretary of the lodge and sent to the secretary of the national lodge without delay.

SEC. 6. Any member who is sick or out of employment during the period of one full month shall be exempt from paying the twenty-five (25) cents per month to the protective fund until he recovers from his sickness or finds employment. But members out of employment must report the fact to their lodge at every regular meeting, or be charged with the twenty-five (25) cents per month to the protective fund.

SEC. 7. All moneys due the national association shall be forwarded to the secretary thereof by draft (on New York, Philadelphia, or Pittsburg), express, P. O. order, or registered letter. For check sent on any bank, except in the city of Pittsburgh, twenty-five (25) cents extra shall be charged for collection.

ARTICLE VII.—*Executive committee, its duty and power.*

SECTION 1. There shall be an executive committee in each district or division, consisting of the vice-president, his deputies, the president of the national lodge, and the president of the lodge where any grievance may arise, except for the signing of the yearly scales. But no person shall be allowed to serve as a member of the executive committee who is personally or directly interested in any grievance that may come before said committee.

SEC. 2. The vice-president of the district or division shall be chairman of the executive committee.

SEC. 3. It shall be the duty of the vice-president, after first having been notified by and under the seal of the sub-lodge, to examine, in conjunction with the mill committee, into both sides of any grievance that may arise before calling the executive committee together to legalize a strike. When a strike has been legalized the vice-president shall notify the general office of the same in writing.

SEC. 4. The executive committee, if, upon investigation, find it to the best interest of the association so to do, shall have full power to declare a strike, which they have legalized, at an end, and the vice-president shall report the same to the general office of the association in writing.

SEC. 5. The executive committee shall have full power to open a mill that goes on strike in violation of sections 3 and 4 of this article.

SEC. 6. All expenses incurred by the vice-presidents, deputies, and presidents of sublodges serving on executive committees shall be paid by the secretary, on the order of the president, attested by the secretary of the national lodge. All bills of deputies and executive committees shall be certified to by the vice-president.

ARTICLE VIII.—*Strikes.*

SECTION 1. No sublodge under the jurisdiction of this association shall be permitted to enter into a strike unless authorized by the executive committee of their district or division.

SEC. 2. When the executive committee of a district or division find it necessary in accordance with the laws of this association to legalize a strike in any one department of a mill or works, it shall be required that the men of all other departments shall also cease work until the difficulty is settled.

SEC. 3. When a strike has been legalized and the general office of the association has been properly notified of the fact, in writing, the secretary of the national lodge shall at once prepare a printed statement of all the facts in the case, as near as possible, and forward the same, under the seal of the national lodge, to all sublodges, warning all true men not to accept work in such mills, shops, or factories.

SEC. 4. Any subordinate lodge entering into a strike in the manner provided by the laws of this association shall receive from the protective fund the sum of four dollars ($4.00) per week for each member actually engaged in the strike in the mill over which the lodge has jurisdiction, provided they remain in the locality of the strike, or notify the corresponding representative of that lodge of their location and their being unemployed each week while on strike, and have held membership in the association for six months, are not in arrears, and the lodge to which they belong is in good standing in the national association. Except a strike has been legalized three months prior to July first, no benefits shall be paid to any member for any strike during the months of July and August. This section also applies to members who are standing turns in the mills on strike, and who hold no other situation except that of standing turns in that mill.

SEC. 5. If, upon investigation, it is found that benefits have been paid to a member not entitled to them, the lodge in which such member or members receiving such benefits held membership, shall be held responsible for the amount thus paid, and said amount shall be charged up to such lodge.

SEC. 6. No member shall be entitled to strike benefits for the first two weeks while on a legalized strike. Payments of benefits shall date from the commencement of the fourth week after the strike has been legalized, and no benefits shall be allowed for the fractional part of the first week.

Sec. 7. A member who has been suspended or expelled shall not receive any strike benefits (whether engaged in a legalized strike or is victimized) until six months after he has been restored to membership.

Sec. 8. If any member or members, while receiving benefits from this association, shall work three or more days in one week, at any job, either in or outside of a mill or factory, he or they shall not be entitled to benefits for that week. And any member on the benefit list, either on strike or victimized, refusing to work a third turn in a week, with a view to securing his benefits, his name shall, if proven against him, be stricken from the benefit list. Members out of employment or idle for repairs when a strike takes place in one department of the mill (those that were idle previous to the commencement of said strike, and were idle at the end of it), can not be considered "on strike," nor entitled to strike benefits.

Sec. 9. No member or members of this association shall be entitled to strike benefits for a strike in any mill or factory in which he or they have the mere promise of a situation. That is to say, if a member has been promised a situation in a mill and said mill should go on strike before he begins to work he shall not be entitled to strike benefits during said strike.

Sec. 10. No member of this association shall be entitled to strike benefits because of his refusal to work in a blacksheep or nonunion mill.

Sec. 11. Any member engaged in a legalized strike, procuring a permanent situation elsewhere, forfeits his claim to strike benefits during the continuance of such strike.

Article IX.—*Victimized members.*

Section 1. Should any member or members of this association be discharged (victimized) from his or their employment for taking an active part in the affairs of this association, either as a member of the mill or conference committees, or for otherwise being active in promoting and guarding the interests of this association, such member or members shall use his or their best endeavors with the manager to get reinstated, and failing in this, he or they shall then and there report such case to the chairman of the mill committee, who shall at once proceed to investigate the case as set forth in sections 2 and 3, of article VII. Should the committee fail to get the brother or brothers reinstated, they shall then carry the case to the lodge in precisely the same manner as in cases where the whole mill is involved in difficulty, and in no case of individual discharge (except the mill committee have good grounds to believe that the brother is discharged *without just cause*) shall such job be declared vacant until the executive committee of the district or division has decided the case.

Sec. 2. Should the executive committee of the district or division, after deciding the brother victimized, deem the organization unable to sustain a strike for his reinstatement, he shall receive from the protective fund of the association six dollars (6.00) per week, for a period of eight (8) weeks and no longer, unless in extreme cases, when it shall be left discretionary with the president of the national lodge, as to the length of time benefits shall be paid. If within the limit of time (eight weeks) prescribed for the payment of victimized benefits a situation has been procured for him, either by himself or other members of the association, payment thereof shall immediately cease. The law applying to the payment of victimized benefits shall be the same as that governing the payment of strike benefits.

Sec. 3. If, upon investigation, it is found that victimized benefits have been paid a member not entitled to them, the lodge in which such member, receiving benefits, held membership shall be held responsible for the amount thus paid, and said amount shall be charged up to such lodge.

Article X.—*Mill committees and their duties.*

Section 1. Each sublodge shall have a mill committee, consisting of three members, on each turn, from each department represented in the lodge, and any member in good standing in the lodge, and holding a job in the mill where the lodge exists, can be appointed on the mill committee, whether at the meeting or not, provided he is twenty-one (21) years of age, and has been a member of this association one year, and all excuses from serving on said committee must be granted by a two-third vote of the lodge. This law shall not apply to newly organized lodges where the members have not held membership for one year.

Sec. 2. It shall be the duty of said committee to superintend and guard the interests of the association in the several departments, and when it becomes apparent that any advantage is being taken of our laws, or any member of this association, and the committee of the department where this occurs has failed to adjust the difficulty, then the committees of the other departments, in conjunction with the committee having the grievances, shall jointly exhaust every effort with the manager of the works to settle the difficulty before reporting the case to the vice-president of their district or division. In case the joint committee fail to meet, the lodge having the grievance shall have power to call on the vice-president of the district or division.

SEC. 3. When the joint committee, after using all honorable means to bring about a settlement of the difficulty, have failed, they shall immediately call a special meeting of their respective lodges, jointly, and all members of each lodge working in that mill shall be notified by the mill committee to attend the same.

SEC. 4. At said special meeting the grievance pending shall be explicitly stated by the members of the joint committee, and if the joint meeting consider the grievance sufficient the corresponding representative of the lodge having the grievance shall, by instructions of his lodge, *under their seal and in no other manner*, notify the vice-president of the district or division, and work shall continue until the vice-president has investigated the case.

SEC. 5. The communication sent to the vice-president, as set forth in section 4, shall in turn be sent to the general office of the association by the vice-president as a guarantee that the sublodge has complied with the law prior to the vice-president going to investigate the case.

SEC. 6. In mills or factories where the manager, superintendent, foreman, or boss absolutely refuses to recognize the mill committee in a settlement of any difficulty in which this association is interested, the committee shall immediately call a special meeting as set forth in section 3, of this article, and carry out the instructions as laid down in section 4.

ARTICLE XI.—*Scale of prices.*

SECTION 1. Wherever practicable, steps shall be taken to provide a scale of prices for every trade or calling in each district represented in this association, but no scale or price shall be considered by the executive committee, or the convention, unless the same has first been presented to and demanded of the firm.

SEC. 2. When it is found necessary that the scale of prices governing any department of a mill or factory needs revision, such department shall submit, in writing, to their lodge the alterations desired in their scale, on or before their first meeting in the month of March. Each lodge shall then consider such desired changes, shall vote by written ballot thereon, and report the result in writing, under the seal of the lodge, to the general office of the association. No sublodge under the jurisdiction of this association, or member thereof, shall countenance the holding of meetings outside the lodge room for the purpose of agitating class legislation for advanced wages, and no lodge in the association shall receive or act upon matter discussed, originated, or in any manner acted upon outside of the association relative to class interests.

SEC. 3. When all desired alterations to the several scales are received at the general office from sublodges, which shall be on or before the first Tuesday in April, the secretary of the national lodge shall get the same printed in pamphlet form, together with the suggested amendments to the laws, and forward a copy thereof to every sublodge six weeks prior to the meeting of the next annual convention.

SEC. 4. The proposed alterations to the several scales and amendments to the general laws, as compiled and sent to sublodges by the secretary of the national lodge, shall then be discussed in each lodge, and the action of the lodge be given to the delegates of the lodge, who shall carry the same to the national convention.

SEC. 5. The suggestions pertaining to the scale of wages, and contained in the programme of business, shall be referred to the wage committees at the annual convention, and the president of the national lodge is empowered to call the wage committees together three or more days prior to convening of the annual convention, at his discretion, for the purpose of considering the scale suggestions and preparing a report thereon for the annual convention.

SEC. 6. In order to aid the wage committees in their work the corresponding representative of each lodge must send to the general office, two weeks prior to the meeting of the committees, a statement giving the condition of their mill, the amount of work done the past year, the feeling of the members of the lodge regarding wages for next year, stocks in hand, if any, and what kind, and any other information that will aid the committees and convention in arriving at a proper understanding on the wage question, and any corresponding representative failing to comply with the provisions of this section shall be fined in the sum of $2.00, and his sublodge shall be notified of the same.

SEC. 7. To change the basis of any scale it will require a two-third vote of all the delegates present at the annual convention.

SEC. 8. In iron rail, steel rail, and converting mills, all departments in said mills shall have their several scales expire on June 30th; and when it is found necessary that the scale of prices governing any department of such mills needs revising, such department shall submit, in writing, to their lodge the alterations desired in their scale on or before the first stated meeting in March. Each lodge directly interested in such scales shall then consider such proposed change at the first stated meeting in April, at which a vote shall be taken by written ballot, requiring a two-thirds majority to adopt, and if the committee appointed by the lodge fail to agree with the company, the case shall be referred to the executive committee of the district or division for final action.

SEC. 9. Unless the scale is signed in conference, three copies shall be sent out by the secretary of the national lodge, and when signed, one shall be kept by the firm, one by the lodge, and the third be sent to the general office of the association.

SEC. 10. The scale, unless signed in conference, shall be presented to the manufacturers for signature by members of the mill committee representing each department, one week prior to July 1st, the commencement of the scale year, and notice shall be given by them that unless the scale of prices besigned on or before June 30th, all departments of the mill and factory will cease work, except roll turners and engineers.

SEC. 11. That when a stock of muck bar is on hand and the company not wishing to boil iron, the finishing mill shall run on after the scale is signed. But when ready to boil, every man shall receive his own job; if he does not the mill shall cease work until he does.

ARTICLE XII.—*Charges and trials.*

SECTION 1. No subordinate lodge shall be expelled or suspended, or deprived of any of its rights or privileges, except as provided in this constitution.

SEC. 2. If any subordinate lodge is found to be violating any of the laws, rules, or regulations of this association, they shall be reported in writing to the vice-president of the district or division in which such subordinate lodge is located, by any member in good standing in this association.

SEC. 3. When the vice-president has received notice of any subordinate lodge violating the laws, &c., as provided in section 2, he shall, as soon as possible, proceed to investigate the case, and if he finds that the charges as reported to him are correct he shall at once notify the president of the national lodge, who shall without unnecessary delay, bring such lodge to trial before a board of investigation, consisting of the president of the national lodge, the vice-president of the district or division, and his deputies, whose decision shall be final, unless non-concurred in by two-thirds of the delegates at the next national convention.

SEC. 4. Before any sub-lodge can be put on trial by the president of the national lodge, the latter shall serve the lodge to be put on trial with a full copy of the charges preferred against it, in writing, not less than two weeks before the time appointed by him for a trial of the case.

SEC. 5. Any sub-lodge put on trial as set forth in this article shall place in the hands of the president of the national lodge such documents as he may desire to further the investigation, and such lodge shall be entitled to produce such testimony bearing upon the case as they may desire, and also to employ counsel, but such counsel must be selected from members in good standing in this order.

SEC. 6. The board of investigations shall have full power to inflict such penalty for violations of laws, etc., as they may deem expedient in the case, and any lodge refusing to pay the penalty inflicted upon it by the board of investigation, their charter shall at once be forfeited until the meeting of the national convention, when if said convention reverse the decision of the investigation board, their charter shall be returned.

SEC. 7. When any member or members of a sub-lodge have violated any of the laws of this Association, charges shall be preferred against them in writing, signed by a member of this order, stating besides the general offense, the specified particulars, with reasonable clearness, a true copy of which shall be placed in possession of the accused at least seven days before the time appointed for trial by committee.

SEC. 8. The charges and certified copy of appointment for trial shall be placed in the hands of a special committee of not less than three members of the lodge, who shall notify both the accused and accuser to appear before the committee for investigation, when they shall present such testimony as will bear upon the case.

SEC. 9. The committee shall keep a correct record of all the proceedings in the case, which they will submit to the lodge, together with a report, embodying their conclusion, in form of resolutions, for the action of the lodge.

SEC. 10. If the accused or accuser fail to appear before the committee when duly summoned, they shall be reported guilty of contempt (if they have not sufficient excuse) and shall be subject to suspension or expulsion, on a vote of the majority present. But their failure to appear shall not preclude the committee from proceeding with the investigation, if the witnesses or other means of investigation are at hand.

Sec. 11. When a committee has reported charges sustained, the accused or accuser may present defense in the lodge, either personally or by counsel (the counsel employed must be members in good standing in this organization) and shall then, with the prosecutor, retire, when a vote by ballot shall be taken: first, whether the lodge will sustain the committee; and second, if the lodge will adopt the recommendation of the committee. On which proposition every member present, except the president, shall vote, and a two-third vote shall determine the result.

Sec. 12. When charges are preferred against the president of the national lodge, the vice-president of the first division, first district, shall select seven lodges, from which lodges one delegate each shall be elected by written ballot. Said delegates shall constitute an investigation board, whose duty it shall be to investigate said charges, and if found guilty said board shall have power to reprimand, suspend, or expel.

Sec. 13. The secretary, treasurer, and trustees of the national lodge, and also the vice-presidents of the several districts and divisions shall be tried as provided in section 12, at which trial or trials, the president of the national lodge shall preside. He shall previously give date, place and hour of meeting.

ARTICLE XIII.—*Penalties and Privileges.*

SECTION 1. The president of the national association shall issue a quarterly password, through the secretary of the national lodge, to each subordinate lodge in good standing. No lodge shall be entitled to or receive the password unless complying with Article IV, section 5. And no member shall communicate the password to another, or use it for any purpose whatever, except to enter a lodge room, under penalty of expulsion.

SEC. 2. Any subordinate lodge disbanding shall immediately transmit to the secretary of the national association all books, seal, charter, and funds in their possession, and in the event of reorganization of said subordinate lodge, they shall be entitled to receive back the same, upon the payment of the usual charter fee, except the funds, which shall stand to their credit on the national lodge book.

SEC. 3. Where there are two or more lodges in one locality and the interests of the organization require their consolidation, they may join in forming a new lodge, by a vote of the majority of the members present: *Provided,* That there shall not be ten members of either lodge who are not desirous of retaining its separate organization; the name of the lodge so formed to be decided by a majority vote of the lodges in joint convention.

SEC. 4. Subordinate lodges shall have the power to reinstate their suspended members by the applicant paying such sum or reinstatement fee as the majority of the lodge may determine.

SEC. 5. Members expelled from a subordinate lodge shall remain expelled for six months, when they may renew their connection with this association on application, in writing, to and on such conditions as may be agreed upon by the lodge to which they formerly belonged. But should the applicant for reinstatement consider the sum demanded exorbitant (or should the lodge refuse to reinstate him for any sum) and the lodge persistently refuses to reinstate him, the advisory board of the national lodge shall, upon application by the person or persons asking for reinstatement, have power to grant such applicant a card for an amount to be determined by said board, and should any sublodge within thirty (30) days after receiving notice from the advisory board of the amount determined upon by them to be charged for reinstatement fail to reinstate such person and grant him or them a card, the president of the national lodge shall issue such card to the person or persons asking reinstatement, collect the amount determined upon by the advisory board, and turn it over to the lodge, and no member shall refuse to work with such person or persons while their case is pending. In all cases, however, where a person applies to the advisory board for a card, the sublodge refusing to grant the same shall be heard in evidence before the board.

SEC. 6. That any member of a former lodge now defunct, and of which the books, etc., have not been returned to the general office (see section 2, this article) who can procure a certificate of recommendation bearing the signature of the president and corresponding representative, together with the impression of the seal of any subordinate lodge to which he may make application, the secretary of the national association shall issue a recommendation for such member to be reinstated into such subordinate lodge, upon payment of such sum as said subordinate lodge may require of him.

SEC. 7. All subordinate lodges having become suspended for nonpayment of dues, or otherwise violating the constitution, meriting suspension, may be reinstated by making proper application to the president of the national association and paying such sums as he may deem proper.

Article XIV.—*Constitutional decisions and appeals.*

SECTION 1. All questions of a constitutional character shall be referred to the vice-president of the district or division having jurisdiction over the sublodge sending it. Sublodges, however, shall have the right to appeal from the decision of the vice-president of their district or division to the president of the national lodge, whose decision shall be final unless nonconcurred in by two-thirds of the delegates present at succeeding national convention.

SEC. 2. Individual members in good standing having a grievance of any kind before their lodge, and not being satisfied with the decision thereof, shall have the same right to appeal from the decision of the lodge through the vice-president of their district or division, as set forth in section 1 of this article. Notice of an appeal by individual members, however, shall be served on the sublodge from whose decision the appeal is made.

SEC. 3. All questions referred to the vice-presidents or president of the national lodge, as set forth in section 1 of this article, shall be in writing, giving full details of the case. These documents shall also bear the impression of the seal of the sublodge and in such cases the seal shall be at the disposal of the individual member the same as with the sublodge.

Article XV.—*Seals.*

SECTION 1. The seal of the national association shall be peculiar to itself; subordinate lodge seals shall be uniform, and furnished by the national association; and all documents emanating from national or subordinate lodge officers shall bear the impression thereof.

Article XVI.—*Cards.*

SECTION 1. This national association shall issue a due card and also a withdrawal card, which shall be in possession of the secretary thereof. He shall distribute them per order of subordinate lodges, for the use of any member in good standing and no subordinate lodge shall have authority to grant or receive any other card but those provided by this national association.

SEC. 2. All members shall provide themselves with a due card, and such card shall show the debit and credit account of such members, in their respective lodges.

SEC. 3. Any person referred to or mentioned in section 1, of article I, must, unless a reasonable excuse is given, produce a card before they be allowed to work; and those not members, who have situations, shall be given four weeks time to join, and the president of the sublodge shall see that this section is enforced.

SEC. 4. Any member of the association going from one locality to another shall provide himself with a withdrawal card. Said card shall bear a certificate of membership from subordinate lodge with a date of initiation, admission by card or reinstatement, and also a certificate of such lodge membership in the national association; and any member obtaining such card must present the same for membership in any other lodge, except the holder of such card works by the day or hour in steel mills, in which case such cards shall be deposited in the lodge composed of men working by the day or hour in said mill—if one be in existence in the mill in which he has obtained employment—and no subordinate lodge shall have power to reject said card. No member shall be entitled to receive a withdrawal card unless he is in good standing and clear on the secretary's books.

SEC. 5. Any member removing from one locality to another and obtaining a situation must deposit his card in the lodge which controls the mill wherein he works, and all cards not deposited within four weeks thereafter, shall be annulled.

SEC. 6. Where there are two or more lodges in one mill controlling the same branch of business, a member who holds membership in any of those lodges shall have a right to demand his withdrawal card from the lodge in which he holds membership, but he must deposit the same in one of the other lodges situated in the same mill, controlling his branch of business.

SEC. 7. Members holding withdrawal cards and not depositing them as provided in section 4 of this article (knowing the existence of a lodge in the locality where they reside or work) shall pay to the lodge in which said card is deposited such fine as said lodge may deem proper to inflict; also dues from the time said card became annulled until it was accepted by the lodge.

SEC. 8. The secretary of the national association shall attach the seal thereof to all cards before forwarding them to subordinate lodges; and all cards granted by any subordinate lodge shall be signed by the subordinate lodge president and financial secretary, and receive the seal of said lodge.

SEC. 9. Any member retiring from the trades represented in this association shall make application for an honorary card at the next stated meeting of his lodge, which shall be granted. Should he at any time desire to deposit said card in any subordinate lodge, the president thereof shall appoint a committee of three to investigate his conduct toward the order and its members during the time he held such card, and if the committee report favorable, a ballot shall be taken, and by a majority vote the applicant shall be admitted to membership. But if the committee report unfavorable, then a ballot shall be taken, and unless two-thirds of the members vote in favor of his admission the president shall reject the card.

ARTICLE XVII.—*Dishonorable members.*

SECTION 1. Any member robbing or embezzling from a brother member, or leaving a member in debt with intent to defraud, by not giving proper notice of his departure, or has been fraudulently receiving or misapplying the funds of the association, or the money of any member or candidate, entrusted to him for payment of the same, or by divulging any of the proceedings of the lodge, or who has slandered any brother member, or advocated division of the funds or separation of lodge districts, or by acting contrary to the established rules of this association on any question affecting the price of labor, or the system of working in any district, if opposed to the interests of his fellow workmen in keeping with the rules of this association, shall, upon trial and conviction thereof, be punished by fine, suspension, or expulsion, as may be determined by two-thirds of the members present.

ARTICLE XVIII.—*Special rules.*

SECTION 1. Every member shall interest himself, individually and collectively, in protecting his trade and the business of all employers who recognize, negotiate, and are under contract with his association. This, however, shall not be construed to mean that a member can work for anything less than the regularly adopted scale of prices, or in any other manner do what is detrimental to the established rules, customs, etc., of this association.

SEC. 2. That in each works the mill committee shall wait on every new workman, when employed, and ask him for his withdrawal card. They shall deliver the same to the secretary. But if he has not got a withdrawal card, and is not a member of the association, steps shall be taken to persuade him to join it. They shall carefully watch, and attend to any complaint that may suddenly arise in the works, or any other matter affecting the interests of the members. And when it is found that a manager, superintendent, or foreman is using his or their influence in persuading men in the mills or factories not to join this association, they shall severally be notified by the mill or factory committee that such action must be stopped.

SEC. 3. When a vacancy occurs in the boiling department the oldest boiler, if he so desires, shall have the preference of the furnace so vacated. Five heats, double turn, shall constitute a day's work for boilers working common iron; six heats, single turn, and not more than ten heats in twenty-four hours, shall be made under any circumstances. Where $1.00 or more per ton is paid extra for boiling charcoal or dephosphorized iron, five heats shall constitute a day's work, single or double turn. The uniform charge for pig iron in a single boiling furnace shall not exceed five hundred pounds per heat, but in neither case shall this apply to furnaces working castings; for a double boiling furnace the charge for pig iron shall not exceed ten hundred pounds per heat; for a double-double boiling furnace the charge for pig iron shall not exceed twenty-one hundred pounds per heat; for a "twin" furnace (where there are two doors on one side only, close together) the charge for pig iron shall not exceed eleven hundred pounds per heat; for a Siemens-Martin furnace the charge shall not exceed fourteen hundred pounds per heat; for a Swindel furnace the charge shall not exceed thirteen hundred pounds per heat. Castings in a single boiling furnace shall not exceed twenty-five hundred pounds per turn on double turn, and thirty hundred pounds on single turn, and sixty hundred pounds for double furnaces on single turn. The product of a single boiling furnace, working cast iron swarth, shall not exceed twenty-eight hundred pounds per turn, a double boiling furnace fifty-six hundred pounds per turn, and a double-double boiling furnace eleven thousand and two hundred pounds per turn. The charge for scrap furnaces on cinder bottoms shall not exceed six thousand pounds per turn for scrap, and not more than three thousand two hundred pounds per turn for one-third scrap and two-thirds swarth, and on sand bottom furnaces nine thousand pounds of scrap per turn; but none of these stipulations apply to other gas furnaces. For fixing furnaces the men shall be given all the necessary ore the furnace requires.

SEC. 4. Any iron worked in a boiling furnace taking more than one and three-quarter hours to make a heat shall be considered a grievance, which, on demand of five members, the mill committee shall report to the boss, and immediately notify the vice-president of the district or division, and on the advice of the vice-president they shall cease work until they get better iron to work. And if at any time within thirty days from the expiration of the above three days' notice the iron shall again be as bad as when the notice was given, the mill committee shall report to the boss, and the night turn, if working double shall finish their turn, and they shall then cease work until they get better iron.

SEC. 5. A fine of five ($5.00) dollars shall be imposed upon any boiler or puddler who is known to put in any "jams" or "cheeks" with brick or fire clay, and upon proof thereof, a fine of five ($5.00) dollars followed by suspension, shall be imposed upon any boiler who is known to violate clauses 1, 2, and 3, of the boiler's (western) scale, or any of them, and the names of such party or parties shall be published in the quarterly statement. Such fines, when imposed, shall be collected from the member at the first regular meeting of his lodge succeeding the violation of this section. This section is not intended to prevent a puddler or boiler from putting a ball of fire clay in the jams during the week in order to keep his furnace working.

SEC. 6. Every member of this association is strictly prohibited from employing helpers at a boiling, puddling, or heating furnace under the age of fifteen years.

SEC. 7. Sheet mills shall be allowed to work three turns, but no turn shall exceed eight hours; and on sheet mills working three turns the number of pairs shall not exceed 180 for single iron or 105 pairs double iron for a turn's work (except in such small sheet mills where orders under fourteen (14) square feet are to be averaged up to twenty-four (24) inches wide by ninety-three (93) inches long, in which cases no heat shall contain more than thirty (30) pairs and no single or double turn sheet mill shall exceed 216 pairs single iron or 120 pairs double iron for a turn's work.

SEC. 8. All iron rolled on sheet and jobbing mills required to be sheared shall be pulled up to the shearman's standing by the company, ready for shearing.

SEC. 9. No nailer shall run his machines (a job) for anything less than full price, or pay more than one half for feeding.

SEC. 10. No nailer under the jurisdiction of this association shall be allowed to buy any part or parts of an automatic feeder, rods or anything pertaining to the same, excepting nipper sockets, in any factory.

SEC. 11. That no member in any works shall render any assistance or loan his tools to any workman who persistently refuses to become a member of this association, or refuses to pay up his arrears to the same, or uses his influence to disorganize his fellow-workmen and make it difficult to carry out the objects of this association.

SEC. 12. Any mill under the jurisdiction of this association running double or treble turn three or four months in one year shall be considered a double-turn mill, and in the event of such mills going on single turn the work shall be divided.

SEC. 13. Should any department of a mill running single, double, or treble turn, be stopped through overproduction or other causes, the work shall be equally divided, except when a furnace is out for repairs, and any person taking a job on conditions shall be branded as a " blacksheep."

SEC. 14. This association will not tolerate any man holding more than one job. One furnace, single turn, one train of rolls double turn, one steel smelting gas furnace one turn, to constitute one job, and all are expected to enforce this rule. Any man holding two or more separate jobs, in violation of this section, shall be stigmatized as a " blacksheep." By " two or more jobs" is meant where one man draws pay for two or more separate jobs at the same time. No person shall be allowed to work two or more consecutive turns at his job in a mill or factory when there are members out of employment, in the immediate vicinity, fully qualified to do the work.

SEC. 15. Any member known to go to his work drunk, or who shall lose any work through drunkenness, and the foreman of the mill discharges him, no steps shall be taken by his lodge to reinstate him in his work. Any member acting in a manner detrimental to the interests of, or that will bring reproach upon this association or its members, shall be reprimanded, fined, suspended, or expelled from the lodge in which he holds membership.

SEC. 16. The members of this association shall not injure each other in their employment, such as undermining or conniving at member's jobs, when such member is known to be standing out for his rights and trying to obtain those privileges which properly belong to the members of this association. Any member taking a job in such a way shall become unworthy of membership, and be expelled from the association.

SEC. 17. The several members of all lodges shall, as much as in their power, endeavor to establish and make permanent the same, and use all honorable exertions to secure employment for any member of this association, in preference to all others. They shall also give a helping hand to each other in the works, as much as it may be in their power so to do.

SEC. 18. Except on questions of wages regulated by scale of prices, two weeks' notice shall be required from employers before a reduction can take place, and two weeks' notice shall be given when an advance is requested, and any rules agreed upon by the mill or factory committee and company, *and ratified by a two-thirds vote of the lodge,* cannot be changed unless two weeks' notice has been given by either party.

Sec. 19. When it shall be found beyond a doubt that any member of this association, in any mill under its jurisdiction, is working below the prices established by it, the men in such mill shall cease work until such prices are rectified.

Sec. 20. No member of this association shall be allowed to change or alter rules existing in any mill before submitting the desired change to the lodge having control of the department for which the change is intended; and if a majority of all members of the lodge vote in favor of said change, the mill committee shall notify the superintendent of said change before the same goes into effect.

Sec. 21. Any member having worked at any of the trades in iron or steel mills or factories shall not be termed green hands, *provided* they are members in good standing in this association.

Sec. 22. Any person employed as foreman, puddle boss, superintendent, or general manager of any mill or factory, or holding any of the above positions, together with a situation in the mill or factory, shall not be eligible to membership in this association.

Sec. 23. That the members of this association shall, at the discretion of the president of the national lodge, refuse to work in any mill or factory where the manager, superintendent, foreman, or puddle boss is deriving a direct benefit from a furnace, rolls, etc., in addition to his position as above, for which he receives a regular salary.

Sec. 24. Should any member of this association undertake to instruct an unskilled workman in any of the trades represented in this association, it shall be the duty of the mill committee to notify him that this association cannot tolerate such proceedings, and should he still persist in doing so, charges shall be preferred against him and he shall be expelled or suspended, as the lodge may determine.

Sec. 25. Any member or members of this association having procured credit for groceries, provisions, or clothing during a strike, and who refuses to pay or make arrangements to pay the same, he or they shall receive no protection from the mill committee or the lodge in case of discharge by the manager, upon the complaint of the person or persons to whom such debt or debts are owing.

Sec. 26. In case one department of a mill is found to be privately working at a less rate of wages than is provided for through the regularly adopted scale of wages of this association, and such terms and agreement coming to the knowledge of the officers, all other departments in said mill shall cease work in order to enforce the price specified in the scale.

Sec. 27. The foreman on each separate job in steel works shall, in conjunction with the mill committee, have the privilege of filling a temporary vacancy.

Sec. 28. In each mill, under the jurisdiction of this association, the weight of each turn's work shall be displayed on a board, in some conspicuous place in the mill, where tonnage men can see the amount of product turned out each turn.

Sec. 29. Wherever practicable any mill, department, or factory under the jurisdiction of this association, desiring so to do, can, upon agreement with the management, arrange to work on the eight-hour system.

Sec. 30. Any member leaving a job to better his condition can not claim his former job if he gets discharged or loses his new job on account of a shut-down.

Article XIX.—*Subordinate lodge officers and their duties.*

Section 1. The elective officers of a sublodge shall consist of a president, vice-president, recording secretary, financial secretary, treasurer, guide, inside guard, outside guard, and three trustees, and in case of the resignation or death of any one of them a successor shall be elected to fill the vacancy.

Sec. 2. It shall be the duty of the president to preside at all meetings of the lodge, preserve order, and enforce the constitution; he shall decide all questions of order, subject to an appeal to the lodge; he shall have the right to vote at the election of officers, and when the members are equally divided on other questions he shall have the casting vote; he shall sign all orders on the treasurer for such moneys as shall by a vote of the lodge be ordered to be paid; he shall call special meetings at the request of the mill committee or by request of ten members of the lodge in good standing, and perform such other duties as the lodge may require of him.

Sec. 3. It shall be the duty of the vice-president to perform all the duties of the president in case of the absence of that officer and to assist in preserving order in the lodge.

Sec. 4. It shall be the duty of the recording secretary to record the proceedings of the lodge in a book kept for that purpose; to read all papers before the lodge, and draw and sign all warrants ordered by the lodge, and perform such other duties as the lodge may require.

Sec. 5. The corresponding representative shall answer all letters and carry on all correspondence which may be deemed necessary, abstracts of which he shall record in a book kept for that purpose, which at all times shall be subject to the inspection of the lodge. He shall also prepare and send to the secretary of the national association a quarterly report, as provided in section 5, and a weekly report, as provided for in section 6 of article IV and section 6 of article XI, and perform such other duties as the lodge may require of him. All necessary expenses incurred by him in the discharge of his duties shall be paid by the lodge.

SEC. 6. It shall be the duty of the financial secretary to receive all moneys due the lodge and pay the same to the treasurer, from whom he shall take a receipt; he shall keep correctly the accounts of the lodge with its members, and shall at all times have his books open for examination by the auditing committee, and perform such other duties as the lodge may require of him.

SEC. 7. It shall be the duty of the treasurer to receive from the financial secretary all moneys collected by him. He shall deposit all moneys belonging to the lodge in bank, in his name as treasurer of —— lodge, No. —, State of ——, Amalgamated Association of Iron and Steel Workers, and before any moneys thus deposited can be drawn each check shall be signed by him as treasurer and countersigned by the president, recording secretary, and chairman of the board of trustees of the lodge. He shall pay all warrants drawn on him by the president and signed by the recording secretary; keep regular and correct accounts of all moneys received and paid by him, and report the same at each quarterly meeting, having his accounts open for examination by the auditing committee at any time when called upon; and at the expiration of his term of office (or sooner if called upon by the lodge so to do) deliver up all moneys, books, papers, and vouchers in his possession to the auditing committee or his legally elected successor. Before entering upon the duties of his office he shall give bond, with such security as may be thought proper by the lodge, for the correct and faithful performance of his duties.

SEC. 8. It shall be the duty of the guide to see that all present are entitled to remain; take up the password; introduce candidates, and attend to visiting members.

SEC. 9. It shall be the duty of the guards to attend properly to the doors, inside and out, and see that none but members are admitted, unless permitted by the lodge.

SEC. 10. It shall be the duty of the trustees to have charge of the hall and all property of the lodge, subject to the direction of the lodge, and perform such other duties as the lodge may require. They shall also hold the bond of the treasurer, and see that said bond is legal.

ARTICLE XX.—*Nomination and election of sublodge officers.*

SECTION 1. The nomination of sublodge officers shall be made at the stated meeting preceding the night of election, also on the night of election. A member can be elected into office while absent, provided he has accepted the nomination.

SEC. 2. To be eligible to the office of president, vice-president, recording secretary, financial secretary, treasurer, or corresponding representative of a sublodge, all candidates therefor must have been members six months. This shall not apply to lodges that have not been organized six months.

SEC. 3. The election of officers, except representative to the national convention (see section 7, article V), shall be separately, by ballot, and shall take place on the last stated meeting in December and June; except the recording secretary, financial secretary, treasurer, and three trustees, who shall be elected annually on the last stated meeting in December.

SEC. 4. The president shall appoint three members, not in nomination for office, one as clerk, and two as tellers of election, who shall receive the votes and count them in the presence of the lodge, and the clerk shall announce the result to the president, who shall, in turn, declare the names of the successful candidates to the lodge.

SEC. 5. The officers elect shall assume their respective duties on the first stated meeting after their election.

SEC. 6. No member shall be entitled to a vote who is three months in arrears for dues, assessments, and fines; and no candidate shall be eligible to office unless he is clear on the secretary's books up to and including the night of election.

SEC. 7. The written ballot shall be used in balloting for all officers, and a candidate must receive a majority of all the votes cast before he can be declared elected. If there should be no election on the first ballot all but the two highest shall be dropped. No member present shall be excused from voting.

ARTICLE XXI.—*Installation of sublodge officers.*

SECTION 1. The installation of sublodge officers shall take place at the first regular meeting after election. Vacancies *pro tem.* may be filled at any regular meeting by appointment by the president.

SEC. 2. Any member accepting an election in any subordinate lodge and failing to appear for installation without a constitutional excuse, shall be fined the sum of fifty cents.

SEC. 3. No officer shall be allowed to vacate his chair until his successor has been installed.

ARTICLE XXII.—*Subordinate lodge meetings.*

SECTION 1. Stated meetings of sublodges shall be held not less than twice a month.

SEC. 2. Special meetings must be called by the president, on application of the mill committee or any ten members in good standing; or at any time the president himself may deem it necessary for the interest of the lodge.

SEC. 3. When special meetings are called there shall be no business transacted except such as is specified in the call.

SEC. 4. Seven members shall constitute a quorum for the transaction of business at stated meetings, and ten members shall constitute a quorum at special meetings.

ARTICLE XXIII.—*Applicants for membership.*

SECTION 1. Candidates for membership to sublodges shall be proposed by a member of the lodge in good standing, which proposition shall be made in writing, entered on the records, and referred to a committee, whose duty it shall be to inquire and report, in writing, at the next stated meeting of the lodge as to the fitness of the candidate for membership. Candidates for membership working by the day or hour in steel mills shall apply to the lodge composed of men working by the day or hour in such mills, if one is in existence, and no lodge composed of tonnage men shall receive application for membership from such men in said mills. The recording secretary shall read the report of the committee, and if it be favorable the candidate shall be balloted for, and if all the balls are white he shall be declared elected; but if two or more black balls appear against him his case shall be referred to a special committee for investigation; and should the persons casting the black balls refuse or neglect to give their reasons for so doing to the special committee for the space of two weeks, and should the special committee themselves find no just cause for this rejection they shall report favorable to his election, whereupon he shall again be balloted for, and if two-thirds of the votes cast be favorable he shall be declared elected, but if more than one-third be unfavorable he shall be declared rejected. Should either committee report unfavorable they shall state their reasons for so doing, and the lodge shall then receive or reject said reasons by a majority vote. Membership shall date from the time of initiation, admission by card or reinstatement, and dues, fines, and other moneys shall be charged accordingly.

SEC. 2. It shall be the duty of the corresponding representative to notify the general office of the rejection of a candidate, and a person who has been rejected in any lodge shall not be proposed for membership in any other lodge for the space of six months thereafter. And should the candidate apply to any other lodge for membership after the expiration of six months, it shall be the duty of such lodge to instruct their corresponding representative to inquire of the sublodge that rejected the candidate the cause of such rejection.

SEC. 3. The member who shall propose a candidate for membership shall, at the time of making the proposition, pay to the secretary one-half the amount of the initiation fee, which shall be returned in case the candidate is rejected. Should the candidate be elected he shall be admitted on payment of the balance of his initiation fee and signing the constitution.

SEC. 4. Should the candidate neglect or refuse to appear and be initiated for the term of one month after receiving notice of his election, unless prevented by sickness or other unavoidable occurrence, he shall forfeit his claim to membership, together with the amount paid at the time of his application.

ARTICLE XXIV.—*Dues and other moneys.*

SECTION 1. Each member of a sublodge shall pay as initiation fee not less than one dollar and such sums as monthly dues as the lodge shall determine, together with fines and other moneys. The due card shall be sufficient notice of his arrears, and any member omitting to pay the same within three months shall be reported to the lodge by the financial secretary; whereupon the president shall, unless otherwise directed by the lodge, declare such members suspended, and the names of such members shall be communicated to every lodge in the district by the corresponding representative of the sublodge from which they were suspended.

SEC. 2. A member suspended for nonpayment of dues shall not be restored to membership except he apply in writing. The said application shall then be referred to a committee whose duty it shall be to investigate his character and fitness for membership and report their opinion in writing at a subsequent meeting of the lodge; whereupon a ballot shall be had, and if a majority of the ballots sustain the committee it shall be recorded as the judgment of the lodge, and any member thus reinstated shall pay such sum as the lodge may determine.

SEC. 3. A member feeling incapable by some unavoidable cause to pay dues, fines, or other moneys, shall report his case to the lodge, which may exempt him from paying the same by a two-thirds majority.

ARTICLE XXV.—*Members in arrears.*

SECTION 1. Any member of a subordinate lodge three months in arrears shall not be recognized by the mill committee in any grievance in which he may become involved during such arrears, even though he pay up his arrearages immediately before or after the trouble arises.

ARTICLE XXVI.—*Funds.*

SECTION 1. The funds of each sublodge shall be used only for its legitimate purpose.

SEC. 2. In order that the funds of the lodge may be had at as short notice as possible when required, it shall be the duty of the treasurer to deposit in bank all moneys over twenty-five dollars. The treasurer shall draw the money thus deposited whenever it may be required to be used to pay orders regularly drawn on him by the proper officers of the lodge.

SEC. 3. All bills and other claims against the lodge must be presented at regular meetings and receive the approval of the same before payment.

ARTICLE XXVII.—*Sublodge auditing committee.*

SECTION 1. At the last stated meetings in June and December, each sublodge shall appoint three members for the purpose of auditing the accounts of the financial secretary and treasurer.

SEC. 2. The auditing committee shall thoroughly investigate the accounts and report the same to the lodge on their first stated meetings in July and January, and the balance that the books call for shall be shown to the lodge by the treasurer, or its equivalent in certificate of deposit, or the account in a bank book.

SEC. 3. Should the auditing committee, through complication of accounts or otherwise, be unable to report, as provided in section 2, this article, they shall nevertheless report to the lodge the condition of affairs, when the lodge shall grant such time as the exigency of the case requires.

SEC. 4. It shall be the duty of all members to render the officers and committees of the lodge proper aid and influence in the prosecution of their duties.

SEC. 5. All committees not otherwise provided for shall be appointed by the president.

ARTICLE XXVIII.—*Fines for various causes.*

SECTION 1. Officers and members of subordinate lodges are required to be punctual in their attendance.

SEC. 2. Officers of subordinate lodges failing to attend the regular meetings of the lodge shall, for each omission, be fined twenty-five cents, unless satisfactory reasons can be shown, in which case the fine shall be remitted.

SEC. 3. Members of subordinate lodges failing to attend meetings of their lodge at least once a month shall be fined the sum of ten cents, unless excused through sickness or some unavoidable cause.

SEC. 4. Any member of a subordinate lodge failing to appear at the last stated meetings in June and December, shall be fined fifty cents, unless he can give satisfactory evidence that it was impossible to attend.

SEC. 5. Any member of a subordinate lodge persisting in using unseemly language, or in an indecent manner give offense to a brother member, or by offensive conduct, shall be fined one dollar for the first offense, and if he still persists in the unmanly use of such language he shall be excluded from the lodge room and will not be permitted to reënter during the meeting.

SEC. 6. The chairman of any committee failing to report at the time required, unless further time be granted, shall be fined one dollar. Such fine, however, shall be remitted when a satisfactory explanation is given.

SEC. 7. Any member entering a subordinate lodge under the influence of liquor, shall for the first offense be fined one dollar, and double the sum for every subsequent offense.

SEC. 8. Any member of a subordinate lodge violating his obligation to this order shall be liable to a fine of not less than three dollars, reprimand, suspension, or expulsion, according to a decision of his lodge on a two-thirds majority vote.

SEC. 9. Any corresponding representative failing or neglecting to prepare and forward the quarterly report of his lodge, or to attend to such other duties as pertain to his office, shall be fined two dollars.

SEC. 10. All fines thus imposed, if not paid at the time, shall be charged by the financial secretary to the person from whom due, and must be liquidated to entitle him to any privileges or benefits of this association.

ARTICLE XXIX.—*By-laws for subordinate lodges.*

SECTION 1. Subordinate lodges shall have full power to make such by-laws for their government as they may deem necessary, provided they do not conflict with any of the laws, rules, or regulations herein contained.

ARTICLE XXX.—*Amendments and dissolution.*

SECTION 1. This constitution shall not be altered or amended except by the national convention, a majority of the members present consenting thereto.

SEC. 2. No subordinate lodge can dissolve so long as there are ten members in good standing who shall be willing to continue it.

RULES OF ORDER OF THE NATIONAL CONVENTION AND SUBLODGES.

Rule 1.—The president having taken the chair, the officers and members shall take their respective seats, and at the sound of the gavel there shall be general silence.

Rule 2. The president shall preserve order and pronounce the decision of the lodge on all subjects. He shall decide questions of order without debate, subject to an appeal to the lodge by three members; on which appeal no member shall speak but once, when the question before the lodge shall be: "Shall the decision of the president stand as the judgment of the lodge?" which question shall be taken by the lodge.

Rule 3.—During the reading of the minutes, communications, and other papers, or when a member is addressing the chair, silence shall be observed in the lodge room.

Bute 4. Any member who shall misbehave himself in the meeting of the lodge, disturb the order or harmony thereof, either by abusive, disorderly, or profane language, or shall refuse obedience to the presiding officer, shall be admonished of his offense by the president, and if he offend again he shall be excluded from the room for the session, and afterwards dealt with as this constitution provides.

Rule 5.—No member shall be interrupted while speaking, except it shall be to call him to order, or for the purpose of explanation.

Rule 6.—If a member, while speaking, be called to order, he shall, at the request of the president, take his seat until the question of order is determined, when, if permitted, he may proceed.

Rule 7.—Each member, when speaking, shall be standing, and respectfully address the president, confine himself to the question under debate, and avoid all personalities or indecorous or sarcastic language.

Rule 8.—If two or more members arise to speak at the same time, the president shall decide who is entitled to the floor.

Rule 9.—No member shall speak more than once on the same subject or question until all who wish to speak shall have an opportunity to do so, nor more than twice, without permission from the president.

Rule 10.—No motion shall be subject to debate until it shall have been seconded and stated from the chair. It shall be reduced to writing at the request of any two members.

Rule 11.—When a question is before the lodge no motion shall be in order except to adjourn, for the previous question, to postpone indefinitely, or for a certain time, to divide, or commit, or amend; which motions shall severally have precedence, in the order herein arranged.

Rule 12.—On the call of five members debate shall cease and a question be taken on the matter or subject under debate.

Rule 13.—On a call of five members a majority of the lodge may demand the previous question, which shall be put in this form: "Shall the main question be put?" and until it is decided, shall preclude all amendments and all further debate.

Rule 14.—When a blank is to be filled, the question shall be taken first upon the highest sum or number, and the longest and latest time proposed.

Rule 15.—Any member may call for a division of the question when the sense will admit of it; but a motion to strike out and insert shall be indivisble, except at the option of the mover.

Rule 16.—Before putting the question, the president shall ask "Is the lodge ready for the question?" If no member rises to speak, he shall rise and put it; and after he has risen to put the question no member shall be permitted to speak upon it. When the president is addressing the lodge or putting a question silence shall be observed in the lodge room.

Rule 17.—All questions, unless otherwise provided, shall be decided by a majority of the votes given.

Rule 18.—Communications, petitions, and memorials shall be presented through a member of this lodge, or by the presiding officer; a brief statement of their contents shall be entered upon the minutes.

Rule 19.—Any member may excuse himself from serving on a committee, if at the time of his appointment he is a member of one other committee.

Rule 20.—The person first named on a committee shall act as chairman until another is chosen by the members of the committee. The mover of a resolution referred to a special committee is usually the first named thereon.

Rule 21.—No committee can be finally discharged until all the debts contracted by it shall have been paid.

Rule 22.—A motion to adjourn is always in order after the regular business is gone through, which motion shall be decided without debate.

Rule 23.—A motion to lay upon the table shall be decided without debate.

Rule 24.—When a motion is postponed indefinitely it shall not be acted on during that or the next succeeding stated meeting.

Rule 25.—No motion for reconsideration shall be received if made by a member who voted in the minority in the first instance.

Rule 26.—On the call of five members present, the ayes and nays shall be ordered. When the question is decided by yeas and nays each member shall vote and the names and manner of voting shall be recorded on the minutes.

Rule 27.—All questions of order not provided for by these rules must be determined by Cushing's Manual, or at the discretion of the lodge.

ORDER OF BUSINESS OF THE NATIONAL CONVENTION.

1. Opening the convention.
2. Calling roll of officers and representatives.
3. Appointing of committees.
4. Report of president of the national lodge.
5. Report of secretary of the national lodge.
6. Report of treasurer of the national lodge.
7. Report of trustees of the national lodge.
8. Report of vice-presidents and special organizers.
9. Reading and referring of the programme of business.
10. Reading the minutes of the previous session.
11. Calling the list of absentees.
12. Reception of communications.
13. Report of committees.
14. Unfinished business.
15. New business.
16. Bills of account.
17. For the general good of the order.
18. Closing and adjournment.

ORDER OF BUSINESS FOR SUBORDINATE LODGES.

1. Opening the lodge.
2. Calling the roll of officers and members.
3. Reading minutes of the previous meeting.
4. Calling list of absentees of the last meeting.
5. Payment of dues, fines, and other moneys.
6. Propositions for candidates.
7. Reports of committee on candidates.
8. Balloting for candidates.
9. Initiation of candidates.
10. Reception of communications.
11. Are any of the brothers sick?
12. Is any brother out of employment?
13. Does any brother know of a vacancy?
14. Has any brother violated his obligation?
15. Reports of standing committees.
16. Reports of select committees.

17. Are there any bills of account?
18. Unfinished business.
19. New business.
20. Has any member anything to offer for the good of the order?
21. Receipts of the evening.
22. Has the treasurer received the same?
23. Closing and adjournment.

By Mr. BOATNER:

Q. Does your order countenance any unlawful or revolutionary efforts to coerce employers?—A. No, sir.

Q. The object of the organization is by organization to protect and maintain the rights of the workingmen?—A. To obtain fair day's wages for labor and to get rules and regulations to enable them to work with comfort.

Q. Well, does your order also reach to any oppression of individual workmen? For instance, say a man is improperly discharged or unjustly dealt with in any way, does your organization take jurisdiction of the case of that man?—A. They make an investigation to find out the cause of the discharge.

Q. And if they find a man is improperly discharged they give him the moral support of the organization?—A. Yes, sir.

By Mr. BYNUM:

Q. How many employés are there in the works at Homestead; how many men work there in the whole mill?—A. From what I learned, perhaps 3,800.

Q. Now, what proportion of them are members of the Amalgamated Association?—A. I am not able to state the number, but there are eight lodges, but what their membership is I could not tell you.

Q. Can you give about the number of men inside the mill who belong to the association?—A. Not positively; that is, I can not give it to you accurately.

Q. I do not ask you to give it to me positively?—A. It may run from 800 to 1,100, but I could not just state.

By Mr. BOATNER:

Q. Do you know how many there are in the county of Allegheny who are members of the Amalgamated Association?—A. There are a good many, but the number I could not give. The sublodges have control over that. They report annually what the members are, but I could not say.

Q. I mean, when I say "Amalgamated men," members of the Amalgamated Association?—A. They are pretty well in; then there are some who are not in.

By the CHAIRMAN:

Q. Are you the president of the National Association of Amalgamated Workmen?—A. Yes, sir.

Q. That extends through how many States, everywhere?—A. Through the entire United States.

By Mr. BRODERICK:

Q. Just one question. The association does not countenance violence of any kind for the purpose of keeping out nonunion men or preventing them from securing employment?—A. No, sir.

Q. Nothing of that kind is sanctioned by the association?—A. They are always advised to be law-abiding people.

H. Mis. 335——11

TESTIMONY OF H. C. FRICK—Recalled.

H. C. FRICK, recalled and examined.

By the CHAIRMAN:

Q. There have been several statements made with reference to the effect upon the workmen in the four departments at Homestead of the scale that your company proposed if that was carried into effect. Can you state with any more particularity than you have already done about that?—A. Yes, I think I can.

Q. I want to call your attention to another thing. Some of the workmen who have testified state that it is not the best paid who are to be reduced, but some of those who have the hardest jobs to perform are the most reduced. I would like to hear your explanation on this point.—A. Well, we will take for instance the 119-inch plate mill. In that department those who receive the highest pay will under the new scale, or the scale proposed, suffer the greatest reduction. I have had here placed beside the earnings of the men employed in that department in the month of May the lowest wages that they would have made under the new scale when the same tonnage was produced. By glancing your eye along this column you will see there are quite a number of men in that department whose wages were not reduced at all. For instance, there is a number here in one list of 25 unchanged by the new scale and whose earnings I suppose, from looking at this, averaged during the month $75 per month. I think it will exceed that.

Q. Let me ask you a question there. Why do you take May; is that an average month, or do you take it because it is nearest to the closing?—A. I take May because it was the nearest month to the one in which we proposed to hold the conference.

Q. Were the earnings in May the average or larger than the average?—A. The earnings in May may have been a little larger than usual; that is, larger than the average. How much I could not say, but not very much. There is another page with about the same number of names on it where there are no reductions. These papers will give you in detail, however, just the number who were reduced. There are a number of men employed in these departments, 30? men I think I am safe in saying in this department, and I find there was but 82 reduced in this department.

Q. Is there a statement on that paper showing just the number, without reference to the names, reduced and the number not reduced?—A. Yes, sir; that statement is complete.

Q. We may not want to publish the whole list, but simply take these numbers.—A. As I say, of the 300 men in this department——

Q. What department is that?—A. In the 119-inch plate mill there are but 82 men reduced; that is to say, where the tonnage rate is affected. The minimum, however, would apply to the tonnage men on the sliding scale only. They are reduced by the changes in the minimum; that is, all of them except those who are employed by the day and by the month.

Q. When you get through with this statement I will ask you some questions.—A. Here is a statement of open-hearth department No. 2. There were employed in that department in the month of May 296 men; 196 were unchanged by the new schedule and 100 were changed. Here is a statement of open hearth No. 1, where there were 172 men employed, 75 of whom are reduced and 97 are not reduced, unless it should be that they are on the sliding scale and would be affected by the change in the minimum. Here is a statement of the men employed in the 32-inch slabbing mill, which some of them have designated as the armor mill. I find that there were 157 employed; 106 are not reduced and 51 are reduced. There are of course a few of the 106 who are on the sliding scale and who will be affected by the change in the minimum.

In that connection, if you will permit me, I would like to say a witness here yesterday, Mr. McLuckie, stated we had purchased the Duquesne steel plant for the purpose of making billets in order to reduce the price of billets and thus affect the wages at the Homestead works, as the wages in these works were based on the price of billets. I might say, to show how absurd this is, our pay roll at Homestead for the month of May was over $200,000. Only about 40 per cent of that pay roll is affected by the sliding scale or by the price of billets, but we will say it is $80,000. We manufacture at Duquesne about 20,000 tons of billets monthly. Say that we reduce the price of billets at Duquesne $1 per ton in order that it might have an effect upon the wages at Homestead. A reduction of $1 would mean a loss of $20,000 at those works to us. We will succeed by that, we will say, in reducing the wages of our Homestead men, which amount to $80,000 a month, 3.78 per cent—we will call it 4 per cent; 4 per cent of $80,000 is $3,200. So, according to the reasoning of Mr. McLuckie, by losing $20,000 at Duquesne we would save $3,200 at Homestead. I think that will be plain to anybody. And so on down. Every dollar we will take off billets at Duquesne we will lose $20,000 per month, to save $3,200 per month; or, in other words, make a net loss of almost $17,000 by that operation every month.

Q. Mr. Frick, what was the real reason of your company for proposing this schedule of pay or compensation to these men. I have reference to the change of the minimum price and the reduction. I understand, I think, from what has already transpired, the desire of the company to change the time of the expiration of the contract from the last of June to the end of the year. Now what I want to know is the reason why the company proposes to reduce the basis of compensation, and, in fact, reduce the compensation to these men, which you admit would be at least 15 per cent.—A. I think, judge, I have answered that, although I will try to do so again. The reduction in the selling price of our product was one reason; another reason——

Q. Will you please state what that was?—A. I gave that; you will find that among my testimony, and I could not repeat it unless I referred to it. Another reason was, we had to put in new machinery, which largely increased the output; that is to say, we had to put in this new open-hearth plant to increase our capacity in that direction, in addition to the No. 1 open-hearth plant we had, changing the method of operation there, casting a larger ingot, so that the tonnage would be larger, and by changes made in this 32-inch slabbing mill we have been enabled to increase the production of the 119-inch plate mill, I think, at least 50 per cent over what it did do at one time. We thought a readjustment was necessary—in fact, we knew it was, for I may say here, we have lost money this year and I think a greater part of last year on every ton of blooms, billets, and slabs that we have sold which were produced at Homestead.

Q. You say you have lost money on them?—A. Yes, sir.

Q. Does the amount which you pay your workmen have any relation to the amount of income or profits of the company, or are these wages fixed arbitrarily?—A. The wages, I may say, with the exception of this 40 per cent that is affected by the sliding scale, are fixed arbitrarily; that is to say, we agree to pay so much, and we pay it through good times and bad, with very little change. The lowest priced labor we have at Homestead that is done by men—of course we have boys who do not get quite as much—is 14 cents an hour. These men, the common ordinary day laborers, usually work ten hours. If they work longer they get paid additional.

Q. Then your laborers share in the matter of profits only in consequence of the sliding scale, which is affected by the market?—A. Exactly. If you will permit me, while we are on this question; if you remember, the witness I referred to stated, if I recollect correctly, that we manufactured so many billets more than other people. Now, I have before me a list of the steel-billet-makers and their daily capacity, and I would state this is approximately correct.

Q. Is that throughout the United States?—A. Yes, sir. I would not swear it was absolutely correct, but I find there is a capacity to manufacture of about 10,100 daily. At the Duquesne works our capacity is about 800 tons daily. I find in this list that Jones and Laughlins, who were referred to on yesterday, manufacture 1,000 tons daily, and so on. This list I will put in evidence, if you wish.

Steel-billet makers and their capacity daily.

	Tons.
Duquesne Works, Cochran, Pa	800
Homestead Works, Munhall, Pa	400
Jones & Laughlin's, Pittsburg, Pa	1,000
Oliver Iron and Steel Co., Pittsburg, Pa	250
Hainsworth Steel Co., Pittsburg, Pa	350
Shoenberger & Co., Pittsburg, Pa	350
Spang Steel and Iron Co., Pittsburg, Pa	250
Riverside Iron Works, Wheeling, W. Va	400
Wheeling Steel Works, Wheeling, W. Va	400
Bellaire Nail Works, Bellaire, Ohio	400
Laughlin & Junction, Mingo Junction, Ohio	400
Middleport, Ohio	350
Ashland Steel Co., Ashland, Ky	400
Belleville, Ill	250
Joilet, Ill	800
South Chicago, Ill	400
Cleveland R. M. Co., Cleveland, Ohio	350
Otis Iron and S. Co., Cleveland, Ohio	250
Cambria Iron Co., Johnstown, Pa	400
Pennsylvania Steel Co., Steelton, Pa	400
Bethlehem Iron Co., Bethlehem, Pa	250
Lackawanna, Scranton, Pa	250
Troy Iron and Steel Co., Troy, N. Y	300
Chester, Thurlow, Pa	250
Pottstown Iron Co., Pottstown, Pa	250
Pottsville, Pa	200
	10,100

In addition to this, there are new works just about completed at New Castle, Pa. Its estimated capacity is about 600 tons per day, and one under contract at McKeesport, Pa., capacity about 400 tons per day.

That is to show we do not by any manner of means control the billet market.

Q. What proportion of the steel billets produced in the United States are produced by your mills?—A. Well, according to that statement, Homestead is put down here at 400 tons; that would make, counting the Homestead Works and the Duquesne Works, 1,200 tons, which would be about 12 per cent.

Q. Twelve per cent of the whole output of the mills in the United States?—A. Yes, sir; I think that is correct.

Q. Will you state, Mr. Frick, for the information of the committee, either at other mills, if you know, in this country, or at your own, the approximate cost of the production of a ton of steel and steel billets?—A. Well, I believe I declined to answer that question the other evening, and I do not like to go into the question of cost.

Q. I am not asking you for a minute detailed account, but if you know what is the cost at other mills, or at your own, the committee would like to know.—A. I might say in a general way in regard to the cost that it is a difficult matter to state exactly what the cost is, and I would like to tell you why.

Q. We would like to know the reasons and elements which enter into it.—A. For instance here are two mills at Homestead, which we call the 33 inch and the 23 inch mills, in which we manufacture beams, channels, and structural material and billets. The 23 and 33 inch is the size of the rollers.

Mr. BYNUM. It does not have reference to the thickness of the plates at all?

The WITNESS. No, sir. Now we find it necessary, owing to the cost of the material there, that we should have a new mill, which we have just about completed. I believe we call it the 35-inch mill. We have completed that mill at a cost I think of something like $800,000, and it has only been in operation about fifty days.

By the CHAIRMAN:

Q. What is the cost of the entire working plant at Homestead; I do not mean to the dollar?—A. That would have to be the cost now, and I could ascertain——

Q. I do not ask you for accuracy.—A. I should suppose $5,000,000 or $6,000,000.

Q. From $5,000,000 to $6,000,000?—A. Yes, sir; exclusive of the land. Now we have completed this new beam mill, but before it was completed we ordered a part of the material for the reconstruction of these mills. Here is a whole list of materials here for that purpose, when the orders were placed, and the name of the contractor with whom they were placed, the date they are to be delivered, and the price that all these articles are to cost. I find the footing to be—I have not gone over it—$159,526.50. I find a list of articles which the contractor has agreed to deliver on the 16th of September, so that from now on until that time and later we will be at work changing these mills. Of course these are mills which in their time were first-class mills. As Mr. Roberts remarked yesterday, Jones & Laughlin he says have a very much better mill than our 23-inch mill. Well, he may be right in that, but we of course are going to enlarge our mill and make it more modern. At the same time he stated the wages which were paid in that same mill—a mill comparing with our 23-inch mill. I do not know that I remember just what percentage of wages he stated they paid more than we paid, but I would like to, if you wish, give you an idea of what wages we pay in that mill.

Q. All right, we will be glad to have it.—A. I find here a list of men employed in the 23-inch mill. The number I suppose would be 200 men. I find that we have 2 rollers in that mill, and that the first one worked twenty-six days in May and earned $285.05, and that the second one worked twenty-two days and earned $247.45. As Mr. Potter explained to you this morning our mills are under the control of superintendents. These rollers retain the money they receive. They have nobody to pay out of that, while at Jones & Laughlin's the rollers, as I understood Mr. Potter to say, and Mr. Roberts also, have to pay out of their earnings. I have given you the earnings of the rollers in this mill. Now I find here the heaters in that same mill; there are 6 of them, and they worked on an average about twenty-three days. Their earnings will average over $130 each per month. Then there are the heaters' first helpers. There are quite a number of them; the average, I should think, would be about $80 per month. Those are the wages we pay in that mill, and in this particular mill we asked no change whatever—no reduction in the minimum at all, until probably when these new improvements are put in, there will be necessarily a readjustment made, but until that was done there was to be no change whatever in this department. So that in a comparison with Jones and Laughlin's mill, Mr. Roberts took up a department of ours in which we proposed no change.

Mr. BYNUM. He did not state that. He was only comparing them as to the wages paid.

The WITNESS. I did not understand Mr. Roberts to state, however, that we did not intend to make any change in that department. Now, in regard to a question which was brought up by one witness in regard to the mortgages which we hold on property in Homestead belonging to our employes, I will say we do this only for the convenience of our employés and to assist them. Any man who will come to us and say that he has a lot he has purchased on which he has paid, we will say, $500, we will advance all the money that he may want with which to construct a house, allowing him to pay it off at so much a month—just whatever he may fix and whatever he thinks he can spare from his earnings. We do that in all cases at all our works. We charge him 6 per cent for the money; and I may say that to my knowledge we have never foreclosed a mortgage, not one, or given any employé the slightest trouble in regard to it. I have before me a statement showing the amounts that we have loaned to the workmen at our Homestead Steel Works, the names and the total amount, which I will file with you.

Statement of principal due on bonds and mortgages, June 1, 1892, Homestead, steel works department.

Robert P. Dickson	$555.00
H. Critchlow	37.50
Jno. Fitzsimmons	396.00
Jno. F. Carney	296.00
Jas. Rushton	100.00
Solomon Walker	151.33
Walter and Annie C. Aston	335.50
Jno. McCallum	175.00
Chas. Stagg	260.00
Jno. Dierken (mortgage paid off)	295.50
F. M. and Kate Topper	110.00
Ezekiel Timmons	68.00
Jno. Geo. Saalmger	50.00
Arthur E. Nicholson	160.00
W. H. Corbett	400.00
Thos. Hutchinson (sick, excused until August)	501.92
Jas. O'Brien	210.00
John Bane	265.00
William T. Harkness	450.00
Charles Wigmore	680.00
Evan E. Jones	160.00
Charles H. Watts	520.00
John Wiesan	100.00

John Marley	$625.00
Richard Barnes (dead)	672.00
William and Margaret McBroom	600.00
Demas Critchlow	615.00
Nicholas Wiesan	300.00
Joseph B. Stewart	220.00
J. Miller Colgan	640.00
W. P. and Maggie E. Thompson	575.00
William R. Thomas	720.00
Jessie S. Lautz	540.00
David and Cath. Lynch	1,075.00
Patrick and Catherine McGee	900.00
Thomas J. Crawford (paid-off mortgage)	80.00
Charles G. Peterson	562.00
Peter Fullard	840.00
Harry W. Wright	2,150.00
James Grose	1,280.00
F. J. Ackerman	505.00
James H. Slocum	1,125.00
Samuel Ellis	1,014.00
Joseph Treusch	304.00
Patrick Philpott	560.00
George Popp	210.00
Bridget and Patrick Tarney	575.00
Casper and Bridget Kramer	230.00
Jacob Schorr	430.00
James Meloy	390.00
Harry G. Taylor	850.00
Geo. A. Todd	1,030.00
Henry Hitzfeldt	1,125.00
Henry Lorener	775.00
Geo. Parker	770.00
Robt. E. McDonald	1,040.00
Jno. Owen Thomas	628.00
Jas. V. Partington	380.00
Jno. A. Hickey	580.00
Lewis Lewis	1,000.00
Geo. Phillips	875.00
Geo. W. Stevick	1,125.00
Jno. Kinnely	750.00
Albion Wiegel	1,375.00
Jas. A. Burns	3,200.00
Geo. W. Hatcher	775.00
Jos. Belvischmitt	715.00
Hiram Hall	980.00
Thos. W. Bowness	800.00
Total	42,796.75

By the CHAIRMAN:

Q. What interest does your company charge?—A. Six per cent; and I may say we allow our employés the same rate.

Q. On deposits?—A. Yes, sir; all of those who desire to deposit with us, and here is a book which shows the terms on which we take these deposits.

Q. State them briefly.—A. We state—

First. No deposits will be received from or held for any person not in the employ of this association.

Second. Every person desirous of becoming a depositor shall at the time of making his first deposit sign a book containing the following rules, and by such act shall signify his willingness to be bound thereby; and every such depositor will receive a numbered book containing these rules, which book shall be inscribed with his name and in which the amounts of his deposits shall be inserted.

Third. Not less than $3 will be received as the first deposit; not less than $1 will be received at any subsequent deposit and fractional parts of a dollar will not be received at any time.

Fourth. Not more than $2,000 will be received for account of any one depositor.

I may say that occasionally we make an exception to the rule and have received a little more, but it is rarely that we do.

Fifth. Interest at 6 per cent per annum will begin with the date of deposit and will be computed to the first days of January and July in each year, payable semi-annually on the regular pay day nearest the 15th day of the same months.

Sixth. All or any part of deposits can be withdrawn only on notice by the depositor or his legal representatives given on any regular pay day, when the amount named in such notice, which must not include fractional parts of a dollar, will be paid on the next regular pay day of the department in which he is employed.

Then there are a couple of more rules here, quite lengthy, and if you want me to read them I will read them.

Q. They are not important?—A. I could give you a list showing the amount of money deposited with us by our workmen at Homestead and the names of the men, but I do not think that would be quite fair to the depositors.

Q. Just state the aggregate amount.—A. The aggregate amount is about $140,000 at present.

Mr. BRODERICK. On that you are paying 6 per cent, the same which you charge on the mortgages?

The WITNESS. Yes, sir. The mortgages amount to about $42,000. That I failed to state, but it is on the list I handed in.

The CHAIRMAN. Will you state to the committee now the cost of producing a ton of steel billets, the basis upon which this sliding scale is put?

Mr. BOATNER. Are you going to answer the question?

The WITNESS. I might give you a general idea of the cost, but I would not say it was exact.

By the CHAIRMAN:

Q. I am not asking you about all your business, but I am asking you about that, as it is the particular article on which the sliding scale is fixed?—A. I will say this. The market price of pig iron to-day is about $14 per ton. I think, taking the mills of the country over, that could not be converted into a ton of billets at a less average cost than $10 per ton, making the total cost in the neighborhood of $24—that is, the country over.

Q. Will a ton of pig iron make a ton of steel?—A. No, sir; about 75 per cent.

Q. If that cost $14 and the other labor and expenses, $10, it would make——

A. That buys enough pig iron; that $10 would buy enough pig iron to make a ton of billets.

Q. You stated that $14 was about the cost of a ton of pig iron?—A. Yes, sir; the market price. I think that is a little less than the cost.

Q. Then the additional expense of turning out a ton of steel billets would be, you say, about $10, making it about $24?—A. That, however, does not include interest on investment or anything of that kind.

Q. If a ton of pig iron would only produce 75 per cent of a ton of steel billets, would it not enhance the cost very much above $24?—A. That $10 would include the purchase of enough pig iron to turn out a ton of billets.

Q. And pay for the labor and expense of converting it?—A. Yes, sir.

Q. You say that without taking into the calculation the cost upon the the investment or plant?—A. Yes, sir.

Q. Well, now, Mr. Frick, you have superior machinery and facilities, would you object to stating what it costs at the Homestead mill, including material and leaving out the cost of the plant, to produce a ton of steel billets?—A. Yes, sir; I think, judge, I have gone as far into the question of costs as I will go.

Q. You are not inclined to state your figures so as to show the profits of the company in the business in which you are engaged?—A. Exactly.

Q. Now, in that connection, your company could not afford to continue their business and pay your laborers whom you have been paying unless there was a profit in it to the company and a fair income on the investment, could they?—A. No, sir; certainly not.

Q. Now, I will ask you this question. Has the amount of earnings in your business here cut any figure in the proposition you made to these men to reduce their wages?—A. The losses, as I stated, we have met with in those three items which I mentioned, blooms, billets, and slabs, of course had their effect in our wanting to have some change in the wages.

Q. That was one of the factors which entered into the consideration?—A. Certainly.

By Mr. BOATNER:

Q. When Maj. McKinley was presenting the bill which bears his name in the House, he declared that the metal schedule had been based on a careful calculation of the labor cost and all other costs of production in this country, so that it would not involve a reduction in the wages of the American laborer. The bill was passed upon that theory and it was supposed it was passed because of that fact. Now, we are instructed to ascertain how far the rate of duty affects the matter; so it becomes absolutely necessary for us to know, under that resolution, what the cost of production is, and I would like to ask you, if the information was given to Maj. McKinley on which he made this calculation and basis, why you object to giving it now.—A. I would give you general information of course, such as I have done, and I have no doubt you could get this information which was given to Maj. McKinley.

Q. But Maj. McKinley's promise seems not to have been made good. He declared the adoption of this schedule would not reduce wages, and you now admit a reduction of wages has become necessary?—A. As I stated, that has become necessary by overproduction, I think. I do not think the McKinley act or the change in the tariff which was made as a rule affected wages.

By the CHAIRMAN:

Q. There were hearings before the Committee on Ways and Means of various persons skilled in these matters. Were you one before that committee?—A. No, sir.

Q. You were not examined?—A. No, sir.

By Mr. BOATNER:

Q. Was your firm represented in a hearing before that committee?—A. I do not think we were.

Q. Was your firm in existence at the time that act was passed, when it was framed?—A. This new concern, the Carnegie Steel Company, Limited, was not in existence.

Q. I saw it stated in a morning paper yesterday that your firm had taken a foreign contract for the delivery of steel rails at a price $7.50 under the American price for that product.—A. That is not true. In the first place, we have taken no contract and have not had an inquiry.

Q. Well, the papers are generally correct, and I took it for granted that was correct.—A. I am very glad you asked me that question.

The CHAIRMAN. Do you know the difference in the cost of producing a ton of steel billets or steel rails in Europe and in this country?

The WITNESS. I could not say that now—no; I might answer you I do not; but I might ascertain in a few moments. If you will pardon me, I see a gentleman in the audience who could give you that information, the editor of the American Manufacturer.

By Mr. BOATNER:

Q. Mr. Potter, the general manager of your mills, stated a few moments ago that owing to the improved machinery in your works at Homestead, you were able to turn out 50 per cent more product with 50 per cent less labor in certain lines. Do you indorse that statement?—A. I think that is substantially correct, in one department.

Q. In other words, with the use of that machinery one man does the work that four men did formerly?— A. I think that is correct.

By the CHAIRMAN:

Q. Which department is that?—A. I think he had reference to the 119-inch plate mill, with the assistance of the other department, the 32-inch slabbing mill.

Q. Can you state independently of other costs the labor cost of producing a ton of steel billets?—A. I could get those figures for you, but I think I will have to decline to give them to you.

Q. You decline to give all the cost to you or your company, but upon what ground do you decline to give the labor cost separate from the other?—A. Well, I do not think we should be asked to give away those details of our business.

By Mr. BOATNER:

Q. You asked the Government for a duty to compensate between the difference in the American labor cost and the foreign labor cost; then upon what principle, receiving from the Government a protection which is ostensibly and avowedly for that purpose, do you decline to give the information upon which that legislation is based?—A. We did not ask the Government for such protection.

Q. You did not?—A. No, this concern did not.

Q. You are greatly misrepresented then if you did not. The press misrepresents you very much.

By Mr. BYNUM:

Q. You spoke of the reduction in the duties on billets in the McKinley bill. The tariff fixed in the McKinley bill is a specific duty, is it not—so much a pound?—A. I believe so.

Q. And the tariff rate in the old law was an ad valorem rate?—A. I believe that is true.

Q. So that the specific duty is an invariable one, is it not?—A. Yes, sir.

Q. If the price of billets goes down low the specific rate is liable to be higher then than the ad valorem rate?—A. Yes, sir.

Q. So it depends upon the price of billets whether it is a higher or a lower tariff?—A. Yes, sir.

Q. The price of billets has been going down ever since the manufacture commenced in this country?—A. They have had their ups and downs.

Q. What is the average price of billets now?—A. I suppose about $24.

Q. Now, in 1887. they were $34, were they not?—A. I think that is correct.

Q. So if they continue to fall as they have fallen within the last ten years, the specific rate would be the higher duty?—A. Exactly.

Q. The rates of duty prescribed in the McKinley bill were satisfactory to the steel and iron industries, were they not?—A. I think so.

Q. Had you any objections to them?—A. No, not to any extent.

Q. Did Mr. Swank represent the steel and iron industry before the Committee on Ways and Means?—A. I think so.

Q. Do you recollect and know the fact that he stated that this schedule was satisfactory to the iron and steel industries?—A. Personally I could not say.

Q. You have not examined the hearings before that committee?—A. No, sir.

Q. Do you not recollect he stated that at a meeting of the iron and steel industries?—A. No; at present I do not recollect that, but I have no doubt he did.

Q. You stated, I think, in answer to Col. Oates, that the importation of billets, etc., had been no greater since the enactment of the McKinley bill than before?—A. Yes, sir; I think I stated that. I think that is true.

The CHAIRMAN. Has it not been something less?

The WITNESS. I think it has.

By Mr. BYNUM:

Q. You spoke of the cost of a ton of billets, and you took pig iron at $14 market price. You did not take the actual cost of a ton of pig iron?—A. No, I think that is less than the actual cost at present.

Q. Have you ever examined and do you know of the investigation made by Mr. Wright in this country and in Europe as to the labor cost of a ton of steel rails?—A. I have seen some statements of Mr. Wright's; yes, sir.

Q. His agent made application to your mill to get the actual labor cost in that industry?—A. I think he did.

Q. They were not given?—A. No, sir.

Q. So those tables were based really on similar mills in the country, where the milling cost is higher than yours?—A. I think his tables are merely guesswork, and I do not think they are reliable at all.

Q. They were taken from actual reports given by manufacturers in the different industries, were they not?—A. Not to my knowledge.

Q. He so states. Now, do you remember that in the production of a ton of steel rails, taking the iron ore in the mines, taking everything, from the material in the ground, limestone to be quarried, and coal to be mined, that the labor cost of a ton of steel rails in this country was only $11.27?—A. I do not remember the figures.

Q. Do you remember that his statement given to Congress was that there was only 27 cents difference in the labor cost of producing steel rails in this country and in Europe?—A. No; I do not remember that.

Q. Are not some manufacturers of steel in this country exporting steel?—A. I believe so.

Q. Where do they export?—A. I think Park Brothers are the only ones I know of, but they make a fine grade of steel.

Q. The finer grades of steel are exported and sent into the markets generally in the world?—A. Yes, sir; the finer——

Q. There is more work on the finer grade of steel than on the lower?—A. I should think so.

Q. The finer you make an article, of course the more work it takes?—A. That follows.

Q. So, upon the very highest grades, in which the most labor is employed, we are absolutely exporting the best qualities and competing with foreign labor—A. There is a small amount of that being done by those gentlemen, I believe.

By the CHAIRMAN:

Q. You put in evidence a contract which you have with the Government for supplying armor plate for war vessels which are being built?—A. Yes, sir.

Q. The prices agreed upon by your company with the Government are fairly remunerative to the company, are they?—A. Well, we are really unable to answer that yet, as we have not gotten along far enough to determine.

Q. The contract was made by your company on that hypothesis?—A. Yes, sir.

Q. Have you not a very large contract with the World's Columbian Exposition at Chicago?—A. Not directly.

Q. For structural material?—A. I believe we failed to secure the contracts there.

Q. You have a great many large contracts, have you not?—A. Oh, yes, sir.

Q. Are those contracts which you have and demands for the product of your mills as great as your company can supply at their various works?—A. No; not as great as we could supply if we were running steadily.

Q. Is there any dearth in the market; have not you a very large trade?—A. We have a very large trade; yes, sir, but the mills are not always kept busy.

Q. Has not your company the largest trade in their products of any company in the United States manufacturing similar products? Do you not do the largest business?—A. I think it is likely we do.

Q. Mr. Frick, does not your company sell at as close a price as they can, so as to control the market?—A. No, sir.

Q. Do you not undersell some other mills in order to do a lively business and find a large sale for your products?—A. Not for that purpose.

Q. It is your purpose to do a large business and a profitable one?—A. Of course we do a large business, but the contractors are in the market, and we name our figures, and keep them as high as we think we should, and very often we do not get the contract. Occasionally we do.

Q. Some other firm underbids you?—A. Yes, sir. And very often we take contracts at what we know is a low price in order to keep the mills running. That is true.

Q. Is it not a fact that your company sells directly the product of your mills by superior machinery for less than other mills bringing forth a like character of product? Do not you claim on account of the superior facilities you have and management, that you can do that, and do you not sell at a less price?—A. No, sir; we do not; we take our chances in the market with other manufacturers, and, as I state, occasionally we secure an order, but, as I say to you, as often we lose it, it being obtained by a competior at a lesser price than the one bid by us.

Q. Well, competition is sufficiently great, however, to keep the price down within reasonable limits?—A. It has been for some time past. I think the lowest prices are prevailing now that have been ever known in the steel and iron business in this country.

Q. Well, prices in everything are lower than they have been for years past, are they not?—A. Well, I only speak in reference to what we manufacture.

Q. Well, you are an intelligent man and you are cognizant of the markets; staple products all over the country have been ranging at lower prices, have they not?—A. In the last year or so the prices for our cereals, etc., and all that sort of thing, have been higher than for some time; that is, wheat, rye, and corn; cotton, I believe, has been lower than it has been for a good many years.

Q. It has been very low, sir, below the cost of production. Mr. Frick, I will ask you this question: Could not the mills of your company at Homestead be continued in the same line of work and without change on the scale of pay to these workmen which expired on the 30th of June, and still the company realize fair profits?—A. No; I think eventually we would have to go into bankruptcy.

Q. That is if you continued on the old scale?—A. If we did not have a readjustment of wages occasionally when it was necessary. That has been the fate of a good many steel concerns whom I know have gotten into trouble.

Q. Can you state what has been the percentage of increase in steel-producing mills in the United States within five or ten years?—A. I think I can give you that. I have here a statement of the production of Bessemer steel in the United States, that is, Bessemer steel ingots, net tons of 2,000 pounds, beginning with 1874 and ending with 1891. In the year 1874, 91,000; in 1875, 375,000; in 1876, 525,000; in 1877, 560,000; in 1878, 732,000; in 1879, 928,000; in 1880, 1,203,000; in 1881, 1,539,000; in 1882, 1,696,000; in 1883, a slight falling off, 1,654,000; in 1884, 1,540,000; in 1885, 1,701,000; in 1886, 2,541,000; in 1887, 3,283,000; in 1888, 2,812,000; in 1889, 3,281,000; in 1890, 4,131,000; and in 1891, 3,637,000. That is taken from Swank's report.

Q. Now, can you give the committee the amounts of the increased consumption or demand for these products for the same period or any part of it?—A. I think that will be shown by the product, which has been about in the same proportion.

Q. Then what reason can you give for a diminution of the price if the demand has kept pace with the production?—A. Well, I might and should say, I guess, within the last year or so the stocks have been increased; consumption has not kept up with production, and consequently stocks have increased and that has forced down the price more or less.

Mr. BRODERICK. I think you stated on yesterday that, in some way, the tariff was not involved in this dispute, as you understand it?—A. I do not think it is.

Q. I presume your offer to reduce wages was based upon the idea that the productive capacity of the mills would be increased by this new machinery and the reduction of the prices of your product?—A. Yes, sir; and I should say also—I did state previously—that this is just a readjustment of the scale on account of the changed condition of our mills, and that I felt satisfied that by next year this time, when we got this into operation, the product of our mills would so increase that the men would be getting as high wages as they did before the reduction. That, I may say, has been the experience of the Edgar Thomson plant, where we work on a sliding scale with our men. We will fix the scale for three years, we will say, and we make improvements increasing the product, but their wages go on and they are paid until the end of the three years, and we then readjust the wages owing to the changes and new conditions, and in the course of time we reach a high point again.

Q. Is there anything the mill produces there upon which the tariff was increased when the McKinley law was passed?—A. Not one article to my knowledge. The McKinley law is there in front of you. On every article we produce there I think there was a reduction. I furnished you with a list in the first part of my testimony.

Q. But that reduction was not sufficient to increase the importation of these products?—A. No, sir.

Q. In your judgment, what would the effect have been had the reduction been sufficient to have largely increased the importation of these products?—A. Then it would have very seriously affected wages.

Q. Is it not true that by reason of holding up the tariff or the duty on these articles that the stock has been increased and the capacity of the machinery has been enlarged by holding up this duty?—A. Yes, sir; I think so.

The CHAIRMAN. You mean production has been stimulated in this country?—A. Yes, sir; I certainly think so.

By Mr. BYNUM:

Q. The iron industry was greatly depressed away back in 1873, up to about 1879, was it not?—A. Yes, sir.

Q. And the revival took place in 1880, 1881 and 1882; those were the most prosperous years?—A. I think 1879 and 1880 were the most prosperous years.

Q. The production increased considerably in this country in these years, and I think it continued up to 1882, when probably there were greater profits in the iron industry than any other years. Now, do not you know those years were the years of greatest importation from abroad?—A. It may be so.

Q. Does not the prosperity of home manufactures, if you have examined the tariff, show that the years of the greatest importation and the years of the greatest exportation are the years of the greatest prosperity of the home industries?—A. It would show a very large demand for such material.

Q. It would show a condition of prosperity of all branches of all industries?—A. It is the high prices of an article that reduce the importation, of course.

Q. And it also increases the home production?—A. Yes, sir; it stimulates it.

Q. So that when it comes about that you find large importations one year, it is good evidence that it was a year of high prices and a great demand at home?—A. Exactly.

Q. The duties on iron are practically prohibitory, are they not?—A. Yes; I think they are at present.

Q. What did you say was the duty fixed on billets?—A. I think I stated six-tenths, but I would have to refer to find out exactly.

Q. And billets are selling for less than a cent a pound, or about a cent a pound?—A. A little over a cent a pound.

Q. So six-tenths would be about 60 per cent duty? You do not claim the difference in the labor cost in Europe and America in making a ton of billets is 60 per cent?—A. I really—I could not answer that question.

Q. It would cost more for coal there?—A. Yes, sir.

Q. For coke?—A. Yes, sir.

Mr. BOATNER. There is some little fog in regard to this matter.

By Mr. BRODERICK:

Q. During the years 1879 and 1880, when there was a greater importation of this material, what was the price of steel rails then, as com-

pared with the present price in this country?—A. Well, I was not then
in the steel business, but I will say generally they were very much
higher than they are now.

Q. You do not know how much?—A. I could not tell you without
referring to the records.

Q. Was not that importation at that time because of the high price
for all those products?—A. Yes, sir.

Q. Can you tell about what per cent or about how much higher they
were?—A. I would just give you a general idea, but I think they were
probably 40 per cent higher than they are now.

Q. Take what you are producing down here. What was the difference on that? How much higher was it then on the product of your
mills?—A. I really could not answer you, but at this date I should
think it was fully what I have said.

Q. Forty per cent?—A. Probably sixty.

Q. Then you attribute the large importation of those years to the
high prices?—A. Yes, sir; and the strong demand there was in the
country on account of the railroad building going on in those years,
which made a big demand for the product.

By Mr. BYNUM:

Q. That importation was of crude metal, principally scrap iron and
pig iron?—A. I could not answer that.

Q. Now, in regard to the price of steel rails you say being higher,
has the price of steel rails fluctuated considerably in the past five or
six years?—A. Yes, sir.

Q. In 1882, and I believe in 1883 and 1884, along there, I forget
exactly which year, steel rails sold as low as $27 a ton?—A. No, I do
not think it was that.

Q. Twenty-eight?—A. They may have reached that.

Q. Do not you recollect there was a great demand for rails in 1887
and 1888?—A. Well, I was not in the steel rail business then.

Q. As a matter of fact, that year we built about 13,000 miles of railroad, and as it takes about 100 tons of rails to the mile, our product
was about 13,000,000, and do not you recollect the fact that the year
before rails sold at $27 a ton, and by reason of the tariff, the tariff ex-
cluding the foreign product, the price of rails went from $27 to $39 a
ton?—A. That is the reason as you state it. I did not go into the steel
business until January, 1889.

Q. You were not manufacturing steel rails at that time ?—A. No, sir.

By Mr. BRODERICK:

Q. Has the price of all the products of your mills decreased within
the last three years?—A. Yes, sir; I think I am correct in saying they
have.

Q. Notwithstanding the tariff is virtually prohibitory?—A. Yes, sir.

By the CHAIRMAN:

Q. At the beginning of your testimony you gave the names of a large
number of the members of your firm, mentioning the different properties they owned. Now, I will ask you to state, if you have no objection, the aggregate value of those properties.—A. Well the capital of
our concern as at present organized is $25,000,000. A large part of
that is made up by these various properties and by working capital to
carry them on. Of course in addition to the capital we have other
money in the business.

Q. You are the president of the company and have the management
of all the different mills?—A. I am chairman of the association.

By Mr. BRODERICK:

Q. Why do you take the month of May to base your estimates upon?—A. For the reason that we expected a final conference with our workmen in the month of June, and I just said to make up the month of May. I do not know how I took that.

Q. Is that a month in which the mills are running to their full capacity?—A. It is one of the months in which they run about as full as any other in the year.

Q. How many months in the year do they run to their full capacity?—A. I think I stated already the average in the whole year is about 270 days. There may be a little more in some departments and a little less in others.

Q. Most of the losses are during the winter season, or, rather, most of the delay, or when does it happen?—A. Well, that I could not say, but I think it would be in the winter months when we would be slacker. In fact I am quite sure it would be.

Q. For want of material?—A. For want of orders; yes, sir.

Mr. BOATNER. You have told us all you know about these matters?

The WITNESS. I think so.

Total pay roll for month of May, 1892.

In ascertaining average earnings it would be necessary to know number of days each employé worked. Some of these worked but one day during month of May. Average, say 18 days.

Department.	No. of employés, men and boys.	Amount earned.
Converting works	350	$18,784.05
Open hearth No. 1	171	10,591.05
Open hearth No. 2	206	17,742.55
28-inch blooming mill	218	9,790.30
119-inch plate mill	276	20,202.95
35-inch and 40-inch mills	110	3,889.15
32-inch slabbing mill	159	2,610.20
33-inch beam and cogging mill	258	16,413.00
35-inch and 40-inch mill yard	290	8,928.30
Fitting shop	132	5,277.23
23-inch shape mill	305	14,330.35
10-inch merchant mill	66	3,283.00
Rivet and bolt shop	4	238.15
General and improvements	405	12,360.35
Armor-plate department	144	8,797.45
Miscellaneous	559	31,196.70
Scott & Co., teaming	38	2,706.80
Total	3,787	193,150.60
City office pay-roll	64	8,637.70
Grand total	3,851	201,788.30

I certify that the within statements are correct and correspond with the time-books and ledgers on file in the office of the Homestead Steel Works.

C. E. McKILLIPS,
Chief Clerk.

TESTIMONY OF CHARLES MANSFIELD.

CHARLES MANSFIELD sworn and examined.

By the CHAIRMAN:

Q. Where do you live?—A. In Homestead.

Q. Were you at Homestead or in that vicinity on the morning of the 6th day of this month?—A. Yes, sir.

Q. Did you see a boat or barges containing Pinkertons and others come to the wharf near the works?—A. Yes, sir.

Q. Did you see them attempt to land?—A. Yes, sir.

Q. Where did you first see the boat?—A. The first time—I went down with this crowd to the river bank and I arrived just near the electric-light plant when I heard whistles blowed—no, I heard whistles blowed which waked me and I got up, dressed, and went down to the river bank outside the mill, and the first I saw of the boat was when it was coming up the river below the town.

Q. Are you a laborer; do you work down there?—A. No, sir; I am employed in a real-estate office in Homestead. Previous to that time I worked for a local newspaper as reporter and had charge of their news route, and my business was to notice these things for the purpose of assisting the people on that paper to get a correct account of it.

Q. Did you hear any firing before you went to the river?—A. No, sir; I was there before the firing was done. I was there when the whistles were blowing, and it was some time about 2 o'clock; probably 3; it was early in the morning, and I could not say exactly now, and the boat did not come until after that.

Q. Where were you when you heard the first firing?—A. Standing on the river bank between the company's fence and Dixon street along the river bank.

Q. Before the crowd had entered the works?—A. Oh, yes, sir.

Q. Did you see any who fired?—A. No, sir; it was impossible to see them, as it was dark; it was early in the morning, and there was a very large crowd, and to say who did the firing would be a thing no person could speak of truthfully.

Q. I am not asking you what particular persons did, but do you know which way the firing was?—A. Yes, sir; the first firing was done outside of the mill probably, and from where I was standing I could see the flashes in the air. They were fired generally most in the air. I did not see any firing done in the direction of the boat.

Q. The firing was from the bank?—A. Yes, sir; into the air.

Q. You went along with the crowd up to where the boat landed?—A. Yes, sir; I did not go up with the first rush.

Q. When you got there did you see the men on the boat attempt to land?—A. Yes, sir; after the crowd run up I went up behind them and stood at the corner of the pump house to be out of range. I did not want to get hurt at all, and I stood there and saw the firing.

Q. Who commenced the firing?—A. The firing was off the boat first. From where I stood the boat was tied above the pump house, and I stood at the corner of the brick pump house, the new one the machinery is not in yet, and from that corner I saw them fire off the corner of the boat. The fire was from the boat first, and a man fell.

Q. Did a man on shore fall?—A. Yes, sir; I did not know who he was at the time, but I learned afterwards.

Q. Did you hear any words pass between the parties on shore and

H. Mis. 335——12

those on the boat?—A. Yes, sir; I could hear them talking, but owing to the confusion and the distance from me I could not hear what was passed because it was done so quick. I could not just recollect.

Q. Was it light or dark?—A. No, sir; it was not dark, but it was not broad daylight and a fog was on the river. It was early in the morning and you could not see as distinctly as you can now. It was early in the morning and it was not really light then.

Q. You testify, then, that you know the first firing was from the boat?—A. Yes, sir.

Q. Did you see the flash and hear the report?—A. From where I was standing I saw both the flash and heard the report and I heard the ball strike; also at the time this man fell the next instant you could distinguish the balls strike the beams above the men's heads. The firing from the boat was against these beams largely, making a terrible racket.

Q. When did the people on shore fire?—A. Just almost immediately after the firing on the boat they opened fire on the shore.

Q. Was there any firing between the time the boat passed where you were up to the landing before that firing you described there?—A. That I could not say, sir. When I left the bank I did not go into the fence there, but I went around the railroad, and of course what transpired then, as it takes a good little time to go around, I could not speak of that, as I do not know. I did not see that at all.

Q. Do you know whether or not there were any shots fired from the shore in the direction of the boat before it came to the landing?—A. Below the town?

Q. Opposite the town or anywhere up to the time it landed?—A. Not that I had knowledge of. Of course it might be possible, but the reason I know they went into the water is I stood with my back to the river and watched the flashes and I could see by the flashes that the revolvers shot up in the air. I suppose there were one hundred shots fired, but it would be impossible for me to say whether anyone fired on the boat or not. The reason they were firing, as it was said afterwards, was to make a noise and alarm the town. That is what they told me.

Q. That was the reason the people on the shore fired?—A. So as to create an excitement and rouse the town.

Q. When you got to the river you found a large number of people down there, did you?—A. Yes, sir; the town was alarmed.

Q. You heard before that the blowing of whistles to give an alarm.—A. Yes, sir.

Q. There was a general understanding or information there that signals would be given in case of an approach of these Pinkertons?—A. Yes, sir; I believe that was published in the papers to that effect before that morning.

Q. What did you say your object was in coming down there?—A. I am clerk in a real-estate office and before that I was employed on a Homestead paper, as a reporter in charge of the news route, to gather news, and my object in going there was to be thoroughly familiar with it so that we could make up an account of the affair.

Q. You were acting as an enterprising news-gatherer?—A. Yes, sir; that is what I was down there for. I thought there would be trouble and I went down there.

By Mr. BYNUM:

Q. Did you see any demonstration made there in the way of throwing stones and missiles, pieces of iron, or anything of that sort?—A.

No, sir.   When the crowd rushed down the bank you know I did not see any thrown against the boat, nor do I think any were thrown.

Q. You do not think any were thrown at all?—A. I do not think there were.

Q. Whereabouts were the men who fired shots from the boat?—A. Up in the bow, where the doors were open.

Q. Were they out on the bank or simply standing on the bow of the boat?—A. Standing on the bow outside the door.

Q. How were the boats fastened there; how did they lie with reference to the post there or to the piling; did they lie up and down or with their ends to shore?—A. By the ends, not parallel, as their sterns were farther away than their bows.

Q. Then how could you see men standing on the bow of the boat?— A. Yes, sir; there was quite a crowd.

Q. What were the men doing on the shore at the time the first firing occurred?—A. They were talking excitedly and gathered together in a crowd.

Q. Did you see any of them have arms?—A. No, sir; I saw no guns at all until after the first firing. I did not see any arms at all in that crowd on the shore until——

Q. You say there was shooting there afterwards?—A. Yes, sir.

Q. What arms did you see then?—A. I could not see from where I was the arms at all, but by the shots they were revolvers.

Q. You did not see any other kind of weapons except revolvers or recognize the sound of anything else from the shore?—A. Not from the shore.

Q. What were these men doing; did you see the man who was shot on the shore?—A. He seemed to be in advance of the crowd on the shore; he was one of the foremost and I saw him fall. I did not know who he was, but I have since understood he was a man by the name of Foy.

Q. What was he doing at the time?—A. The crowd was talking excitedly and he was in there talking with the rest.

Q. Do you know what was said?—A. No, sir; I could not distinguish what was said; everybody it seemed in that crowd was talking.

By Mr. BOATNER:

Q. Could you see the kind of gun which was used; the first gun which was fired, was it a gun or pistol?—A. From the boat.

Q. Yes, sir.—A. I judge it to be; I am slightly familiar with firearms; I judged it to be a rifle from the sound of the firing.

Q. Could you see the man who fired it?—A. No, sir; I could see it was fired at the crowd. You will understand me a little better when I tell you the boat is narrow and these persons were huddled close together.

Q. How far was the man who fired the gun from the crowd into which he fired?—A. Well, sir, he could not have been more than 5 or 6 feet.

Q. Not more than 5 or 6 feet. What did you say was the name of this man who was shot?—A. I learned afterwards that it was a man by the name of Foy who was wounded the first fire.

Q. Was he shot through and through?—A. All I know is from the newspaper reports, that he was shot in the side, shot through the lower part of the lung and the ball lodged somewhere in his body. I only know that from reading the newspapers.

By Mr. BRODERICK:

Q. I believe you stated you heard the firing commence down on the bank to bring the people together?—A. Yes, sir; that is where the first firing was done.

Q. Was that kept up until the boat landed?—A. No, sir. I say that I did not follow them right away as the boat went up. Some of the crowd rushed around to get up to the railroad and then shortly after that I followed that crowd up and I knew nothing of what occurred after I left the river bank until I came back to the river bank again.

Q. Did you hear shots from that time occasionally?—A. I did not notice them. I was running rapidly and would not have noticed them if there had been.

By Mr. BYNUM:

Q. Did you see anybody hurt on the boat?—A. No, sir. I might say after this firing occurred that everything got comparatively quiet and I walked to the edge of the bank, as there was no shooting going on, and one of the gentlemen in charge of the men on the boat came out and said to the crowd, "Men, there is no use disguising the fact. We are every God damned one of us Pinkertons and we intend to go up to that mill in spite of everything and we will give you fifteen minutes to get out of that yard." Some one answered that they did not see any necessity for waiting that long to go in there, and——

Q. That is not what I asked you; I asked you if there was anybody hurt there?—A. No, sir; I did not see anybody hurt there on the boat.

TESTIMONY OF A. J. TAYLOR.

A. J. TAYLOR sworn and examined.

By the CHAIRMAN:

Q. Were you at Homestead on the morning of the 6th of July?—A. Yes, sir.

Q. Did you see the trouble between the men on the boats and barges and the people on the shore?—A. Yes, sir.

Q. What was the first you saw of it?—A. Well, sir, I was awakened at about 2 o'clock. I could not sleep, and I thought I might as well get up and see what was going on. I will say I am not engaged in the mill there at all.

Q. What is your business?—A. I am a groceryman, sir; I went down to the river, and I guess it was between 2 and 3 o'clock, and I could not see any trouble down there. I saw a lot of men gathered around the river bank, and I said to another fellow there, "I am not going to stay here; I am going home and get some sleep." I went home and went back to bed, and from that time to the time the whistle blowed, I did not think it was any more than a minute, but it must have been about an hour——

Q. No matter about that; just tell what you saw when the boat arrived.—A. I got up and dressed and started for the river again and when I got to the corner and looked down I saw the boat coming up the river, which I took to be a barge as it was kind of big, and I saw a mass of people following it. I walked on Fifth avenue and I went with the crowd and by the time I got to the Penickerty bridge there was an immense crowd, and I stopped on the Penickerty bridge. The boat by this time had got tied and I could see the barges plain, and they were saying something; I could not understand what they were saying. Those men were all excited and you could not tell much about what was said there. Then some man went down to the plank and this man started off——

Q. The gangplank, you mean?—A. Yes, sir; that was launched for the Pinkertons to come off, and I saw a man throw his hand up that way and fall and then I saw another man who was on the shore—no more than that much difference between them [snapping his thumb]—throw up his arms.

Q. Did you see any firing?—A. I saw firing on both sides after that.

Q. After that both from the boat and from the shore?—A. They opened fire on the men on the shore, I suppose.

Q. Which side fired first?—A. The first man I saw fall was one of the strikers; one man who had hold of the plank.

Q. You heard a report and saw the flash of the guns?—A. Yes, sir; I saw the flash.

By Mr. BYNUM:

Q. I understood you to say you saw a man come out on the plank, throw up his hands, and fall before you heard any firing?—A. No, sir. I said there was a man on the plank and a man who had hold of the plank——

Q. Throw up his hands and fall?—A. Yes, sir.

Q. There was no firing up to that time?—A. No, sir.

Q. You do not know what occasioned his fall. Then I understand you to say another man afterwards on that plank threw up his hands and fell?—A. A man back of him fell after him.

Q. Up to that time there had been no firing?—A. No, sir.

By the CHAIRMAN:

Q. Was that on the plank or on the boat?—A. The second man? He was on the plank ready to come down.

Q. You saw them fall before you saw any firing?—A. Yes, sir; that is what started the firing.

By Mr. BOATNER:

Q. Was there any firing simultaneously; did they fall because they were shot?—A. Yes, sir; because you could see the smoke of the firing.

Q. Did the first flash come from the boat or the shore?—A. Well, it came from the boat.

By the CHAIRMAN:

Q. How far were you from it?—A. I was about as far as from here down to the wharf there [looking out of window].

Q. Fifty or sixty yards away?—A. I guess it would be about that. I was right parallel with them; I was out on the Penickerty bridge, and they were in that direction.

Mr. BYNUM. I want to get another answer from you with regard to this. I understood you to say that men were coming out of the boat and the first thing you saw was a man throw up his hands and fall?

The WITNESS. My illustration was this: That a man who had hold of the plank fell first, and he was the one I said I could not think who he was.

The CHAIRMAN. He was on shore?

The WITNESS. Yes, sir.

By Mr. BYNUM:

Q. He was a man helping to put out the plank?—A. No, sir; I said——

Q. I just want to know what you saw there at that time; now, who was it that first fell there?—A. I could not give his name.

Q. I do not mean his name, but was he one of the crew on the boat?—A. No, sir; he was one of the strikers on the shore.

Q. What plank did he have hold of?—A. The gang plank that was throwed out to let the Pinkertons come out on.

Q. What was he doing with that plank?—A. I could not tell you that, sir. There was such a fuss and everybody was making such a fuss you could not understand what was said from the distance I was at.

Q. He fell?—A. Yes, sir. He throwed up his hands and fell.

Q. Now, then, who was the next person you saw fall?—A. I seen a man on the barge throw up his hands after this man fell, and the two fell.

Q. When did you hear the first shot in relation to these incidents?—A. I heard the first shot when this man fell on shore, and then right after that this man on the gang-way plank who was there ready to come off, he fell. There was not very much difference between them, but still there was some, and then they opened fire; and I could not state who was firing.

Q. That is what I do not understand; I want to know after the firing commenced did these men fall?—A. No, sir; they did not.

Q. Do you know in which direction the shot came which struck the first one?—A. Yes, sir; it came from the boat.

Q. The first shot then was fired by the boat according to your statement?—A. Yes, sir.

Q. Where was the next shot fired from?—A. It seemed to come from the shore.

By Mr. BRODERICK:

Q. Do you know what took place before the boat got to the landing, 200 yards or more away?—A. No, sir; as I stated I was not down along the river there.

Q. You did not go there until the boat was landed?—A. No, sir.

By Mr. BYNUM:

Q. How far were you from the boat at the time you saw this?—A. As I stated before, about as far from here down to the wharf here.

Q. This edge or the far edge of the wharf?—A. (Standing up and looking out the window.) About where that lumber is lying down on the wharf.

Q. You were on the railroad bridge?—A. Yes, sir; I was out to the first pier, that is, the structural work.

Q. Now, from where you were standing the bow of the boat was the end farthest from you?—A. Yes, sir.

Q. How could you see a man on the bow of the boat standing on that pier of the bridge when the boat was lying lengthwise from you?—A. Say there was the bridge here, and the barge was swung kinder out that way, with the stern of the boat towards me and the pier was out like this [illustrating].

Q. That bridge runs at an angle across the river?—A. Yes, sir.

Q. How far out is the first pier.—A. It is right here [illustrating], at the low-water mark.

Q. Now, standing there you would look to the right in a direct line north to where the boats were, and if the stern of the boat was lying out in the river, it would be pointing towards the first pier?—A. No, sir; the second pier.

Q. Does not the river make a bend around where the landing is there?—A. The bridge comes in this direction [illustrating] and then goes down this way [illustrating].

Q. The bridge comes down this way, but still after you pass it the river makes a turn where you land the boats?—A. No, I suppose it is about straight.

Q. Did not you notice this piling around there makes a turn where the boats land?—A. No, sir; I do not think it does.

Q. You think the river runs straight there?—A. Just about straight; down below there is a little bend.

The CHAIRMAN. It was the bridge pier you were out on?

The WITNESS. Yes, the bridge pier.

TESTIMONY OF GEORGE F. RYLANDS.

GEORGE F. RYLANDS, sworn and examined.

By the CHAIRMAN:

Q. What is your name?—A. George F. Rylands.

Q. Now you may make your statement which you desire?—A. I want to make a statement about the improvements which they assert have been made in this mill. I have been in that mill nearly four years, four years next month and since I have been there——

Q. State what mill that is.—A. It is the 119-inch plate mill; from that time there has not been added a wheel to it. There is one improvement they have made there and that is in regard to the slabbing mill. Now, in all mills that roll ingots that ingot is cast from the open-hearth furnaces and brought into the plate mill. Up there they cast in a larger ingot, and probably they will have one or two ingots, and in other mills they will have twelve or fifteen. The 32-inch mill can pass from $3\frac{1}{2}$ up to 8 and 10 inches thick, according to the size plate you want. Of course this is an advantage to us, but still it is an advantage to the mill and to the company, and the men on the furnaces have to work so much harder. As they get it hot from the 32-inch mill they have to keep watch of that stuff so much closer and it adds to the work and keeps them more continuously at work than any other mill in the country of its kind. Now, up there we make sometimes as many as twenty-three to twenty-five heats for a day's work, and other mills, such as the Shoenberger, make four heats for a day's work of twelve hours.

Q. Before you began your testimony you said something about May being the largest month in regard to earnings?—A. Yes, sir; since the mill has been built.

Q. State what that was; state what the average was, if you know.—A. The average of the year has been 1,300 tons per month.

Mr. BOATNER. Have you tables there showing the production for each month?—A. Yes, sir.

Comparison between the month of May as given before the Congressional Committee and the average.

	Wages earned in May.	Average monthly wage.	Showing proposed minimum $23, taking above average.*
Roller	$278.50	$171.73 = 15	$157.95
Screwdown	214.05	141.05 = 5	129.77
First shearman	217.50	159.38	140.78
Second shearman	141.55	104.26	195.94
Tableman	108.85	122.59	112.73
Heaters	190.65	134.87½	124.15½
Hookers	153.25	104.26	95.04
Heaters' helper	135.00	91.97½	84.61½
First sweeper	109.00	73.58	67.74
Second sweeper	97.60	67.37	62.01
First leader	129.65	95.03	87.43
Second leader	121.40	88.92	81.88
Shear helpers	95.00	67.37	62.00

*From these figures should be deducted the cut in the rates, averaging 15 per cent.

Average tonnage per month per turn...tons.. 1,300
Average tonnage per turn..do... 57½
Average number of turns per month.. 22½

Average output of 119-inch plate mill since July, 1890, at which time the eight-hour arrangement commenced, up to and including June, 1892, a period of twenty-three months.

Average per month...tons.. 1,300½
Average per turn..do... 57
Average number of turns worked per month... 22

This would give an average rate per day to the following-named workmen on the present scale of $25 per ton.

	Per day.	Per month.	Per ton.
			Cents.
Roller	$7.60	$171.73	13.21
Screwdown	6.23	141.05	10.85
First shearman	7.04	159.38	12.26
Second shearman	4.61	104.26	8.02
Tablemen	5.40	122.59	9.43
Heaters	5.96	134.87½	20.75=2
Hookers	4.61	104.26	8.02
Heaters' helper	4.07	91.97½	14.15=2
First sweeper	3.25	73.58	5.66
Second sweeper	2.98	67.37	5.19
First leader	4.19	95.03	7.31
Second leader	3.93	88.92	6.84
Shear helpers	2.98	67.37	5.19

The proposition from the firm calls for a reduction on the minimum basis (from $25, at present, to $23) of 8 per cent for each man. This, coupled with a reduction on the rate, means a cut which varies from 15 to 30 per cent.

The CHAIRMAN. Do you know the average per cent of the reduction proposed by the company?—A. Well, it will run in our mill, I should judge, about 22 per cent, that is, including the reduction on the basis, the minimum.

Q. Just give the average rate per day for the twenty-three months.—A. Well, the roller, $7.60 per day; the screwdown, $6.23; first shearman, $7.04; second shearman, $4.61; tableman, $5.40; heaters, two heaters per turn, $5.96; hookers, two to a turn, $4.61; heaters' helpers, two also, $4.07; first sweeper, $3.25; second sweeper, $2.98; first leader, $4.19; second leader, $3.93; shearman's helpers, ten in number, $2.98 each.

Mr. BOATNER. Is that their average wages per day?

The WITNESS. Yes, sir; for twenty-three months.

The CHAIRMAN. For twenty-three months prior to the last day of June.

The WITNESS. Yes, sir; for the days they worked.

By Mr. BOATNER:

Q. And you say their average has been twenty-two days?—A. Twenty-two and a half days. They work eight hours and they work three turns.

Q. Eight hours a day?—A. Yes, sir; but we start Sunday night at 11 o'clock in that mill, in order to get the tonnage out. The night turn works from 11 o'clock until 7 o'clock.

Q. The mill runs all the time, night and day?—A. Yes, sir; it stops at 3 o'clock Saturday afternoons and starts at 11 o'clock on Sunday night. The mill is gotten in shape and on Sunday at 11 o'clock it starts up.

Q. That is, you get it heated up?—A. They start to rolling at 11 o'clock Sunday night. The paper I hold in my hand is the proposed scale for the 119-inch plate mill. In this scale they take in all the labor, that is, the men directly connected with that mill, upon the furnaces, shaping and making and placing on the cars. That includes pull-ups, markers, gaugers, stampers, painters, helpers at scales, millwrights, millwright helpers, line drawers, greasers, etc. There are twelve of those men who would be on twelve hours a day working, and the tonnage men would be on eight hours under the proposed scale.

Now here is a statement which was printed in last Sunday morning's paper, which is an answer to their proposition, and which I would like to have go in my testimony.

The statement was as follows:

[From the Pittsburg Dispatch.]

Shortly after the return of the committee which waited upon Governor Pattison at Harrisburg, a statement was prepared in answer to the Carnegie Company and given out last evening by the workers. This statement was as follows:

HOMESTEAD EMPLOYÉS' ANSWER TO THE CARNEGIE COMPANY.

The differences existing between the Carnegie Company and their employés at Homestead have drawn from Mr. H. C. Frick a statement of the points in dispute which makes necessary a reply in order that wrong impressions of the conditions may not be received by the public.

It is asserted that the employés combined with others of their trade, forming the Amalgamated Association, with absolute control over the Homestead Works. This charge can only be supported to the satisfaction of those who deny the right of the employé to enter objection to any conditions offered by the employer. The workingmen at Homestead, nor any other of the hundreds of mills organized into the Amalgamated Association, have no desire to dictate the wages they shall receive; but they see no good reason why they should not exercise the privilege of engaging with their employer in the controversy through which the rate of compensation for their labor is fixed.

PREPARED TO DISCUSS THE SCALE.

The workmen are now, as they always have been, prepared to meet the representatives of the company and discuss the provisions contained in the scale submitted by them. If the conferences already having been held failed to bring about a settlement, it can not be said that this was the fault of the workingmen.

The scale under which the men at Homestead were working was arranged in July of 1889. The rate of wages was fixed according to the selling price of four-by-four Bessemer steel billets, the wages advancing and declining with the selling price of that article; it was provided that the minimum should be $25. Complaint is made that no minimum should have been insisted upon. It is the experience of the iron and steel workers that some prevention is necessary to protect themselves from being reduced to an extremely low rate of pay by the acceptance by manufacturers of sales below current rates; as the workingmen do not sell the product, there must be a point where reduction in wages by reason of low-figured sales shall cease.

It is alleged that labor organizations are injurious alike to the toiler and those by whom they are employed; in substantiation of which it is cited by the firm that there is no organization amongst their employés at Braddock nor Duquesne steel works; that the men there are satisfied; that they get good wages, and that no strike has occurred at those works since the institution of that management.

SATISFACTION AT OTHER MILLS DISPUTED.

It may be said that the satisfaction of which Mr. Frick speaks as existing at the above works is forced, rather than voluntary, as may be proven by the many efforts of the men in these mills to organize themselves in secrecy. Knowledge of such intentions coming to the ears of the company would be and was followed by discharge. The wages enjoyed by the men at Braddock and Duquesne are the direct result of the rate of compensation sustained by the organized iron and steel workers. While they are not organized in these mills, the rate of pay for the class of work done by them, fixed by their organized fellow-tradesmen, determines the pay that can command their services.

It is the custom of the employers of nonunion men in the iron and steel trade to pay the rates provided by the Amalgamated scale, in order to secure the services of men of that trade; it is found, however, to be invariably the case that these employers, while they pay the rates provided by the Amalgamated Association, the men are required to accept conditions which are tantamount to a reduced rate, although not appearing on the face. We have reasons to believe that the nonunion plants of Braddock and Duquesne can be proven to be no exception to this rule.

ALL OF THE WORKMEN AFFECTED.

The introduction of improved machinery, to which reference is made by the company, has displaced men that were necessary before the introduction of such machinery, and in this manner repays the cost of the investment. The output of a mill is always considered when arranging scales, and if increase of output without increase of labor to the workmen is brought about by improvement, there is every opportunity offered by the workmen to arrive through conference at an equitable rate, but when the employer refuses to engage in discussion with the employé on the matter all hope of a just settlement is lost.

An attempt is made to lead the public into the belief that the number of men affected by the reduction are few. Here again it becomes necessary to impress on the public mind the fact that there are three distinct propositions contained in the dispute, namely: A reduction in the minimum, another reduction on the proportionate rate of pay (thus making a double reduction), and that the scale terminate December 31, 1893, instead of June 30, 1894. It must be understood that while all of these propositions do not affect the whole of the Homestead workmen, few of the 3,800 employés of that place escape without being affected by one or more of its provisions.

WHAT MUST BE CONSIDERED.

What does not affect the one does affect the other, and it might be said that instead of the company's proposing altering the condition of employment of 325, the change is general, and the whole are involved. It is stated by the company with much force that it is not their desire to reduce their workmen below others. The cost of production to the Carnegie Company at Homestead is decidedly in favor of the company as compared with mills of that character. It can now be shown that they can not establish a complaint in that direction.

In arranging scales of wages to govern iron and steel workers there are innumerable things which must receive attention if justice must prevail. The intricacies referred to are such as to render liable erroneous views to be drawn by those not familiar with the trade from their discussion in the public press. There can be no legitimate reason why the Carnegie Company should deny their Homestead workmen a conference, where the things of which they complain could be analyzed, and if found unjust made right.

PLEAS FOR PROPER ARGUMENT.

The men make no fairer proposition than this, for the simple reason that none fairer is possible. If argument and honest reasoning were substituted for the reserve and coldness of manner as seen in the company's present attitude, there can be reason to expect an end of this deplorable state of affairs. Does it not seem strange that the Carnegie Company looks with distrust upon the organization of its Homestead employés, while several of its large mills have for several years encouraged the organization of the men, and at this moment are getting along satisfactorily together?

Surely it will not be charged that the men at Homestead are less intelligent or less entitled to those rights which are the principles of organized labor, and which are inseparable from their citizenship. There are none who regret the lamentable occurrences of the past few days more than those whom the Carnegie Company charges with having been instrumental in bringing them about. We are willing to allow the public to judge, after the evidence is all in, whether these charges are true. We feel that the erroneous statements given out relative to our conduct will be removed by impartial investigation in due time. Until then we prefer to forget our recent sad experience.

Q. Is there anything else you wish to state?—A. Nothing, unless you wish to ask some question. If there is anyone who would like to ask me some questions I would like to answer them if possible.

TESTIMONY OF WILLIAM McQUADE.

WILLIAM McQUADE, sworn and examined.

By the CHAIRMAN:

Q. What is your name?—A. William McQuade.

Q. You can proceed and make such a statement as you wish.—A. In contradiction to Mr. Frick's statement about the improved machinery in the 119-inch mill, our tonnage has not been so great when we were working what we called double turn or two turns, one of ten hours and the other of eleven hours, which left three hours of the twenty-four unoccupied in that mill, and I will state that we have not had any improvement in machinery there at all, but the advancement in the tonnage there has been due partly to slabs and partly to the three turns placed there in operation. We had three hours per day and also had eight hours for Sunday. That gave them a big advance in their tonnage and put the output so much greater.

Previous to that time we did not work so hard; we had an hour's time for dinner and an hour's time for supper, and that time was lost to the mill, and the management of the mill proposed it to us jointly, and we had agreed to it also, and we could produce more tonnage in that mill by the use of three turns there, and that has been one of the great factors in putting so large a tonnage, so much greater than it was before, and I state positively from five years' experience in that mill that there has not been any improvement made in the machinery in that mill. Now, he says there are; I say there are not. To that is due their increased tonnage. We work these eight hours consecutively right straight through, we stop only the time it takes to oil the engine, and our time is more occupied in those eight hours than what it was before, and therefore we are working more steady and harder right along to produce this tonnage.

MR. BOATNER. How long do you stop during those eight hours?— A. While they are oiling they eat, at least some of the boys, some of them; a great many of them in the mill do not carry anything to eat at all, because they haven't got time to eat. The duration of the stop is from three to five minutes, and they eat what they can in that time with their hands full of grease, and if they are not through eating they have to go and begin work again.

By the CHAIRMAN:

Q. They work for the eight hours continuously?—A. Yes, sir. I have worked in that mill and labored there when I was throwing up, sick, and I could not leave my post. There is another statement there Mr. Potter made to me. I was one of the committee who went up there to interview them on this new scale and he said as soon as he got this scale in vogue that every man would be affected by this tonnage, that it would be possible to put on tonnage rates, and to substantiate that statement I will ask for Mr. Ryland's scale of Carnegie, Phipps & Co. there, that is, their proposed scale. The tonnage rates paid the men in that mill now are rollers, screwmen, tablemen, hookers, sweepers, shearmen, that is, including first and second shearmen, helpers, heaters, heaters' helper, cranemen, and scrap crew. Now, the others they proposed to put on tonnage at this reduction. That goes contrary to his statement that it is only the tonnage men who are affected by this. He has got other men whose positions are, pull-up——

Q. They are not tonnage men now, but he proposes to put them on?—A. Yes, sir. You understand this will affect three hundred and some odd according to the statement he has made to you. Cranemen, pull-ups, marker, gauger, stamper, painter, line drawers, helpers at scales, millwright, millwright's helper, scrap crew and greaser. These men heretofore have not been paid tonnage rates, but as soon as this new scale gets in vogue he will compel all those men to accept tonnage rates, and by giving them that to receive on this sliding scale the minimum which affects them as well as it does the others.

Mr. BYNUM. About how many in number would it add to the tonnage rate?—A. By Mr. Potter's own statement to me it would affect every person he could possibly put under it who handled a ton of steel.

By the CHAIRMAN:

Q. What do you say about the number?—A. Well, I do not know exactly.

Q. They claim it will only affect 325. Now, how many additional do you claim?—A. Well, it would affect every man in the mill outside of the common laborer, that is, what we call dinkey men, etc. I do not know exactly how many, but it would affect the greater number of them. It would affect all but the common laborer that he could put under this.

Mr. BYNUM. Can you not tell us just about what proportion of the number in the mill? I do not ask you to be accurate at all. Would it affect one-fourth or one-half?—A. Yes; it would affect nine-tenths of the men there. I do not think there is any more than one-tenth of the men connected with that mill who are on common labor.

Mr. BRODERICK. Would it affect them at once?

The WITNESS. It would affect them after the scale came in vogue, according to Mr. Potter's statement to me. This is the great idea. You will see the association never runs this mill; it will be placed in vogue and——

Mr. BOATNER. Your idea is that the proposed change in the rate of wages would affect all the skilled labor in the mill injuriously?—A. Yes, sir.

Q. And reduce their wages?—A. Yes, sir; that is Mr. Potter's statement to me that it would. That is the idea of the firm and what they are governed by, and every man would be affected by this minimum employed there except the common laborer, who is paid $1.40 per day of ten hours' work, or fourteen cents an hour.

The CHAIRMAN. Is there any additional statement you wish to make?—A. No, sir; I think not.

Q. You have no further testimony?—A. No, sir; not in that line.

By Mr. BRODERICK:

Q. Is there any department where new machinery has been put in since the last scale was signed?—A. Not in our department, there has not been.

Q. Well, in any department there?—A. I know of no improvements made there since our mill has been put in operation at all.

Mr. BYNUM. The trouble is, we confuse the term of mill; we take the whole plant and understand it as a mill, and you separate it into different departments down there and call each one of them a mill, and that is confusing to us.

The WITNESS. Yes, sir; there is great confusion in this thing, and they understand that point, too, when they put these scales out for the public to be confused.

The CHAIRMAN. Well, gentlemen, the committee think they have gone through with the investigation, of this part of it, at least, which we propose conducting here. We have a further inquiry to make at other places concerning the Pinkerton organization and their methods, etc., so the committee will now adjourn its work at this place.

COMMITTEE ROOM OF COMMITTEE ON JUDICIARY,
Washington, D. C., July 22, 1892.

The subcommittee of the Committee on the Judiciary appointed to investigate the employment of Pinkerton detectives in connection with the transportation of interstate commerce the recent labor troubles at Homestead, Pa., this day met at 10 a. m., Hon. Wm. C. Oates in the chair.

Present, the chairman, Mr. Bynum, and Mr. Broderick.

TESTIMONY OF ROBERT A. PINKERTON.

ROBERT A. PINKERTON, sworn and examined.

By the CHAIRMAN:

Q. Please give the stenographer your full name and residence.—A. Robert A. Pinkerton, 39 Eighth avenue, Brooklyn.

I desire to present a statement which I have drawn up and which I hand to the committee [handing statement to the chairman of himself and William A. Pinkerton].

At this point John Devlin, A. W. Wright, and John W. Hayes, secretary general executive board of the Knights of Labor, presented to the committee a list of questions which the said Devlin and his associates desired answered. They made the request on behalf of the Knights of Labor.

The committee retired to examine the statement of the Messrs. Pinkerton and the list of questions offered and on their return the statement was allowed to go in as a presentation of their case and not as evidence and the questions were allowed to be put. The statement of the Pinkertons is as follows:

WASHINGTON, D. C., *July 22, 1892.*

To the Judiciary Committee of the House of Representatives:

You have asked us to appear before you and testify in regard to the business conducted by us under the name of Pinkerton's National Detective Agency. The present inquiry by your committee arises from the recent deplorable events at Homestead, in the State of Pennsylvania, and we are informed that a statement on our part of our connection with strikes and of the general method of carrying on this branch of our business will aid the committee in its investigation.

The agency was founded in 1850 by the late Allan Pinkerton, and during the last twenty years it has frequently furnished private watchmen to protect the property of individuals and corporations during strikes. The men employed by us in this strike work are selected with great care and only after a full investigation of their characters and antecedents. Not a single instance can be cited where we have knowingly employed unreliable or untrustworthy men, or where any of our watchmen have been convicted of a crime. Moreover, we have seldom permitted our watchmen to carry arms for the purpose of protecting property and life unless they were authorized by the proper legal authorities or sworn in as deputy sheriffs. Our men have never wantonly or recklessly fired a single shot in any of these strikes, and have only used their arms as the last extremity in order to protect life. We have consistently refused to permit our watchmen to bear arms without special legal authority or as deputy sheriffs even when on private property, and we had no intention of varying from this rule in the Homestead strike.

When first requested to send watchmen to protect the Homestead plant and property of the Carnegie Steel Company, Limited, we refused to do so unless all our men should be sworn in as deputy sheriffs before going to Homestead. We were then assured that the sheriff of Allegheny County, Pa., knew that our men were going to Homestead to act as watchmen and to guard the property of the company and protect its workmen from violence. We were further assured that the sheriff had promised, immediately upon any outbreak or disturbance, to deputize all our watchmen as sheriff's deputies if it became necessary for the protection of life and property. On that condition only did we consent to furnish about three hundred watchmen. A large number of these men were our regular employés, who could be thoroughly trusted for integrity, prudence, and sobriety. The remainder were men whom we employed from time to time or who were known and recommended to us. They did not go into the State of Pennsylvania as an armed body or force, and we should not have permitted or assented to this. There was no intention or purpose whatever of arming them until they were on the property of the company at Homestead and until and unless they had been sworn in as the sheriff's deputies.

The Sheriff's Chief Deputy Gray accompanied our men, being on the tug towing the barges, and it was distinctly understood that he had authority to duly deputize them in case of necessity. The boxes containing the arms and ammunition were shipped from Chicago and were to be delivered at the Homestead yards. The instructions to our men were that they should not be armed unless previously deputized by the sheriff. As a matter of fact, the boxes on board the barges were not opened and the arms and ammunition were not distributed until after the strikers had commenced firing on the watchmen and it became evident that it was a matter of self-defense, for life or death. Klein had been murdered by the strikers and about five other watchmen shot and wounded before our men began their fire in self-defense. Even then it was impossible to attempt to shoot those firing at the barges, because the strikers made a breastwork for themselves by placing women and children in front and firing from behind them. Not a single woman or child was injured by our men.

When our men surrendered, the leaders of the strikers solemnly promised full protection to property and life. They knew that our men surrendered because the wounded required attention and for the purpose of saving further loss of life. After the surrender all our men, including the wounded and helpless, were brutally beaten and robbed by the strikers, and the leaders made no real or honest effort to protect them. Our men were robbed of watches, money, clothing, in fact, everything, and then mercilessly clubbed and stoned. Conners, unable to move or defend himself, was deliberately shot by one of the strikers and then clubbed. Edwards, also wounded and helpless, was clubbed by another striker with the butt end of a musket. Both died, and subsequently another watchman became insane and committed suicide as a result of the fearful beating after having surrendered. All our men were more or less injured. The acts of the strikers, after our men surrendered, would be a disgrace to savages. Yet, because done in the name of organized American labor, sympathy, if not encouragement, is shown for such deeds by part of the press and by political demagogues.

We do not shirk responsibility for any of our acts in this or any other strike. The coming murder trials ought to bring out the truth and uphold the law. Our actions will then be shown to have been legal from beginning to end. Whatever may be the present prejudice against our agency, we shall patiently wait the sober reflection of the country in the confidence that the enormity of the wrong and outrage, done to our men at Homestead will be ultimately recognized, although the example will in the meantime have caused incalculable injury to the community.

The principle involved is of far more importance than are the merits of the present controversy between the Carnegie Company and its workmen. We have no quarrel with organized labor, and they have no cause of complaint against us except in so far as they attempt to destroy property and life and to violate the law. If the owners of mills, factories, mines, railroads, and other valuable property can not employ watchmen to protect life and property, then all capital so invested is practically at the mercy of secret labor organizations, whose tyranny and despotism exceed anything ever known in the history of the world. These societies intimidate whole communities by threats of murder, and are determined upon ruin and destruction of property if their demands, no matter how unreasonable or impracticable, are not complied with.

In the case of the Mollie Maguires, they terrorized the public authorities, and for years were absolute in their rule of murder and destruction of property. Every large strike has shown that these labor organizations will murder and destroy property out of sheer wantonness and revenge. During the Chicago Stove Company's strike, the strikers concealed explosives in a mould in order to cause an explosion when the molten metal was poured in. During the strike on the Chicago, Burlington and Quincy Railroad, dynamite was put under trains by leaders of the strike in the expectation that trains would be blown up and innocent passengers killed. During the recent strike on the New York Central obstructions were repeatedly placed on the track by strikers, and in one instance a train of sleeping cars, filled with sleeping passengers and running at a high rate of speed, was thrown down a steep embankment. In another instance during the same strike, the strikers attempted to wreck the Chicago express going down a steep grade into West Albany, and would have succeeded in killing or maiming a great number of passengers, if one of the railroad ties, with which the obstruction was made, had not been rotten. In the city of New York, during the stonecutters' strike, strikers, in order to kill non-union men, unwound a part of the rope of a windlass and during the night poured acid on the rope and then rewound it so that the next day nonunion men might be killed in ascending with the stone or by the falling stones. These fiendish acts were done by members of labor organizations in the promotion of their strikes, and the only grievance which the men had was that the employer was seeking to hire men who were perfectly willing and eager to take the places of the well-paid strikers.

These are but a few instances where strikers, controlled by secret labor orders, have sought to murder and to destroy property. It was morally certain, from the threats of the men themselves, that the strikers at Homestead would resort to similar violence and attempt to destroy the property of the Carnegie Company if any attempts were made to supply their places by nonunion men. At the present time, thousands of men would go to Homestead, attracted by the high wages paid there, if they were assured of protection in the right to earn their living.

The business of watching and guarding private property is now extensively carried on in large cities in this country, not only by ourselves, but by many other reputable concerns. Thousands of banks, residences, warehouses, offices, stores, etc., are thus protected and guarded by private watchmen. If men can not lawfully act as private watchmen in a large manufacturing plant, then it must follow that the bank or the private house or office can not be protected or guarded. It would, we think, surprise the community if it should be declared by Congress that the right to protect one's property and to hire servants and agents to assist in so doing no longer exists in this country.

We were advised by our counsel, Messrs. Seward, Guthrie & Morawetz, of New York, that we were not violating any law of the United States or of the State of Pennsylvania; that our acts were lawful; that we had the right to employ and send men to Homestead to act as watchmen; that if they were attacked they had the right to kill, if absolutely necessary for self-defense; that they had the right to bear arms on the premises of the Carnegie Company in order to protect life and private property whether or not they were deputized by the sheriff of Allegheny County; that we had the right to ship arms from Chicago to the Carnegie yards at Homestead for the purpose of arming our men if and after they were deputized by the sheriff; that in view of the attack on the barges our men had the right to bear arms and to defend themselves, and that all their acts in firing in self-defense from the barges, after the attack on them, were legally justifiable under the laws of the United States and of the State of Pennsylvania.

Yours, respectfully,

WM. A. PINKERTON,
ROBERT A. PINKERTON.

At this point the committee took a recess until 1 p. m.

AFTER THE RECESS.

The committee met. Present, the chairman, Mr. Boatner, Mr. Bynum, and Mr. Broderick.

The CHAIRMAN. I will state for the information of the reporters that, as we began, a committee representing the Knights of Labor, Mr. John Devlin, Mr. A. W. Wright, and Mr. John W. Hayes, presented several questions which they desired the committee to propound to the witness. Under our rules and practice we do not allow any parties not members of the committee to put questions. The committee examined the questions and have submitted them to the witness for answer and the witness has no objection to answering all of them and he proposes now to make his answers.

The chairman then proceeded to read the following questions and the witness made the following answers:

Q. State the names and residences of the principals composing the so-called Pinkerton agency.

A. Pinkerton's National Detective Agency is owned and conducted by William A. Pinkerton, of Chicago, and Robert A. Pinkerton, of New York, as copartners, and as survivors and successors of the late Allan Pinkerton.

The CHAIRMAN. There are no other persons members of the association or business?

The WITNESS. Except the employés.

The CHAIRMAN (reading):

Q. State the number and location of the offices, principal and subordinate, of the agency.

A. There are two principal offices, situated respectively at New York and Chicago. The Chicago office is under the immediate direction and control of William A. Pinkerton, and the New York office of Robert A. Pinkerton. We have six regular branches situated in Boston, Philadelphia, Kansas City, St. Paul, Denver, and Portland, Oregon.

Q. What is the nature of the several branches or kinds of business which the agency undertakes to conduct?

A. The nature of our business in all its branches is that of a general private detective business. We supply watchmen to protect and guard banks, private residences, offices, stores, warehouses, etc. We also supply men to act as watchmen for race tracks, summer resorts, fairs, exhibitions, theaters, etc.

Q. What number of firearms and weapons of offense, of all kinds were subject to your control or owned by your agency on the 4th day of July, A. D. 1892, and where were they deposited?

A. Our agency owned about two hundred and fifty rifles, about four hundred pistols, and about an equal number of clubs, and they were deposited at Chicago.

Q. State the number of the persons regularly in your employ on the said 4th day of July, or formerly.

A. We had in our employ at that time not to exceed 600 employés, including clerks, stenographers, typewriters, etc., detectives, night and day watchmen, 600. To the best of my knowledge and belief we have never had more than 800 persons in our employ at any one time at all the offices in the United States.

The CHAIRMAN. Would it be practicable for you to give the names and places of residence of these people at present?

The WITNESS. Well, it would not.

Mr. BOATNER. Do you think it would be well to load down the report by printing the names and addresses of 800 people?

The CHAIRMAN. I do not.

Mr. BOATNER. It does not seem to me to be relevant to the investigation. You might inquire as to the class of people they employ and you can inquire about that without requiring him to give their names and residences.

Mr. BYNUM. Could we get about the number employed in each city?

By the CHAIRMAN:

Q. Can you give about the number employed in each office?—A. Well, it is according to the season. We have more employés in the summer time than we do in the winter months, and I suppose I could give an estimate of what there were at each office——

Q. Just give that.—A. Well, at the present time there are employed in New York—there may be from 100 to 125; in Boston, 20 to 25 ; in Philadelphia, possibly 40; in Chicago, possibly 125 to 150; in Kansas City, possibly 30; in Portland, Oregon, possibly 15; in Denver, possibly 30, and in St. Paul, possibly 20.

The CHAIRMAN (reading):

Q. What authority do you exercise, or claim to exercise, over your employés as to obedience of orders? Are they required to bear arms and go wherever ordered by the principals of the agency, and perform whatever service is imposed upon them?

A. The only authority we ever exercised, or claim to exercise, is that of any employer exacting obedience, attention to duty, honesty, and sobriety. They are not required to bear arms or to perform whatever service is imposed on them. They are always advised of exactly what they are expected to do, and are at perfect liberty to refuse any employment to which they object.

Q. Are any of your contracts with your employés in writing? If yea, produce one or more of them.—A. Our contracts with many of our employés are in writing. They provide for honesty, sobriety, and attention to the duties for which they are employed. We decline, under advice of counsel to produce these contracts because they are matters of private agreement between ourselves and our employés.

Mr. BOATNER. I desire to enter my protest against any such style of proceeding as to propound these questions at the beginning of the examination of this witness. It appears to me it is an usurpation of the powers of this committee. It is a reflection upon the committee in that it takes for granted that the committee will not make a proper investigation. The very purpose for which we summoned Mr. Pinkerton is to investigate the participation of the Pinkerton Company with the late riots and disturbances at Homestead, and I do not like to be put in the position of having a reflection thrown upon us that we would not ask the proper questions. If I had been present this morning I would have opposed these questions coming in at this time. After we had examined the witness, then if there were any questions which they desired to have put not covered by our examination, the questions could have been asked.

The question was discussed by the committee and it was decided as the examination had been begun in this manner it would be continued and the balance of the questions put.

The CHAIRMAN (reading):

Q. State under what circumstances you entered into the agreement with Mr. Frick, or his associates, to guard the works at Homestead, Pa. Who first broached the negotiation ending in the employment? Produce all correspondence relating thereto.

A. We were requested by the Carnegie Steel Company, limited, to furnish about 300 watchmen to protect the property of the company at Homestead and the lives of their employés. The negotiations were first broached by the company's representative. The correspondence relating thereto is not in my possession here.

Q. Was this your first agreement to supply men to Mr. Frick or his associates? How many men and on what terms did you supply them in the matter of the difficulty in the Connellsville coke regions?

The CHAIRMAN. You may answer that or not, as that is something we are not charged with inquiring into.

A. Our firm had been previously engaged by Mr. Frick, or the Coke Company with which he was connected in Pennsylvania. During the coke strike we supplied between 150 and 200 watchmen, as nearly as I can now recollect, and the terms were $5 per day. These men were ultimately all sworn in as sheriff deputies, and some of them were given State commissions under the Pennsylvania Coal and Iron Police Law.

The CHAIRMAN (reading):

Q. How many men were you requested to furnish in the Homestead matter; within what time, and from what localities did you obtain them?

A. We were requested to furnish about 300 watchmen; they were to be supplied by the 6th of July; we had about ten days' notice, and the men were obtained from Chicago, Philadelphia, and New York. All these men knew exactly the nature of their employment, and many of them had been for some time regularly in our employ. All of these men had recommendations as to their character and antecedents, or were personally known to us. Their references are always investigated, and we use the utmost care in selecting as reliable and trustworthy men as possible.

Q. How were the barges on which your men were transported to Homestead constructed as to the defense and protection of persons upon them?

A. I do not personally know anything about the barges, but so far as my firm are concerned the barges were not constructed for the purpose of defense and protection. They were simply ordinary barges, used for transportation.

Q. Were not the barges lined with iron or steel plates of sufficient strength to resist small arms of every kind?

A. I am informed and verily believe that the barges were not lined with iron or steel, and were not of sufficient strength to resist small arms.

Q. Were not the men on the barges entirely secure from any attack from the union men of Homestead, so long as they remained behind the protecting sides of the barges?

A. To the best of my knowledge and belief the barges were not secure from attack, and the great amount of wounds inflicted on our men should conclusively establish that they were not a sufficient protection. We would never have allowed our men to start on the expedition had we known they were going to be attacked before landing.

Q. Why were barges employed to transport the men from Pittsburg to Homestead instead of the ordinary modes and means of travel by land and water?

A. Barges were employed instead of the railroads because the Carnegie Company and ourselves expected that thereby our watchmen would be enabled to land upon the company's property without causing any breach of the peace or tending to excite the men who had gone on strike. The landing was made at night, and at an hour when we expected the strikers would be in bed, because we believed that after the experience of the sheriff's men an attempt might be made to forcibly prevent our men entering the works if we came by railroad in the day time. Our sole desire was to avoid by all means a breach of the peace and inciting or aggravating a riot. Had we known, when the men started, that they could not land without a breach of the peace, we should have refused to permit them to go unless authorized by the governor of the State or deputized by the sheriff.

Q. State the number of men on the barges, the amount of fixed ammunition, and the number and kind of firearms of all kinds, and by whom the said ammunition and arms were supplied.

A. There were about 310 men on the barges. There were about 250 rifles, about 300 pistols, and ammunition and night clubs. The clubs are what are usually known as watchmen's sticks or police batons.

Q. How many of the men on the barges were old and trained employés of your agency? What authority had they over the recruits in respect to requiring them to bear and use firearms at their command and direction?

A. About two-thirds of the men had previously been in our employ. They had no authority over the other men in any way, and could not have given them any orders in respect of bearing or using firearms. All the men were under the charge of F. H. Hines, who had been in our employ for many years, and whom we knew to be trustworthy, prudent, and reliable in every way.

Q. State with particularity where the men who were finally taken to Homestead were assembled together, through what States, and by what lines of railroad they were transported to Pittsburg.

A. About 120 men were sent from Chicago; they passed through Illinois, Indiana, and Ohio. About 76 men were sent from Philadelphia, passing through New Jersey, New York, Ohio. About 120 men were sent from New York, passing through New York, Ohio, and Pennsylvania. All the men met at Ashtabula, Ohio; went from there to a point near Youngstown, Ohio, where they were put aboard the barges. The Chicago men left by the Lake Shore road; the New York men went over the West Shore road and the Lake Shore; the Philadelphia men went over the Pennsylvania road, the Lake Shore and the West Shore.

Q. State precisely the object in placing the large number of firearms on the barges, and whether it was not understood between the principals of the agency and Mr. Frick and others representing the Carnegie Works at Homestead that the men on the barges were to commit a breach of the peace, or to use force to recover possession of these works if necessary.

A. The arms placed aboard the barges were in boxes and were destined for the yards and private property of the Carnegie Company. Our positive instructions were that they should not be used or distributed to the men until after they had been sworn in by the sheriff, and we were assured that the sheriff had promised to swear them in upon the first sign of trouble or disturbance. Our men were not, under any circumstances, to commit a breach of the peace, and there never was any such understanding, directly or indirectly, with any one connected with the Carnegie Company or with anybody else. We would not permit them to use force to recover possession of the works if they had been in possession of the strikers, unless they had been duly authorized and sworn in by the sheriff. Our only purpose was to go upon private property and then protect it from attack.

Q. State whether it was not the intention of the superior officers on the barges, and whether they had not been instructed to fire on the so-called locked out union workmen at Homestead and to take life if it were necessary, to obtain possession of these works.

A. They were not so instructed, and would not have fired upon the locked out men except as a matter of self defense after they had been

Q. Did you not know that it was your duty to first apply to the courts for assistance and secure the usual process and writs before you were authorized to employ force to reach the Carnegie steel and iron works at Homestead?

A. We understood that our employers, the Carnegie Company had duly applied to the proper legal authority, and that we were going to Homestead with the consent and approval of the sheriff and our watchmen would be sworn in in case of any outbreak.

Q. What right did you believe you had to assemble men at various places outside of the State of Pennsylvania, and to carry them within that State armed or with stores of arms conveniently at hand, without the request or consent of the authorities of the commonwealth of Pennsylvania, or of any municipality therein?

A. We were advised by counsel that we had a perfect right to send watchmen from one State to another. We did not attempt and have never attempted to send any armed body, and the arms on the barges would not have been distributed if the men had not been attacked. There was every reason to believe from the threats from the strikers themselves that our men would be attacked, and that attempts would be made to destroy the property of the Carnegie Company. The principal deputy of the sheriff of Allegheny County, Mr. Gray, accompanied our men, and we distinctly understood that he would be authorized and prepared to swear our men in as soon as there was any outbreak or indication of trouble.

Q. Did your agency, before taking armed men into Pennsylvania, make any effort to obtain the consent or authority of the executive of the commonwealth of Pennsylvania? or did you ever, upon any occasion before taking armed men into any State or commonwealth, ask for or obtain the consent or authority of the executive of such State or commonwealth?

A. This question is a matter of law, and it would be a waste of time for us to attempt to instruct the committee.

Q. Would you not have the same authority or legal right to place 10,000 armored barges on the navigable waters of the United States equipped with men and loaded with arms and ammunition, that you had to place these barges so manned and loaded upon the waters of the Monongahela River?

A. This question is a matter of law, and it would be a waste of time for us to attempt to instruct the committee.

Q. How many human lives have your employés taken since your agency first entered upon the business of supplying men to protect the property of corporations and employers against so-called "strikers," or to make effective so-called "lockouts?"

A. During the twenty years that we have been engaged in this strike work, not a single instance can be cited where our men have fired upon the strikers except as a last extremity in order to save their lives. During these twenty years three men have been killed by our watchmen in these strikes, up to the time of the Homestead affair. In each instance our men were sworn in as deputy sheriffs or peace officers, and whenever tried have been acquitted.

By the CHAIRMAN:

Q. As I understand you you are engaged in the regular detective business, and in addition to that furnish guards to corporations and others who desire to employ them to guard property in case of strikes, disturbances, etc.?—A. We are engaged in the general detective business. The watch business is a separate business, but controlled by ourselves, and we furnish watchmen for private parties or corporations.

Q. Will you mention the number of strikes or disturbances between corporations engaged in the transportation of interstate commerce or carrying the United States mails and their employés wherein you have interposed and furnished men as detectives or as guards to such corporations and their property?—A. I can not state the exact number of railroads, corporations, or individuals we have been employed by or furnished with watchmen in the twenty years since we commenced it.

Q. State the principal ones within your recollection, and give the committee an account of the character of them?—A. The ones that I recollect are the Chicago, Burlington and Quincy; the Lake Shore——

Q. When did that occur, take them one at a time?—A. I can not give the date.

Q. What year.—A. I can not give you the year. It was about four years ago; that was the Burlington strike. The Lake Shore Road was about five years ago, and the New York Central Road about two years ago. There have been other roads but I do not call them to mind. There was the Union Pacific seven or eight years ago.

Q. You furnished men, did you not, at a strike, or a series of strikes, occurring, I believe, in 1886 and 1887 out west; that is, west of the Mississippi River?—A. West of the Mississippi?

Q. Yes, it was investigated by a committee of Congress.—A. I do not call it to mind; I do not know of any investigating committee who investigated any strike which we were engaged in.

Q. Have any of your men ever been indicted or tried for killing or wounding any people while engaged in the duties which you employed them to perform?—A. Yes, sir.

Q. Will you state the cases and the results?—A. In the strike—there is another road I had forgotten, and that is the Delaware, Lackawanna and Western—there were several arrested, one for shooting, who was tried and acquitted. At the stock-yard strike in Chicago, there were two or three arrested, tried, and acquitted. In a number of strikes there have been parties arrested on charge of assault. None have been convicted, except two before a magistrate or justice of the peace, and the judgments have been reversed.

Q. What cases are they?—A. That was on a strike on the New York Central Road.

Q. What year?—A. Two years ago.

Q. What was the charge against the men, or how many charges?—A. Simply assault. Some were acquitted. Those who were taken into the higher courts were acquitted, but some being tried by local magistrates the men were committed for trial, but never were tried; that was the result of that, or if tried were acquitted.

Q. Have you ever furnished guards to travel on trains which were engaged in the transportation of interstate commerce and the United States mails between different States?—A. Yes, sir.

Q. In what cases?—A. In the cases of the Burlington strike and the New York Central strike. I think, wherever we have done strike work for railroads at the time we furnish men to ride the trains.

Q. Do these men go armed?—A. I should think they did; I do not know positively.

Q. What were your instructions in such cases?—A. It was allowing to the circumstances. In the New York Central strike the men who rode freight trains were armed. They were obliged to protect themselves from parties shooting out of buildings at them and throwing stones from an elevation down on the company's employés or on themselves. In the New York strike a number of men were knocked off freight trains, off trains while in motion, by stones, and some were shot.

Q. About what number would be furnished for a train?—A. It would be according to the length of the freight train. I suppose that one man would probably cover five cars—five, six, or seven cars. There would be a man, anyhow, to every brakesman on the train and one in the caboose, and probably one riding with the engineer.

Q. Can you give the date——?—A. (Continuing.) I will say these men were sworn in, all of them, as peace officers.

Q. Can you give the date of the negotiations between you and Mr. Frick, chairman of the Carnegie Steel Company, at Homestead, with reference to furnishing men who were sent there subsequently; I mean the men who were sent to Homestead and got into trouble on the morning of the 6th of July?—A. Yes, sir; I think the negotiations commenced eight or ten days previous to that.

Q. Some eight or ten days previous to that?—A. Yes, sir.

Q. With whom did you negotiate?—A. My negotiations were conducted through Mr. Schoonmaker, who was in consultation with Mr. Frick; he is the vice—I think the assistant to the president of the Carnegie Steel Company.

Q. Mr. Frick testified that he contracted to pay you $5 a day per man and feed them—board them; was that the contract?—A. Yes, sir.

Q. How many did you say were furnished?—A. I say 310. There may have been 312 or 315, along there. I say under 316 men limit.

Q. Who had charge of these men; did you not have some one who controlled their action and directed them?—A. Yes, sir; F. H. Hinde, an employé of ours at New York, was to be in charge of the men.

Q. Did he go in charge of them?—A. Yes, sir.

Q. What became of him?—A. He was shot down in attempting to land at Homestead.

Q. Did he recover?—A. He is still in the hospital at Pittsburg; he was shot twice.

Q. You have no personal knowledge of the barges or of any transaction which occurred in taking the barges up the river and in the landing or attempted landing at Homestead?—A. Nothing except from the reports which have been made to me.

Q. You have no personal knowledge?—A. No, sir.

Q. Have your men, while in the employ of railroads and on trains running through the country, ever been engaged in any fight or battle with other people other than you have stated, that in some instances they were fired upon by unknown parties and had stones thrown at them?—A. Well, we have a good deal of work, and I guess we do most of what they call train-robbery work—where trains are robbed by train robbers. We work for all express companies and where there is a robbery we go out—and in this case, in speaking of men who have been killed by our men, I leave the train robberies outside. I mentioned three men who have been killed in connection with strikes, but I did not mention the men killed while being arrested for holding up trains and who resisted arrest.

Q. Do you know how many people of that character, train robbers, have been killed by your men?—A. No, sir; I would have to look up the papers to see it. I think there were in 1866, at the time of the Adams Express robbery at Seymour, Ind., two or three killed while attempting to rob the train.

Q. By your men who were on the train?—A. Well, there were a

number of our men on the train, and there were others on the train, and it was done at the nighttime, and whether they were killed by our men or not I could not say.

Mr. BYNUM. Those who were not killed were hung to a limb of a tree on the edge of Seymour the morning afterwards.

The WITNESS. Yes, sir; there were a number hung out there. In replying further to the question I desire to state that at any time we have ever had trouble in connection with strike work on railroads it has always been where it has been brought on by the strikers or their friends, and in riding trains, where strikers have come out and put obstructions on the track to stop trains from moving and take possession of freight yards and driven off switchmen, our duties have always been to put the trains in motion and to clear the yards of strikers and allow the trains to move; never to stop a train or obstruct it.

By the CHAIRMAN:

Q. Have your employés in any case within your knowledge fired upon or made an assault upon any citizen of the United States or other people while in the discharge of these duties or in the employ of corporations; have they ever made any assault upon them or begun any riot, or shot, or abused them?—A. Not begun it. They have fired when they have been fired at; when they thought their lives were in danger.

Q. Is it not a habit of your men while thus employed to go armed?—A. Well, where they have been sworn in as peace officers, yes, sir; and where they have been actually on the road, protecting the property and the lives of employés or traveling through the country; but traveling through the country like transporting the men from Chicago or New York or Philadelphia to the Carnegie works they did not carry arms. The arms are sent and they are generally put on the company's property and are not used except where some necessity arises to use them. We do not carry armed guards through the country.

By Mr. BOATNER:

Q. You have charge of the New York office, I believe?—A. I have charge of what we call the eastern division; New York, Boston and Philadelphia.

Q. Mr. Frick put in evidence a letter, I think, of your agency dated on the 25th day of June, in which he made formal application to be supplied with men. Was there any agreement between your agency and Mr. Frick prior to that time that men should be furnished?—A. I do not believe there was an agreement at that time. I had declined to furnish men unless they could be sworn in. I had positively declined to furnish them unless that should be done.

Q. Mr. Frick testified that several days before the 25th a representative of your agency came from Philadelphia and had an interview with him in regard to these men; that your representative had stated the terms upon which they would be furnished, and that he had accepted the terms by making no objection?—A. I said that to the best of my recollection it was eight or ten days before that consultations had been going on. I now remember that Mr. Hinde was sent on from New York, at the request of either Mr. Frick or his representative, to come to Pittsburg for the purpose of an interview.

Q. What I want to get at is the date when Mr. Hinde went to Pittsburg?—A. What was the date of Mr. Frick's letter?

Q. Mr. Frick's letter was dated the 25th of June. He said Mr. Hinde had been there prior to that but we could not get out of him just how long prior to that. A.—I could not state now; it may have been four, five, or six days prior, but there was no understanding at that time that our men were to be employed. The understanding was that in case circumstances arose which warranted it, they would be employed. Terms were mentioned, no doubt, but there was no understanding they were to come in and go to work at that time. It was simply a general conversation that in case the men were to be employed that a man had been on the ground and looked it over, and it was for consultation only that Mr. Hinde went to Pittsburg.

Q. Had Mr. Hinde returned to New York before the 25th?—A. Oh, yes, sir. He went away with these men when they left.

Q. He went away with the men?—A. Yes, sir.

Q. When he returned to New York you received this letter which was dated on the 25th of June and that was after he had had an interview with Mr Frick?—A. Yes, sir, my recollection is that that is what led up to the letter. I declined to furnish the men unless they could be sworn in. After Mr. Hinde's return I declined to furnish the men unless they could be sworn in.

The CHAIRMAN. As deputy sheriffs?

The WITNESS. As peace officers or deputy sheriffs.

By Mr. BOATNER:

Q. Did you reply to Mr. Frick's letter of the 25th of June?—A. My recollection is I did, but most of our negotiations were done through Mr. Schoonmaker through the telephone or over their private wire. Mr. Schoonmaker would come to me and then he would go back, and whether he would telephone or use the private wire I could not say.

Q. I would like for you to be certain if you can whether you did reply to his letter of the 25th of June?—A. I think it is very likely.

Q. Well, that still leaves it in a condition of uncertainty?—A. I do not think there is much doubt about it myself; I believe I did; that is all I can say.

Q. Do you recollect having written the letter or dictated it yourself?—A. I did not write it myself; if I did send one, I dictated it.

Q. Do you recollect having dictated it?—A. I have a recollection I did. My recollection is I did.

Q. Do you recollect the substance of the letter?—A. Well, I can only say I think it applied to the swearing in of the men; that if we furnished the men they must be sworn in.

Q. Could you furnish us with a press copy of that letter?—A. I could furnish you with a copy of that letter if it was necessary.

Q. We would like to have it. Mr. Frick has furnished us with a letter to you, and we would be very glad to have a copy of your reply. Now, it was testified to by the captain of the boat who took those men to Homestead that the arms were turned over to him with the supplies, and that they were delivered to him in ordinary boxes, which did not show what they contained. Will you state to the committee who sent those arms to the city of Pittsburg?—A. We sent them.

Q. From what point?—A. From Chicago.

Q. To whose care did you ship them at Pittsburg?—A. To the Union Supply Company.

Q. Did you give the Union Supply Company instructions as to the disposition to be made of the arms?—A. No, sir.

Q. You gave them no instructions?—A. No, sir.

Q. How did the Union Supply Company come to deliver them to the captain of this boat?—A. I have no personal knowledge how it was, but I could assume how it was done.

Q. How would you assume it was done?—A. I assume they got instructions from the Carnegie people, from some one of them.

Q. Had you given the Union Supply Company instructions to act on the orders of the Carnegie Steel Company?—A. No, sir.

Q. How do you account for the fact that the Supply Company accepted instructions from the Carnegie Steel Company about your property?—A. I do not know they accepted instructions. I assume that they did, but I can not account for why they were delivered there.

The CHAIRMAN. Mr. Boatner, I think there is something in the testimony taken out there that Mr. Frick or some of those people are members of the Union Supply Company.

By Mr. BOATNER:

Q. What sort of an organization is the Union Supply Company—what business does it do?—A. I do not know.

Q. You do not know?—A. No, sir.

Q. At whose suggestion did you send those arms and ammunition to the Union Supply Company?—A. The instructions came from the Carnegie people.

Q. And you merely obeyed their instructions in regard to the shipment of their arms?—A. Yes, sir; that is, to ship anything we had to ship.

Q. You have testified at considerable length about the object of having these arms on board; under what contingencies were these arms to be used?—A. In case that their lives—we positively instructed the men and officers that the arms were not to be used except they were sworn in by the sheriff and their lives were in danger. I desire to say that I did not know that the arms were to go up on the boat, but I have understood that the reason they were sent up on the boat was it was impossible to get anything inside of the works otherwise. I had nothing to do with putting the arms on the boat.

Q. Then as I understand, your instructions were that the men in the event resistance was made to their landing should not use the arms unless their lives were in danger?—A. Or unless they were sworn in, and then only when their lives were in danger.

Q. They were not to use the arms unless they were sworn in and their lives were also in danger?—A. Yes, sir; unless their lives also were in danger.

Q. Do you mean if they had been attacked and their lives were threatened before they were sworn in that they had no right to protect themselves?—A. Not with arms.

Q. Even if they were attacked with arms?—A. If they were attacked with arms, and the men's lives were in danger they were to protect themselves.

Q. Were not arms furnished?—A. They were to protect themselves, those were the instructions to the men.

Q. But they were provided with those arms?—A. They were not; the arms were sent up to be put inside the Homestead works.

Q. But the evidence which was furnished there at Homestead shows this state of facts, when the provisions were put on board the barges the arms were put on also, that the sheriff was instructed not to swear these men in except in case of trouble, and there is a good deal of doubt, and the sheriff himself did not seem to know what instructions he had given, but that was the contention of the Frick people.

Mr. BYNUM. Pardon me, Mr. Boatner, without any intention you might mislead him, and you should state to him that that was the testimony which was elicited at Pittsburg.

Mr. BOATNER. I am now stating to him what testimony was stated there; you understand that?

The WITNESS. Yes, sir.

Q. Now, I want to know what use would be made of those arms in the event an attack should be made upon the boat in advance of those men being sworn in. You say to this committee the men were instructed they were not to use the arms until after they were sworn in and then assailed?—A. I desire to say this: I had no reason to anticipate an attack on the boat, and therefore gave no instructions on that point. We had every reason to believe that they could land on the company's property without trouble.

Q. You thought they could get there without the Homestead men knowing anything about it?—A. That was the object.

Q. Without the strikers ascertaining that fact?—A. That was the object.

Q. That was the object in sending them up by boat?—A. Yes, sir; by boat.

Q. Then the object of furnishing them with arms was to resist any forcible attack which might be made on the works after obtaining possession?—A. Made on the works, or any forcible attempt which was made on themselves where their lives were in danger.

Q. Well, now, let me see if we can get at what your understanding was. These men you supposed were to begotten into the works without the strikers knowing it?—A. That was what we hoped to do.

Q. That was what you expected?—A. That was what we expected.

Q. They were then furnished with arms?—A. They were not; no, sir, the arms were shipped by the Union Supply Company.

Q. We have gotten way past that; the arms were put upon the boat, you do not deny that?—A. No, sir; I do not.

Q. And the arms were issued to the men?—A. Yes, sir; but I had nothing to do with issuing them.

Q. Was it not contemplated when you shipped the arms that they were to be issued to the men in the event it became necessary to issue them. A. Yes, sir; when they were on the company's property.

Q. That was the understanding when you sent them?—A. Yes, sir.

Q. Now, then, in the event any attempt should be made by the Homestead workmen to dislodge your men from those works or dislodge the employés of the Homestead Company from those works, was it not expected your men were to use the arms with which they had been provided?—A. No, sir; not unless their lives were in danger.

Q. Then if the Homestead strikers had come to the works and undertaken to put your men off without endangering their lives they would not have been authorized to use those guns?—A. No, sir; they would not.

Q. If the strikers had come there with sufficient force just to shove them out of the works they would have gone?—A. Well, I suppose if there had been trouble there they would have fought there, but there would have been no arms used.

Q. What did you expect them to fight with?—A. They had three hundred what we call night sticks, night clubs.

Q. They were then to use the sticks unless the Homestead people resorted to arms?—A. They were to protect themselves and they were to keep tresspassers off the company's property.

Q. How?—A. Well, at the first sign of trouble the understanding was that they were to be sworn in. And after that if anyone attempted to come on the property of the company they would be then peace officers, and anyone committing a breach of the peace should be arrested.

Q. It was supposed then if anyone attempted to enter those works they would be sworn in as peace officers and they would have author ity to arrest them?—A. Yes, sir.

Q. And in the exercise of that authority they were authorized to use the arms if their lives should become endangered—is that the way of it?—A. If their lives were in danger and they were fired on, and perhaps some of them were killed, and they supposed their lives depended upon their firing back, they were authorized to use their arms.

Q. You stated something about the Chicago, Burlington and Quincy strike; how many men did you have in the service of the company on that Burlington strike?—A. Well, it extended from Chicago to Denver, and I suppose that, guessing at the number, there may have been 300 men employed there.

Q. Were those men sworn in as peace officers on that occasion?—A. At different parts of the road they were; yes, sir.

Q. Were the men considered as employés of the road or as your employés?—A. At some parts of the road they were not.

Q. Were those men armed?—A. The men riding trains and the men doing duty at different points of the road where there had been trouble were armed. Where there had been no trouble they carried clubs.

Q. What was the purpose of having men armed on that occasion?—A. Well, to protect their own lives and to protect the company's employés.

Q. In other words, to resist any armed attack upon the road or its employés?—A. To drive off any armed attacks.

Q. By the use of arms?—A. Well, if arms were used, the men would be expected to protect themselves rather than be killed.

Q. Well, as a general rule, it is too late for a man to use arms after he is fired upon. Were your instructions to your men that they had to be fired upon before they could return the fire?—A. There has never been a case where that has not been the case that I know of. They have always been assailed first. If a man is standing on top of a freight train and another man is standing upon a bank above him, and he takes a bowlder and throws it down on him he might as well shoot at him with a rifle bullet.

Q. Would it not be too late to shoot the man after he had thrown the bowlder?—A. I think if the man got away it would not be too late.

Q. What is the use of a man being armed if it is not for the purpose of preventing these assaults?—A. They are to defend themselves with.

Q. It seems to me there is an inconsistency in your statement. You say that your men are armed for the purpose of defending themselves, and yet you say they are not to defend themselves until after they are fired upon. Now, down in my part of the country it is generally too late for a man to defend himself after he is fired upon; he is generally hors de combat afterwards?—A. There is quite a difference between where you live and up here, although the law may be the same.

Q. Then they are not as good shots here as they are down there?—A. No, I do not think they are. In fact, if the firing at Homestead had been done to kill there would have been a great many more people killed than there were. I have no doubt if the men had wanted to use those arms they would have obtained possession of that yard, but they would have had to sacrifice a great many more lives to do it.

Q. You also stated you served the New York Central Railroad. How many men did you have in the service of that road during the strike?—A. Possibly 350.

Q. Were those men considered as employés of the company, or your employés; from whom did they get their orders while they were in that service?—A. Well, they got their orders from me.

Q. Were they sworn in as peace officers?—A. Yes, sir.

Q. Well, after having been sworn in as peace officers, did they continue to get their instructions from you?—A. Yes, sir; and the sheriff was in consultation——

Q. The sheriff was in consultation?—A. Yes, sir; at times.

Q. Yet you say you continued to give orders to the men?—A. Simply in regard to the protection of the property and the protection of the employés.

Q. Now, by what legal authority are you advised that you have the right to instruct a sworn officer of the law; you had no official position, had you?—A. I was sworn in.

Q. Were you sworn in also?—A. Yes, sir.

Q. In what capacity?—A. As a peace officer.

Q. What sort of a peace officer?—A. A deputy sheriff.

Q. Then I suppose you got your orders from the sheriff and gave them to the men?—A. Yes, sir; I got orders from the sheriff and I also gave orders to the men.

Q. Did you have any participation or did your men have any participation in the strike which occurred at St. Louis two years ago?—A. No, sir.

Q. You did not?—A. No, sir. You mean where the trouble was on the bridge—what was known as the Missouri Pacific strike, where the trouble was on the bridge.

Q. Yes.—A. No, sir.

Q. Are those two strikes, the Chicago, Burlington and Quincy and the New York Central the only strikes you have had connection within the last six or seven years?—A. No, sir; we have had connection with a good many strikes.

Q. Well, railroad strikes?—A. I mentioned, I think, the Lake Shore, and the one I did not mention at the time was the Delaware, Lackawanna and Western.

Q. State if there has been any instance in which you have furnished men as guards or policemen under such circumstances as have been detailed unless they have been sworn in as deputy sheriffs; in other words, have you made it a rule that your men shall be sworn in as deputy sheriffs?—A. We made it a rule. Possibly at some point on the Burlington road where there was no trouble the men have acted as watchmen without being sworn in, but only at those points where there has been no trouble.

Q. You have stated that three men were killed by your people in these strikes, and I have been requested to ask you if you know of any women who have been killed?—A. Never, to my knowledge; there never was. It was stated in the papers that was so, but it is not a fact. It was stated that women were killed at Albany, but that is not the fact.

The CHAIRMAN. Have you any women detectives in your employ?

The WITNESS. No, sir.

By Mr. BOATNER:

Q. How many similar agencies are there to yours in the United States, or are there any others of which you know?—A. There are a very large number of what they call private detective agencies in the United States, in New York, and all the large cities.

Q. Are there any other agencies besides yours of which you know which furnishes men, such as you furnish, to aid corporations in resisting strikes or maintaining lockouts?—A. There have been other agencies who have furnished men to do this work.

Q. In late years?—A. Yes, sir; in the Lake Shore strike before we took hold of it there were other parties contracting to do the work.

Q. Can you state any other such agencies?—A. Well, there was a firm called Mooney & Boland, of Chicago, who furnished men for the strike; also in the street-car hands' strike in Chicago, and the Lake Shore. There are other parties who are not known as being in the detective agencies who have contracted to supply men in small numbers as watchmen at different points. That is men who have been officers. There is an agency called Field's who have supplied men to some roads there in the Northwest and to mining companies in the Northwest.

The CHAIRMAN. Have you furnished any men in the case of the troubles in Idaho which are now going on there?

The WITNESS. No, sir.

By Mr. BYNUM:

Q. Is your organization in the form of a corporation or a mere company?—A. It is a copartnership.

Q. You have stated fully, I presume, the object of that copartnership?—A. It is for the carrying on of the general detective business and having a watch force.

Q. What was the object of your furnishing men, for what purpose have you furnished men to railroad corporations transporting interstate commerce and carrying the mails; in other words, I want to know what was the object for which these men were furnished?—A. In strike work, strike troubles.

Q. Well, at any time, what was the purpose for which they were employed?—A. Well, of course we do other work for railroad companies outside of strike work; we do detective work.

Q. But in strike work, say?—A. Well, we have furnished them for the purpose of protecting the property and employés, for the moving of trains, and seeing that trains were kept moving; for clearing yards of strikers and switch yards and protecting life and property generally, and passengers.

Q. The purpose was for the movement of trains upon schedule time and to prevent interference with them?—A. Always so.

By the CHAIRMAN:

Q. Have you ever supplied men for the inteference with the running of trains or the transportation of interstate trade or commerce?—A. Never. Our whole work in connection with strikes on railroads has been to raise blockades and move trains, never to stop them.

Q. To allow trains to run on their regular time?—A. Yes, sir; where trains have been obstructed by strikers and discontented employés, or for any other causes which might arise during the strike, our duties have been to get the trains started and kept moving, all freight, passenger, and mail trains, as rapidly as we can.

Q. You do that for a consideration; the companies pay you, I suppose?—A. Yes, sir.

By Mr. BRODERICK:

Q. Where is your principal office?—A. Our principal office? We call Chicago our principal office, as that is where we originated from, but the business now is such we call New York and Chicago our principal offices.

Q. You stated, I believe, that it was a partnership; have you never had a charter from any State?—A. Never.

Q. Does the law of Illinois require a partnership to be in writing and recorded?—A. I think not.

Q. I refer to the articles of copartnership?—A. I think not.

Q. Do you know whether the articles of copartnership are in writing or not?—A. Yes, sir.

Q. Have you a copy, and could you furnish the committee with a copy?—A. I have a copy.

Q. Have you one with you?—A. No, sir; I have not seen the articles of copartnership for many years.

Q. Can you state, in substance, the object of the copartnership more definitely than you have?—A. Only that the copartnership is for the carrying on of the general detective business and the private watch force.

Q. When you first inaugurated your enterprise, the only object was to establish and maintain a detective agency?—A. And a private watch force. I think the agency was started in 1850 by my father, and in 1857 he established a private watch force; that is what we call the merchant's force, to watch stores, banks, and private residences.

By the CHAIRMAN:

Q. Allen Pinkerton was the father of you and William A. Pinkerton?—A. Yes, sir.

Q. You and he are brothers?—A. Yes, sir.

By Mr. BRODERICK:

Q. The original purpose was to establish and maintain a detective agency?—A. Yes, sir; that was the original idea at the time it was started.

Q. But the scope of your organization has been enlarged?—A. Yes, sir.

Q. Are you required to report, or do you report to any authority in the States where you operate?—A. When we are sworn in, if at any time we are sworn in, we report; if not, no, sir.

Q. Have you ever been subject to the order of the governor in any State in which you have operated?—A. Occasionally. If we serve the governor's warrant we are supposed to report on it and we do report on it; that is, in criminal cases.

Q. Have you ever been authorized by the governor of a State to do anything other than serving of a warrant?—A. Yes, sir.

Q. What other service have you been authorized to do?—A. Our men have been sworn in as coal and iron policemen under the State law.

Q. In what State?—A. In the State of Pennsylvania. I think we organized the first coal and iron police in the State of Pennsylvania at the time of the Molly McGuire troubles.

Q. The governor there exercises some control and authority over the police?—A. Over the coal and iron police; that is, their commission comes from the governor.

The CHAIRMAN. There is a statute there which authorizes the governor to appoint men railroad police and coal and iron police?

Mr. BRODERICK. I have understood there was.

The WITNESS. When I spoke of his swearing us in I referred to our men, our employés.

Q. From what State were those men brought to serve as coal and iron police?—A. When the coal and iron police were first organized the men came from Chicago and part of them from Philadelphia. At that time it was not probably known that they were our men. I do not know whether the governor understood they were our men or not.

Q. Has your association ever been recognized as an association by the governor of any State?—A. Only to the extent we have been working for the governors of different States, a great deal of it.

Q. What sort of work?—A. Detective work.

Q. Nothing more than detective work?—A. Detective work.

By Mr. BOATNER:

Q. Is it true you were employed to police this city, or to assist in policing this city, at the last inauguration?—A. To this extent—that I selected a number of men who were brought in from the outside, from the different cities, for the purpose, during the inauguration, of picking out thieves, pickpockets, and confidence men, but only in the detective line; in no other way.

Q. At whose suggestion?—A. I think it was the board of police.

Q. The strikers, I believe, or Mr. Weihe, who is a representative of the Amalgamated Association, claimed that the methods of the strikers are purely peaceable; that they only persuade people not to accept the positions which they vacate, or from which they have been locked out, and that they did not encourage any sort of violence or countenance it. Now, I understand you to say your men are never authorized to use arms or force until they are attacked, and I want you to explain to us how you and your men and the strikers get together under those conditions?—A. Well, I never knew a strike in my life, and I have seen and had to do with a great many of them, where these labor organizations have not taken hold of nonunion men who wanted to go to work and caught them and beaten them. I have seen men's faces beaten into a jelly; I have seen men knocked off freight trains and shot off the top of freight trains; I have known of strikers, members of this very Knights of Labor, putting obstructions on the tracks to throw off trains moving on the railroad at night time, on a part of the road where they run the fastest down an embankment and where there were nothing but sleeping cars on the train; I know of members of this same Knights of Labor who have been convicted and sent to State prisons for that very offense. I have seen men who wanted to work treated worse than savages by those very representatives of these secret labor organizations and there has never been a case, and they can not cite a case, where they have not been the means of bringing on trouble, and I notify them to do it if they can. I have known of them putting, in the strike at Chicago—the iron strike—where stoves were molded, high explosives in the molds so that when the hot iron was put in the molds it would explode. On the Chicago, Burlington & Quincy strike members of this very organization were arrested and convicted for putting dynamite under cars. There were two trains wrecked on the Central road, one a fast express on the way from Chicago, and the men who committed these acts were convicted and they were members of the Knights of Labor, and they confessed they were furnished money by the Knights of Labor.

Q. There is one other question I wanted to ask you. Knowing the hostility of the Knights of Labor people and organized labor generally to your force, and knowing that in all probability sending your men to Homestead would result in a collision, why did you send them there without the authority of the officers of Allegheny County, and without stipulating that they should be qualified as officers before they approached the Homestead works?—A. I stipulated that as far as possible. I had no reason to know that our men would go and be assaulted; we supposed our men would be landed on that property without assault.

Q. You only supposed that because you would slip right in there without the strikers knowing it?—A. We expected to get them in there without being noticed.

Q. You knew you could not get them in over any of the railroads or that they could be brought there by daylight, and therefore you tried to get them in there at night?—A. Yes, sir.

Q. That shows you were fully aware that an effort to send them there would result in a collision. Now, why did not you see the sheriff or some other legal officer of that county, and have your men, if they were going to send them there, qualified as officers of the State of Pennsylvania?—A. That is what we did do.

Q. Did you see the sheriff?—A. No, sir, the Carnegie people did.

Q. You took the word of the Carnegie people for it?—A. Yes, sir; the sheriff, I believe, testified to it.

Q. But there is a difference in the testimony. Did you see anyone there or seek the sheriff or any other officer of the county of Alleghany to have him authorize these men to be sent there?—A. No, sir.

Q. Have you got any such paper in your possession?—A. No, sir; from the sheriff, no, sir.

Q. Or any other officer?—A. No, sir.

Q. Then you merely accepted the verbal statement of the Carnegie firm?—A. Of their representative.

Q. And you acted entirely upon their representation?—A. As they represented it to me.

By the CHAIRMAN:

Q. How many detectives did you furnish here in Washington at the last inauguration? I understood you to say you furnished some.—A. I think we furnished anywhere from sixteen to twenty. They were detectives selected from different parts of the country, as I say, for the purpose of keeping away thieves.

Q. With whom did you contract to furnish those men?—A. There was no contract as you might call it—that is, a signed contract. It was simply a notice sent.

Q. Somebody paid for it?—A. Yes, sir; it was paid for by the order of the Board of Police Commissioners.

Q. And application was made by the chief of police?—A. I could not say whether application first came through the chief or secretary, but they have the letters which would show, I suppose. It was somebody in authority there, and I think the board authorized them to be employed.

Q. They were here for duty only as detectives?—A. Yes, sir; to pick out professional thieves who gather where great crowds gather at any time, and they arrested, I think, about forty.

By Mr. BOATNER:

Q. Did you ever detail any of your men for services as Knights of Labor?—A. Well, not services as Knights of Labor. I suppose we have got men who have been members of the Knights of Labor.

Q. My question was whether you ever detailed them to become Knights of Labor and to serve in that direction?—A. Well I—

Q. You may be like Mr. Frick, and it may be a secret which you do not care to give away?—A. If I can I should prefer not to answer that question.

H. Mis. 335——14

The CHAIRMAN. That would go into one of the private methods of transacting your business.

The WITNESS. Yes, sir—that is, the detective part of it.

By Mr. BYNUM:

Q. Those detectives you furnished here at the inauguration I understood you to say were simply furnished to detect thieves, etc. That is the custom in all the great cities in the country where large crowds gather together?—A. Yes, sir; where unusual crowds gather together.

Q. Where the municipal authorities in those localities call on the police officers from different cities who are acquainted with professional thieves?—A. They make what they think is the best selection, and that is the only work that we have done in the District of Columbia that I know of.

Q. You say you know of only three persons having been killed by your men?—A. Yes, sir.

Q. Do you mean the only persons killed where your employés were engaged?—A. Yes, sir.

Q. How many men were killed at the coke strike?—A. None, I think.

Q. How many people were killed at the Connelsville strike?—A. I do not remember of anybody being killed there, that is, killed at the time. Of course men might have been killed by railroad trains or something of that kind, but I do not remember.

Q. Do you know of anyone having been killed in a collision between your men and strikers?—A. No, sir; not there. Our watch service and our detective service are entirely separate; the detective business is one thing and the watch is another, and they are the same as two different institutions.

Q. I understand that. The watch service finally grew and developed with the necessity for sending watchmen to protect property?—A. Yes, sir; these men who go out on strike work—the papers call them detectives, but they are none of them detectives. They are simply watchmen, as none of the detectives go on that kind of work.

By Mr. BRODERICK:

Q. You spoke of furnishing the last inauguration with some men. Has that been the custom heretofore, or has this been the only case?—A. I think on one or two previous occasions we have furnished men, but not to the extent we furnished them at this time, on this last occasion; and whether it was because their services were satisfactory on the previous occasion I can not say, but on this last occasion it was given to me to select the men who were to be brought from the outside.

Q. Do you remember on what other occasion you furnished them, or what other inauguration?—A. Well, I suppose it was the one before that.

Q. The one before the last?—A. It was either that or when there was some large crowd of people here, but that was only two or three men and on the last occasion we furnished, I think, anywhere from 16 to 20.

Q. You furnish men to State fairs and gatherings of that nature?—A. Yes, sir; where we are applied to.

By the CHAIRMAN:

Q. You say you do not employ any women?—A. We do as typewriters and clerks.

Q. Not as detectives, nor in the guard business.—A. No, sir.

Mr. BOATNER. I suppose if women possessed the necessary qualifications you would not debar them on account of their sex?

The WITNESS. We do not employ them. Those who want to go into detective business are sort of unreliable and you can not depend on them, you can not bet on them.

By the CHAIRMAN:

Q. Here is a statement which you and your partner furnished to this committee. I see by the character of it that you could not testify to all of it because a good deal of it is argumentative. Do you swear that the statement of facts which it contains are true?—A. Yes, sir.

Q. And you desire it to go along with your testimony as a statement of your case?—A. Yes, sir.

By Mr. BOATNER:

Q. There is one single question I want to ask, with the chairman's permission. Do you conduct your business in any State where the laws of the State prohibit it, as far as you know?—A. I do not exactly understand the question. I do not know of any State which prohibits our carrying on a detective business.

Q. That is what I wanted to get at; but what I mean is, in the way of furnishing bodies of men for the protection of property in case of strikes or lockouts such as you have named, have you been stopped from that business by the officers of any State?—A. No, sir.

Q. As being contrary to the laws of the State?—A. No, sir.

Mr. BYNUM. The only laws which have been passed are those which prohibit police powers being conferred upon others than residents of the State.

The WITNESS. That is it; residents of a county.

Mr. BYNUM. That is a law of Indiana, I believe.

Mr. BOATNER. Have such laws been passed in some counties?

Mr. BYNUM. Indiana has a law which prohibits them from conferring police powers on any others than residents of a county, and he must be a resident for a stated length of time.

By the CHAIRMAN:

Q. What is your method of recruiting men for this service as guards or watchmen?—A. Well, take for instance, the Carnegie strike. There are all the time constantly applying to us parties who want employment as watchmen or detectives. Each one who applies is furnished an application, a printed application, and he writes out his application. These application blanks ask certain questions, which are to be answered. He writes out his application, and on the margin of the application the superintendent or assistant superintendent, who has examined the man, must state what his impressions are in regard to the man as he sees him and talks to him. If at any time we propose to employ that man we then go into his references, which he gives in his application. For instance, in the Carnegie strike, if we wanted additional men than what we had ourselves we used those applications. We went back to those applications. We sent for the men to explain what we wanted them for. If they wanted the employment they took it. If they did not want it they did not take it. It has been stated I advertised in New York; I did not do that.

Q. How many of the 310 or 312 men there were your regular employés, or what portion were recruited who had not served you before?—A. I think two-thirds fully were men who were in our employ and had been in our employ and whom we knew. The others were men who had been got on these applications to us and whose references we looked into.

Q. One of the witnesses who testified before us, Mr. Kennedy, a boat-man, who was on the barge, testified that not more than 40 or 50 of your men were on the deck of the barge and fired at the time when the strikers on the shore or the mob were firing; that it was a sudden fusil-lade and both parties ran; the strikers on shore fled in every direction and your men ran back into the barges and hid, many of them stating when he suggested to them just afterwards that they might go out and take possession of the property that they did not come there to fight; that they only came there to stand guard; and he said, furthermore, that he never saw such cowardice in his life. What do you say in re-gard to that?—A. I have heard the stories in regard to the matter. I have also questioned the officers who had charge. They stated to me they could have taken possession of the yard right at the start, almost any time before 10 o'clock, with 50 or 75 men, but they would have had to kill a number of people, and among them women and children, and they concluded not to do anything of the kind. They say the force down there was firing over their heads and it——

Q. Over whose heads?—A. Over the strikers' heads—and it goes to show that must have been so or there would have been more killed than there were.

Q. What kind of arms did your men have?—A. Winchester rifles.

Q. They are powerful weapons.—A. I understand at the start there were not over 20 men who were given arms, and afterwards when the thing got to be pretty hot there were about 40 men armed; but when it started there were not over fifteen or twenty armed.

Q. The testimony was they were getting arms out after they had seen this hostile demonstration and some shots had been fired at the boat coming up the river, and that they were unboxing their arms when the boat landed?—A. That is the way I understand it.

By Mr. BRODERICK:

Q. Are there similar agencies to yours in this country?—A. There are large numbers of detective agencies. There is hardly a city of any size in the country that has not got them.

Q. Do you know whether any private agencies are chartered by the State?—A. Some are, I think. I am not sure of that. I think that is so.

Q. Are they generally organized——
The WITNESS (interrupting). That is what we call a license.

Q. Are they generally organized and incorporated like yours?—A. We are not incorporated, sir; we are just a copartnership.

Q. That is the rule, is it, simply to form a partnership?—A. Some are incorporated and some have licenses to operate.

By the CHAIRMAN:

Q. Yours is simply a private partnership between you and your brother?—A. Yes, sir.

Q. In the case of the New York Central Railroad strike did you have any correspondence with any officers of that company prior to the em-ployment of your men?—A. Oh, no, I think it was all done by personal interviews.

Q. With what officers or employés of the company or agents?—A. Personally I was up on the line of the road attending court in a burglary case when the strike came on the Central Railroad, and it was not ex-pected at all; it was very sudden. It came on within two or three hours when the order making the strike was given and the trains were all tied up and as soon as I could get to Albany I went there to get directions from New York by telegraph and I staid at Albany during the whole strike.

Q. From whom did the telegram come?—A. Mr. Bangs, who was our superintendent in New York; he was in consultation with the officials of the railroad.

Q. Who were the officials of the railroad who negotiated for the employment of your men?—A. I think that Mr. H. Walter Webb, the vice-president, was probably the one who did it, but I did not see him until after the strike was over, or rather, I saw him when he came up the road on one or two occasions, but I staid in Albany and was not in New York.   •

Q. Have you the letters and correspondence touching the matter of your employment, or any directions, printed or written, or contracts in in writing which you can furnish?—A. From the officers of the company?

Q. Yes; between you and them.—A. No, sir; there was nothing of the kind.

Q. The negotiations you say were not carried on by written correspondence?—A. No, sir; it is simply an understanding.

Q. Did your employés come into collision with those strikers of the railroad, and was there any killing done on either side?—A. We had two men killed up there, but I will say there were no men killed on the strikers' side. These men were not killed either by the strikers. They were killed by the railroad trains while they were patrolling along the tracks at night time.

Q. You testify that your men did not kill anybody there?—A. Not a one.

Q. Never have killed but three except in the matter of train robberies?—A. Outside of the Homestead strike.

Q. I mean up to the Homestead strike; is that your testimony?—A. Yes, sir; that is my recollection; three is the limit in twenty years.

Q. You say that during the years you have been in the business that some of your men have been indicted and tried for shooting or for assaults, but you have never had one convicted by a superior court or on final trial?—A. Before a jury; no, sir.

Q. Never had one convicted?—A. No, sir; not one.

Q. They have always been acquitted?—A. Yes, sir; they have always been acquitted.

TESTIMONY OF WILLIAM A. PINKERTON.

WILLIAM A. PINKERTON, sworn and examined.

By the CHAIRMAN:

Q. Please give your place of residence?—A. 196 Ashland avenue, Chicago.

Q. You have heard the testimony of Mr. Robert A. Pinkerton?—A. I have.

Q. You are a brother of his?—A. Yes, sir.

Q. And business partner?—A. Yes, sir.

Q. What do you have to say as to the statement he has made as to the business that you are engaged in and the manner in which it is carried on?—A. I should verify his statement, sir, in every particular. One thing he appeared to neglect, and that is the question of riding men on trains which probably——

Q. Will you state about that?—A. Well, off and on for the last twenty-five years all over the United States, particularly in the west and southwest, we have furnished men to guard against the attacks of train robbers. We have furnished men to act as guards to express messengers and take care of their money.

Q. How many railroad strikes and strikes of other corporations do you remember that you have furnished a guard or detective force, and when and where was it and the extent, to the best of your recollection?—A. Well, in the Burlington, Lake Shore and Michigan Southern—they were the two which came under my personal observation—and the Union Pacific.

Q. In what years?—A. Well, the Union Pacific matter was nearly eight years ago, the Burlington was about four years ago, and the Lake Shore about five years ago. It was a switchmen's strike on the Lake Shore Railroad.

Q. Did you furnish armed men to those corporations, and if so, about how many to each?—A. Well, I do not recollect now, but it might have been between 200 and 300 in the employ of the Burlington. In the Lake Shore and Michigan Southern there were probably anywhere from 75 to 90 men, but they only went to work after the road had been blocked up for five days and not a wheel turned on the road.

Q. What did they go there to do?—A. To open up the yards, clear men out of the yards who did not belong there, allowing engineers and firemen to go on the trains unmolested to pull the trains out. For five days there had not been a train taken away from there.

Q. In doing that did you shoot anybody or were they shot by anybody?—A. They did not shoot anybody.

Q. Did they have any personal collision or conflict or blood letting?—A. Well, up in the town of Lake there were three men caught turning a switch, which was for the purpose of wrecking a train which was due, and the men were caught and resisted, and they fought when they attempted to make them prisoners, and they were handled with a night stick. The town of Lake was then on the outskirts of Chicago and is now a part of Chicago.

Q. Do you know of any instance where your men in the employ of corporations, companies, or private individuals have taken life or killed anybody?—A. Well, the three instances which my brother mentioned is all I recollect. We canvassed the matter over together.

Q. Do you know the names of those men and where those killings occurred?—A. I know the name of one of them, and the other occurred down in New York, and we are not sure in regard to the third one, even, and that took place down in Ohio in the Hocking Valley coal strike nine years ago.

Q. Were your men tried or indicted for the killing of either one of those three men?—A. The men in Jersey were indicted and tried and acquitted. The men in Chicago were arrested, and after examination before a magistrate the case went to the grand jury, and the grand jury returned no bill.

Q. How about the Ohio case?—A. There was never any one punished for that.

Q. No trial had there?—A. My recollection of that is, it was a charge of shooting and not of killing, but I will not be positive. I think there were only two, the case in New Jersey and the case of the Union stock yards in Chicago.

Q. What was your practice in regard to sending out men with guards? Do you send them armed or box up their arms and send them along·

with the men, or do you depend upon their employers to furnish arms?—
A. Well, the way we got the arms in the first place was the employers
bought the arms.

Q. In what case do you refer to?—A. Well, this is one; two or three
different cases, where they bought arms in small quantities and when it
was over the arms were thrown on their hands and they said, "What
will we do with them;" so we bought them up in that way and latterly
we have furnished the arms.

Q. What amount of arms and the character of them belong to your
company?—A. Well, we had about 250 or 260 rifles.

Q. Enfield?—A. No, sir, Winchester; and I think between 400 and
500 revolvers of all sizes and all kinds.

Q. You divided your arsenal and kept some at one place and some
at another?—A. They are all kept at Chicago.

Q. That is headquarters and the arsenal or arms are kept there?—A.
Well, as you like; the arms were there.

Q. Do you keep on hand a good supply of ammunition?—A. No; it
is not necessary; you can buy that at short notice.

By Mr. BRODERICK:

Q. You stated you owned some arms which were kept at Chicago;
are your men drilled?—A. No, sir; not with arms; not at all, and never
have been drilled. All that is newspaper talk in which there is no
truth, and as a matter of fact they have never been drilled.

Mr. ROBERT A. PINKERTON. Where there has been a strike and they
go armed they went through a certain drill.

The WITNESS. But at the headquarters of the organization there has
never been anything of the kind.

Q. There has never been any drilling of arms?—A. No, sir; nothing
of the kind in the world.

Q. Any drilling without arms?—A. The patrol force in Chicago
amounts to upwards of 100 watchmen now; they are drilled in the
method of marching, etc.

Q. Some of your men have been with you a good many years?—A.
Yes, sir; a good many of them.

Q. About what proportion of your force have been with you two
years or more?—A. Well, sir, I should judge four-fifths of the men
have been with us for five years or more, and from that up to thirty
years.

Q. How are they paid?—A. Paid a salary, sir.

Q. Monthly?—A. Weekly.

By Mr. BYNUM:

Q. There is one question I will ask, to see if I understand the testimony of you and your brother. In cases where you furnish men as
watchmen your instructions have been that they shall only use force
to resist force?—A. That is right.

Q. And only so much as to protect themselves?—A. Yes, sir. I have
always told them in going away, and when I have been present myself,
that because a man blackguards and throws a stone and women use
a stick or stone that is not occasion to go back at them, but to try to
get along without any trouble, and never more so than in this last case.

By the CHAIRMAN:

Q. Part of the men who went to Homestead were sent by you?—A.
Yes, sir.

Q. What number?—A. Well, there were over 100.

Q. You shipped the arms from Chicago down there, did you?—A. Yes, sir.

Q. Was that a part of the contract?—A. I do not know anything about the contract personally, sir; that was not made with me; but I shipped them under instructions from New York; boxed them up and sent them to the Union Supply Company. I did not know they were even on the boat, and there was no intention to put them on the boat, and I was surprised at their being on the boat, and the only reason that that was done was because they could not get anything on the company's property.

Q. What is the general character of the men you employ and use as watchmen?—A. Good.

Q. Are the men of good character?—A. Yes, sir; they can not get there unless they are, neither. They must be sober, industrious, reliable men.

Q. You say you would not employ men of doubtful character or bad habits?—A. No, sir; we never have.

Q. How do you ascertain when you are employing your recruits as to their reliability?—A. The same way a bank president would ascertain the habits of a clerk in regard to reliability, by making him give references and looking up the references and examining to see if he is all right.

Q. Does that habit prevail—is this the practice in all your offices?—A. Yes, sir.

Q. That has been your practice heretofore?—A. Yes, sir.

Q. Are you or your brother regarded as the head of the firm?—A. Neither one, it is a copartnership.

Q. All of these other offices have to be operated under your direction and head?—A. Under our head. He takes the Eastern one, and I take the West.

Have you ever furnished any men to prevent railroad trains from running, and obstructing them?—A. Never in the world.

Q. Or to prevent any particular class of men from working in a factory or furnaces or mines?—A. Never, sir.

Q. Then for what purpose do you hire and furnish men to these various corporations?—A. To protect property and life.

Q. And to enable them to pursue——A. (Interrupting). To enable them to conduct their business without interference; that is, unauthorized interference.

Q. Did you ever see that book before (handing book)?—A. Yes.

Q. What book is that?—A. This is an ordinary time book.

Q. Used by whom and for what purpose?—A. By us.

Q. Used by your firm of Pinkertons?—A. Yes, sir.

Q. To keep the time for the men in your employ?—A. Yes, sir.

Q. Is that a list of the names of the men who went to Homestead?—A. Some are in there which I recognize. I think that is an old list, sir, of men that have been used at fair grounds or race tracks, although there is quite a number of men there I know who are among the number that went to Homestead.

Q. That book then was a book with which the accounts of men in your employ were kept?—A. Yes, sir; the same as an ordinary time book would be kept as to how many days the men worked.

Q. The entries in that book seem to be the time of men in 1890?—A. It is an old book, probably taken along for the purpose of filling up, that is all. There is nothing relating to anything very recent in there,

Q. That book was said to have been captured when the men surrendered at the barges?—A. I do not doubt it, sir.

Q. Do you recognize any of those names (handing sheet)?—A. Yes, sir; I know the handwriting.

Q. Whose handwriting is it?—A. It is in the handwriting of one of the men who was shot there; his name is Hoffman. I suppose he appeared before the committee as he was supposed to appear. These things here (exhibiting blank) are forms of pay orders. If a man is away from home and he wants to send the money to his family he fills up a duplicate and sends it to the office to be paid to whom he pleases, and the office turns it over to whoever he wants it turned over to.

By Mr. BRODERICK:

Q. Have you any means of giving the names of those who were at Homestead, all of them?—A. Yes, sir.

Q. Can you furnish the list?—A. I guess I could furnish the list from Chicago.

Q. You have no means of doing that now?—A. No, sir; I could not give it here; no, sir.

Mr. ROBERT A. PINKERTON. There is one thing I want to explain to the committee, and that was in regard to the answer that has been given that we have employed no one whose character was not all right. That had reference to strike work, and that answer is correct. There have been occasions in bank robberies where we have bought information from criminals, and where we have used criminals where we have been obliged to do it and where the men have had bad characters.

Mr. BYNUM. That is in the detection of crime and not as peace officers?

Mr. ROBERT A. PINKERTON. Not as peace officers; no, sir.

By the CHAIRMAN:

Q. (To Mr. Robert A. Pinkerton.) Do you testify that you send out as guards or watchmen men of good character?—A. As far as we are able to investigate they are, and I do not believe you can find any instance where that is not the case. They have been called thieves, thugs, and ex-convicts, but they can not cite a single case of that.

Q. I do not know of any complaint of your work within the province of detective work; it is only where you have furnished these guards or watchmen.—A. I also desire to state, as far as we are personally concerned, that we have no feeling against labor organizations and never had, and all we have ever done in connection with labor work or with these strikers is simply to protect life and property. We have no quarrel with labor organizations. I believe that labor organization is a good thing, and I believe if a man wants to strike he has a right to strike, but if a man wants to work he has a right to work, and a labor organization has no right to interfere with him; but we have no quarrel with any labor organization that I know of and we have no feeling against them.

Q. And you carry on the business which you have described, as a matter of course, for the money that is in it for you?—A. Yes, sir; as a matter of business.

By Mr. BRODERICK:

Q. About what proportion of your men which you have employed are citizens of the United States?

The WITNESS. All of them. I take it all of them are; I do not know of any who are not.

By Mr. BOATNER:

Q. Do you inquire about a man's citizenship when he applies to you for work?—A. Yes, sir.

Mr. WILLIAM A. PINKERTON. You are referring to watchmen?

Q. Yes, sir. Where you are sending out men like those in this Homestead case.

Mr. ROBERT A. PINKERTON. They have all got to be citizens as far as we know.

Q. Do these strikes furnish you with a considerable part of your business?—A. No, sir; it is an outside branch of the business entirely.

The CHAIRMAN. The detective business pays better than that?

Mr. ROBERT A. PINKERTON. We have never looked for any strike work, but it is something which has grown up on our shoulders.

Mr. BOATNER. I suppose you take that sort of employment from a sense of duty?

The WITNESS. Yes, sir.

The CHAIRMAN. Well, I believe we are through with the examination of these gentlemen.

Mr. ROBERT A. PINKERTON. Then we are free to go home if we want to do so?

The CHAIRMAN. Certainly; and we are very much obliged to you for your prompt attendance.

Mr. ROBERT A. PINKERTON. I want to thank the committee for their giving us this hearing, and this is the first chance we have ever had to have one, and I am very glad to have had an opportunity of appearing before this committee.

The CHAIRMAN. I bear testimony to the fact when I wrote to you gentlemen about this committee being raised, I received letters from each of you manifesting your perfect willingness to come before the committee and testify and make disclosures about your business.

Mr. WILLIAM A. PINKERTON. I am only sorry, as I was expecting the committee to come to Chicago or New York, and make a personal investigation of the books and papers of our establishment.

Thereupon the committee adjourned, subject to the call of the chairman.

WASHINGTON, D. C., *Friday, July 29,* 1892.

The subcommittee of the Committee on the Judiciary, having in charge the investigation of certain labor troubles at Homestead, Pa., met in the room of that committee at 2 p. m., Hon. William C. Oates in the chair.

Present, Messrs. Oates, Boatner, Bynum, Broderick, and Ray.

The CHAIRMAN. The stenographer will note that Mr. Ray is substituted as a member of the subcommittee in place of Hon. E. B. Taylor, who is absent.

Mr. BOATNER. Mr. Chairman, it seems to me that it would be saving the time of both members of the committee and Mr. Powderly if we would permit him to furnish a statement. The object of this investigation is to ascertain all the facts which we can, relative to the employment of the so-called Pinkerton force by railroads, corporations and other persons during strikes. We are not concerned with their employment as private watchmen for residences and banks, or in their employment for the detection of ordinary crimes. It is only so far as that force is used in bodies in strikes, and in the prevention of strikes that we are concerned. And it has occurred to me that Mr. Powderly might prepare a statement of what he knows about the matter, giving the instances and the manner in which they have been employed, what they have done which may be considered unlawful and illegal, giving us the names of witnesses from whom he has obtained the information in cases where he does not speak from his own personal knowledge, or furnish reports in cases where he relies upon reports, after receiving which, we may investigate further in reference to the facts which he may furnish. It appears to me that that would facilitate the furnishing of the information, and save his time as well as ours. I make a motion that he be asked to prepare and furnish such a statement.

The CHAIRMAN. I think it would be well to swear Mr. Powderly, and examine him to a limited extent, which will develop what his statement will be.

Mr. BOATNER. I imagine that Mr. Powderly has very little personal knowledge in these matters.

The CHAIRMAN. We will soon learn that.

Mr. BOATNER. His statement might be such as he has learned from the public prints.

The CHAIRMAN. I think that would properly come a little later on. (To Mr. Ray.) What do you say?

Mr. RAY. I think Mr. Powderly should be examined long enough to develop whether or not he has any personal information. If he has, he should be allowed to give it to us, and be fully examined; but if he has none, and can give us the names of witnesses, that would put us on the track of evidence that would throw light on this subject, he should be allowed to state all he knows in reference to it. If he has nothing to give us, except hearsay, I do not know what business he has before us.

Mr. BYNUM. I think we would get along faster if we would hear Mr. Powderly's statement. He can make his statement just as full here as elsewhere.

TESTIMONY OF T. V. POWDERLY.

T. V. POWDERLY, sworn and examined.

By the CHAIRMAN:

Q. Please give us your name and address.—A. T. V. Powderly, Scranton, Pa.

Q. Do you hold any official position with regard to labor organizations? If so, state what it is.—A. I do; General Master Workman of the Knights of Labor.

Q. Of the United States?—A. Yes, sir—of everywhere.

Q. It extends all over the United States?—A. Yes, sir.

Q. (After reading the resolution authorizing the appointment of the committee.) Do you know of your own knowledge of the employment of persons said to belong to the Pinkerton detective force or guards, (or whatever it be called,) in any of these connections wherein violence has been done and general complaint made of their employment?—A. Am I to understand that I must see things in order to be able to testify to them?

Q. Yes, or have knowledge of them.

Mr. BOATNER. I do not know that I so understand it. I understand this investigation we are pursuing is for the purpose of obtaining information.

The CHAIRMAN. I want to ask the witness if he knows anything of his own knowledge.

Mr. BOATNER. I think Mr. Powderly may state anything he knows from information.

The CHAIRMAN. Of his own knowledge.

Mr. BOATNER. I take it for granted——

The CHAIRMAN. Let him answer.

Mr. BOATNER. If he has not that knowledge he can give us information as to where he gets it.

The CHAIRMAN. I think you are raising that question in advance.

Mr. BOATNER. He raised it himself.

The CHAIRMAN. I want to know if he knows of his own knowledge.

The WITNESS. Being under oath I want to know my position.

Mr. BYNUM. He is asking what you know, and if you know any facts.

The WITNESS. I am somewhat at a disadvantage here, because when your telegram went to Scranton last evening I was not there, and I have had no opportunity of examining the records since I received the telegram, or I would have brought them with me, or at least have fortified myself with the facts.

I have had experiences with the Pinkerton people for over six years, and for that reason I can speak somewhat knowingly. I saw the published reports of the statements submitted by the Pinkerton brothers, which is contained in your document. On seeing that in the papers last Saturday, I hastily prepared a statement contradictory of the allegations made by the Pinkertons, and I mailed it to the chairman of the Judiciary Committee, not knowing his name, as I do not keep track of these matters. I sent it on to Washington, with a copy of a secret circular sent out by Pinkerton's Agency.

Q. Your answer is that you have some personal knowledge, and you have other knowledge that has come to you from various sources which you believe to be true?—A. Yes, sir.

Q. You have stated that you saw some account of a statement made by the Pinkertons. We have here the statement received by the committee, and in order that you may not be misled I will state that the statement of the Pinkertons was not received as evidence, but only as a presentation of their case.—A. Their testimony, unfortunately, never went to the country, while this statement was published broadcast. In that statement they have taken to deliberate slandering and lying. I want to state that distinctly.

Q. If the testimony was not sent out it was because the reporters did not do it.—A. I am not blaming reporters. I simply say the Associated Press carried it, and it was received as the testimony of the Pinkertons.

Q. It was not received by the committee as testimony, and was so announced at the time—that it was a mere presentation of their case, more by way of argument than anything else. They were asked before they concluded their testimony if they swore to those facts set forth as true, and they said, yes, they did.—A. They swore to the facts as set forth in the statement.

Mr. BYNUM. It is nothing more than fair that Mr. Powderly should be allowed to make a statement in answer to theirs, and that it should be put in the record.

The WITNESS. I have a statement, and shall I leave it with the committee, or read it?

The CHAIRMAN. You may read it.

The statement was read as follows:

MR. POWDERLY'S ANALYSIS OF THE PINKERTON TESTIMONY—AN END MUST BE PUT
TO PINKERTONISM BEFORE IT INVOLVES US IN CIVIL WAR—CAPITAL HAS BEEN
THE LEADER AND TEACHER IN DISREGARDING AND DEFYING THE LAW—CON-
GRESS MUST ACT AT ONCE.

SCRANTON, PA., *July 23, 1892.*

To the Judiciary Committee of the House of Representatives:

In view of the fact that the Messrs. Pinkerton were permitted to submit a
statement concerning the affairs of the Pinkerton detective agency, I feel that in
equity I should be accorded a like privilege. The relations existing between
capital and labor will not become more friendly by the constant interference of a
force that always takes sides with the former, no matter what the justice of the claims
of the latter may be. If the Pinkerton detective agency was influenced by the philanthropic motives which its managers would have us attribute to it, we would
find its employés taking sides with laboring men occasionally. Surely, workingmen
and workingmen's organizations are right once in a while, and, if the cause of right
alone attracted the attention and won the service of the employés of the Pinkerton
agency, those who belong to organized labor would have had tenders of disinterested
service ere this.

It is not philanthropy, it is not a sense of duty, nor is it patriotism that actuates
the institution under discussion. To make the record read accurately it must be
written that the Pinkerton detective agency operates for gain, and that cause or
object which can command the most money will find the employés of the Pinkerton
agency arrayed in its service and in opposition to the interests which are not influ-
ential or wealthy. If labor organizations could command the wealth that employers
of labor do at this day, we could hire the services of "watchmen" from the Pinkerton agency by offering a higher reward for such service.

I have no hesitation in asserting that many of the statements made in the written
document submitted by Messrs. Pinkerton are inaccurate; others are deliberately
false and can not be proved before any fair tribunal in the land. Let me quote one
section of the statement:

"The men employed by us in this strike work are selected with great care, and
only after a full investigation of their characters and antecedents. Not a single instance can be cited where we have knowingly employed unreliable or untrustworthy
men, or where any of our watchmen have been convicted of a crime. Moreover, we
have seldom permitted our watchmen to carry arms for the purpose of protecting
property and life, unless they were authorized by proper legal authorities or sworn
in as deputy sheriffs. Our men have never wantonly or recklessly fired a single shot
in any of these strikes, and have only used their arms as the last extremity in order
to protect life."

All who are familiar with the character of work which has been done by the alleged
"watchmen" during the past few years will bear testimony to the fact that but little, if any, care is exercised in the selection of those who are employed as "watchmen" by the agents of the Pinkertons. In the New York Central strike, to which
they refer, I would call your attention to "a single instance" in which an unreliable
man was selected to act as a "watchman."

On the 16th of August, 1890, Adolph Polletschek, a native of Austria, aged 45, and
but four years a resident of the United States, made affidavit that he was employed
by the Pinkerton agency and sent to the Albany yards to do duty as a "watchman."
In that affidavit, which was sworn out in my presence and which I still hold, Mr.
Polletschek swears that he was armed, and told by the Pinkerton officer in charge,
that he was to interfere with the strikers in order to cause them to engage in riotous
action. It was impossible for either William or Robert Pinkerton to know anything
about the antecedents of Polletschek, as he had no relatives in this country, was unknown to them previous to that strike, and was engaged by their agent, who made
no inquiry as to who or what he was. This one illustration is at least sufficient to
cast a doubt on the accuracy of the statement submitted, but not sworn to, by the
Messrs. Pinkerton. The Messrs. Pinkerton can very conveniently assert that they
have never "knowingly employed unreliable or untrustworthy men,"for they know
little, if anything, about the men who are engaged by their agents, their assertion to
the contrary notwithstanding.

The assertion that their "men have never wantonly or recklessly fired a single
shot" is unqualifiedly false, and if the Judiciary Committee will now continue the
investigation at points where the Pinkertons operated and take the testimony of
workingmen, business men, and clergymen, who can not afford to go to Washington
to give their evidence, it will be provided with abundant proof that their statement
was not founded on fact. On Saturday, August 16, 1890, two Pinkerton "watch-

men" occupied positions on the top of a freight car which was moving through the
West Albany yards. As the car neared the Van Woert street crossing a small boy
threw a stone and struck one of the "watchmen." Instantly the fellow brought his
rifle to his shoulder and fired. The ball missed the boy, but struck a man named
John McCarthy, who was walking about inside of the fence which surrounded his
residence. McCarthy had nothing to do with the trouble, knew nothing about the
coming of the Pinkertons, and had no idea that the boy intended to throw the
stone. This will serve to illustrate that wanton and reckless firing by Pinkerton
"watchmen" does take place. The statement that none of their men have been
convicted of a crime is true, and about the only true statement they make.

When the Pinkertons fire upon the people they do so from behind the breastworks
of capital. Those upon whom they fire are too poor to indulge in litigation. The
law protects the rich without question, but the poor must pay for the justice they
obtain. As a matter of fact, it would be next to impossible to convict a Pinkerton
of any crime, for he operates against the poor. The man who would prosecute would
be poor, his employment would depend on his action, and very few men are self-
sacrificing enough to act as prosecutors when the blacklist confronts them. There is
a reason why none of the "watchmen have been convicted of a crime." The statement is artfully made—to be a criminal and be convicted of the crime are two different things.

It amounts to conviction in the minds of workingmen that where the Pinkertons
gain a foothold they incite to riot for the purpose of lengthening their term of service.
The workmen at Homestead gave assurances that they would protect property; it
was clearly to their interest to do so. On the contrary, it would be to the interest
of the "watchmen" to start fires, drive away imaginary intruders and perform other
services in order to prejudice the public mind against the strikers. This, if you will
pardon the expression, is the old game of the regulation Pinkerton "watchman."

During the continuance of the Denver and Rio Grande strike, some years ago, we
employed watchmen to watch the Pinkerton "watchmen," and discovered them in
the act of placing dynamite on the tracks. I believe you will have no trouble in
securing this evidence.

The statement of the Messrs. Pinkerton is not consistent. It says: "They did not
go into the State of Pennsylvania as an armed body or force, and we should not have
permitted or assented to this." That is exactly what they did permit. And further
on in the statement it is admitted that "the boxes containing the arms and ammun-
nition were shipped from Chicago, and were to be delivered at the Homestead yards."
Technically, these men did not go armed into Pennsylvania; the arms were boxed
up and were not distributed until at the scene of trouble. Why should they be
armed in Chicago and sent across two States in order to reach Pennsylvania? The
Governor of Pennsylvania may also assert that he did not send armed men to Homestead, or that the militia "did not go armed." The men rode in one car and the
arms were transported in another, but they were to be given into the hands of the
men at Homestead. This mere quibbling on the part of the Messrs. Pinkerton is simply intended to deceive.

If you will turn to the constitution of Pennsylvania you will notice that section 3
of Article XIV reads as follows:

"No person shall be appointed to any office within any county who shall not have
been a citizen and an inhabitant therein one year next before his appointment if the
county shall have been so long erected; but if it shall not have been so long erected,
then within the limits of the county or counties out of which it shall have been
taken."

The men transported by the Pinkertons from New York and Illinois were not citizens
of Pennsylvania; they could not become so in a night; they were not amenable to
the laws of Pennsylvania, except for offenses committed while in this State. They
were strangers, and as such could more easily escape detection than well-known
residents. They were in no way identified with the interests of the State or its people, and would not take the same interest in preserving the peace or the same precaution in protecting property as if they were residents and citizens. It was a wise
thought that preceded the adoption of that particular section of the constitution of
Pennsylvania, but it was violated in letter and spirit in assigning strangers (to the
Commonwealth) to duty at Homestead. To be elected to office a man must be known
to possess the necessary qualifications to fit him for the office, and in order to perform
the most insignificant of duties the official must be sworn. Whether elected or appointed, the official must be sworn; but in this case it does not appear that the Messrs.
Pinkerton took the precaution to have them sworn in, even though the performance
of that act would have been in direct violation of the fundamental law of the State.
The sending of these men into this State was illegal; it was invasion of our rights
as citizens of Pennsylvania. Under Section 4 of Article IV, Constitution of the United
States, each States is guaranteed freedom from invasion. It reads:

"The United States shall guarantee to every State in this Union a republican form of government, and shall protect each of them against invasion; and on application of the legislature, or of the executive (when the legislature can not be convened), against domestic violence."

Under these two sections of the Constitutions of Pennsylvania and the United States the legal pathway is pointed out in cases where domestic violence is threatened. Under these two sections the necessity for the presence of the Pinkerton "watchman" is disposed of, and he has no legal standing before the law. If he goes above the law, and that has been done in this case, then more than a mere investigation will, it seems to me, be necessary.

Speaking of secret labor organizations, this remarkable statement goes on to assert: "All capital so invested is practically at the mercy of secret labor organizations, whose tyranny and despotism exceed anything ever known in the history of the world, These societies intimidate whole communities by threats of murder, and are determined upon ruin and destruction of property if their demands, no matter how unreasonable or impracticable, are not complied with."

I have for twenty-two years been connected with labor organizations, and during that time have gained an experience which warrants me in stamping the brand of malicious falsehood upon the above-quoted assertion. It goes without saying that either the Messrs. Pinketon have not read the history of the world or else they know but little about labor organizations. It is the part of policy for the Pinkerton agency to terrorize timid capital by making it believe that it is at the mercy of labor organizations; it is also to their interest to cause men of wealth to believe that their wealth is not safe while labor organizations exist. There is no labor organization on this continent to-day which could not be made a most beneficial ally of capital were it not for the pernicious meddling of the detective agencies of the land, which, in order to prevent their occupations from vanishing, must conjure up the imaginary where the real would not answer their purpose. Labor organizations are recognized by law; they may or may not be sworn, but whether sworn or not, the man who takes an obligation in order to gain information and then sells that information is a perjurer. I place in your hands a copy of the Pinkerton secret circular to employers. I hold the original. In it you will find this clause:

"Corporations or individuals desirous of ascertaining the feeling of their employés, and whether they are likely to engage in strikes or are joining any secret labor organizations with a view of compelling terms from corporations or employers, can obtain, on application to the superintendent of either of the offices, a detective suitable to associate with their employés and obtain this information."

If suboration of perjury is not contained in that section, then it comes amazingly close to it. Read still further in that secret circular, and you will not wonder that employers of labor have been disturbed and restless of late:

"We suggest whether it would not be well for railroad companies and other corporations, as well as individuals who are extensive employers of labor to keep a close watch for designing men among their own employés, who, in the interest of secret labor societies, are inducing their employés to join these organizations and eventually to cause a strike. It is frequently the case that by taking a matter of this kind in hand in time and discovering the ringleaders, and dealing promptly with them, serious trouble may be avoided in the future."

That the Pinkerton agency has not been idle in suggesting to employers of labor that they will ferret out designing men and expose them is morally certain; their existence as a detective agency depends upon their detecting something; and reasoning men will not have to ponder long over the very apparent bitterness shown to their deadly and uncompromising enemy—the labor organizations—by the Pinkerton brothers.

Who is to prove that it was not a paid agent of the Pinkerton agency who placed the explosive in the mold during the strike at the Chicago Stove Works? Was it not proved that Pinkerton agents made efforts to induce men to place obstructions on the tracks during the Chicago, Burlington and Quincy strike? During the stone-cutters' strike in New York the Pinkerton "watchmen" were on guard when the "acid was poured on the rope." Why were they not watchful enough to do detective duty then and arrest the perpetrators of the dastardly deed? Is it not wonderful that the alleged damage is discovered, just before the final catastrophe takes place, by the Pinkertons?

The statement goes on to say that during the recent New York Central strike "obstructions were repeatedly placed on the track by strikers." That is not true, and it is doubtful if the one fatal accident would have happened had not the desire to keep up the turmoil actuated either the Pinkerton detective agency or the management of the New York Central Railroad. The first attempt, or rather the first reported attempt, to place obstructions on the track of the New York Central, and the one to which the Messrs. Pinkerton refer in their statement, was without foundation. Lurid reports of its fiendishness were scattered broadcast, however, and these no doubt promoted the deed at Castleton later on.

To prove that the Messrs. Pinkerton do not adhere closely to the truth in making allegations, let me give you the facts in that particular case: On August 30, 1890, the east-bound Chicago Express, when nearing the West Albany yards at a place called Karner, came to a standstill, and several passengers alighted and walked forward to see what the trouble was. Next day's papers contained a detailed account of the discovery of obstructions on the track and the imaginary fiend who perpetrated the deed was severely arraigned, while the undersigned was also editorially condemned and called on to "ferret out the Knight of Labor who did the deed and deliver him up to justice." I did investigate, secured the name and address of one man who was on that train and who walked forward when it stopped. The New York World, then as now in favor of right, contained a statement, made by a gentleman named Bosch, to the effect that the train stopped because of want of steam or for some other cause; that he went to the front of the engine with five others, and that there were no ties or other obstructions in sight, much less on the track. I cut that clipping from the World, mailed it to Mr. Bosch with request that he verify the statement, and this is a copy of his answer:

ALBANY, N. Y.,
September 3, 1890.

T. V. POWDERLY, Esq.:

DEAR SIR: I have just received your letter of September 2, and I hereby agree to swear to the statement made in clipping which you sent me from yesterday's World to be true in every way. Five of my companions will do the same.

I am very truly yours,

JOHN BOSCH.

I did not ask Mr. Bosch to swear to the truth of the World's report; his letter and guaranty that five others would swear to its truthfulness were sufficient. I have in this letter refuted every specific allegation made by the Pinkerton brothers, and you have but to subpœna parties who were residents of the localities where these transactions occurred to establish the proofs without question.

If organizations of capital are necessary, organizations of labor are doubly so; but there exists no necessity whatever for the existence of a wandering army of vagabonds raked together from the four quarters of the earth, to engage in labor disputes. Capital makes a mistake in engaging these vagrants, but it can not be blamed so much when one reads the alarming secret circulars issued from the headquarters of the Pinkerton detective agency.

At the time the New York Central strike was in progress, Mr. Quinn, of New York, offered the following resolution in Congress:

"*Resolved,* That the Committee on the Judiciary be instructed to inquire and report, by bill or otherwise, what legislation within the province of the Federal Government may be proper and necessary to prevent corporations engaged in interstate-commerce traffic from employing unjustifiably large bodies of armed men denominated 'detectives,' but clothed with no legal functions. The employment of such so-called 'detectives' operates at the city of Albany and other places, as recently demonstrated, to place the lives of peaceable and unoffending citizens at the mercy of persons acting without legal authority, direction, or responsibility, and to the local injury and detention of interstate commerce."

With the end of the New York Central strike interest in that resolution ceased, and since then nothing has been done to carry out the spirit of the resolution until the Judiciary Committee entered upon its present duty. I, in common with a large number of citizens who take an interest in this question, feel that it is dangerous to allow any agency other than the United States Government to transport armed bodies of men across State lines. If a detective agency has that right other agencies have just as good a right, and soon we will find ourselves living under, not a government of the people, but a government of those who have the money to pay for these hireling armies when they wish to encroach on the rights of others. If Pinkerton has the right to arm men to engage in strikes, the strikers have the right to meet them with arms in their hands, and to such extremities we should not be driven. Congress should protect this and all other States from invasion.

At the last session of the Pennsylvania legislature the Knights of Labor presented a bill having for its object the abolition of the system of introducing armed bodies of men to the scenes of labor troubles, except as provided by the constitution, but the same power that procured the services of the invaders at Homestead prevented the reporting of that bill from committee, and it was not passed.

There is no doubt in my mind but that the Messrs. Pinkerton will continue to arm and transport troops from one State to another unless prevented by a national law. The effect of such a system will lead to the arming of other than the State or United States troops, and this arming will come as a right if due and proper protection be not afforded by the proper authorities. Who undertakes to do wrong should be punished, but if I offend against the State a private citizen should have no right to shoot me to death for it merely because other men are wealthy enough to disregard the law in hiring him. That workingmen, whether organized or not, have the legal right to protect themselves can not be questioned, and in basing my opinion that others have as equitable a right to carry arms as the Pinkerton "watchmen" on the wording of a letter received during the New York Central strike, I can not be much in error. Roger A. Pryor, whose qualifications to render a legal opinion can not be questioned, wrote as follows:

"I mean the enlistment of banded and armed mercenaries under the command of private detectives on the side of corporations in their conflicts with employés. The pretext for such an extraordinary measure is the protection of the corporate property; but surely the power of this great State is adequate to the preservation of the public order and security. At all events, in this particular instance, it was not pretended either that the strikers had invaded property or person, or that the police or militia in Albany had betrayed reluctance or inability to cope with the situation. On the contrary, the facts are undisputed that the moment the men went out Mr. Pinkerton and his myrmidons appeared on the scene, and the police of Albany declared their competency to repel any trespass on person or property. The executive of the State, too, denied any necessity for the presence of the military.

"I do not impute to the railroad officials a purpose, without provocation, to precipitate their ruffians upon a defenseless and harmless throng of spectators; but the fact remains that the ruffians in their hire did shoot into the crowd without occasion, and did so shed innocent blood, And it is enough to condemn the system that it authorizes unofficial and irresponsible persons to usurp the most delicate and difficult function of the State and exposes the lives of citizens to the murderous assaults of hireling assassins, stimulated to violence by panic or by the suggestion of employers to strike terror by an appalling exhibition of force. If the railroad company may enlist armed men to defend its property the employés may enlist armed men to defend their persons, and thus private war be inaugurated, the authority of the State defied, the peace and tranquility of society destroyed, and the citizens exposed to the hazard of indiscriminate slaughter.

Unfortunately labor is not provided with the means to defray the expenses of thorough investigations, legal or otherwise, which would place the terrible truths before your committee. This is not necessary at this time, for the fact that men and arms were transported from Chicago to Homestead, across three States of the United States, is admitted by the Pinkerton brothers; and if it can not be shown that their action was based on law, and that law published to the world, they should be punished for usurping the functions of the President of the United States, who alone is authorized by law to order armed men from State to State. Mere censure will not atone for the wrong; it should be punished according to its enormity.

That this letter is lengthy is true, but the necessity for it is so great that I trust your committee will pardon me for trespassing so long upon their time and patience. Respectfully submitted.

T. V. POWDERLY,
General Master Workman.

During the reading of the statement Mr. Powderly made the following explanations of it:

The strike at Chicago was of several weeks' duration, and was not ordered or countenanced by the Knights of Labor. The Chicago, Burlington and Quincy strike was a strike of the Brotherhood of Locomotive Engineers, in which the Knights were not interested. The letter which I have in this statement was written during the time of the New York Central strike, and was read at a public meeting in Union Square, New York.

After reading the statement, Mr. Powderly said:

Here is a statement he makes, that "it is only after a full investigation of their character and antecedents that men are employed by Pinkertons." I have an affidavit here which shows that they appointed a bad man. This affidavit is dated Philadelphia, July 28. That is the case of Mr. Frank Webb, who recently figured in the Pinkerton affair at Homestead, and whose wife was murdered. This is one illustration which goes to show that during the strike at Homestead Pinkerton men were employed who were not of good character, as stated by the Pinkertons in their testimony.

H. Mis. 335——15

By Mr. BOATNER:

Q. What is it you have to say about that man Webb?—A. Webb was the murderer of his own wife. He had not been living with his wife for about eighteen months, and was implicated in her murder. He was not a very good character, and was one of the men selected by the Pinkertons to go to Homestead. We are gathering the testimony, and we find that one is accused of wife murder, four of burglary, two of wife-beating, and one of arson. I think that is the list. We propose to do a little detective work of our own, and we will do it without arms, in order to find out what the charcters of these men are. We will prove beyond the shadow of a doubt that in a great many cases the claim that the characters of the men are good is without the slightest foundation.

During the New York Central strike I stood on the street in Syracuse one day and saw two men talking to an official. I was introduced to one of them and he told me that he had just served his term in the State penitentiary. I do not remember that he stated what the crime was, but he had been liberated only a few days before, and was then employed by the Pinkertons to go to Albany and take charge of some men on a strike.

Q. Take charge of men on a strike?—A. To take a rifle and do Pinkerton duty.

The CHAIRMAN. I want to say, as a member of the committee (speaking for myself, and I believe also in speaking for every member of the committee), that from the beginning of this investigation I have had no purpose or object in it except to get at the bottom facts without regard to whom they hurt or help. I have no feeling or preference and no interest at all in this matter. The committee has not been informed as to any considerable number of witnesses (we have had witnesses the best we could get) who would give us information, and I would be glad if you would furnish the committee with names of witnesses, and their places of residence, who of their own knowledge could give important evidence touching these matters. We would be glad if you could do so.

The WITNESS. I could not do it offhand. I can do it by reference to my files.

By the CHAIRMAN:

Q. How much time do you think would be necessary in order to enable you to do that?—A. I did not intend to go home until next week, but I can go there from here, and as soon as I get back I will send you the information you desire.

Q. I think I ought to say that the committee is somewhat at sea in this investigation, because it is supposed Congress will adjourn in a few days. We have already taken all the testimony which we deemed necessary in order to have a full explanation of the whole thing as to the matter of the transportation of these men to Homestead. We have heard since we returned to Washington the testimony of the Pinkertons themselves, and we now hear you. We can, I suppose, make a report upon the Homestead branch, and, if the House gives us permission, we can go on and investigate the Pinkerton branch of it to the very bottom. That, however, might be a matter for future legislation, if the committee agree upon it. I do not know what the opinions of the other members are. What do you wish to say about this?—A. I notice a question here by Mr. Boatner: "Did you ever detail any of your men for service for the Knights of Labor;" and he tries not to answer that question. The Pinkerton Agency has detailed men to join the Knights of Labor. I know of the case of a man named Frank McGrane or McCrane. He became a member, under another name, of a local assembly of the Knights of Labor, and personally confessed to me that he was prompted to join it by the Pinkerton Detective Agency, in order to worm himself into the confidence of my friends in Scranton, members of the organization, and, if possible, to implicate me in some unworthy transactions.

By Mr. BOATNER:

Q. Can you give us the present address of that party?—A. I do not know, but I will try to find it. This was in 1886, during a trouble in the Northwest, or shortly after that trouble.

By Mr. RAY:

Q. Is this gentleman living?—A. He was recently. I saw him not long ago. He is in the neighborhood of Scranton, and I think I will have no difficulty in finding him.

As to the other matter to which he refers, that of the New York Central strike, telling of Knights of Labor being imprisoned, I will say that as to one man, Judge Griffith, in passing sentence on him, said:

> The evidence adduced leads me to believe that you are the moving spirit in this trouble, and that you are the man who has concocted this diabolical scheme; still you have proved yourself to be not the hardened criminal that should receive the severest penalty.

It was afterwards proved that he was a Knight, and had prompted others to do deeds, and it was afterwards stated by men who gave testimony, and was proven that he was in the service of the Pinkerton Company.

By Mr. BOATNER:

Q. That was the party who was sentenced for some offense?—A. He was putting obstructions on the track at Castleton and other places.

Q. How long ago was that?—A. That was in September, 1890.

Q. You say you can give the names of witnesses who can furnish evidence tending to show that he was in the employ of the Pinkerton agency?—A. Yes, sir; there are two others, including this one. Their names are Reed, Cain, and Buett. The other two were not Knights of Labor. They had been expelled from the organization for misconduct. Judge Griffith, in speaking to Reed, said:

> You have joined an organization of honest men who have banded together for their common interest, but you have left their principles and become a murderer, plunderer, and pillager.

These men to whom Mr. Pinkerton referred in his testimony in which he stated he knew of obstructions being placed upon the track knew nothing of the fact, for in the trial he was forced to admit that he knew nothing at all about it, and that what he stated was hearsay upon the statement of such a man as this. Yet he comes here before this committee and says that these things are true. The one Knight of Labor, Kiernan, was on the trial acquitted. They did not have a particle of evidence against him. In fact it was proven that he did everything in his power to prevent that.

I have letters from attorneys which it is not necessary to read, but I have a circular of August 21, 1890, since the necessity that existed for keeping it secret has ceased, I will put in the testimony. This was a secret circular sent to our people on the New York Central, and it speaks the sentiments of the Knighs of Labor.   The circular was read, as follows:

SECRET CIRCULAR.

NEW YORK, *August* 21, 1890.

To the Knights of Labor on the New York Central
and Hudson River Railway, greeting :

Yesterday the general executive board of the order made a final effort to adjust the difficulty into which you have been precipitated. Arbitration was offered and refused, an investigation was asked for and that too was rejected, an opportunity was sought to question the discharged men in presence of Mr. Webb and that was denied. We have consequently officially decided to support the striking men, and will do every legitimate thing to make your cause successful. We will do what lies in our power to aid you and win that recognition you seek, and in thus pledging ourselves we feel that we speak for the whole order. But a solemn duty rests, for fulfillment, with the striking men: Keep away from the company's property. Do not congregate in groups anywhere except in your sanctuaries. Make no threats either against the company or any other person or thing. If it comes to your knowledge that property is in danger, it is your duty to notify the civil authorities to take steps to prevent the doing of damage, for, bear in mind, that that very property was created by your own labor. Have no altercations with the Pinkerton men; keep away from them when there is danger of a rupture. And when opportunity offers have some of your coolest members reason with those who have taken your places, with a view to convincing them that they are acting unmanfully. Necessity may have driven them to take your places, and they must be treated as kindly as possible.

Remember that every man of you is being watched, your footsteps are being dogged, and even a joking remark may serve to fasten upon you a crime of which you would scorn to be guilty. Keep away from the rum shops, and frown down every attempt to induce your brothers to even enter saloons, at least until this trouble ends. By taking this course you will strengthen our hands, and public opinion, always fickle, will be borne to your aid by the shifting winds which guide its movements more often than if any other course is taken. Let me now sum up:

Keep sober.
Do no loud talking.
Have no intercourse with strangers.
Keep your own counsel.
Make no threats.
Allow no damage to be done to the company's property if you can prevent it.
Assert your right to organize and the right to be heard in your own behalf.

Your orderly conduct since the strike began has been a source of great gratification to myself and of just pride to our order. Let the wise counsels which have hitherto guided you continue to prevail.

Expressing the deepest sympathy with each one of our members engaged in this just struggle and the hope that success will come to us, I remain,

Sincerely and fraternally, yours,

T. V. POWDERLY,
General Master Workman.

(After reading.) That was lived up to to the letter.

By Mr. BYNUM :

Q. Who were the officials on the New York Central Railway at that time?—A. Chauncey Depew was president, H. Walter Webb was vice-president and was in charge of the company.

Q. Were Pinkerton men employed in that strike?—A. They were employed even before the strike took place, which caused Webb to say that he knew nothing about it. He was led to remark that the strikers did a very scurvy trick, or something of that kind, to stop work without letting him know anything about it.

By Mr. BOATNER :

Q. I suppose in this remark you refer to Mr. Chauncey Depew, the great orator and prominent after-dinner speaker?—A. Yes, sir. I have no hesitation in saying that Mr. Depew was the man who ordered the strike, and that he did that before he went to Europe.

By Mr. RAY:

Q. Do you say that he ordered the strike ?—A. I do.   I will explain that. The men were thoroughly organized on that road, and by leaving orders with the subordinates to harass the men, getting up contentions, goading them where it was unnecessary, and imposing penalties where none should be imposed, and doing other mean and harassing things of that kind, the men were finally driven to desperation, and went on a strike. When the time came that the men were ready to strike, Mr. Depew took shipping for Europe.

By Mr. BOATNER:

Q. You are surely mistaken about that. Mr. Depew has stated publicly that that system had been brought to perfection, and was so fairly and justly regulated toward the men, and so entirely satisfactory was their situation, that their position depended entirely upon a proper discharge of their duties; and that so universal was their satisfaction that there was absolutely no conflict existing between the employers and employed. I am surprised at your statement.—A. One man who had been in the employ of the New York Central road for twenty-three years, one of the most cautious men, was discharged simply because he was a Knight of Labor.

By Mr. RAY:

Q. In that connection, I will ask you if you think that Mr. Depew ordered the strike; or do you think that his conduct was such as to incite it ?—A. He desired it.

By Mr. BOATNER:

Q. He adopted a line of policy which he knew would result in a strike ?—A. Yes, sir.

Q. And he went away ?—A. He went to Europe.

By Mr. RAY:

Q. Have you any evidence of that fact, except that certain orders were given, of which you presume he had knowledge ?—A. The whole history of that strike can be obtained.

Q. This charge is that you conclude from certain facts and circumstances that he ordered the strike ?—A. I do; from an intimate knowledge of the affairs of that strike as they were disclosed to me after it took place.

Q. Were you acquainted with Mr. Depew ?—A. I never met him.

Q. You can not base your opinion on anything that he said in your presence ?—A. No, sir. As president of the road, he must have had knowledge of those things.

Q. Did you visit Albany during that strike ?—A. Yes, sir.

Q. And you were there while it was in progress ?—A. Yes, sir.

Q. Did you see any of the conflicts between the people or the strikers and the Pinkerton men ?—A. No, sir; I did not.

Q. Did you observe any shooting, or was there any shooting when you were there?—A. No.

Q. Had it occurred previous to your visit, or did it occur subsequent to it?—A. I was there twice or three times. The first time I was there, there had been no shooting. The second time I was there, shooting had taken place, and afterwards there was some shooting. Two boys and one man were shot.

Q. Did you see any of these Pinkerton men there ?—A. Yes.

Q. What were they doing ?—A. I saw but two. They were standing in the Albany yard. They were not doing anything there.

Q. The property was in the possession of the company at that time?—
A. Yes, sir.

Q. Did you have any conversation with these Pinkerton men?—A.
No, I did not.

Q. Did you know either of these Pinkerton men?—A. No; I could
not swear they were. They were appointed as such.

Q. You have never had any conversation with either of them?—A.
No.

Q. Did you know of any other men who have been in their employ?—
A. Yes, sir.

Q. How many?—A. This man Polletschek.

Q. Did you know any other person who has been in their employ?—
A. I am not personally acquainted with any.

Q. This man you did know?—A. Yes, sir. He made an affidavit in
my presence.

Q. He is the only one who has been in their employ that you have
ever had any conversation with?—A. Yes, sir; to the best of my knowledge.

Q. And this is the same man you say you saw in Syracuse?—A. No,
sir; I forgot about the man in Syracuse, This man in Syracuse told
me he was in the employ of the Pinkertons; but Pollitschek I met in
the city of New York.

Q. You made the statement that you saw a man in Syracuse, and
that he stated he was employed by the Pinkertons, and that he was
but a short time out of States prison.

Mr. BYNUM. I suggest that Mr. Powderly be permitted to complete
his statement. I asked the question as to officials of railroad company
because it bore upon the New York Central strike, about which witness
was testifying.

Mr. RAY. I supposed that he had finished his statement.

The WITNESS. A certain Peter McCallam was said to be in the employ of the Pinkertons at the time of the New York Central strike, and
having performed duty for them. I have an affidavit of Thomas Stokes
to that effect.

The affidavit was read as follows:

STATE OF NEW YORK, *Duchess County:*

Thomas Stokes, being duly sworn, deposes and says: That he is a resident of the
city of Poughkeepsie, in said county, and has been for a period of twenty years; that
on or about the 3d day of September, 1890 (about the hour of 7 o'clock p. m.), said
deponent was standing on the Church-street bridge, overlooking the New York Central Railroad in the city of Poughkeepsie, N. Y., and that while on the said bridge at
said time he was approached by one Peter McCallan, who said to deponent, "Stokes,
less go and throw a switch to-night," or the same in substance; deponent replied,
"You must be getting crazy," to which the said Peter McCallan replied, "You need
not throw it; I'll throw it, and you be there to help me," to which deponent replied,
"You do not know what you are talking about," whereupon deponent walked away.

THOMAS STOKES.

Sworn to before me this 6th day of September, 1890.

CHARLES A. HOPKINS,
Commissioner of Deeds in and for the city of Poughkeepsie, N. Y.

I introduced that for the purpose of showing that this man whom I
believed to be a Pinkerton man was inducing others to do these acts
and to bring discredit upon the strikers. The other affidavit here simply is a continuation of that. If my knowing the men to be Pinkertons—that is, having absolute knowledge that they were such—is necessary, so far as that is concerned I could not swear that these men were

Pinkerton men. We simply saw them there acting in that capacity; and the fact that Pinkerton was there himself would lead us to suppose that he was in charge of these men. I did not see that, but simply read the testimony taken in the trial, and formed my conclusions accordingly. Of the Southwest strike the same was true.

By Mr. BYNUM:

Q. Probably I can suggest to you something the committee wants to know. Did that strike extend to East St. Louis as well as to West St. St. Louis?—A. Yes, sir.

Q. I want to call your attention to one thing in reference to which the Pinkertons testified, and that was that in all the engagements in which their men were engaged up to Homestead trouble, there have been killed but three men. My recollection is that there were a number killed in East St. Louis?—A. I think there were seven.

Q. Seven or eight. Do you know anything about the particulars of those cases, as to who was responsible?—A. I can get particulars. That testimony was taken by the Curtain committee.

The CHAIRMAN. Here is the report of the Curtain committee.

By Mr. BOATNER:

Q. In your statement a while ago, you referred to an "official indorsement" of the strike, and the information to the men that the strike would be "supported." Will you be kind enough to give the committee what you consider to be the legitimate methods of "supporting" a strike? How can a strike legitimately be made effective? There is a difference between the statements of some witnesses we have had and the Pinkertons upon that subject. Please inform the committee what acts of striking workmen are approved by the Knights of Labor in making a strike effective.—A. None. We provide no laws for the government of strikes. We have none on our books, but what we call "supporting" a strike is simply to provide them with funds.

Q. While out of employment?—A. Yes, sir.

Q. Does your organization countenance the prevention of nonunion men taking the places of striking or locked-out men?—A. We agree with Andrew Carnegie—"Thou shalt not take thy neighbor's job."

Q. Does your organization countenance the enforcement of that unwritten law?—A. If we can do so peaceably, yes.

Q. Do you justify force in preventing nonunion men from accepting work?—A. No.

By the CHAIRMAN:

Q. How would you prevent it, if the former employés saw proper to use it?—A. I can not just now recall a case, but on several occasions we have met men and advised them to go away, and have succeeded; but now, in order to prevent them communicating with us, it is the custom to have Pinkertons in close proximity and get up a row.

By Mr. BOATNER:

Q. Then, you attribute these conflicts between workingmen to the interference of the Pinkertons?—A. Most assuredly.

Q. Is it your idea that if the Pinkertons were not employed employers could successfully and peaceably replace their striking workmen with nonunion men, if they saw proper?—A. I believe they could. There might be a broken head occasionally, but it would not lead to the great violations of the public peace that we have read about lately.

Q. Do you think that the Carnegie Company could have introduced

nonunion workmen into their Homestead mills to take the positions of
their locked-out or striking employés?—A. They would have been able
to have introduced a few people, but not a sufficient number to have
defeated the Amalgamated society.

Q. How would your Amalgamated society have prevented the operation of mills, if it had adhered to the rule which Mr. Weihe testified
before us they were using—only moral suasion?—A. I do not know
what Mr. Weihe testified to, but I do know that the rule among workingmen is (it is an unwritten law) to meet nonunion men wherever
they can, and they have been known to pay them wages, and to send
them away from the scene of trouble. That has been done repeatedly.

Q. Suppose they can not persuade them away; are they justified in
using force to make them go away?—A. I should think not.

Q. Are they maintained in such a system by organized labor?—A.
No.

Q. I understand you now to state, after a proper investigation into
their character and antecedents, that the assertion of the Pinkertons
that they employ only reputable men is false?—A. Yes, sir.

Q. You also state that their assertion that they never act except
under legal authority and for the protection of property, is untrue?—
A. I do. I believe that is what they do. I do not know what authority
they have had to act in Homestead. In reading the papers I have seen
no authority at all.

Q. It was stated here by the Pinkertons that in the New York Central strike, all their men were sworn in as peace officers, and acted under the authority of the sheriff. Do you know whether or not that is
true?—A. I believe that many of them were; but in Pennsylvania no
man can hold an office unless he has been a citizen in the county one year.
If the people are not allowed or permitted to elect a man, certainly
Robert Pinkerton should not be permitted to go into Pennsylvania and
have a sheriff swear them in.

By Mr. BYNUM:

Q. The effect of the decisions of the courts as to these positions is
that they are not offices under that section of the law. The position of
a deputy is not held to be an office. It is not the construction which
the law or the courts of that State give it.—A. Well, then, in what
capacity can they come?

Q. Your opinion is that it excludes them from holding office. It
would not apply to the places of deputies, but it would apply to the
position of the sheriff. No man would be eligible to that office unless
a citizen of the county.—A. But the law says a man shall not be appointed to any office in Pennsylvania unless he has been a resident a
year.

Q. But you take the position that a deputy could not be appointed
who was not a resident. Is not that the construction you put upon the
statute—that it is an office?—A. I do not know about that.

Q. Is it your idea that they are officers? Are not the rulings of the
courts to the contrary?—A. I do not know.

By the CHAIRMAN:

Q. That question may be considered possibly as relevant, but in the
testimony it is not shown that the Pinkertons taken to Homestead were
sworn in as deputies. The deputy sheriff was present, but when the
emergency arose, he did not do it.—A. If it were necessary to import
men to any State in the Union, the Pinkertons could go over to Canada,

get men, and be authorized to bring them here and shoot down our citizens.

By Mr. BOATNER:

Q. They could not be authorized to come here and shoot down our citizens.—A. He testified that these men were citizens of other States.

By Mr. BYNUM:

Q. The point to which I desire to call your attention is not important at all; but pretty nearly every State has had provisions that no one shall hold office, except he be a citizen of the county; but I think you will find the construction of such provisions by the courts of all the States is that the position of a deputy is not an office. A provision of the statute that no man shall hold two offices may exist, and yet a man may be an officer and a deputy. It would require a broader provision of the statute in order that no man who was a nonresident should be appointed as a deputy.—A. I do not know how it strikes the members of the committee, but to my mind, that makes it stronger against the Pinkertons. Under that construction of the law they may be taken from Canada as well as from a State.

Q. Unless there is some other provision besides that?—A. Yes; or they may be taken from England or Russia.

Q. There have been a great many cases in the United States in which foreigners have been appointed deputies?—A. Adam Pollitscheg was not only appointed by the Pinkertons and sent up to Albany, but he was a foreigner, and it can be proven. He was not a citizen, and was only four years in this country. I have the evidence of that.

By Mr. BOATNER:

Q. I understand you to say that in your opinion a number of these cases of violations of the law, to which the Pinkertons have referred in their testimony as having been committed by Knights of Labor, or instigated by them, were committed by his own people, that his own men have sworn to some of these disturbances?—A. That is not only my impression, but it is the conviction of organized labor.

Q. Will you be kind enough to furnish us the instances in which you know, or have reason to believe, that has been done, or give us the names of persons who will substantiate it?—A. I will endeavor to do so.

By Mr. BYNUM:

Q. I notice in the Congressional Record of Wednesday a quotation from you, made by Mr. Hale in the Senate. I wish you would examine it and state whether this is a correct account of your statement, or whether it is a product of yours [handing witness a copy of the Record].—A. (After examining it.) Yes, sir; I wrote that.

Partisan papers are endeavoring to make political capital out of the terrible scenes which took place at Homestead the other day. The Democratic papers are vehement in their denunciation of the Republican party for enacting a tariff law under which protection was afforded to manufacturers. There is no love for workmen in the hearts of these editors; a desire to serve party interests alone actuates them. Let us review the situation in brief. Tariff laws could not be passed without discussion, and in all of the debates which took place in Congress over the Mills and McKinley bills I can not find that a single amendment was offered by a Democrat to give the workmen a certain portion of the tariff when collected.

The Mills bill and the McKinley bill differ very little in the duty on steel rails, plates, etc. One was a Democratic bill, the other a Republican. The McKinley bill reduced the duty on the articles manufactured at Homestead, and Democratic papers, in asserting that the trouble at that point is due to the McKinley bill, are but condemning the very thing that they themselves advocate and on which they base their claim to power—a reduction of the tariff. The Pinkertons existed before the Mills bill was introduced in Congress, and that institution continues to flourish now that the McKinley bill is in force. Whether the tariff went up or down, disputes between employer and employed would continue. Workingmen are not the fools that politicians believe them to be, for we do not feel that the coming of the millennium depends upon the way Congress legislates on the tariff.

If our Democrats who are so eager to make political capital out of this difficulty will lend me their ears, I will whisper to them that Representative Watson, of Georgia, has had a measure before Congress for the last four or five months which aims at the abolition of the Pinkertons as a factor in the industrial life of the United States. The Democratic party has a sweeping majority in Congress; it has a full knowledge of the acts of the Pinkertons on previous occasions. I have presented evidence enough to Congress to prove that Pinkerton is an enemy to American liberty. That Democratic majority has a knowledge of the existence of Watson's bill, and it has up to the present time dillied and dallied with it, and has no idea of passing it. "We have petitioned for redress," have endeavored to get the ear of Congress, but "our repeated petitions have been answered only by repeated injury," and civil war at Homestead.

Q. I desire to know whether you had reference to House Bill 5680. Please examine that bill and see whether that is the bill referred to.— A. [After examining the bill.] I never read this bill before, but I should judge that is the one.

A BILL to regulate the employment of certain persons to do the work of guards, and so forth, and for other purposes.

Be it enacted by the Senate and House of Representatives of the United States of America in Congress assembled, That whenever any persons shall be employed to guard or defend property of any kind, the persons so employed shall be residents of the State where the property to be guarded or defended is located, and for the conduct of the said employees the employer and the owner of the property shall be responsible both civilly and criminally while the employment exists.

SEC. 2. That no private person shall employ any private citizen, directly or indirectly, or arm and equip anyone already employed, to make arrests without warrants, to disperse mobs or quell disturbances, to establish martial law, to aid in the operating of engines, cars, or boats, by force of arms; or to do any other acts within the scope of the legal duties of the militia or the authorities and officers of towns, cities, counties, States and the United States.

SEC. 3. That no person shall organize, keep, or maintain any force of employees, agents, or associates for the purpose of hiring said force, or any part thereof, to private citizens or corporations to make arrests without warrant, to disperse mobs or quell public disturbance, to make forcible evictions, to establish or enforce martial law, or to do any other acts properly within the province of the militia, or of the lawful authorities of towns, cities, counties, and States, or of the United States.

SEC. 4. That any person violating any of the provisions of the foregoing sections shall be guilty of a misdemeanor, and upon conviction shall be punished by fine of not less than one hundred dollars nor more than ten thousand dollars, and by imprisonment for not less than three nor more than twelve months.

Q. This committee desires to formulate legislation on this subject if it possibly can find authority upon which to base it. Will you state the article and section of the Constitution giving to the Congress of the United States the power to pass such a measure as that?—A. I do not know that I can point out any other facts than those I have pointed out; I do not think that I can point out any better one than section 4, Article IV of the Constitution, which guarantees to each State a republican form of government, and says that they shall be secure against invasion.

I would like to say that I think this is an invasion of the State of Pennsylvania, and that we must so regard it. We feel, also, that if men had been selected in the neighborhood, they would have some regard for the people and the property of the neighborhood. They would have been more honest and not so reckless, and would not have permitted such violations as have recently occurred. We feel that each locality should take care of its own affairs. We feel that this is an invasion of the State, and that under that section the people could legislate; but we do not think that if legislation were enacted outside of that, that it would be unconstitutional.

Q. The Federal Government is one of delegated powers, and we must find the power in the Constitution, or it does not exist.—A. That we believe.

Q. Section 1 of this bill provides that no person shall employ any private citizen, directly or indirectly, to aid in operating engines, cars, or boats by force of arms. Do I understand you to mean that any citizen has not a right outside of the armed force of the State to protect his own property against the attacks of others?—A. I regard institutions such as railroads and other corporations of that kind to be more than private property.

Q. But this applies to persons and not to corporations. For instance, I will ask you this: Have you not a right to employ an individual and put him in your house to protect it against attack? Have you not a right to defend it without calling upon the militia of the State or the sheriff of the county?—A. I do not think so.

Q. That is all.—A. I believe that if I have reason to expect at any time that my property is in danger, I should notify the proper authorities, and look to them for protection. I believe furthermore that in this Homestead matter it was the duty of the sheriff to call in the regular force; that he was authorized to call in the *posse comitatus*. He had that right. The law provides that those refusing to go shall be punished.

Q. But they can not call on it to guard the property against supposed attacks.—A. No; nor were there any attacks threatened on this property. We must go further and find out if threats were made. On the contrary, the strikers assured the company that they would enter into bond to protect the works.

Q. It is not necessary that you should be threatened or be in danger in order to justify you in putting a guard in your house. You have a right to act on your own impulses, and to protect your castle without waiting until its destruction is threatened. Your servant has a right to make the same defense that you have, even to taking life.—A. I do not know the intricacies of the law, as I am not a lawyer. I simply know what I would do, and I do not know what provocation would lead me to take life. You will have to ask a more bloodthirsty man than I am. But I regard this as an entirely different thing.

Q. But we are confining it to the question of our power to pass this bill.—A. I am not talking about that bill.

Q. That is what you were talking about a moment ago.—A. I am speaking now on the broad principle. I did not know what was in the bill.

By Mr. BRODERICK:

Q. This bill seems to prohibit persons being employed to do any sort of guard duty. If Congress has power, and should enact that law to prohibit the employment, or the shipment of armed men from one State to another, would not that furnish a remedy?—A. That is my suggestion. I do not think the United States should be called upon to interfere, except where it is an interstate matter.

Q. You do not believe that the Government ought to interfere in the employment of detectives in work on private residences, or the employment of detectives in ferreting out crimes and collecting evidence?—A. No, sir. We readily recognize their proper duties in such work as furnishing detectives for balls—that of the "400" for instance. Of course, they know who need watching. That is quite another matter. We regard the detective business and the business of shipping troops as distinct and separate.

Q. There is no objection to the employment of detectives when necessary ?—A. We regard it as a questionable occupation to be spying into other people's affairs.

Q. What do you think of arbitration as a medium for the settlement of these difficulties ?—A. I have been quoted so often and called a crank so long that I do not know as I ought to repeat my views on that point. The Knights of Labor make a demand upon their members to work for the passage of laws providing for arbitration between employé and employer, and they believe that it should be made compulsory. We believe that it is a matter that should be legislated upon, and that capital should not have a right to decide these questions as it pleases.

The CHAIRMAN. It is a difficult matter, if not impossible, to enact a law and enforce it, for compulsory arbitration.

Mr. BRODERICK. I do not contend that the Government can do that at all, but I am of the opinion that the States can do it.

The CHAIRMAN. I have examined the law of Pennsylvania upon the subject, and I see many difficulties in the way.

The WITNESS. Our arbitration in Pennsylvania is practically a dead · letter.

The CHAIRMAN. It is so in all the States. We have one in the statutes of the United States that grew out of that strike in the West, and was the outcome of a report of the Curtin Committee, but it does not amount to anything.

By Mr. BRODERICK :

Q. Are you familiar with that volunteer arbitration ?—A. It has no operation. Neither side is in favor of it.

Q. That kind of arbitration never accomplished anything, did it ?—A. I believe, with proper provisions for appeal, that enforced arbitration could be accomplished.

By the CHAIRMAN :

Q. With reference to the testimony of the Pinkertons about the good character of those they employ: Did you notice that they made a distinction here in their testimony before the committee ? They said that they inquired about the character of their men, and employed only men of good standing as "watchmen;" but that they did sometimes employ disreputable people in their detective business. They stated that the two businesses were separate.—A. It is fortunate that they made that statement.

By Mr. BYNUM :

Q. It is only in special cases, they say, where they make use of disreputable characters to ferret out crime.—A. If the right of the Pinkertons is conceded to arm men at will as watchmen, all they have to do is to establish their agency in Detroit across the river from Windsor, arm men in Canada, pick up a fuss in Detroit, and march their men in there.

Q. An armed force violating the laws, and an armed force which claims to be executing the laws, are quite different things.—A. We do not consider that the Pinkertons are executing any law.

Q. The Pinkertons claim that they are in the employ of persons engaged in the enforcement of private rights. The question at Homestead does not relate to the present question as to whether they should have been sworn in as deputy officers. Carnegie & Co. claim they had the right to employ men and put them upon their private property to guard it, and that the clothing of them with powers of deputy officers would have added nothing to their authority, because that right exists in every individual—the right to protect his property. When you speak of the Pinkertons as an armed force invading a State, if that force went there to protect property under its laws, and not to make an attack upon the authorities or the laws of the State, would not that be legal ?—A. We certainly regard it as an invasion. I believe the civil law is adequate to the case. If the civil law can not protect them, then they have a right to apply to the proper authority.

Q. That leads us to this : That the entry of a body of armed men from one State into another, is a violation of law, no matter what the purpose is ?—A. Yes, sir.

Q. The purpose, I think, and the intention for which they were going, must constitute the crime, whether it is an invasion or not. The gathering of men in a State for the purpose of making an attack in violation of law would be just as much treason as if they came into the State and were levying war against it. If the attack was made on the laws, it would be treason, whether it was made by residents or nonresidents.— A. I do not know what the law of Pennsylvania on that point is; but I do know that we regard it as insurrection. Take an insurrection like that at Harpers Ferry; it was treason, because it was an attack upon the laws of the State; but if it had been an effort to defend the laws and protect private property against destruction, it would not be treason.

The CHAIRMAN. I think, Mr. Powderly, I see one difficulty you are laboring under in this matter. I will agree with you that it is bad policy to allow private citizens to keep bodies of armed men, whether they go armed, or are armed after they come into the State, for the purpose of private employment. The question of the right, as it now exists, and what the law should be, may be two entirely different things. The law may permit it, and the question before this committee is as to whether, if the law does permit it, that law ought not to be changed, and, if it should be changed, what the remedy is. That is what we are seeking to ascertain, in the first place, whether it be lawful or unlawful, and no matter whether it is lawful, if it is an evil, the evil ought to be corrected.

Q. There is no division of sentiment as the committee is now constituted, or as it has been heretofore constituted, as to the bad policy that is complained of, and which we desire to remedy.

The WITNESS. I am very glad to hear that.

The CHAIRMAN. While there may be power to employ these men, we believe it is bad policy, and that such things are liable to bring on trouble.

The WITNESS. It is liable to lead to civil war.

The CHAIRMAN. I agree with you as to that. This committee is compelled to meet the question of law, and that is the reason why I am directing your attention to these matters, in order that you may investigate them, and if you have any suggestion to make we will hear you.

The WITNESS. As to the right of a man to protect his own property, I will say that I do not remember ever having been at Homestead, but I do know the location of certain mills in other places. I know a mill situated in a hollow and the homes of the workmen are upon a hill. The Pinkerton plan, as we understand, and as it has been carried out, aims at some one person and shoots another. What is to prevent the workingmen from arming themselves and staying away from the property, and, when the Pinkertons come, stand upon their own hillsides, shoot at somebody else and hit a Pinkerton man?

The CHAIRMAN. That would be a violation of the law.

The WITNESS. That is exactly the point. That was done, and the testimony went to prove it in the case of McCarthy. He was a man who was recognized as a man against whom they had a grudge. They fired at a child, but, in reality, they fired at McCarthy.

Mr. BYNUM. If a man is engaged in an unlawful act and accidentally takes life, it is quite a different matter from a case in which he is engaged in a lawful act.

The WITNESS. The wealthy company can get a sight of the man in the jury box, and McCarthy had no redress.

Mr. BYNUM. A man shot at could have full redress.

The WITNESS. Well, it is like the man who killed the "nigger" in San Francisco harbor: "Did he kill the nigger?" It is done every day.

By Mr. BYNUM:

Q. Here is the point. Supposing these watchmen had landed in those barges unarmed on the property of the Carnegie Company, right where they attempted to land, what right had anybody to prohibit them from going ashore?—A. I do not know that anybody would have that right. As I said before, I do not know the law, but I know what is the unwritten law. I know people may be called "cranks," but labor made these mills more than the Carnegies, and that while the men inside of the works were engaged in a dispute as to prices with Mr. Frick, and the question of rates of wages was up, before a conclusion could be reached boards were being nailed on the fence. It was a menace, and when night came the men were locked out.

These men found that these preparations had been going on. They knew that their labor had created these mills. I believe that those workingmen had some rights, which, possibly, the law could not give them. They felt that they ought to defend these rights and that their reputations were at stake. They had proposed to guard this property, and that was the reason that led people to believe that these men would not attempt to attack the property.

By the CHAIRMAN:

Q. The sheriff testified (and Hugh O'Donnell also, for there is no difference between them) that they offered, when the sheriff came up there, to furnish any necessary number of guards to be put into the property to take care of it, and that they would enter into bonds that the property should not be injured in any way. The sheriff declined to accept their offer, because, he said, those who were put in there would prevent the company from putting other men there to work.—A. He assumed that.

The CHAIRMAN. They did not deny that. What the company wanted to do was to put in nonunion men, but that was what the strikers did not want, so that while the sheriff seems to have been inefficient he was right in that particular. It would not have been consistent with his duty to have accepted the men as guards and put them in there, because it would have defeated the object the company had in view. There is no evidence that there was a disposition on the part of the strikers to destroy any of the property.

By Mr. BYNUM:

Q. I do not wish to be understood as assuming any facts. I made a hypothetical statement, but what I wanted to get at was, under your theory, if these workingmen held possession of the property and the owners did not agree with them upon terms as to rates of wages, what remedy was there for the owners of the property except to take it by force?—A. Is it not a fact that this institution was protected by United States laws?

By the CHAIRMAN:

Q. Have you reference to the tariff laws?—A. Yes, sir.

Q. It is in evidence that it is so protected.—A. Is it not a fact that the Carnegie Company gets the benefit of this protection?

The CHAIRMAN. Yes, sir.

The WITNESS. Then, is not the Government obliged to go still farther and see that that protection is properly distributed? We want protection to protect, if that is the theory.

The CHAIRMAN. I think that is one of the absurdities of the doctrine of protection.

Mr. BYNUM. We might come together on that.

The WITNESS. I am not pressing that point. I am not clashing with free-traders, protectionists, or capitalists. I simply say it goes to show that the Government should go a step farther. From statements made in all the speeches in Congress when these laws were under discussion, I did not find anybody asking for protection for the poor manufacturer. The claim always was that the workingman should be protected; but when the duties are collected at the port of entry, somehow the protection gravitates into the pockets of the manufacturers. I am of the opinion that if some must be robbed to protect others, we want to get our share of the spoils, to use plain English.

Mr. BYNUM. I am one of those who do not believe that protection protects the workingman.

The WITNESS. Another thing. They claim that those men at Homestead were receiving very high wages. I do not know whether that is true or not; but I learn that they live but 7 or 8 years with good eyesight.

The CHAIRMAN. There is evidence tending in that direction.

The WITNESS. There is good reason that those men should have high wages.

The CHAIRMAN. It occurred to me (and this is a good time to introduce it, as this is somewhat of an irregular talk) that while these men were getting pretty high pay, an inspection of the work showed that they were men of very high skill.

The WITNESS. Yes; very high skill, as I am informed.

Mr. BYNUM. I do not think the testimony discloses that they received very high wages. The wages are high as compared with what unskilled labor gets, but compared with skilled labor, they are not getting as high wages at Homestead as in the other mills around Pittsburg.

The WITNESS. But our chief bone of contention is the Pinkerton interference. I do not know that I can advance a proper remedy, but I feel that the system is a standing menace to order and good government in this country.

Mr. BYNUM. I agree with you; but I think it is a matter for the States, not a matter for Congress.

The WITNESS. I think it would be bad for us to be compelled to exterminate them ourselves. If some laws of the States or of the nation are not passed—we never object to any kind of force being used by proper authorities—but if something is not done to prevent the introduction of Pinkerton interference in labor affairs, there will be trouble the character of which no man can predict.

Mr. BYNUM. I understood you to say that an effort had been made in Pennsylvania to pass a law in reference to that matter, but that it was defeated. When was that effort made?

The WITNESS. It was made at the last session of the legislature. It could not be reported from the committee.

By Mr. BYNUM:

Q. You are aware that the State of Indiana enacted a law at the last session of the legislature prohibiting any persons from being clothed with police powers, except men who have been citizens of the State for a certain length of time?—A. I have read of it. That was done in New York and Massachusetts recently.

Q. Would not a law of that kind be effective in Pennsylvania?—A. If the managers of such institutions as the Carnegie works could keep away from legislative halls we would pass it.

Q. If it were enacted, I mean, would it not be effective?—A. Yes, I think there is no doubt of it.

By the CHAIRMAN:

Q. There is no doubt that if private companies or private persons may employ or furnish as guards, as was done at Homestead, men to the number of 300 or 1,000, they could do it to the extent of many thousands. While they may not violate any law in doing it, it is something which, if extended, will result in evil, and, therefore, it ought to be regulated or suppressed by law. The only question with us is, I think, as to how it can be done.

Mr. BRODERICK. That is one of the things we have to make some recommendation upon.

By the CHAIRMAN:

Q. I wish to ask a question in reference to the Knights of Labor in order that it may go into the record. The committee are unanimously in favor of legislation against the practice of the Pinkertons in hiring bodies of men and transporting them from one State to another. We are satisfied of this with the evidence now before us. Is there, in your opinion, any necessity for taking further testimony?—A. I do not think there is. I would be very happy to say no to that.

Q. If it is only a question among the members of the committee as to how that legislation could come, we are agreed, practically, that it is an evil; additional testimony is not likely to affect our opinions any further?—A. No, sir.

Q. Now, I have no doubt (not knowing the opinions of the other members of the committee, for this is the first expression that has been given) that some outside people have very much misjudged the committee?—A. I have not heard of any criticisms.

By Mr. RAY:

Q. These gentlemen have broached the question of the tariff. I desire to ask you if you think that there is any possible connection whatever between tariff laws and the Homestead troubles?—A. No, I do not know that there is, except the one particular that I have mentioned. I believe that a man who gets wealthy by any means will become arrogant in time, and will feel that he has a right to manage his property as he pleases.

Q. You think it has no earthly connection, unless it be that the Car-

negie Company becoming wealthy have consequently become tyranni-
cal with their men?—A. I contend that all of these things come through
protection. When protection is given in the interest of a certain institution, I think that the benefits should be evenly distributed.

Q. If it be true that a high tariff, made for the purpose of protection,
builds up manufactories, and if it also be true that, at the same time, it
increases the wages paid to laborers in those manufactories, then it does
benefit the laborer, does it not?—A. It makes it absolutely necessary
that labor should have an organization that will be two-edged—to keep
the manufacturers from getting all the benefit of the protection, and to
keep out hundreds of thousands of laborers who may be brought in to
take their places. The manufacturers will send across the water to obtain low-priced men.

Q. I will ask you the question again. If the protective tariff does
builds up manufactories, and if it does increase correspondingly the
wages paid to labor engaged in those manufactories, that it protects
both the employé and the employer?—A. Yes; I suppose so.

Q. And would be a just law. Of course your idea is aimed at this,
the building up of the price of labor, and as the increased prices paid
to labor would encourage immigration from foreign lands, you believe
that the importation of foreign cheap labor should be restricted?—A.
I do.

The CHAIRMAN. We are in accord on that.

Mr. RAY. I am in accord with that idea. [To the witness.] Is there
any connection between the Amalgamated Society that we read about
as in existence at Homestead and the Knights of Labor?—A. No.

Q. They are entirely independent?—A. Yes, sir.

Q. Do you know whether any Knights of Labor are also members of
the Amalgamated Society?—A. I believe not, although there may be
some. There is nothing in our organization to prevent it.

The CHAIRMAN (to Mr. Ray). We have got that in evidence; and
you will find the constitution and by-laws in the record.

By Mr. RAY:

Q. Do you know of any case where the Pinkertons have been used
excepting to protect property and enable the owners to run and conduct
their property in their own way?—A. I do not know of any cases other
than those I have given.

Q. In the case of the Albany strike, that was a strike of the employés
of the New York Central and Hudson River Railroad?—A. Yes, sir.

Q. In that case was it not true that the employés of the railroad
company ceased work and refused to let other workmen come in and
run trains?—A. No.

Q. They ceased work?—A. They ceased work.

Q. Do you not understand also that they refused to permit the officers
of the railroad company to put on engines and run trains by new workmen?—A. They did not refuse to permit it. They did everything in
their power, however, to induce these men not to take the trains.

Q. Didn't they do that by force?—A. No.

Q. Didn't these nonworking employés refuse to work, and did they
not obstruct the running out of the trains in Albany?—A. Not that I
know of.

Q. Didn't you understand that to be the fact?—A. No; on the contrary, the very moment that the men struck the Pinkertons were on
the ground.

Q. Supposing they were on the ground the minute that the men

H. Mis. 335——16

struck, did not the company undertake to run their trains?—A. Yes, and did run their trains.

Q. With men who did not strike?—A. Yes, sir.

Q. Then where is there a clash between the company and the workmen?—A. The clash was no more between the company and the workmen than between the company and the citizens, for in shooting they shot no strikers. Crowds would line bridges of railroads where trains were being made up, and strikers would pass remarks, causing the men to fire, and fire just as much at those who were not strikers as those who were.

Q. Then you claim that armed Pinkertons were put upon moving trains, and that the Pinkertons would fire upon crowds of citizens, and that these Pinkertons had come from other States?—A. Yes, sir; that is the way it was done. That was brought out in the trial.

Q. Was there not evidence that the running of trains was obstructed?—A. Only at one place; I do not know whether it was the case at Castleton or not.

Q. You would not defend the idea of strikers obstructing the running of trains, would you?—A. In what way? Yes, in a certain way, I would.

Q. In what way?—A. In inducing those who had taken the places of the men to leave.

Q. Inducing them by talk and persuasion?—A. Yes.

Q. You would not justify them in preventing by force the running of trains?—A. No; I would not countenance that. It would be against the law, and that is the only reason why I would not.

Q. If it were not against the law would you countenance it?—A. Certainly I would. I believe in keeping within the law.

Q. In the Homestead matter do you think the striking workmen had the moral right to go outside of the law to take possession of the property of the Carnegie Company and prevent the incoming of other workmen?—A. No: that was not the idea.

Q. You do not sustain that idea?—A. That was not the idea. This is the idea with organized labor. They find two men to every place made vacant, and these men may be obtained to take the places of strikers. If every man who was thus deprived of work were morally certain that he would never get employment again, it would not make him feel half so sore as to feel that the Pinkertons were brought there. It resolves itself upon that one pivot.

Q. I understood that the striking workmen at Homestead refused to permit other workmen who had been employed to go into those mills?—A. I had not heard anything of that kind.

Q. Did you not understand that these striking workmen even refused to permit the sheriff and his deputies to go in and take possession of the Carnegie works?—A. No; I did not understand that. I believe they entered the town and were sent home again. They were not near the works.

By Mr. BYNUM:

Q. The testimony is, they went up to the gates. At first O'Donnell told them to go and take the works, but when they went up to the gates there was a large party of men between them and the gates, and they were refused admittance.—A. I understood the Amalgamated Society were satisfied for them to take possession of the works.

By Mr. RAY:

Q. Would you justify the striking workmen in taking possession of works where they had been employed?—A. No.

Q. Would you justify their action in refusing to permit the owners of those works to fill them with workmen wherever they could get them?—A. No; except in the way stated.

Q. In any way?—A. No.

Q. Would you justify the owners in defending the works by an armed force, if the striking workmen undertook to take possession by force?—A. Take possession under the laws of the country, I would not. Certainly it is admitted that the employés agreed to guard these works and protect them.

Q. What objection can there be to their bringing men from any place inside of the United States where they could obtain them, for the purpose of protecting their property against force?—A. There is an objection. When the trouble begins, the idea is uppermost in the mind of the employer that he must win by any means, fair or foul, and if he employs men who are known to the neighborhood, and they do any unlawful act, they will be apprehended and punished under the law, but if he becomes a partner with Pinkertons in procuring criminals who will come there and perpetrate crime, so that nobody can prove who they are, they can not be brought to justice, but escape punishment.

Q. Then your opposition to the Pinkertons is not aimed against the right of the owner of the property to guard it against force by armed men?—A. We never questioned that right.

Q. But your opposition is aimed against the employment of irresponsible parties from abroad?—A. Yes, sir; hirelings and roughs.

Q. I would like to ask a question or two in regard to this Hudson River Railroad strike. You threw out, as I understood you, a pretty broad accusation against Mr. Depew. Do you mean to be understood as alleging that you believe that Mr. Depew, before he went to Europe, so acted, or acted with a design, to bring on a strike of the employés of that railroad company?—A. I stated it, but I will state it again. I believe all these things were done with the full knowledge of Mr. Depew; that he knew that the ultimate result would be a strike; and I believe he felt that under the conditions the strike would be a failure to the men, and that he desired it.

Q. He believed there would be a strike?—A. I believe he wanted it to be done in a more quiet way, possibly, but that was the only way it could be done. I believe I can prove this statement.

By the CHAIRMAN:

Q. Was that strike on the question of the reduction of wages?—A A dozen and one things entered into it.

By Mr. RAY:

Q. Do you know that that strike arose out of a question as to the rates of wages paid to the employés?—A. There were other questions.

Q. Discipline and wages?—A. Discipline, wages, and promotion of men. New men would be taken on in defiance of the laws of the company, and new men would be given the preference.

Q. It was a difference between the company and the men as to whether the company were to run the property in their own way or whether the employés should dictate?—A. The company professed to run it in a particular way, but did not run it that way.

Q. Then you think that one of the causes of the strike was that the company violated its own rules?—A. Not only that, but violated a written agreement with the men. If the agreement was wrong it should not have been entered into, but having been entered into it should have been respected.

Q. Then you think the company violated a contract with its employés?—A. It violated an agreement. I do not know whether it would be called a contract.

Q. Was it such a violation that the employés could have gone into the courts and asserted their rights?—A. Oh, employés have no business going into the courts in this country to get their rights.

Q. You think not in the State of New York?—A. Not in the State of New York, and you know that, if you live in New York.

Q. I do live in New York, and my experience is that any suit brought against a railroad company in that State is generally successful?—A. In that case the employé of the company never works for that company any more, and that is true in Pennsylvania as well as New York.

Q. Do you not think that public sentiment does not uphold any intolerance on the part of a railroad company?—A. Public sentiment will allow you to be hung up by the thumbs. Public sentiment is a very fickle jade. Men must have a well filled pocket if they want to win in the courts.

Q. Do you think the decisions of juries sustain that view of the matter?—A. It depends upon who sees the jury.

By the CHAIRMAN:

Q. You mean sensibly?—A. I mean financially and otherwise. There is a jury fixer in New York. It is the consensus of opinion of the press in New York State and city that a poor man has no business going into court to fight a corporation.

By Mr. RAY:

Q. Do you not think that the sentiment and sympathy of juries, outside of the big cities, are altogether against the railroad companies and other corporations?—A. No; I do not think so.

Q. Take the same question in regard to the large cities?—A. Let me go on a little further with that. No employé of a railroad company would be on a jury and render a verdict against the company. Shippers of freight would not dare do it. The farmers along the road are in the same position.

Q. Do you not think that almost universally in New York State in jury cases against railroad companies the verdict is against the company?—A. I am not disputing that fact. I am talking about employés of the company who bring suit.

Q. Employés who bring suits do so mostly for damages in cases of accident?—A. Almost universally in cases of accident. They would not dare bring suits against a company and hope to keep their places.

Q. Do you not think the sentiment of people who make up juries and the sympathy of the public is almost universally in favor of the employés of the company?—A. I do; but sympathy and sentiment will not keep a man in bread after he is discharged.

Q. Do you not believe in the right of a railroad company or any other corporation to discharge an employé in case they can not agree?—A. I should judge that is their right, and they have freely exercised it.

Q. Where they do not agree?—A. Yes, sir; we have to admit it as a right.

Q. It is a natural right?—A. No; I do not call it a natural right, by any means.

Q. Would you think any employé would have a right to remain when he did not agree with his employer?—A. I will answer that in this way: As an employé of a company I enter into an agreement; I use no force; that agreement is violated; then I enter the courts for redress;

if I obtain redress I am discharged. I do not believe it is a natural right of the company to discharge me for that reason.

Q. If the company only employed you for a limited time, and the time had expired, would the company be under obligation or compulsion to keep you longer?—A. They do not employ men in that way. I never was employed in that way in my life.

Q. They employ men for an indefinite time?—A. Yes; and can discharge them when they please.

Q. Then the remedy for the working men is to refuse employment unless the company will make a contract for a definite length of time—that is, band themselves together and agree that they will not enter the employ of a railroad company unless the company will agree to employ them for a definite length of time.—A. That sounds very nice and would be ideal if necessity did not interpose. Give them the same wealth and they will agree entirely. It is simply the demands of wealth. The Knights of Labor have a remedy for this and they will come forward with it some day.

Q. What is that remedy?—A. Government ownership of the railroads. We believe the railroads are public highways. Then the Government will have a right to interfere.

Q. Would not the Government ownership of railroads so increase the number of Government officials and the power of the Government that there would be greater complaint than now exists and would not greater injustice be done?—A. There would be greater complaint than now exists. We hear very little complaint now. They are doing the robbing of the people all the same, and the people have no authority over them. There is no use in complaining, but establish Government ownership once and it will be just exactly as it is to-day with you gentlemen when you run for office—all your bad deeds are made known and a great many more. I suppose you have found that out. It is a good deal like the case of the colored woman who had four children and one was a little whiter than the others. She said she always despised that brat, because he showed dirt so easy.

Q. Suppose the telegraph and railroads were under Government ownership and the number of employés should be so great that if either party got into power and secured control of this vast machinery, this patronage should be used to keep it in power?—A. Then we would have still another remedy.

Q. What is that?—A. That is the referendum—that all laws shall be acted upon or voted upon by the people.

Q. Do you think that is practicable?—A. Yes, sir; I most assuredly do.

The CHAIRMAN. I am glad you have mentioned that, for I saw it stated the other day, and I did not understand it.—A. It means that all laws shall be originated by the people, or rather be approved by them, before they become operative.

By Mr. RAY:

Q. How many laws are presented to this House?

The CHAIRMAN. No member knows all of them.

Mr. BYNUM. We would be compelled, then, to know them all by memory.

The WITNESS. Then ignorance of the law would not be an excuse. Take the ballot law of Pennsylvania—the Baker law. I asked a gentleman who voted for it about a certain section of it. He was a gentleman who was talking very loudly about the Force bill. I read him a section from the Baker law of Pennsylvania, and I said to him, "This is a section of the force bill." He said, "It reads like it." And yet that man voted for the very same bill in the legislature, and did not recognize it.

By the CHAIRMAN:

Q. We have gotten away from the question into the domain of politics and general philosophy. You have explained the referendum, which I did not understand. Now, in reference to the ownership of railroads by the Government, how do you propose that the Government shall obtain the ownership of all the railroads and telegraph lines? How are we going to get them?—A. Can not the Government buy them?

Q. Where is the money to come from?—A. Do not the railroads earn money?

Q. Of course they earn money.—A. The Government's credit is good.

Q. Would you buy them on the Government's credit?—A. They would soon pay for themselves. I would not buy the "water" in them. It is not necessary to buy them all. You could establish one line east and west and make that a standard. The others would follow suit. It is not necessary to buy them all at once. We do not mean that that matter shall be side-tracked in any way. We could buy the older railroads first. We believe that the time to begin is very near at hand.

By Mr. BRODERICK:

Q. How would it do to begin by foreclosing on the Union Pacific?—A. I think that would be justifiable. The people really and morally own the railroads.

By the CHAIRMAN:

Q. Have you examined the answers of Robert Pinkerton and his brother to the questions which were propounded to them by the executive board of the Knights of Labor through this committee, in reference to which you may have seen some newspaper comments?—A. I simply saw some garbled extracts. I did not see the whole of it.

Q. You probably have seen that objection was raised to the answers on account of the manner in which they were gotten up, because the committee after agreeing to propound these questions, and paying deference to the wishes of that board, in letting them come in before the members of the committee propounded any questions at all, and that I, as chairman of the committee, allowed the counsel of the Pinkertons to take these questions away and prepare answers to them. No doubt you have seen that statement?—A. No, sir; I have not.

Q. That is a fact. I did that, and I take all the responsibility myself. If you have not seen the criticism, I do not know whether you can answer it. You know that it is very common in answering interrogatories in court, to allow the witness' lawyer to prepare his answers. That is a very common proceeding in all equity practice in court.—A. I do not know as to that.

Q. It certainly is.—A. I have not read this at all. I got to Philadelphia yesterday and saw the newspapers, but they did not have a full account of it. These things are new to me.

Q. I read the questions and Robert Pinkerton read his answers which appear under them.—A. I simply read the statement in the paper. This matter was only brought to my attention yesterday, or last night, when I looked over it on the train coming here.

Q. Members or representatives of the Knights of Labor have taken exceptions to the methods of this committee on that account.—A. I do not know anything about that.

Q. I wanted to say this, that there was no intention of unfairness or impropriety about it.—A. I was not here, and did not know of it.

Q. I would ask you if you do not think the answers by the Pinkertons were full to the questions?—A. I have not read them at all.

Q. After twenty-four questions were put, against the protest of Mr. Boatner, a member of the committee, who thought it was entirely improper to allow those questions to be put in preference to the committee's examination, but a majority of the committee thought that those questions ought to be put, and as we had agreed to do that, it was done. After that the Pinkertons were questioned on every conceivable matter that we thought of relative to the investigation. I have called your attention to it for the purpose of showing you what were the facts in the case.—A. Of course I do not know anything about it, as I have said.

The CHAIRMAN. It is worth nothing except to show you and the country that this committee is not guilty of any unfairness and does not intend to be.

By Mr. BYNUM:

Q. What positions do Devlin, Hayes, and Wright hold in the Knights of Labor?—A. They are members of the general executive board; that is, Wright and Devlin are, and Hayes is general secretary of the organization.

The CHAIRMAN. I do not know of any other questions that we desire to ask you. I wish to say to you that this subcommittee is a creature of the full committee, and also that the full committee is under the authority of the House, and I can not say to what extent this investigation may be protracted or what it may be directed to do. Therefore, if it is not too great a trouble to you, we would like to have you send us the names and addresses of any parties who may be in possession of information bearing upon the matter we are investigating.

A. All right.

Q. Do you know whether a protracted investigation would affect the final action of this committee?

Mr. BYNUM. In justice to other members of the committee who may be put in a false attitude, I would say that we are perfectly willing to hold this matter open, and give them an opportunity to be heard in their defense—not only willing, but anxious to do so.

Mr. BRODERICK. Whatever we do, we ought to close next week.

By Mr. RAY:

Q. Have you stated everything you know personally embraced within the scope of these resolutions?—A. I do not know that I have.

Q. You have given everything you recollect?—A. I have given everything that I recollect. I am much obliged to the committee, and I hope its labors will be fruitful.

Mr. RAY. If you can suggest the names of any further witnesses, you should make them known to us.

Hereupon the committee adjourned.

The taking of testimony will be resumed and a report made to Congress early in the next session.

WM. C. OATES,
Chairman subcommittee of Committee on Judiciary,
House of Representatives.

www.ingramcontent.com/pod-product-compliance
Lightning Source LLC
Chambersburg PA
CBHW020854270326
41928CB00006B/692